CASTE AND DEMOCRATIC POLITICS IN INDIA

edited by

Ghanshyam Shah

Anthem Press
London

This edition first published by Anthem Press 2004

Anthem Press is an imprint of
Wimbledon Publishing Company
75-76 Blackfriars Road
London SE1 8HA
or
PO Box 9779, London SW19 7QA

This edition first published in 2002 by
Permanent Black, Delhi, India.

British Library Cataloguing in Publication Data
Data available

Library of Congress in Publication Data
A catalogue record has been applied for

1 3 5 7 9 10 8 6 4 2

ISBN 1 84331 085 6 (Hbk)
ISBN 1 84331 086 4 (Pbk)

Typeset by Pentagon Graphics Pvt. Ltd., Chennai, India
Printed in India

CONTENTS

Anthem South Asian Studies

Series editor: Crispin Bates

ACKNOWLEDGEMENTS

For permission to reprint material in this book, thanks are due to the following: Popular Prakashan, Mumbai, for the material by B.T. Ranadive, J. Manor, Pushpendra, and G. Shah's 'Social Backwardness and the Politics of Reservations'; Centre for the study of Developing Societies, Delhi, for the material by G. Omvedt and S. Kumar; the author and Cambridge University Press for the material by O. Mendelsohn.

Every effort has been made to contact copyright holders. Perceived omissions will be rectified in future printings if brought to the notice of the publisher.

LIST OF CONTRIBUTORS*

Rajni Kothari, an eminent political scientist, is Founder Director and former Chairman of the Centre for the Study of Developing Societies, Delhi.

Sanjay Kumar is a faculty member at the Centre for the Study of Developing Societies, Delhi.

James Manor is Professor at the Institute of Developing Studies, Sussex, UK.

Rushikesh Maru worked at the Centre for the Study of Developing Societies, Indian Institute of Management, Ahmedabad.

Oliver Mendelsohn is associate Professor at the School of Law and Legal Studies, La Trobe University, Australia.

Gail Omvedt has taught at the University of Pune. She is currently Senior Fellow, Nehru Memorial Museum and Library, New Delhi.

Pushpendra is working with Action Aid India, at its Bihar Office.

B.T. Ranadive was a leading member of the Communist Movement in India.

Ghanshyam Shah is Professor, Jawaharlal Nehru University, New Delhi.

D.L. Sheth is Professor, Centre for the study of Developing Societies, Delhi.

* The internationally eminent, such as Gandhi, Ambedkar, Dumont etc., are for obvious reasons not part of this page.

1

Introduction: Caste and Democratic Politics

Ghanshyam Shah

The struggle for power and the distribution of power and resources constitute the major domain of politics. In democratic political systems, participants assert their individual and/or collective rights and aspirations. They articulate an ideology and evolve strategies for maintaining the status quo in the social order, or for bringing about social transformation. To attain these objectives they compete for power and influence. One of the important spheres of politics is the governance of society through the state and the social institutions of civil society. This involves the identification of corporate needs and the resolution of conflict among various interests. Such needs cannot all be met at the same time. It is the task of those who are responsible for governance to sort out priorities, corresponding to the availability of resources. Policies for production systems and the distribution of resources are therefore evolved and a consensus is created to give them legitimacy. In short, who gets what, when, and how in society are some of the central concerns of politics.

Politics notwithstanding, the ideals set out in the Constitution and theorised by leaders and philosophers do not function devoid of the social system, the cultural ethos, and the social milieu. Though decisions related to governance are taken by the state, in a democratic system people get involved in decision-making processes. They elect their rulers, and while electing these representatives they express their needs, expectations and aspirations. These expectations are not necessarily personal; they are also diverted to the well-being of the community—the immediate primordial group, the caste, the larger society which includes region and country. In fact the line dividing personal and community interests is thin. People put pressure on decision-makers to get things done via organised or unorganised struggles, persuasion, and many other means. Political elites cannot ignore social forces for they themselves are part of them. It is imperative for decision-makers in a democratic system to seek and extend the support of their constituents in order to preserve their political power.

Politics is not of course a mere blueprint of social forces and the conflicts therein. Democratic politics with a constitutional framework has its own agenda for social transformation, for the creation as well as management of surplus and its use. It creates new institutions and a value system suited to its own ends. These institutions and ideologies get shaped and reshaped within specific contexts, and in the process, politics generates changes in the social system. There is thus a constant and complex interaction between society and polity. For meaningful understanding, this interaction has to be contextualised and understood from specified perspectives.

THE CASTELESS SOCIAL ORDER: AN IDEAL

India became a republic in 1950. The Preamble and Directive Principles of the Constitution envisage building a social order around the principles of equality, liberty and fraternity. The intervention of the state in social transformation for an egalitarian and secular social order is the core and the spirit of the Constitution. Echoing this, Article 38 reads: 'The State shall strive to promote the welfare of the people by securing and protecting as effectively as it may a social order in which justice, social, economic and political, shall inform all the institutions of the national life'. Adult franchise has been the first step towards attaining this goal. For the first time in Indian history, adult citizens of the country gained the right to vote and elect representatives to decision-making bodies from the village panchayat to the Lok Sabha. They also have the right to contest elections so as to become rulers. As a result, a large number of social groups hitherto deprived of political power began to realise that they could compete with the traditionally dominant power elite and wield power so as to redress their grievances and express needs, priorities and aspirations; in short, decide their destiny. Politics is now more competitive and open.

The Indian Constitution derecognises caste as an ideal and also strives through various provisions to build a casteless social system. It prohibits discrimination in the public sphere on grounds of religion, race, caste, gender or place of birth. It directs that there shall be equality of opportunity for all citizens in matters relating to economic aspirations or to the appointment of any office-of state. It lays down positive measures for ameliorating the socio-economic condition of traditionally deprived social groups so that, eventually, they do not suffer caste-based discrimination. Further, the Constitution makes preferential provisions for the socially and economically backward strata of society—Articles 330 and 332; 15 (2)(4) and 29, 29(2); 16(4), 35, 244, 320(4), 333 and 335. This was considered necessary because of a scarcity of opportunities and the prevalence of age-old caste/community-based discrimination. The fathers of the Indian Constitution had hoped that overall conditions in the country would improve within ten years, rendering reservation unnecessary. H.V. Kamath, a member of the constituent assembly, expressed the hope in the following words:

> I only wish to express the hope that, before ten years have expired from the commencement of the Constitution, in this country of ours which is ancient, but ever young, there will be no socially and educationally backward classes left, but that all the classes will come up to a decent, normal human level, and also that we shall do away with this stigma of any caste being Scheduled. This was a creation of the British regime which happily has passed away. We have taken many strides forward in removing or doing away with the numerous evils that were associated with the British regime: that is one of the few that still remain. I hope that ere long, this stigma too will disappear from our body politic, and we shall all stand before the world as one single Indian community.[1]

There is a near consensus among the educated political elite of all political shades that caste is antithetical to the idea of India's democracy. Jawaharlal Nehru argued in the 1950s:

> The conception and practice of caste embodied the aristocratic ideal and was obviously opposed to democratic conceptions. It had its strong sense of *noblesse oblige,* provided people kept their hereditary stations and did not challenge the established order. India's success and achievements were on the whole confined to the upper classes, those lower down in the scale had very few changes and their opportunities were strictly limited. These upper classes were not small, limited groups but large in numbers and there was also diffusion of power, authority and influence. Hence they carried on successfully for a very long period. But the ultimate weakness and failing of the caste system and the Indian social structure were such that they degraded a mass of human beings and gave them no opportunities to get out of that condition educationally, culturally or economically. That degradation brought deterioration all along the line, including in its scope even the upper classes. It led to the petrification which became a dominant feature of India's economy and life.[2]

In the early 1950s many scholars, social workers and some leading political personalities of the ruling party believed that caste and all that goes with it 'are wholly incompatible, reactionary, restrictive and barriers to progress'. Without the complete annihilation of the caste system, democracy was doomed. This view continues to prevail and is often expressed in political and academic discourse. But the discussion is more often than not rhetorical. There is very little deliberation around questions such as: Can caste be annihilated? If yes, how? What kind of cultural, political and economic interventions might weaken the caste structure and its value system? What kind of alternative social formation can emerge?

Parliamentary democracy has survived in India for five decades. Economic development and 'modernisation', of course not of the expected nature and speed, have taken place. At the same time, caste has survived, though its institutions and values have undergone changes. Students of Indian politics grapple with the riddle of how caste and democracy have gone together.

This volume focuses on the role of caste in Indian democratic politics. What role does caste play in elections, decision-making processes, institutional functioning, and the distribution of resources? At which level and in which sphere of politics is the role of caste more visible and relatively more decisive than others? In the process of interaction among various forces—caste, religion, economy, polity, etc. what happens to caste—its structure, functions, and value system? How much, and in what way, has the power structure in society undergone change with the assertion for political power among traditionally deprived castes? Is caste still omnipresent in politics?

DEFINING CASTE

All Indians including non-Hindus have jati (that is, caste) by birth, as an identity for social interaction. But the meaning of jati is not the same among Hindus and non-Hindus: caste does not have a religious sanction among the latter, it is merely a social stratum of which they are a part. Among Hindus it is believed that one's jati is a reward or punishment for one's karma.

Sociologists find it difficult to arrive at a definition of caste for it involves the subjective identification of caste via data that varies from group to group and from time to time. J.H. Hutton, the census official who collected and compiled massive data on caste concluded that: 'The truth is that while a caste is a social unit in a quasi-organic system of society and throughout India is consistent enough to be immediately identifiable, the nature of the unit is variable enough to make a concise definition difficult.'[3] G.S. Ghurye observes: 'It appears to me that any attempt at definition [of caste] is bound to fail of because of the complexity of the phenomenon.[4]

The meaning of jati is not always uniform and consistent. It varies with the purpose for which the tag is used. Jati has a specific social meaning, identifying a person's place for everyday interaction in the social order of a village society. For instance, a villager in central Gujarat might identify himself as a Khant when he interacts with another villager of a neighbouring locality who calls himself a Bareeya. The two will not have a relationship which permits dining together. They do not belong to a common matrimonial network. In terms of jati, they consider themselves part of distinctively separate social groups within a village. At the same time, they identify with each other outside the village for political reasons against upper-caste Patidars or Banias and against lower jatis such as Bhangis and Chamars. Both introduce themselves as Kshatriyas when they attend a political party meeting at a taluka or district headquarters. They would describe their caste as falling under Other Backward Caste (OBCs) when they visit a government office to get a loan or a subsidy for a government-sponsored programme or if they apply for scholarships for their children. There is thus one meaning of jati in the context of matrimonial and kinship relationships, a different meaning for economic interaction, and a third meaning for political purposes. Jati does not necessarily have the same meaning even within the political context: The two exemplars above could team up as Kshatriyas for Parliament or state assembly elections but remain as Khant and Bareeya for village panchayat elections.

Caste is often considered a subunit of varna. According to scriptures like the *Gita* and the *Manusmriti* there are four varnas: Brahmin, Kshatriya, Vaishya and Sudra. This classification is used as an ideal model by one school of Hindu social reformers: Mahatma Gandhi was one of them. Scholars and administrators often collate various jatis into four or five varna categories. The fifth category is of the Ati-Sudras or Avarnas, that is, those outside the varna social order. In the real world, however, several castes do not fit exclusively into any of these categories, nor are all individuals aware of varna categories. What matters to them is their jati, which defines social interaction and status.

The discussion on caste among sociologists is centred on its features. G.S. Ghurye discusses six broad features of the caste system. Though these are found throughout the subcontinent, the caste structure has not evolved uniformly in all regions. It is relatively less rigid in Assam, more in Uttar Pradesh and Bihar. The observation of caste rulers also varies—not only from region to region but also caste to caste. Moreover, some of the features of caste have changed considerably during the past five decades.

The number of castes varies across regions. Gujarat has a larger number than West Bengal. The different historical experiences of various Indian regions have contributed to the shaping of present-day socio-political processes, complicated by the uneven economic development of the country, leading to uneven economic opportunities available to different social groups. Castes have never had a uniform numerical strength or spread. Some are scattered throughout a region, some are heavily concentrated in a few geographical pockets. The complications in describing, defining and locating caste are therefore very considerable. In brief, the role and position of caste in relation to politics varies from time to time, area to area, and caste to caste.

Caste Ideology

Notwithstanding different perceptions of caste and the difficulties of definition, there is a consensus among scholars regarding the central ideological thrust which underlies the caste social order. Most sociological writings on caste conclude that *homo hierarchicus is* the central and substantive element of the caste system which differentiates it from other social systems–particularly those of the West. Broadly speaking, the caste system has been governed by the concept of purity and pollution; by interpersonal relationship among individuals being dictated in terms of blood, food and occupation; and by rituals related to them being divided into pure and impure. It is obligatory for each Hindu to confine her/his relationship and interaction within the restricted circle called jati so as to maintain purity in marriage relationships, in exchanges of food, and in the pursuit of occupations.

Chapter 3 examines the ideology of the caste system, which provides an overall framework to the system. It is shared, according to Louis Dumont, by those who are at the helm and at the bottom of the hierarchy. 'The principle of the opposition of the pure and impure', he argues, 'underlies hierarchy, which is the superiority of the pure to the impure; underlines separation because the pure and impure must be kept separate; and underlies the division of labour because pure and impure occupations must likewise be kept separate. The whole is founded on the necessary and hierarchical coexistence of the two opposites.'[5]

Theoretically, as propounded by the shastras, all jatis are hierarchically placed with prescribed social status. The place of the jati is determined by its ritual status, based on the observance of customs for interpersonal relationship. Hierarchy within the caste system is viewed by some scholars as a positive value which maintains social harmony and the social division of labour. The value system is seen by these as satisfying for actors throughout the system, even for those at the bottom.[6] Following this theoretical framework, Michael Moffatt argues that:

> Untouchables do not necessarily possess distinctively different social and cultural forms as a result of their position in the system. They do not possess a separate subculture. They are not detached or alienated from the 'rationalisation' of the system. . . . They recreate among themselves the entire set of institutions and of ranked relations from which they have been excluded by the higher castes by reason of their extreme lowness. Replication is a stronger indicator of cultural consensus than complementarity, since it operates within the untouchable subset of castes, where the power of the higher castes does not directly operate.[7]

This view has been contested by a number of scholars who hold the consensus theory to be a view from the top. Kathleen Gough observes that 'the low castes place much less emphasis than do Brahmins on otherworldliness and on the fate of the soul after death'.[8] Joan Mencher argues that Pariayans in south India have a more 'explicitly materialistic' view of the system and their place in it than do those at the top, and that 'those at the bottom of the hierarchy have less need to rationalise its inequities'.[9]

Moreover, the prevalence of a caste hierarchy does not imply that lower castes also give legitimacy to the theory of karma—the acceptance of one's station in life as given, as the result of deeds in previous births. Had this been the case, Dalits would not have waged struggles against dominant castes to improve their life chances in the here and now. In a study of the Pariayars of a Tamil Nadu village, Robert Deliege observes that hierarchy did not permeate all social relationships among Pariayars: they 'fiercely' defend equality among themselves. The Pariayars 'have internal laws which are much less constraining than those of the high castes and much weaker social control. They exult-in a greater freedom, notably on a moral and sexual level, in greater laxity in religious beliefs even among the Catholics, and in a certain offhandedness with respect to social and religious rites.'[10]

The practice of hierarchy among them is a cultural imposition, not their own preference. Their status is thanks to the hegemony of the dominant castes, and to the milieu in which they live. Dalits do not always imitate Brahmins and the Brahmanical ideology. They may perform some of the rituals of the upper castes but they do not necessarily attach to them the same meanings. Dalits worship Ram and Krishna but, in the contemporary period, neither accept the karma theory nor are willing to achieve equality. At the same time, they often emulate the dominant caste which is in their immediate vicinity—be they Kshatriyas or Sudras. Such imitation primarily denotes the existence of a power relationship. N. Sudhakar Rao observes that Dalits 'emulate the power structure and power relations of the dominant caste in the village and the territory, rather than accept religious values and their exclusion as "impure".'[11]

It is certain that traditional rules for purity and social status have been eroded over the past five decades thanks to the greater penetration of the market economy, 'modern' administration, and expanded communication networks. Traditionally, caste members have been forbidden to accept cooked food from jatis they considered lower than theirs. These rules too have weakened, particularly in public spheres and in urban areas. In their bid to gain a broad support base, the political elites at the district and state levels do not hesitate to accept food cooked by caste members of lower strata.

At the empirical level, caste hierarchy has never been static. Like all social systems it has been shaped and reshaped in local milieus. The caste structure, in terms of hierarchy and boundary for interaction among social groups, can be more or less neat and identified without much difficulty at the village level. But it is not so easy at the regional level. To draw an empirically based macro picture of castes at the national level is all the more difficult.

Though the upper castes try to maintain their higher status, the middle and lower castes have successfully improved their status. With improvements in their economic condition, a dominant section of some of the low castes— including groups that were at one time treated as untouchables—imitated the customs and norms of the upper castes residing in their vicinity. Sociologists call this process sanskritisation.[12] We also have instances of some castes, and even individuals, particularly from the middle rank, who have succeeded in improving their status without adhering to the norms and rituals of the upper castes. Political authority facilitates not only the power holder—ruler—but also his kin and relatives: they enjoy higher social status in caste hierarchy. One can cite instances in history to show that Sudras and Ati-Sudras occupying positions of power have acquired the status of Kshatriyas (though not of Brahmins) even without following the path of sanskritisation.

The process of sanskritisation, which was prominent among lower castes at one point of time, particularly in the nineteenth and early twentieth centuries, slowed down in the 1960s and 1970s. Earlier, many castes hesitated to be called 'backward' despite their poor economic condition. They feared they would not improve their social status by identifying themselves as backward. But this is no longer true, now that the state has provided certain benefits to backward castes. These castes realised that they could improve their status by improving their economic condition rather than by observing rituals followed by the upper castes. But this does not mean that they have given up the caste framework. They continue to maintain their caste identity and prefer to have certain castes below them–lower in social status. Notions of hierarchy remain but not necessarily the belief in purity and pollution. It seems that rituals and social status are becoming separate issues. One can acquire higher social status by making money and acquiring political power, while ritual status in the caste hierarchy remains the same. There is also competition among the castes to be termed 'backward'. Even some of the Brahmin and Rajput jatis, who traditionally enjoyed high status, have approached the government to be classified as 'backward'. Economic benefits are here the prime mover. Does it mean that they compromise ritual status? And what does ritual status mean in this context? We do not have studies which would help answer this question.

Several castes have evolved and/or changed their nomenclature, thus asserting their rights and status. Officials and scholars have also evolved categories which club several castes together, and have identified some castes as subcastes or sub-subcastes. Sometimes this has changed their official identity. Often, this has been done to simplify reality so that the data can be handled easily. Sometimes it is done with political considerations, for mobilisation, or to stall the process of social change, or to win over groups, distribute largesse, and punish others. Thus, new castes are created and other castes dismantled. For example, the Kolis of Gujarat are the creation of a census category which clubs together castes such as the Patanvadia, Bareeya, Khant and Thakor. Initially, these separately followed the rituals of Rajputs and struggled for three decades to be acknowledged as Kshatriyas, so as to get high social status. They felt insulted if they were called Kolis, which indicated a group with low social status. But now they have started calling themselves Kolis so that they can garner material benefits, which is the surest way to improve social status. Social status based on the observance of rituals has become increasingly redundant.

CASTE AND CLASS

According to several scholars, the caste system is essentially a class system. Stratification is based on occupation and the economic position of the group. In the formative years, during Vedic times, these classes were the Rajanyas or the Kshatriyas, the aristocracy; the Brahmins, the priests; the Vaishyas, the people at large, mainly peasants and traders; and the Sudras, the service communities. Kosambi argues that caste did not arise out of any internal division of the varna of Vedic society; the literal meaning of varna is colour. The divisions were the result of external forces. With food surplus, which could be exchanged for commodities, a new social organisation began to form among the Aryans around 1000 BC:

> The principal change in the productive relations was the formation of a servile class from the conquered *dasa* population. . . . The *dasa* by caste had not the right to initiation, nor to bear weapons; he had no property; being himself the property of the Aryan tribe as a whole, much the same way as cattle. . . . It may be supposed that those *dasas* were the descendants of the Indus settlers who had provided the surplus for Indus cities; being persuaded thereto by some method other than force, say religion.

Later, with regular settlement, a 'new class division' within each Aryan tribe evolved. This came into existence to manage the inner struggle among various groups, and to establish the power of the ruling classes. 'The Vaisya (settler, husbandman) and the sudra (helots) are to be exploited for the advantage of the ruling warrior caste, the kshatriya with the brahmin priest's help.... One of the major purposes of the sacrifice was to make the other castes obedient to the kshatriya rulers. Rituals related to sacrifice were evolved to make the vaisya and the sudra submissive and thereby to control the new class structure that had developed within the tribe.'[13]

Morton Klass, a social anthropologist, argues that 'the South Asian socioeconomic system is structurally inseparable from "the caste system". Whatever else caste may be on sociological or ideological levels, it is clearly the crucial element of the economy.'[14] Caste originated with the development of an economic surplus. It was the means by which tribal societies, consisting of originally egalitarian clans, adjusted to the inequality generated by this surplus. According to some historians, the caste-based production and distribution system was strong in Bengal, south India and certain other parts of the country in the eighteenth and nineteenth centuries.[15] Some believe this continues in post-independence India also. Though in some ways jati still plays an important role in the distribution of opportunities, it is an oversimplification to say that caste is the determinant of the means of production in contemporary India, for the capitalist mode of production so clearly dominates.

A number of village studies carried out in the post-independence period show an overlap between the twin hierarchies of caste and landownership.[16] M.N. Srinivas observes: 'The village community consisted of hierarchical groups, each with its own right, duties and privileges. The caste at the top had power and privileges which were denied to the lower castes. The lower castes were tenants, servants, landless labourers, debtors and clients of the higher castes.'[17] Data from two Tamil Nadu villages show that 59 per cent of the Mudaliyars (upper castes) and 4 per cent of the Palli (untouchable castes) are rich peasants or landlords. No Mudaliyar is engaged as an agricultural labourer, whereas 42 percent of Palli households earn their livelihood as farm labourers. A study of six Rajasthan villages in the 1970s shows a similar pattern. 'Only 12.5 per cent of the lower class households belong to upper castes, 60 per cent of the higher class households belong to the upper castes, 24 per cent of the upper castes belong to the higher class, whereas among the intermediate and lower castes only 6.2 per cent and 1.3 per cent belong to high class respectively.'[18]

The Anthropological Survey of India, in its 'People of India' project has studied 4635 communities/castes. Its work confirms that highly placed castes are marked by

> (i) a higher position in the regional socio-ritual hierarchy (ii) better control over land and other resources and (iii) non-commercial relations with other communities of inferior status . . . [the low castes] are placed at the bottom due to their (i) abject poverty caused by less possession of land and less control over economic resources (ii) socio-ritual degradation based on the notion of purity and pollution and (iii) traditional engagement in occupations which are considered ritually unclean.[19]

Aggregate data at the regional and national levels on caste and occupation/ landholding give us a similar picture, though the contrast between high and low castes is blurred. Table 1 presents caste and occupation data at the all-India level covering 113 parliamentary constituencies and more than 400 polling booths, collected as part of a voting behaviour study carried out by the Centre for the Study of Developing Societies, Delhi, in 1999. The data show a positive relationship between caste and occupational status. The small and marginal farmers and agricultural labourers belong mainly to the low or backward castes, and to Scheduled Castes; 34 per cent of the SCs, as against only 7 per cent of the upper castes, are engaged as agricultural labourers. On the other hand, a third of the upper-caste households, as against less than 10 per cent of the OBCs and SCs, are professionals, white-collar employees or big- or medium sized businessmen. The data give a broad pattern of economic differentiation between the upper and middle as well as low castes. The data also point out that the upper or lower castes are not monolithic in occupational status. There is a small proportion among the OBCs and SCs who are relatively better off in terms of landownership and non-farm occupation. There are a few upper castes in some parts of the country, the majority of whose members do not belong to the upper class. Rajputs (upper caste) of Gujarat are a case in point. One-fifth of them are landless. And among the landless 72 per cent are agricultural labourers. Only 2 per cent are in white-collar jobs. The condition of the Kolis is more or less the same. This is the reason that the Kolis and Rajputs are in alliance in the political sphere, despite the gap in ritual status.

Industrialisation and a penetration of the market economy in rural areas have affected the traditional occupation of several castes. As early as 1957, F.G. Bailey observed, in a village situated in the relatively backward Orissa: 'Not every person works at his traditional occupation. The distillers do not touch liquor. The Knod potters do not know how to make pots. The fishermen do not fish. The warriors are cultivators. Everywhere there is a scope for practicing an hereditary occupation and not all members of caste engage in the work.'[20] In the 1950s Kathleen Gough observed a similar pattern in Tamil Nadu. She noted:

> The caste community is no longer homogeneous in occupation and wealth, for caste is today a limited rather than a determining factor in the choice of the occupation. Exactly half of Kumbarpettai's adult Brahmins are now employed in towns as Government servants, school teachers or restaurant workers. Of the remainder, some own up to thirty acres of land, others as little as three. One runs a grocery store and one a vegetarian restaurant. Among the non-Brahmins, the fisherman, toddy-tappers, Marathas, Kallans, Koravas and Kuttadis have abandoned their traditional work.[21]

Table 1: Caste and Occupation

Occupation/landholding	Castes/Communities								
	Brahmin	Rajput	Other upper castes	Peasant middle castes	Peasant OBCs	Other OBCs	Scs	STs	Other minorities
Higher professional (1)	3.8	0.6	3.5	0.7	0.5	0.8	0.3	0.5	3.8
White collar employees (2)	34.7	21.3	21.2	14.4	7.5	9.0	10.0	7.2	14.6
Large business	3.6	2.0	10.1	2.0	0.9	1.6	0.2	1.6	2.8
Petty business (3)	13.4	7.0	25.8	6.3	5.8	10.0	5.3	12.5	14.6
Artisan/Blue collar workers/Service providers (4)	9.0	8.7	9.5	13.6	14.6	34.1	25.5	23.7	20.5
Landholding (Acres)									
0 acres +	2.0	9.0	0.8	5.7	1.1	0.7	0.9	1.3	4.2
10–19 acres	3.4	5.0	0.9	8.0	2.7	1.09	0.5	2.6	2.4
5–9 acres	3.4	11.8	2.4	11.4	7.6	3.7	2.5	4.9	3.5
Less than 5 acres	15.2	23.8	9.5	25.2	27.8	13.5	15.0	15.8	10.1
Tenants 0–5 acres	3.2	2.2	2.5	1.1	4.3	2.0	2.31	2.4	
Agri. labourers	3.6	5.6	10.6	9.6	22.6	20.6	34.3	25.5	15.6
Other workers	0.4	0.6	0.5	0.5	2.4	1.0	1.5	1.0	1.7
Non-workers	4.4	2.5	2.8	1.4	2.0	2.0	1.6	1.8	3.8
Total	100	100	100	100	100	100	100	100	100
	(501)	(357)	(633)	(804)	(1875)	(1469)	(1489)	(1630)	(288)

1. High professionals include medical doctors, engineers, lawyers, chartered accountants, university and college teachers.
2. White-collar employees include government and non-government officers, teachers, clerks, and managers.
3. Petty business includes small shop-owners, hawkers, salespersons, shop assistants, etc.
4. Blue-collar and artisan workers include traditional artisans such as carpenters, barbers, washermen, scavengers, etc.; and tailors, weavers and factory workers.

Source: National Election Study, 1999, Centre for the Study of Developing Societies, Delhi.

Village studies of the 1950s and 1960s in different parts of the country bear out this trend. And, diversification of occupation in the non-farm sector has increased within most castes with the spread of the green revolution, resulting in capitalist farming.

There are still several jatis whose members do not have the opportunity for upward mobility: their economic status has remained more or less the same. One can find such instances among several SCs and numerically small OBCs. Such castes have, even now, a rate of literacy lower than 10 per cent, and all households depend on manual labour for their livelihood. Bavris, Chunara, Khant, Nat, Waghari, etc. in Gujarat are examples.[22] On the other hand there are castes which are internally stratified. There are three types of economic differentiation within these different castes: (1) a caste characterised by sharp polarisation; (2) a caste with the majority of members from the upper strata; (3) a caste with the majority members in the poor strata. Rajputs and Thakurs of Rajasthan, Uttar Pradesh and Gujarat fall in the first category. Some households within these castes own large estates and factories while a large number of caste members are agricultural labourers. Differences in their economic conditions reflect in the social status within the caste. Though estate owners and manual labourers alike call themselves Rajputs, both have hardly any social intercourse with each other in day-to-day life. They do not intermarry; their bonds are historical and perhaps residually emotional.

Most households among several castes, such as Brahmins, Banias and Kayasthas, are well off. On the other hand backward castes comprise an overwhelming majority of households that are poor—small and marginal farmers, tenants, and agricultural labourers. At the same time, a small but vocal middle class has emerged within these castes. D.L. Sheth argues in Chapter 9, that their low ritual status has not prevented their upward mobility. Increasing economic stratification within caste affects political preferences, behaviour, and the unity of caste members on political issues. The dominant stratum of the caste often projects its interests as the interests of the whole caste, and gives it priority while bargaining with the government. For instance, the elites of the SCs and OBCs emphasise reservation in government jobs, higher educational facilities, and more berths in the state cabinet and other public institutions rather than the implementation of land reforms, the distribution of land, and higher wages for labourers—issues which affect most members of the caste. At the same time, while bargaining with the authorities, they do talk about poverty and deprivation. They use ethnic symbols and idioms to seek the backing of a large number of caste fellows. Economic differentiation has led to tensions within the deprived castes. Though they look towards the educated and relatively well-placed members of their castes for help, the poor complain that the latter corner benefits provided by the government. In some regions they have begun to assert themselves against the elites of their castes.

They have been lukewarm in their support to white-collar employees of their castes who fought against the upper castes on the issue of reservation in Gujarat in the 1980 anti-reservation agitation.[23] The middle class of the deprived communities has been alienated in day-to-day life from commoner caste members. At the same time, the upper castes prevent their integration into the middle class.

Though upper castes enjoy a higher social status, it is very difficult to say whether their higher status is because of their ritual status or their economic power—their ownership of land. In Gujarat, Brahmins have not occupied a dominant political position in rural areas. As a group they were not a major landowning caste. Earlier, Rajputs were landlords with much power. Power has been shifting to the middle peasant caste, that is, Patidars, since the mid-nineteenth century. For Uttar Pradesh, Lewis observes: 'While the landowners are generally of higher caste in Indian villages, it is their position as landowners, rather than caste membership per se, which gives them status. In Karimpur where Brahmins are landowners, the traditional caste hierarchy prevails. But in Rampura, the Jats own the land and Brahmins are subservient to them.'[24] Brahmins have not been the dominant landowning caste everywhere in the country. The situation varies from region to region.

CASTE ASSOCIATIONS: THE PRESSURE GROUP

The numerical strength of a group is important in a democratic polity. All jatis are not equal in number or in their spread over region—village, cluster of villages, taluka, district. Some are concentrated in a village/taluka and some scattered in four to five households in a village. Large jatis have an edge in political bargaining with the government and political parties. Therefore there is a tendency among several jatis to expand their network at the district and regional levels, beyond the cluster of village confined by endogamy. Some such jatis form caste associations called a *sabha* or *sangam,* consisting of a cluster of jatis with similar social ranking in a region. More often than not, they are an agglomeration of jatis. There are also a few caste association of multicastes that have different social rankings in the traditional order. They may be called caste 'federations'. More than one caste association for a single caste is not uncommon. Some of these associations are 'horizontal', catering to different areas; some compete with each other.

A caste association is not the same as a traditional caste panchayat or council. Generally, the office-bearers of a caste council enjoy a hereditary position. This is not the case with an association. Often, the latter has a written constitution specifying the power and responsibilities of office-bearers. The former has judicial authority in dealing with ritual and social aspects related to marriage, divorce and family disputes among members. Its decisions are binding on all caste members. Caste associations carry out social, economic, educational and political functions. All members of the caste are not members of *sabhas*; the decisions of the *sabha* are not binding on all caste members. In this sense a caste association is closer to a voluntary organisation. Many caste associations hold out the objective 'to promote and protect the interests and rights of the community' but do not necessarily directly involve themselves in electoral politics.[25] They stay distant from day-to-day politics. They mainly carry out educational (distribution of scholarships, and books, running of schools and hostels), economic (financial assistance to the needy and employment), health-related (offering medicine and healthcare facilities), social (organising marriage functions, get-togethers, constructing and maintaining community halls for the celebration of festivals) and religious activities (organising *bhajans* and *kathas*, religious festivals, managing temples). Many of them publish journals. In 1954 G.S. Ghurye counted no less than 1700 registered caste organisations in Bombay.

The upper castes, with a sizeable well-off section, can mobilise resources and run a number of economic and educational activities. This is not the case with castes that have the majority of households in abject poverty. Their members have to depend on the charity of other organisations run by non-governmental organisations (NGOs), on upper-caste and religious organisations, and on welfare programmes of the state for health and education. Their caste associations too undertake social and religious programmes. These activities sustain and strengthen bonds among members. Most such organisations do not directly get involved in electoral politics. The caste association of those jatis which can muster large numbers and cover a wide geographical area are frequently active in electoral politics. For Rudolph and Rudolph the participation of caste associations in politics is 'the democratic incarnation of caste'. Kothari calls it the 'democratisation' of castes.

The history of caste associations goes back to the late nineteenth century, though their number has increased after independence. They are found in all states. Let us take a few examples. In Maharashtra, the Kshatriya Sabha came into existence in the early 1880s to unite various subcastes among them and 'carry on propaganda for the acquisition of higher social status'.[26] In Uttar Pradesh the Sardar Kurmi Kshatriya Sabha was formed in 1884 to protest against the government decision debarring Kurmis from being recruited in the police service. Another example are the Nadars of Tamil Nadu. In order to augment their economic development, the wealthy Shanars of Tamil Nadu formed the Nadar Mahajan Sangam in 1895.[27] In Gujarat, Rajputs constitute 4 per cent of the population. Politically aspirant Rajputs, having lost political power as rulers of erstwhile states and threatened with loss of land under land-reform legislation, felt the need for a larger numerical support base. They formed the Gujarat Kshatriya Sabha. The caste organisation embraced various jatis of Kolis, who aspired to Kshatriya status. Caste pride and sentiments were invoked in various ways among the Rajputs and Kolis as the Kshatriyas' brethren.[28]

Various activities of caste associations, as of other pressure groups, instil consciousness among the members of their unity, strengthening their bonds and protecting their interests. They make representations to the government, demanding educational facilities, land and its distribution, government jobs, and so on, for caste members. Some submit memoranda or organise public meetings demanding infrastructure facilities such as irrigation, electricity, loans, subsidies for agricultural development. Others bargain with political parties for seats in state assemblies and Parliament, or for other political positions. They are actively involved in politics to mobilse caste members in elections to Parliament. The Gujarat Kshatriya Sabha was a major force in Gujarat politics in the 1960s. In the process, the leaders of the sabha split among various parties, and several parallel caste associations of the Kshatriyas have come into existence supporting the Congress and the BJP. Rajni Kothari and Rushikesh Maru present, in Chapter 10, a detailed study of the political role of the sabha till the early 1960s.

POLITICAL PARTNERS

Several castes join together and launch movements for social reform, for the assertion of their rights and justice, and for political power vis-à-vis the dominant castes. Non-Brahmin movements in Tamil Nadu and Maharashtra are examples. Jyotirao Phule organised the Satyashodhak Samaj in Maharashtra in 1873, challenging Brahminical hegemony. Though non-Brahmins, particularly Marathas, did not form a party of their own, they captured power within the Congress party. The movement changed the course of politics in the region. In Tamil Nadu several peasant castes, such as Vellala, Gaunda and Padayachi; trading castes such as Chetri; artisan castes such as Tachchan (carpenter), Kollan (blacksmith), and Tattan (goldsmith), individually and jointly initiated non-Brahmin movements. The movement followed several caste associations such as Parayan Mahajan sabha and Adi-Dravin Mahajan Sabha in the 1890s. In 1916 the non-Brahmin manifesto was brought out, highlighting the dominance of Brahmins in government services, and injustice to non-Brahmins, who constituted a vast majority. The formation of the Justice Party followed in 1916. The party sent a delegation to England in 1919 to present the non-Brahmin case before the Joint Parliamentary Committee that was responsible for the preparation of the Government of India Bill. The Dravida Munnetra Kazhagam (DMK) is its offshoot. Two factions of the Vanniyaakkula Kshatriya Sangam of the Nadars formed the Tamil Nadu Toilers' Party and Commonwealth Party and fought the 1952 elections. They then bargained with the Congress for position in the state cabinet. The Scheduled Caste Federation was formed in the 1940s by Ambedkar. Later, in 1956, the Republican Party was formed; these primarily remained the parties of and by the Dalits. The Jharkhand Party was formed by Adivasi leaders in Bihar, and confined to Adivasis. The Bahujan Samaj Party (BSP), launched by Kanshi Ram in 1984, is a party of Dalits aiming at forming alliances of Dalits, minorities and OBCs.

After independence, certain caste associations were formed with the political objective of competing in elections. In Gujarat some of the leaders of the Kshatriya Sabha contemplated, in the early 1950s, forming a party of Kshatriyas. They soon realised they could not muster enough support to contest elections only on the strength of Kshatriyas. Similarly, the political elite of the Kurmis, Yadavas and Koeris formed the Bihar State Backward Caste Association in 1947 to contest elections. The plan did not take off thanks to the resistance of Congress leaders belonging to these castes.[29]

Caste associations of traditionally deprived communities asserted, alongside different leading political parties, to see that their caste members were given party tickets to contest elections. The parties initially resisted pressures from these castes because of the countervailing forces of the dominant castes that controlled the party. Leaders of the upper castes realised they had to share power with lower-caste party members. The numerical strength of the deprived groups became a threat to their position. The party elite accused the new aspirants backed by caste associations as 'casteist' or 'communal'. They prevented the new entrants on 'secular' grounds, such as merit, seniority and party commitment. While nominating candidates for elections, the party's consideration, it was argued, was the aspirants' seniority and commitment to the ideology of the party. In some places, members of the deprived groups were prevented from becoming party members under one pretext or another.[30] But as the competition intensified and as the caste associations of the deprived castes successfully mobilised members for political activities, all parties began to woo leading aspirants of the caste who could mobilise caste votes. Such political aspirants joined different political parties. As they were primarily interested in wielding political positions for themselves rather than serving the social or ritual interests of the caste, they either launched a new association or split the existing one. For them a caste association has been one among several instruments to gain political power.

Some political parties identify with certain castes over the nomination of party candidates and mobilisation in elections. They declare that they stand for protecting the interests of certain castes and communities. The Bharatiya Kranti Dal, under the leadership of Charan Singh, stood for the interests of peasants. It evolved an alliance of four major peasant castes of Uttar Pradesh in the 1969-elections. The alliance was called AJGAR: Ahirs, Jats, Gujjars and Rajputs. In 1977, in Gujarat, the Congress (I) formed Kham, an alliance of Kshatriyas, Harijans, Adivasis and Muslims, for the distribution of party tickets and electoral mobilisation. The party took a pro-poor posture by undertaking a 20-point poverty alleviation programme. It introduced reservation for OBCs in government jobs and for admission in higher studies. Later, it increased the quota of reservation for OBCs to strengthen its base. The Lok Dal was identified with Jars in Uttar Pradesh in the 1977 and 1980 parliamentary elections. The Samajwadi Party in Uttar Pradesh was identified with backward castes in general, and Yadavas in particular, in the 1997 state assembly elections. In Karnataka, Vokkaligas and Lingayats; were the support base of the Congress till the 1960s. Devaraj Urs, who became chief minister in 1972, broadened the base of the party by implementing land reforms and social welfare programmes, as James Manor shows, to aid the disadvantaged backward numerically small castes. The Congress, however, could not maintain this base in the following years.[31] The BJP is generally identified with the upper castes and the Congress with the middle and backward castes. This was reflected in their support base in the 1980s in Gujarat and Maharashtra. In the 1990s the BJP followed the strategy of the Congress—of accommodating backward-caste candidates in elections and successfully getting the support of their backward caste fellows.

There were three consequences of interaction between caste associations and political parties. First, caste members, particularly the poor and marginalised who had hitherto remained untouched by political processes, were politicised and began to participate in electoral politics with an expectation that their interests would be served. Second, caste members got split among various political parties, weakening the hold of the caste. Third, numerically large castes got representation in decision-making bodies, and the strength of traditionally dominant castes was weakened. This explains the rise of middle and backward caste representations in most state assemblies. In Uttar Pradesh the proportion of the upper castes in the state assembly went down from 42 per cent to 17 per cent between 1967 and 1995; whereas the members of the OBCs increased from 24 per cent to 45 per cent during the same period. A similar pattern is found in Bihar and other states. Backward castes have been asserting themselves into political space.

CASTE IN VOTING BEHAVIOUR

As mentioned above, parties accommodate various castes in distributing party tickets. While nominating candidates they take into consideration the caste of the aspirant candidates and the distribution of the numerical strength of different castes within a constituency. Caste leaders also mobilise their followers on caste lines so that they show their strength. In the 1950s wherever caste associations were able to maintain their unity and did not formally ally with any one party, they appealed to their members to vote for their caste fellows, irrespective of their party affiliation. In Rajasthan, Meenas were told: 'Do not give your daughter or your vote to anyone but a Meena.' Similar slogans were used in Tamil Nadu: 'The Vanniya vote is not for anyone else.' But wherever caste associations allied with a particular party, caste leaders asked caste members to vote for that party. The Kshatriya leaders of Gujarat, in the 1952 elections, told Kshatriya voters it was their Kshatriya dharma to vote for the Congress because it was 'the great institution and working for the development of the country'. In the subsequent elections, as the caste leaders split, some Kshatriya leaders said: 'It is our pledge that the Kshatriya of Gujarat vote for the Congress, and not for anyone else.' The others said it was the dharma of the Kshatriyas to vote for the Maha Gujarat Janata Parishad (a regional party).

Though there is a trend among caste members to vote for a particular party, there is never *en bloc* caste voting. Some castes traditionally identify with a particular party. The Jats in Uttar Pradesh identified with the Lok Dal not only because the leaders of the party were Jats, but also because the party raised issues affecting peasants. But all the Jats did not vote for the party because there were some traditional supporters of the Congress, or who perceived their interests differently from other Jat peasants. In Uttar Pradesh, 51 per cent of the SC voters voted for the BSP in the 1998 state assembly elections; 18 per cent voted for the BJP. The vast majority of the BSP SC voters belonged to the poor strata. Middle-class SC voters voted for the BJP. While analysing the election data, Pushpendra observes: 'Occupationally, the BSP's voters are mainly unskilled workers, agricultural and allied workers, artisans, and small and marginal farmers. Persons engaged in business and white-collar jobs constitute only 2.6 and 1.6 per cent of the BSP voters [in Uttar Pradesh].'

In the National Election Survey of 1971 carried out by the Centre for the Study of Developing Societies, it was asked: 'What were your considerations for voting for this candidate/party/symbol?' In that election *garibi hatao* was the dominant issue. The hurricane was in favour of Indira Gandhi. In such a situation caste was not the major issue. This was reflected in the voting preference. The study shows that only less than 1 per cent of voters reported that the candidates' caste was their prime consideration. This has to be read in context, and keeping in mind the limitations of the survey research method: some of the respondents might have voted for people who happened to belong to their caste. But it should be noted that, in their perception, it was not essentially caste-based voting. They voted for the candidate not because he/she was of their caste irrespective of the latter's party and ability. They voted for him/her because he/she was the candidate of the party to which the respondent felt closer for a variety of reasons, including feeling that the party would 'protect his/ her' interests or because the party had done good work for the people. Or, they were in touch with the candidate who might have helped them, or they felt would later help them. Their primary consideration was their perceived interests, and the perceived ability of the party/candidate to protect them. If the candidate happens to be of their own caste, and his/her party is the party which they identify as theirs, they vote for that candidate. If they feel the candidate belongs to a party which is either not able to serve their interests or is hostile or insignificant in politics, they do not vote for that candidate even if he/she belongs to their caste. That is the reason, why several caste leaders, when they change parties or if their party loses popularity, lose elections predominantly in the constituency of their caste members, at one time or another. Therefore, there is no one-to-one relationship between a candidate's castes and that of the voters. In-depth constituency studies of the 1962 elections show that party organisation, leadership and local factors constantly cut across caste loyalties and evolve autonomy of party and secular interests.[32]

We do not have similar data for subsequent elections. During the past three decades the Congress, the Janata Dal and several other political parties have addressed the interests of certain castes. They have mobilised voters on the issues of deprivation and social justice in order to appeal to Dalits and OBCs. Caste-based parties of Dalits or tribals have been formed. In such a situation, what is the role of caste in voting behaviour? We have no data to ascertain the extent to which caste is the prime consideration during voting. During the 1999 Lok Sabha elections people were asked: 'One should vote the way one's caste community votes. Do you agree or disagree?' A third of the respondents (35 per cent) agreed with the statement—one should vote with the caste. This preference is proportionately higher (40 per cent) among the OBCs than among the upper castes. However, we do not have the means to know their meaning of 'caste'—that varies from endogamous group to caste cluster. In short, caste cannot be ignored in understanding electoral politics; at the same time, caste is not everything, and its role cannot be oversimplified as the determining factor.

CASTE CONSCIOUSNESS AND POLITICS

It is the contention of several scientists, political leaders and the media that 'caste consciousness' has increased in democratic politics during the post-independence period. They are uneasy with this development and consider it dangerous for democratic polity. In the 1950s the leading English newspapers said political competition in a representative system has given caste consciousness a new lease of life. Newspapers, by and large, continued to make similar comments in the 1990s. Selig Harrison, a leading American journalist, argued that in post-independence India caste reinforces economic and political conflict. Sriman Narayan, Congress secretary in the 1950s, observed that 'the present system of elections has undoubtedly given strength and encouragement to casteism.'[33] In the late 1970s M.N. Srinivas observed:

> I have referred to the phenomenon of the coming together of cognate jatis by the term 'horizontal stretch': 'horizontal stretch' has resulted in the emergence of huge, monster castes such as Jats, Ahirs, Rajputs, Okkaligas, Lingayats, etc., and they play a vital role in state politics, and through politics in the allocation of resources, and in the distribution of benefits to followers. In each state there are several castes which constantly jockey for power, and the caste idiom is ubiquitous in mobilising people. This occurs in spite of the fact that castes are economically and socially heterogeneous, and that frequently the most bitter rivalries exist within caste. A 'consciousness of kind' is shared by members of a caste and it is pointless to dismiss this as 'false consciousness'.[34]

These observations need qualification and further probing. First, presumably 'increased caste consciousness' contrasts with secular consciousness, implying that, in the past, secular consciousness had greater sway than caste consciousness. This opinion is not supported by evidence. Second, there is no rigorous attempt to define 'caste consciousness'. It is true that, in the past, dominant castes shared resources among themselves, but the visible and vocal aspirants for political power and resources were small and belonged to the upper castes. Decision-makers of that time therefore believed they were making decisions on secular considerations, and that caste was not the criterion. Caste was not talked about in the political sphere and commentators did not think it important. In actual fact, dominant-caste members were cornering the benefits among themselves. Members of the middle and lower castes were, at the time, not forcefully asserting their rights. The caste consciousness of the dominant castes was latent and in the absence of challenge they were able to suggest that their decisions and actions were 'secular'. But this was never so. Democratic politics and the capitalist economy have expanded the base of politics. The bourgeois values of equality and social justice have gained political legitimacy, invigorating the consciousness of traditionally deprived groups. Interaction, including struggles for resources among caste members of a variety of social classes, has increased. Confrontations have become common; a latent consciousness has come out into the open.

As pointed out above, caste also has different meaning, drawing on context. Caste is a primordial localised group; caste is also a broader cluster (though not universal) beyond the kin relationship and endogamy network. Are the former and latter increasing simultaneously? If so, how do they reconcile in a conflicting situation? What happens in the process: what kind of consciousness evolves? We do not have studies of these questions.

Finally, is caste consciousness increasing in all spheres—social, economic and political? And within the political sphere in voting behaviour, party factions, policy-making and the distribution of resources? Empirical studies are needed to probe into such aspects of caste consciousness. We are not clear that caste consciousness for political power and economic benefits among the Brahmins and the Dalits is considered in the same way. The caste consciousness of Brahmins strengthens ritual aspects of caste and helps the status quo; it aims at perpetuating the power of the few. Caste consciousness among Dalits challenges the Brahminical ideology and seeks social transformation towards an egalitarian social order. The latter is a product, and part of the process of, democratisation.

CHALLENGES

Politics does not function in a vacuum. It operates in society, where it is influenced by social forces. Politics influences social forces and changes them. If political institutions and political leaders make a conscious effort to change society, they can influence and bring about changes in the social order and its relationships to a considerable extent. We can see that democratic politics in India has been influenced by caste but it has also changed the traditional caste system and its values. Its traditional concern with purity and impurity has been considerably weakened. Caste has provided an institutional mechanism to the poor and traditionally deprived groups for political participation. Caste has been made instrumental in the pursuit of economic and social rather than ritual concerns. In that sense we are witnessing the democratic incarnation of caste. But this process has reached an impasse and been caught in a vicious circle. Political leaders use caste consciousness for mobilisation but do not really work to solve economic and social problems. So, the framework has definite limitations; it is divisive and hierarchical. This is the challenge facing caste-oriented politics.

The present volume is divided into four parts. The first has six essays by sociologists and political leaders. It is not my contention that political analysis has no sociological perspective and data. The essays here are written mainly with a political purpose, to influence policy for social transformation and strategies for mobilisation and political action. Similarly, sociological writings are never apolitical. The difference between the two is in emphasis and rigour.

Part Two has three essays. They analyse the diffusion of power—the changing nature of dominant castes in rural India and increasing stratification within castes—during the post-independence period.

Part Three has four essays examining caste and political processes in different parts of the country. They deal with the changing nature of caste in relation to politics; caste in relation to political parties and representation; and the assertion of the traditionally deprived groups through electoral processes.

Part Four discusses the politics of reservation and social transformation.

ACKNOWLEDGEMENTS

I thank the Centre for the Study of Developing Societies in Delhi for permitting me to use their election data. I also thank Rajeev Bhargava for his comments on an earlier draft of this chapter.

Part I

THE MEANINGS OF CASTE

Introduction

There is no precise definition of caste. And there is no single definitive theoretical perspective on the caste system in India. Those who look from above, from the vantage point of Brahmins, view caste-based social order differently from those who look from below, from the vantage point of Dalits. Differing perspectives not only influence different understandings of the system, but also the prescriptions and strategies for maintaining or changing it. This outlines a few major perspectives which have influenced the course of Indian politics.

Sociological literature on the ethnographic description and structure of the caste system is very large. It includes individual caste and kinship studies, village studies, and studies on social change focusing on behaviour, value systems and interpersonal relations. G.S. Ghurye, doyen of Indian sociology, published *Caste and Race in India* in 1932. This has appeared in several editions and with new titles: *Caste and Class in India*, and *Caste, Class and Occupation in India*. Ghurye gives a detailed ethnographic account of six important characteristics of the caste system.

Louis Dumont, the eminent French sociologist, greatly influenced the discourse in Indian sociology in the 1970s. In his famous book *Homo Hierarchicus: The Caste System and Its Implications,* he constructed an overall framework for the caste system. In one chapter, titled 'The Theory of the Varnas: Power and Priesthood', he examines the relationship between power and hierarchy in the varna system. Hierarchy in the caste system is not the same, he says, as in the 'social stratification' of Western society; nor is it graduated authority or power, as in a 'military hierarchy'. Hierarchy in caste is the principle by which the elements of the whole are ranked in relation to the whole. He argues that it need not be seen as a linear order, but as a series of successive positions. In the varna theory, power is ultimately subordinate to priesthood: spiritual and temporal authority are not one and the same. Unlike the West, in the varna system spiritual power, that is, supreme spiritual authority is not necessarily expressed politically. Of course, there are many critics of this view.

Mahatma Gandhi was, among other things, a social reformer and visionary. His philosophy and practice have had a considerable influence on Indian politics. Gandhi called himself a Sanatani Hindu. He believed in 'the Vedas, the Upanishads, the Puranas, and all that goes by the name of Hindu Scriptures and therefore in Avatars and rebirth'. He believed in the varna system and *varnashram dharma*. But he was against the caste system, which, according to him, is a degeneration of the varna system. He was particularly strongly against untouchability, apart from wanting abolition of the caste system. The chapter presented here argues that 'Caste Must Go' while the varna system remains.

Dr B.R. Ambedkar, the leading Dalit leader, rejected Gandhi's views on caste and the varna system. He argued that the caste system has religious legitimacy and sanction; he therefore rejected Hinduism. He argued further that the caste system was anti-progress and perpetuated the dominance of Brahmins, and is therefore politically unacceptable.

For most Indian Marxists, caste is an Indian version of class. Here the caste system is seen as a product of pre-industrial class society. It will disappear, Marxists expect, with the ultimate success of the class struggle. Hence they concentrate on class analysis and class struggle and pay little attention to the *issue* of caste. However, a small section of Marxists did give importance to understanding caste in Indian politics. B.T. Ranadive, a leading political leader and theorist, in 'Caste, Class and Property Relations', argues that anti-caste struggles by the oppressed classes should be supported even when they apparently take the form of a demand for the reservation of jobs. He calls for deeper struggle, embracing the oppressed of all castes, against the present socio-economic system based on property and production relations that sustain both caste and class oppression.

Ram Manohar Lohia was the important socialist leader who addressed caste issues in democratic politics. He found that the class view of politics was multidimensional and ignored social realities. He was a champion of the struggles of oppressed castes for reservations for them in legislative bodies and government employment. D.L. Sheth has excerpted Ram Manohar Lohia's writings on 'Caste, Class and Gender in Indian Politics'. Sheth's brief Introduction helps the reader contextualise Lohia's writings on the issue.

2

Features of the Caste System*

G. S. GHURYE

Hindu society is divided into groups, known as castes, with varying degrees of respectability and circles of social intercourse. Baines observes: 'It needs but a very short time in the country to bring home to the most casual observer the ubiquity of the institution, and to make him acquainted with some of the principal exoteric features.' This is due not only to the fact that caste is the most general form of social organisation in India but also because it presents such a marked contrast to the social grouping prevalent in Europe or America. Owing to these two features—ubiquity and strangeness—the institution has found many able scholars devoted to its study. With all the labours of these students, however, we do not possess a real general definition of caste. It appears to me that any attempt at definition is bound to fail because of the complexity of the phenomenon. On the other hand, much literature on the subject is marred by lack of precision about the use of the term. Hence I propose to give a description of the factors underlying this system of castes.

The earliest account of this institution, given by a foreigner of the third century BC, mentions two of the features characterising it before it was modified by close cultural contact with Western Europe during the last century. 'It is not permitted to contract marriage with a person of another caste, nor to change from one profession or trade to another, nor for the same person to undertake more than one, except if he is of the caste of philosophers, when permission is given on account of his dignity.' Though this statement of Megasthenes brings two of the most salient features of the institution to the forefront, yet it falls to give a complete idea of the system.

The outstanding features of Hindu society when it was ruled by the social philosophy of caste, unaffected by the modern ideas of rights and duties, may be discerned to be six.

---

*Caste and Race in India, Bombay: Popular Prakashan, 1969, pp. 1–15.

Segmental division of society: This caste-society was not a more or less homogeneous community in which, whatever distinctions of social status may exist, they are so much in the background that a special inquiry has to be made in order to realise their presence, but a society in which various groups with distinct appellations were prominent. Castes were groups with a well-developed life of their own, the membership whereof, unlike that of voluntary associations and of classes, was determined not by selection but by birth. The status of a person depended not on his wealth as in the classes of modern Europe but on the traditional importance of the caste in which he had the luck of being born. On the distinction between caste and class, as far only as cleavage into well-marked groups is concerned, MacIver observes:

> Whereas in eastern civilisations the chief determinant of a class and status was birth, in the western civilisation of today wealth is a class-determinant of equal or perhaps greater importance, and wealth is a less rigid determinant than birth: it is more concrete, and thus its claims are more easily challenged; itself a matter of degree, it is less apt to create distinctions of kind, alienable, acquirable, and transferable, it draws no such permanent lines of cleavage as does birth .[3]

To restrict myself to the Marathi region, a person is born either a Brahmin, Prabhu, Maratha, Vani, Sonar, Sutar, Bhandari, Chamar, or a Mahar, etc. If he chances to take a vocation which is not earmarked for a particular caste—say the military—he remains a casteman all the same. A Brahmin general and a Maratha general, though of equal status in the army, belong to two different status-groups in their private life and there could not be any social intercourse between them on equal terms. But this is not the case in a class-society where status is determined by vocation and consequent income. A class has no council, standing or occasional, to regulate the conduct and guide the morals of its members, apart from the laws of the community as a whole. Members of one class follow different vocations and, when organised, have standing executive committees, which govern the members of their profession according to their rules. These rules generally exclude the legitimate province of the wider community, and refer only to processional etiquette or economic gain. 'In the case of the brain-working profession, these common rules and this authoritative direction seek to prescribe such matters as the qualifications for entry, the character of the training, the methods of remuneration, the conditions of employment, the rules of behaviour towards fellow professionals and the public, the qualifications and methods of selection for public appointments, and the terms of service, the maintenance of the status of the profession, and the power of expulsion.'[4] Most of the castes on the other hand, excepting the high ones like the Brahmin[5] and the Rajput, have regular standing councils deciding on many more matters than those taken cognisance of by the committees of the trade unions, associations, or guilds, and thus encroaching on the province of the whole community. How the Brahmin and other castes manage their affairs is not quite clear, but in the case of the Brahmins of southern India at least, it seems from an epigraphic record that as occasion arose they used to call a special meeting of the members of the caste.[6] The assembly could get its decree executed by the king's officials. The governing body of a caste is called the panchayat. Some of the offences dealt with by it are: (a) eating, drinking, or having similar dealings with a caste or subcaste, with which such social intercourse is held to be forbidden; (b) keeping as concubine a woman of another caste; (c) seduction of or adultery with a married woman; (d) fornication; (e) refusal to fulfil a promise of marriage; (f) refusing to send a wife to her husband when old enough; (g) refusing to maintain a wife; (h) non-payment of debt; (i) petty assaults; (j) breaches of the customs of the trade peculiar to the caste; (k) encroaching on another's clientele, and raising or lowering prices; (l) killing a cow or any other forbidden animal; (m) insulting a Brahmin; (n) defying the customs of the caste regarding feasts, etc., during marriage and other ceremonies.[7] It will be seen from this list that some of the offences tried by the governing bodies of castes were such as are usually dealt with by the State in its judicial capacity. Thus, a caste was a group with a separate arrangement for meting out justice to its members apart from that of the community as a whole, within which the caste was included as only one of the groups. Hence the members of a caste ceased to be members of the community as a whole, as far as that part of their morals which is regulated by law was concerned.[8] This quasi-sovereignty of the caste is particularly brought to notice by the fact that the caste council was prepared to retry criminal offences decided by the courts of law.[9] This means that in this caste-bound society the amount of community feeling must have been restricted, and that the citizens owed moral allegiance to their caste first, rather than to the community as a whole. By segmental division I wish to connote this aspect of the system. The punishments that these councils awarded were: (1) outcasting, either temporary or permanent; (2) fines; (3) feasts to be given to the castemen; (4) corporal punishment; and (5) sometimes religious expiation. The proceeds of the fines were generally spent on a common feast. Sometimes the perquisites of the panchayat were bought out of them and sometimes again they were donated to charitable purposes.[10] This description of the activities of a caste-council will enable us to appreciate the remark, 'The caste is its own ruler'.[11] The diversity in the administration of law necessarily led to differences in moral standards of the various castes. There was thus created a cultural gulf between the castes. I may note some of the items of cultural differences among the castes to bring out clearly the implications of the segmentation. Many of the castes have their special deities. Among such castes the following may be noted from southern India, Komati, Kamsala, Gamalla, Idiga, Mala and Madiga;[12] from the Central Provinces, Ahir;[13] from Uttar Pradesh, Aheriya, Baheliya, Kharwar, Korwa, Chero, Bhuiyar, Dom, Musahar, and Nai;[14] and from Gujarat, the Vaishyas.[15] About the differences in religious outlook of the Madras castes it has been said: 'Amongst the Brahmin community this one fact stands off clear and distinct, that they do not indulge in the worship of Grama Devata, the village gods, to which the aboriginal population almost exclusively bows down.'[16] The customs about marriage and death vary widely among the different castes. Brahmins did not permit widow-marriage nor tolerate concubinage as a caste-practice. This could not be said of many lower castes. Not only were there such differences in cultural matters among the different castes, but in theory also different standards of conduct were upheld. Thus the Brahmin Government of Poona, while passing some legislation prohibiting the manufacture and sale of liquors, excluded the Bhandaris, Kolis and similar other castes from the operation thereof, but strictly forbade the use of drink to 'Brahmins, Shenvis, Prabhus and Government officers'.[17] These differences of morals and customs were so manifest that the early British courts in India not merely asked the opinion of their pundits, but took the evidence of the heads of the castes concerned as to their actual usages. The collection of laws and customs of Hindu castes, made by Steele under the orders of government, was intended to help the courts to ascertain the diverse customs. The Hindus have no standing arrangements for the disposal of their dead. When any person dies it is the caste-fellows who are to be invited to carry the corpse to the cremation ground and to dispose of it. At the time of marriage a feast has, by common consent, to be given to all the members of one's own caste resident in the village or the town. At the preparation of these feasts as well as in connection with other items of the marriage ceremony it is again the caste-people who run to one's help. These and similar affairs of day-to-day life require the co-operation of one's caste-people. Hence castes are small and complete social worlds in themselves, marked off definitely from one another, though subsisting within the larger society.

Hierarchy: In my discussion of the subject so far I have used the comparative degree with reference to the status of different castes, thus assuming beforehand one of the principal characteristics of the caste-society, namely, the hierarchy of the groups. Everywhere in India there is a definite scheme of social precedence amongst the castes, with the Brahmin at the head of the hierarchy. Only in southern India the artisan castes 'have always maintained a struggle for a higher place in the social scale than that allowed to them by Brahmanical authority ... There is no doubt as to the fact that the members of this great caste (Kammalan) dispute the supremacy of the Brahmins, and that they hold themselves to be equal in rank with them.' John Fryer, who visited India in

1960, seems to refer to this attitude.[18] In any one of the linguistic divisions of India there are as many as two hundred castes which can be grouped in classes whose gradation is largely acknowledged by all. But the order of social precedence amongst the individual castes of any class cannot be made definite, because not only is there no ungrudging acceptance of such rank but also the ideas of the people on this point are very nebulous and uncertain. The following observations vividly bring out this state of things: 'As the society now stands ... the place due to each community is not easily distinguishable, nor is any common principle of precedence recognised by the people themselves by which to grade the castes. Excepting the Brahmin at one end and the admittedly degraded castes like the Holeyas at the other, the members of a large proportion of the intermediate castes think or profess to think that their caste is better than their neighbours' and should be ranked accordingly.'[19] Martin remarks about Bihar that the Shudras there were usually divided into four classes, but adds: 'The people, who assisted me in making up this account, could not with certainty refer each caste to its class; for they never had bestowed pains to enquiry concerning the various claims of such low persons.'[20]

   Restrictions on feeding and social intercourse: There are minute rules as to what sort of food or drink can be accepted by a person and from what castes. But there is very great diversity in this matter. The practices in the matter of food and social intercourse divide India into two broad belts. In Hindustan proper, castes can be divided into five groups; first, the twice-born castes; second, those castes at whose hands the twice-born can take 'pakka' food; third, those castes at whose hands the twice-born cannot accept any kind of food but may take water; fourth, castes that are not untouchable yet are such that water from them cannot be used by the twice-born; last come all those castes whose touch defiles not only the twice-born but any orthodox Hindu.[21] All food is divided into two classes, 'kachcha' and 'pakka', the former being any food in the cooking of which water has been used, and the latter all food cooked in 'ghee' without the addition of water. 'As a rule a man will never eat "kachcha" food unless it is prepared by a fellow caste-man, which in actual practice means a member of his own endogamous group, whether it be caste or subcaste, or else by his Brahmin "Guru" or spiritual guide.'[22] But in practice most castes seem to take no objection to 'kachcha' food from a Brahmin.[23] A Brahmin can accept 'kachcha' food at the hands of no other caste; nay, some of them, like the Kanaujias Brahmins, are so punctilious about these restrictions that, as a proverb has it, three Kanaujias require no less than thirteen hearths.[24] As for the 'pakka' food, it may be taken by a Brahmin at the hands of some of the castes only. On the whole, however, as E.A. Blunt has made out, there is 'no relation between a caste's social position and the severity of its cooking taboo'; as many as thirty-six out of seventy-six castes of Uttar Pradesh take 'kachcha' food from only their own members and none others.[25]

The ideas about the power of certain castes to convey pollution by touch are not so highly developed in northern India as in the south. The idea that impurity can be transmitted by the mere shadow of an untouchable or by his approaching within a certain distance does not seem to prevail in Hindustan. No Hindu of decent [upper] caste would touch a Chamar, or a Dom; and some of the very low castes themselves are quite strict about contact. Thus 'The Bansphor and Basor, themselves branches of the Dom caste, will touch neither a Dom, nor a Dhobi, whilst the Basor, with all the intolerance of the parvenu, extends his objections to the Musahar, Chamar, Dharkar and Bhangi.'[26]

In Bengal the castes are divided into two main groups, the Brahmins and the Shudras. The second class is further divided into four subclasses, indicating their status as regards food and water: (a) the Sat-Shudra group includes such castes as the Kayastha. and Nabashakh; (b) then come the Jalacharaniya Shudras, 'being those castes, not technically belonging to the Nabashakh group, from whom Brahmins and members of the higher castes can take water', (c) then follow the jalabyabaharya-Shudras, castes from whose hands a Brahmin cannot take water; (d) last stand the Asprishya-Shudras, castes whose touch is so impure as to pollute even the Ganges water, and hence their contact must be avoided. They are thus the untouchables.[27] In the matter of food western Bengal resembles Hindustan except in this that in Bengal there are some people who will not accept any 'kachcha' food even from the hands of a Brahmin. 'pakka' food can be ordinarily taken not only from one's own or any higher caste, but also from the confectioner class, the Myras and Halwais.[28] As regards the position of the untouchables, the following observation will give a clear idea. 'Even wells are polluted if a low caste man draws water from them, but a great deal depends on the character of the vessel used and of the well from which water is drawn. A masonry well is not so easily defiled as one constructed with clay pipes, and if it exceeds three and a half cubits in width so that a cow may turn round in it, it can be used even by the lowest castes without defilement.' Certain low castes are looked down upon as so unclean that they may not enter the courtyard of the great temples. These castes are compelled to live by themselves on the outskirts of villages.[29]

In eastern and southern Bengal[30] and in Gujarat and the whole of southern India there is no distinction of food as 'kachcha' for the purposes of its acceptance or otherwise from anyone but a member of one's own caste. In Gujarat[31] and southern India, generally speaking, a Brahmin never thinks of accepting water, much less any cooked food, from any caste but that of the Brahmins, and all the other castes or groups of castes more or less follow the principle of accepting no cooked food from any caste that stands lower than itself in the social scale. This rule does not apply with the same strictness to accepting water. Again as a rule, a lower caste has no scruples in accepting cooked food from any higher caste. Thus all the castes will take cooked food from the Brahmin.

The theory of pollution being communicated by some castes to members of the higher ones is also more developed in Gujarat. Theoretically, the touch of a member of any caste lower than one's own defiles a person of the higher caste; but in actual practice this rule is not strictly observed. In the Maratha country the shadow of an untouchable is sufficient, if it falls on a member of a higher caste, to pollute him. In Madras, and especially in Malabar, this doctrine is still further elaborated, so that certain castes have always to keep a stated distance between themselves and the Brahmin and other higher castes so as not to defile the latter. Thus the Shanar, toddy-tapper of Tamilnad, contaminates a Brahmin if he approaches the latter within twenty-four paces.[32] Among the people of Kerala, a Nayar may approach a Nambudiri Brahmin but must not touch him; while a Tiyan must keep himself at a distance of thirty-six steps from the Brahmin, and a Pulayan may not approach him within ninety-six paces.[*] A Tiyan must keep away from a Nayar at twelve paces, while some castes may approach the Tiyan, though they must not touch him. A Pulayan must not come near any of the Hindu castes. So rigid are the rules about defilement which is supposed to be carried with them by all except the Brahmins, that the latter will not perform even their ablutions within the precincts of a Shudra's habitation.[33] Generally the washerman and the barber that serve the general body of villagers, will not render their services to the unclean and untouchable castes. 'Even a modern Brahmin doctor, when feeling the pulse of a Shudra, first wraps up the patient's wrist with a small piece of silk so that he may not be defiled by touching his skin.'[34]

Civil and religious disabilities and privileges of the different sections: Segregation of individual castes or of groups of castes in a village is the most obvious mark of civil privileges and disabilities, and it has prevailed in a more or less definite form all over India. Southern India, in the matter of ceremonial purity and untouchability, stands out distinct in the rigidity of these rules. In northern India generally, in the Maratha country and, as it appears, sometimes in the Telugu and Kanarese regions, it is only the impure castes that are segregated and made to live on the outskirts of villages. It does not seem that other groups of castes have distinct quarters of the town or village allotted to them excepting in, parts of Gujarat. In the Tamil and Malayalam regions very frequently different quarters are occupied by separated castes or sometimes the village is divided into three parts: that occupied by the dominant caste in the village or by the Brahmins, that allotted to the Shudras, and the one reserved for the

---

* For a slightly different scale of distances, see M.S.A. Rao's *Social Change in Malabar*, 1957, p. 21.

Panchamas or untouchables. In a village of Ramnad district, the main portion is occupied by the Nayakars, shepherds, artisans, washermen, and barbers, forming a group living in the northeast corner of the village, while the untouchables ply their trades in the northwest and the southeast corners.[35] In Trichinopoly district the villages have the houses arranged in streets. 'The Brahmin, Shudra and Panchama quarters are separate, and in the last of these the Pallans, Paraiyans and Chakkiliyans live in separate streets.'[36] In Madras, Pallis or agriculturists live in separate quarters 'distinctively known as the Palli teru'.[37] Sometimes, as in the district of Bellary, it is only the untouchable, like the Madiga, that is singled out for segregation, all other castes living in close proximity to one another.[38] In some parts of the Maratha country castes have been allotted distinct quarters of the village called by the name of the caste: Brahmin-ali, or wada, Prabhu-ali, Sonar-ali, etc. The depressed classes, like the Mang, Mahar, etc., are forced to live on the outskirts of the village.[39]

In southern India certain parts of the town or village are inaccessible to certain castes. The agitation by the impure castes to gain free access to certain streets in Vaikam in Travancore brings into clear relief some of the disabilities of these castes. It is recorded that under the rule of the Marathas and the Peshwas, the Mahars and Mangs were not allowed within the gates of Poona after 3 p.m. and before 9 a.m. because before nine and after three their bodies cast too long a shadow, which falling on a member of the higher castes— especially Brahmin—defiles him.[40] However, in the Dravidian south,[*] the very land of the supreme dominance of the Brahmin, the Brahmin was restricted in his rights of access to any part of the village. It is well known that in a village which is a gift to the Brahmins, a Paraiyan is not allowed to enter the Brahmin quarter; but it is not known to many students that the Paraiyans will not permit a Brahmin to pass through their street; so much so that if one happens to enter their quarters they would greet him with cow-dung water. 'Brahmins in Mysore consider that great luck will await them if they can manage to pass through the Holeya (untouchable) quarter of a village unmolested.[41] All over India the impure castes are debarred from drawing water from the village well, which is used by the members of other castes. In the Maratha country a Mahar—one of the untouchables—might not spit on the road lest a pure-caste Hindu should be polluted by touching it with his foot, but had to carry an earthen pot hung from his neck, in which to spit. Further he had to drag a thorny branch with him to wipe out his footprints and to lie at a distance prostrate on the ground if a Brahmin passed by, so that his foul shadow might not defile the holy Brahmin.[42] In the Punjab, where restrictions regarding Pollution by proximity have been far less stringent than in other parts of India, a sweeper, while walking through the streets of the larger towns, was supposed

---

* Specially speaking Tamilnadu.

to carry a broom in his hand or under his armpit as a mark of his being a scavenger and had to shout out to the people warning them of his polluting presence.[43] The schools, maintained at public cost, are practically closed to such impure castes as the Chamars and Mahars. 'Both teachers and pupils in the schools make it most difficult for low-caste boys to sit in the class-room.'[44] In Gujarat the depressed castes used to wear a horn as their distinguishing mark.[45] From certain decisions noted by the Peshwas in their diaries one can form some idea about the disabilities of some of the castes in the Maratha country. The rulers upheld the claim of the potters, opposed by the carpenters, that they could lead their bridal processions on horseback, and that of the coppersmith, against the Lingayats, to go in procession through public streets.[46]

In Dravidian India the disabilities of the lower castes went so far as to prescribe what sort of houses they should build and what material they might employ in the construction thereof. The Shanars and Izhavas, toddy-tappers of the eastern and the western coasts, were not allowed to build houses above one storey in height.[47] In Malabar the house is called by different names according to the occupant's caste; and peoples of inferior castes dare not refer to their own homes in the presence of a Nambudiri Brahmin in more flattering terms than as 'dung-heaps'.[48]

The toddy-tappers of Malabar and the east coast, Izhavas and Shanars, were not allowed to carry umbrellas, to wear shoes or golden ornaments, to milk cows or even to use the ordinary language of the country.[49] In Malabar, Brahmins alone were permitted to sit on boards formed in the shape of a tortoise, and if a member of any other caste were to use such a seat he was liable to capital punishment.[50] Members of all castes, except the Brahmins, were expressly forbidden to cover the upper part of their body above the waist.[51] In the case of women also, until 1865 they were obliged by law to go with the upper part of their bodies quite bare, if they belonged to the Tiyan or other lower castes.[52] Under the Peshwas a greater distinction was made in the punishment on account of the caste of the criminal than of the nature of the crime itself. Hard labour and death were punishments mostly visited on criminals of the lower castes.[53]

In Tamilnad there has been for ages a faction among the non-Brahmin castes dividing most of them into two groups, the right-hand castes and the left-hand castes. The 'right-hand' castes claim certain privileges which they strongly refuse to those of the 'left-hand', namely, riding on horseback in processions, carrying standards with certain devices, and supporting their marriage booths on twelve pillars. They insist that the 'left-hand' castes must not raise more than eleven pillars to the booth nor employ on their standards devices peculiar to the 'right-hand' castes.[54]

Brahminic ceremonies are to be performed with the help of a ritual, and two types of rituals have been evolved: the Vedic and the Puranic. The Vedic ritual is based on the Vedic mantras and is regarded as of great sanctity, while the Puranic is based on formulae of less sanctity, and not on revealed knowledge. How great this feeling of sanctity about Vedic lore was can be gauged from the fact that in 1843 a Brahmin professor advised the Bombay Board of Education not to publish a certain book because it contained quotations from Panini's grammar which, if printed, would be desecrated.[55] The Shudras are asked to content themselves with the Puranic ritual, while for the impure castes, a Brahmin, unless he is a pseudo-Brahmin or an apostate, would not minister at all. During the career of Sawai Madhavrao, the Peshwa government had decreed that the Mahars, being *atishudras*, 'beyond Shudras', could not have their marriage rites conducted by the regular Brahmin priests. They were asked to content themselves with the services of their castemen- priests, the Medhe-Mahars.[56] It is only from the hands of the clean Shudras, again, that a Brahmin will accept any gifts which are meant to store up merit for the donor. Such an advanced caste as the Prabhu in the Maratha country had to establish its right of carrying on the sacred rites according to the Vedic formulae which were being questioned during the period of the later Peshwas.[57] Certain sacraments cannot be performed by any other caste than the Brahmins. The most sacred literature cannot be studied by the Shudras. No caste can employ any other priests than the Brahmins, with very few exceptions, in southern India. The artisans of Madras seem to employ their own priests; and the goldsmith caste of the Maratha region established their right of employing their caste-fellows as priests during the last part of the Peshwa rule.[58] The innermost recesses of temples can be approached only by the Brahmins, clean Shudras and other high castes having to keep outside the sacred precincts. The impure castes, and particularly the untouchables, cannot enter even the outer portions of a temple but must keep to the courtyards. In south Malabar, the high castes do not allow the Tiyans to cremate their dead.[59]

A Brahmin never bows to anyone who is not a Brahmin, but requires others to salute him; and when he is saluted by a member of a non-Brahmin caste he only pronounces a benediction. Some of the lower castes carry their reverence for the Brahmins, especially in northern India, to such extremes that they will not cross the shadow of a Brahmin, and sometimes will not take their food without sipping water in which the big toe of a Brahmin is dipped. The Brahmin, on the other hand, is so conscious of his superiority that he does not condescend to bow even to the idols of gods in a Shudra's house.[60] The Brahmin has been regarded as the most important subject, needing protection from the king, so much so that the king is styled the protector of the Brahmins and the cows, other subjects being regarded as too insignificant to be mentioned.

In the Maratha country, at the beginning of the seventeenth century, the great preacher Ramdas tried to inculcate in the minds of the people the idea of unity based on the bond of common locality. During the latest period of the Peshwa rule (latter half of the eighteenth century), however, this ideal dwindled into the orthodox one wherein Brahmins figure prominently, the State having no higher function than that of pampering them.[61] Under the Hindu rulers the Brahmins must have secured for themselves many pecuniary privileges, denied to others, on the strength of this orthodox theory of the proper function of the State, and perhaps more because they happened to occupy the posts of importance. Thus in the Maratha region during the period referred to above, the Konkanasth Brahmin clerks obtained the privilege of their goods being exempted from certain duties and their imported corn being carried to them without any ferry charges. Brahmin landholders of a part of the country had their lands assessed at distinctly lower rates than those levied on other classes. Brahmins were exempted from capital punishment, and when confined in forts, they were treated more liberally than the other classes.[62] Forbes makes the following observation: 'The Brahmins of Travancore, as in most other parts of India, have taken care to be exempted as much as possible from punishment; at least, their sentence is far more lenient than that passed on the other castes for the same crimes.'[63] In Bengal the amount of rent for land frequently varied with the caste of the occupant.[64]

Lack of unrestricted choice of occupation: Generally a caste or a group of allied castes considered some of the callings as its hereditary occupation, to abandon which in pursuit of another, though it might be more lucrative, was thought not to be right. Thus a Brahmin thought that it was correct for him to be a priest, while the Chamar regarded it as his duty to cure hides and prepare shoes. This was only generally true, for there were groups of occupations like trading, agriculture, labouring in the field, and doing military service which were looked upon as anybody's, and most castes were supposed to be eligible for any of them.[65] Among the artisans, occupations which were more or less of the same status were open to the members of these castes without incidental degradation. No caste would allow its members to take to any calling which was either degrading, like toddy-tapping and brewing, or impure, like scavenging or curing hides. It was not only the moral restraint and the social check of one's caste-fellows that acted as a restraint on the choice of one's occupation, but also the restriction put by other castes that did not allow members other than those of their own castes to follow their callings. Of such restrictive regulations there were in operation only those concerning the profession of priests, no one not born a Brahmin being allowed to be a priest. The effect of these rules was that the priestly profession was entirely monopolised by the Brahmins, leaving aside the ministrants of the aboriginal deities, while they were seen plying any trade or calling which suited their tastes and which was not polluting. The majority of the Konkanasth and Deshasth Brahmins of the

Maratha country were devoted to secular pursuits filling offices of every kind, including the village accountantship.[66] During the Maratha upheaval and after, the Brahmins entered the profession of arms in fairly large numbers. Before the Indian Mutiny the Kanaujia Brahmins used to enter the Bengal army as sepoys in large numbers.[67] Some of the Rarhi Brahmins of Bengal accepted service under Mohammedan rulers.[68] Some of the Brahmins of Rajasthan served their Marwadi masters.[69] The majority of the Brahmins in the lower Karnatak, according to Buchanan, almost entirely filled the different offices in the collection of revenue and even acted as messengers.[70] Of the Hindustani Brahmins of central India it is said that a considerable population of them are concerned in trade.[71] The Havig Brahmins of the Tulu country did all kinds of agricultural labour excepting holding the plough.[72] About the Kanaujia Brahmins of Uttar Pradesh it is asserted that they even till the soil with their own hands, while shop-keepers and hawking form the main source of livelihood for the Sanadhya Brahmins of that region.[73] In Rajasthan the Brahmin is not only willing to do all the labour that his piece of land requires, but is also ready to sell his labour to other more fortunate occupants.[74] Brahmins in Madras appear as civil, public, and military servants, traders, cultivators, industrialists, and even labourers.[75] It seems that in the days of Akbar, too, the Brahmins were engaged in trade, cultivation, or any advantageous pursuit in general.[76]

More castes than one are engaged in agriculture. Thus we have the Vellalas, the Pallis, the Agamudaiyans, the Malaiyalis in Madras.[77] As regards the five artisan castes, grouped together as Panchakalsi, it is observed that it is not impossible for individuals to pass from one occupation to another without any alteration of social status or loss of right of intermarriage.[78] Weaving is practised by many of the menial castes including even the impure castes of Mahars and Chamars. If one looks at the census reports, especially those for 1901, one finds groups, which are regarded as separate castes, following more callings than one. The following remark of Russell is very instructive from this point of view. He observes: 'Several castes have same traditional occupation; about forty of the castes of the Central Provinces are classified as agriculturists, eleven as weavers, seven as fishermen and so on.'[79] In 1798 Colebrooke wrote:

Daily observation shows even Brahmins exercising the menial profession of a Shudra. We are aware that every caste forms itself into clubs or lodges, consisting of the several individuals of that caste residing within a small distance, and that these clubs or lodges govern themselves by particular rules or customs or by-laws. But though some restrictions and limitations, not founded on religious prejudices, are found among their by-laws, it may be received as a general maxim that the occupation appointed for each tribe is entitled to a preference. Every profession, with few exceptions, is open to every description of person.[80]

When Irving says,[81] [i]f we except the priesthood, caste has not necessarily any effect on the line of life in which a man embarks', he certainly overstates the position, and the following observation of Baines strikes the true note. 'The occupation, again, which is common to the latter [the caste] is a traditional one, and is not by any means necessarily that by which all, or even most, of the group make their living in the present day.'[82]

Restrictions on marriage: Most of the groups, whose features I have attempted to characterise above, are further divided into a number of subgroups every one of which forbids its members to marry persons from outside it. Each of these groups, popularly known as subcastes, is thus endogamous. This principle of strict endogamy is such a dominant aspect of caste-society that an eminent sociologist is led to regard endogamy as 'the essence of the caste system'.[83] There are, however, a few exceptions to this general rule of marrying within one's own group which are due to the practice of hypergamy. In some parts of the Punjab, especially in the hills, a man of a higher caste can take to wife a girl from one of the lower castes, while, in Malabar, the younger sons of the Nambudiri and other Brahmins consort with the Kshatriya and Nayar women, among whom mother-right prevails. Excepting for these cases of intercaste hypergamy each group has to contract matrimonial alliances within its own limits. Outside of this practice the only other authentic case where intercaste marriage is allowed is that of some of the artisan castes of Malabar.[84] Any man venturing to transgress this law will be put out of his own subcaste and it is doubtful if he would be admitted into the fold of any other respectable caste. To illustrate from the Maratha region, a Konkanasth Brahmin must marry a girl born in a Konkanasth Brahmin family, while a Karhada Brahmin must similarly seek his partner from amongst the Karhada Brahmins and so on, the principle being that marriage must be arranged within the group which is most effectively considered to be one's own. If this rule is violated expulsion from the membership of the group is generally the penalty which the offending parties have to suffer. In Gujarat the unit within which all matrimonial alliances must be contracted is very often still smaller than the so called subcaste of the Maratha region. Among the Banias, the trading caste, for example, there are not only the divisions of Shrimali, Porwal, Modh, etc., but there are further subdivisions like Dasa Porwal and Visa Porwal.[85] This is not all. The Dasas are still further required to contract their marriages either from amongst the Dasas of Surat or of Bombay according as they belong to Surat or Bombay. When the groups are so much subdivided the penalty for transgressing the rule of endogamy in reference to the smallest unit is not expulsion of the offending parties but the gratification by them of the offended group.

To regard endogamy as the chief characteristic of a caste is to treat all so-called subcastes as the real castes. Gait[86] advances two reasons against this procedure of raising subcastes to the position of castes, namely, it would be 'contrary to the native feeling on the subject', and would be 'highly inconvenient in practice, as it would create a bewildering multiplicity of castes'. As for the second objection, we may safely pass it over, as it concerns only an administrative difficulty. As regards the Indian sentiment against making a subcaste into a caste, it must be pointed out that, at best, this is the representation of only one side of the problem; for if, to confine myself to the Maratha country, a Saraswat Brahmin is known to the outsiders as a Saraswat, to a Saraswat he is better known either as a Shenvi or as a Sashtikar or Pednekar. Stated generally, though it is the caste that is recognised by the society at large, it is the subcaste that is regarded by the particular caste and the individual. It is mainly indifference towards others, so characteristic of the Indian system, that is responsible for this attitude. For a Brahmin most others are Shudras, irrespective of high or low status; and for two or three higher castes that are allied to the Brahmins in culture, the rest of the population, excepting the impure castes and some other specific groups, is Kulwadi or Shudra—a generic term for manual workers. The higher castes are grouped together as either Ashrafin in Bihar,[87] Bhadralok in Bengal, or Pandhar-peshe in Maharashtra. Further, if we are to take some kind of Indian sentiment as our guide in our analysis, then, as according to the orthodox theory on this matter there are only two, or at the most three castes in the present age, we shall have to divide the whole population of any major linguistic province into two castes, Brahmin and Shudra, or at the most three, where the existence of the Kshatriya is grudgingly granted. Evidently no scientific student of caste, not even Gait himself, has proposed to follow Indian opinion on this matter. There is ample reason why, to get a sociologically correct idea of the institution, we should recognise subcastes as real castes.

Of the features of caste-society dealt with so far three pertain to the caste as a whole; for the status in the hierarchy of any subcaste depends upon the status of the caste, from which follow the various civil and religious rights and disabilities, and the traditional occupation is determined by the nature of the caste. The other three features, which are very material in the consideration of a group from the point of view of an effective social life, namely, those that regulate communal life and prescribe rules as regards feeding, social intercourse and endogamy, belong to the subcaste. In the matter of the panchayat or the caste-council, which is the tribunal for enforcing the moral and economic rules of the group, the subcaste generally possesses its own council. In the Punjab this is the case in all castes, except the artisans and menials. 'Where the subdivisions are not very clearly defined or where the numerical strength of the whole caste is small, there is one governing body for the whole caste.'[88] The following description of the subcaste in Bengal clearly brings out the function I have mentioned as peculiar to it. 'Almost every caste is divided into a number of smaller groups which will only marry amongst themselves. Usually these groups will not eat together and often they will not even take water from each other or smoke from the same "hukka". These endogamous groups are generally known as subcastes. Each subcaste manages its own affairs quite independently of the others, and in the case of the lower castes each has its own separate panchayat or standing committee, by which all social questions are decided.'[89] In Uttar Pradesh it is the subcaste that forms the unit of social organisation, and as such has its own council to look after its affairs quite independently of the similar councils of the other subcastes.[90] Further, inter-dining and interdrinking are restricted to the group which is endogamous.[91] About the Central Provinces Russell observes:[92] 'The real unit of the system and the basis of the fabric of Indian society is this endogamous group or subcaste.' Though this group is usually little known outside a man's own caste, yet it is the members of the subcaste that attend 'the communal feasts held on the occasions of marriages, funerals and meetings of the caste (subcaste) panchayat'. The remark of the Census Operator for Madras that it is the small endogamous subdivisions 'which are for all social purposes the real castes[93] is corroborated by F.J. Richards in the case of Salem district when he observes: 'The Unit of Hindu society is the endogamous group or subcaste.[94] The description of the subcaste of a Hindustani caste given by Sherring will illustrate this. He observes about the Barhai or carpenter caste of Hindustan that its seven subcastes 'are so distinct from one another that they hold no direct social intercourse with each other, either by marriages, or by eating or smoking together'.[95] Further, some of the subcastes have such a distinctness about their cultural items, as for example among the Vellalas, that it is not possible to give a general account of the marriage and other customs applicable to all the subdivisions. While some of them recognise freedom of divorce and remarriage and even polyandry, others strictly follow strictly the Brahmanic rules.[96] The remark of Gait that 'as a rule the prohibition of intermarriage between members of the different subcastes is far less rigid than it is between members of different castes, and when the rule is broken, the penalty is usually not expulsion, but merely some form of atonement, after which the member of the higher of the two subcastes concerned, and possibly his or her parents, take rank in the lower',[97] may be urged as a potent reason why subcastes; should be treated as strictly subordinate to a caste. Here it must be pointed out that in Uttar Pradesh at least 'the penalty for breaches of subcaste endogamy appears to be as severe as the penalty for similar breaches of caste endogamy', and that, though the penalty for the transgression of rules about subcaste commensality varies in different castes, it seems that generally caste and subcaste commensality is much on a par in this respect.[98] Hence it is but proper to treat endogamy within each of the groups constituting caste-society as one of its principal features.

3

Hierarchy: The Theory of the 'Varna'*

LOUIS DUMONT

ON HIERARCHY IN GENERAL

We have encountered hierarchy but we have not defined it. Hierarchy must be our starting-point for two connected reasons: first, it is none other than the conscious form of reference of the parts to the whole in the system; second, it is the aspect of the system which escapes modern writers.[1]

For modern common sense, hierarchy is a ladder of *command* in which the lower rungs are encompassed in the higher ones in regular succession. 'Military hierarchy', the artificial construction of progressive subordination from commander-in-chief to private soldier, would serve as an example. Hence it is a question of systematically graduated authority. Now hierarchy in India certainly involves gradation, but is neither power nor authority; these must be distinguished. We can already do so within our own tradition. Thus the *Shorter Oxford Dictionary* says under 'hierarchy': '(1) Each of the three divisions of angels ... (2) Rules or dominion in holy things ... (3) An organised body of priests or clergy in successive orders or grades. (4) A body of persons or things ranked in grades, orders, or classes, one above another.'[2] It can be seen that the original sense of the term concerned religious ranking. We shall keep to this sense here, making it somewhat more precise. We shall admit that, any idea of command being left aside, the religious way of seeing things requires a classification of beings according to their degree of dignity. Yet the presence of religion is not indispensable, for the same applies whenever the differentiated elements of a whole are judged in relation to that whole, even if the judgement is philosophical as in Plato's *Republic*. So we shall define hierarchy as the *principle*

---

* Extracts from Louis Dumont, *Homo Hierarchicus: The Caste System and Its Implications*, Chicago: University of Chicago Press, 1970, pp. 66–72.

by which the elements of a whole are ranked in relation to the whole, it being understood that in the majority of societies it is religion which provides the view of the whole, and that the ranking will thus be religious in nature.

We are concerned in this case with concepts which have become totally foreign to us, for our egalitarian society adopts their opposites, as Tocqueville has shown us. In the modern age, hierarchy has become 'social stratification', that is, hierarchy which is shamefaced or non-conscious, or, as it were, repressed. The notion has become incomprehensible even to many of the Indian intelligentsia, brought up as they are in the European tradition and subjected to the influence of modern political ideas for more than a century.[3] Consequently, it is not surprising that hierarchy should be the stumbling block for modern writers studying the caste system, as has been seen in the case of the earlier writers, and as will be seen in the case of the more recent.

Once hierarchy has been isolated as purely a matter of religious values, it naturally remains to be seen how it is connected with power,[4] and how authority is to be defined. The principle of hierarchy is linked with the opposition between the pure and the impure. Now we cannot but recognise that this opposition, a purely religious one, tells us nothing about the place of power in society. On this question we must resort to a traditional Hindu theory which, while not dealing with caste (jati) *stricto sensu*, yet has an intimate bearing on it, I mean the classical theory of the varnas. In any case, one cannot speak of the castes without mentioning the varnas, to which Hindus frequently attribute the castes themselves. Thus there are good reasons for studying the varnas, even in ancient India, and then specifying the relationship between varna and caste, especially from the angle of the relationship between hierarchy and power. This will enable us to consider some regional or local examples of caste ranking.

THE THEORY OF THE VARNAS: POWER AND PRIESTHOOD

There is indeed in India a hierarchy other than that of the pure and the impure, namely, the traditional hierarchy of the four varnas, 'colours' or estates (in the sense the word had in France in the *ancien régime*), whereby four categories are distinguished: the highest is that of the Brahmans or priests, below them the Kshatriyas or warriors, then the Vaishyas, in modern usage mainly merchants, and finally the Shudras, the servants or have-nots. This is only a preliminary enumeration, and we shall have to specify the content of these categories in historical terms. There is in actual fact a fifth category, the Untouchables, who are left outside the classification. Now the relationship between the system of the varnas and that of the jati or castes is complex. Indologists sometimes confuse the two, mainly because the classical literature is concerned almost entirely with the varnas. Following Senart, one must certainly keep the two distinct.[5]

On the other hand, it seems that recent anthropological literature does not give the importance of the traditional schema its full due, even from the point of view of castes in the strict sense. There has been too great a tendency to consider the classification of the varnas as nothing but a survival without any relation to contemporary social reality, as Hocart observed.[6] Nearer our own time, it has been recognised that the theory of the varnas has certain functions in the modern age but there has been little attempt to account for this fact. In this connection one must first draw attention to a similarity in the constitution of the hierarchy of the varnas and that of the castes.

Thanks to Hocart and, more precisely, to Dumezil, the hierarchy of the varnas can be seen not as a linear order, but as a series of successive dichotomies or inclusions. The set of the four varnas divides into two: the last category, that of the Shudras, is opposed to the block of the first three, whose members are 'twice-born' in the sense that they participate in initiation, second birth, and in the religious life in general. These twice-born in turn divide into two: the Vaishyas are opposed to the block formed by the Kshatriyas and the Brahmans, which in turn divides into two. Let me simply say here that the lot of the Shudras is to serve, and that the Vaishyas are the grazers of cattle and the farmers, the 'purveyors' of sacrifice, as Hocart says, who have been given dominion over the animals, whereas the Brahmans-Kshatriyas have been given dominion over 'all creatures'. We shall return to the solidarity between the two highest classes and the distinction between them: the Kshatriya may order a sacrifice as may the Vaishya, but only the Brahman may perform it. The king is thus deprived of any sacerdotal function. It can be seen that the series of dichotomies on which this hierarchy rests is formally somewhat similar to caste hierarchy, and it also is essentially religious; but it is less systematic and its principles are different.[7]

It seems that this fourfold partition of later Vedic society can be regarded as resulting from the addition of a fourth category to the first three, these corresponding to the Indo-European tripartition of social functions (Dumezil) and to the triad found in the first books of the *Rig Veda*: *brahman-ksatra-vis* or: the principle of priesthood, that of *imperium*, and the clans or people. The Shudras appear in a late hymn of the *Rig Veda* and seem to correspond to aborigines (like the *dasa* and *dasyu*) integrated into the society on pain of servitude.[8] It must be noted that the Brahman is the priest, the Kshatriya the member of the class of kings, the Vaishya the farmer, the Shudra the unfree servant. This classification has remained identical in form throughout all the literature right up to modern times, though naturally with shifts and modifications in the contents of the categories. In particular, this is the only conceptual scheme which is made use of by the classical texts of Hinduism in order to characterise persons and their function in society, even though actual groups do appear otherwise in these texts, and sometimes have an ambiguous place in the scheme. In all likelihood these texts are contemporaneous with the development of castes in the strict sense of the word, yet they always refer castes to the varnas, and see them, as it were, as varnas. First and foremost, these texts were to mask the emergence, the factual accretion, of a fifth category, the Untouchables, each emulating the others in proclaiming that 'there is no fifth . . .' Note that this amounts simply to applying the existing scheme: the Untouchables are outside the varnas just as the Shudras were outside the 'twice-born'.

It is worthwhile to follow Professor Kane[9] and see how the classical texts define the duties and occupations of the varnas. For the Shudras, the matter is perfectly simple: their only task is to obey or serve without envy (susrusam anusuyaya, Manu I, 91). In contrast to these, the twice-born are vigorously characterised as alike in virtue of a threefold common duty: study, sacrifice, and gift (adhyayanam ijya danam, Gaut. X, 3), that is, to study the sacred texts, offer sacrifices, and give to the Brahmans. They differ in their sources of income, which correspond to *optional* activities or occupations; in this field, the Brahman has the privilege of teaching, performing sacrifices, and receiving gifts, the Kshatriya of protecting all creatures, the Vaishya of living from the land, commerce, grazing and usury (Gaut. ibid.). Manu says the same in a scarcely different way: the Brahman's three ways of making a living are optional for him, but forbidden to the Kshatriya, the common duty (dharma) of the twice-born contrasts with what they do for a living (ajivanartham) (X, 76–7, 79). The Brahman is characterised by six actions (X, 75; I, 88) of which only three are common to the other twice-born (I, 88–90). The first verse, in which the six actions of the Brahman are enumerated, must be translated literally in order to understand how the Brahman's activity is complete, and forms a totality; this idea is expressed by the pairs of opposites 'make others study and study, makes others sacrifice and sacrifice, give and receive . . .' (repeated word for word in X, 75). It can be seen that the ancient conception has been preserved in its essentials: the order of increasing status comprises service, economic activity, political dominion, priesthood. At the same time, with imperturbable logic, the sources of income, so far as they are optional, are subordinated to the religious ends, even if this involves what we tend to consider a contradiction, namely, that the Brahman as compared to the other twice-born, is characterised by inessential (optional) activities, or even, so far as instruction and sacrifice is concerned, by service—albeit religious.

Apart from the implicit statement that the different sorts of twice-born are essentially homogeneous, the feature which most contrasts with the caste system is perhaps the stress laid on function rather than birth.

There are some details to be noticed in connection with the hierarchy of the varnas in classical Hinduism. The Brahman naturally has privileges, and these are listed in the literature. He is inviolable (the murder of a Brahman is, with the murder of a cow, the cardinal sin), and a number of punishments do not apply to him: he cannot be beaten, put in irons, fined, or expelled. The learned Brahman (*srotriya*) is in theory, and the Brahman is specially favoured by the law about lost objects, which generally, when they are found, revert mainly to the king, and which only a Brahman finder may keep in part or whole; similarly, if a man dies intestate, only if he is a Brahman do his goods not accrue to the king (here one can see a certain mixing of the two functions).

It should be recalled that although the Brahman is characterised in the Vedic period by his sacrificial function, in the Hindu period, in harmony with the decline of sacrifice in favour of other rites, the Brahman is, above all, purity. Further, the Brahmanic varna became segmented, even in the classical period, and the priests in charge of public temples, the *devalaka*, were despised by their colleagues. Today the Brahman lineages are graded in virtue of the rank of the castes they serve as domestic priests (*Panjab Census Report*, 1911, I, 310), the highest being the learned Brahmans who do not serve at all.

Generally speaking, the hierarchy of the varnas is expressed in many ways by the differentiated treatment that each is accorded. The punishment of Brahmans just mentioned is an example of this. Whilst there is generally privilege or immunity, at the same time *noblesse oblige*, and a Brahman thief, for example, is punished more severely than his inferiors. Some points are difficult to interpret. Thus Manu lays down that a Shudra may not carry a Brahman's corpse (V, 104), which is incomprehensible from the point of view of purity. But above all, starting from the Dharmasutras of Gautama and Vasistha, one finds seemingly illogical injunctions, which later became very widespread. These are those which prescribe, all other things being equal, an increasing period of impurity for a decreasing status: in the case of death, close relations are impure for ten days for Brahmans, twelve for Kshatriyas, fifteen for Vaishyas and thirty for Shudras. Even nowadays, where orthodoxy prevails, the proportion goes in the same direction (the longest periods are often reduced). But, going by the nature of the system, we would expect the contrary, for impurity is more powerful than purity, and the higher the degree of purity to be regained, the more severe should be the effect of impurity. Either we have not yet managed to enter into the spirit of the system, or else the Brahmans have here transformed into a privilege what ought to be a greater incapacity. This view is reinforced by the fact that, while other prescriptions go in the same direction (for example, how far water must reach to purify someone, Manu, II, 62), we find the gradation reversed in certain cases; thus in the case of stillbirth, Brihaspati (*Asauca*, 34–5) prescribes respectively ten, seven, five and three days for the Brahmans and the following varnas.

We have said that the classical texts described in terms of varna what must surely have been at that time a caste system in embryo. The word jati does occur, but it is generally confused with varna (except in Yajnavalkya, II, 69, 206) and, according to Kane, the emphasis is on birth rather than function. Moreover, concrete names of reference groups are encountered, as in the case of the Chandala, and so are names of other groups, either equivalent in status (placed outside the village, Manu, X, 36, 51) or else of distinctly superior status. Although from a very early epoch the Buddhist texts confirm the actual existence of despised castes and inferior occupations, the normative Hindu texts mostly present the groups they name as if they were products of crossing between varnas. This is the very detailed theory according to which the 'mixing of varnas' gave birth to mixed categories, inferior and more or less hierarchised. It is generally admitted that this theory was used to refer real jati to the varnas. It is difficult to say how these groups come into the classification of the varnas. At least the lowest of them seem outside it, and yet it is repeated that 'there is no fifth (varna)', and there is a tendency to associate them with the Shudras. Already in Panini (500 BC) this produced a distinction among the Shudras, since one hears of 'excluded' (niravasita) Shudras. Later, expressions like 'the last', 'the outsiders', etc., increase, and the word 'untouchable' (asprsya) is not quite unknown. The distinction which people had for so long refused to make in theory finally compelled recognition: the Shudras have acquired rights, they have become in fact members of the religious society, and those excluded are now the fifth, the Untouchables.[10]

A point which must be emphasised in connection with the varnas is the conceptual relationship between Brahman and Kshatriya. This was established at an early date and is still operative today. It is a matter of an absolute distinction between priesthood and royalty. Comparatively speaking, the king has lost his religious prerogatives: he does not sacrifice, he has sacrifices performed. In theory, power is ultimately subordinate to priesthood, whereas in fact priesthood submits to power.[11] Status and power, and consequently spiritual authority and temporal authority, are absolutely distinguished. The texts called the Brahmanas tell us this with extreme clarity, and, whatever has been said to the contrary notwithstanding, this relationship has never ceased to obtain and still does. For example, the obligation of the powerful and rich to give, as is prescribed in the texts, has not been a dead letter. On the contrary, sovereigns have always supported the Brahmans—and their equivalents in this respect—by endowments of land which, as the inscriptions show, may be under two different rubrics (donations to the tompice, and the establishment of Brahman settlements). The difference with the West, let us say Catholic Christianity, seems to consist in the fact that in India there has never been spiritual *power*, that is, a supreme spiritual authority, which was at the same time a temporal power. The supremacy of the spiritual was never expressed politically.

Thus in the theory of the varnas one finds that status and power[12] are differentiated, just as the general consideration of hierarchy seemed to require. This fact is older than the caste, and it is fundamental to them in the sense that it is only once this differentiation has been made that hierarchy can manifest itself in a pure form. We shall return to this fact in the following section. This is not all, for we must remember that these two entirely distinct principles are nevertheless united in their opposition to the other categories which constitute society. As early as the Brahmanas, these are 'the two forces', represented by the men who, according to Manu, have been given dominion over 'all creatures'. In submitting to priesthood, royalty shares in it.

CASTE AND VARNA

We must try to indicate the main features of the relationship between jati, caste, and varna, category or estate, or more precisely, the relationship between the caste system as it can be directly observed, and the classical theory of the varnas. This task is necessary if we remember that the classical authors scarcely speak of anything other than the varnas, and that even nowadays Hindus often speak of castes in the language of the varnas.

In the first place this translation is quite comprehensible, not only in virtue of the traditional prestige of the varnas, but also in view of the homology already mentioned between the two systems, both of which are structural, and both of which culminate in the Brahmans, either as a varna or as a particular caste or subcaste of Brahman which may be regarded as the representative of the varna in a given territory (the highest if several are found there). In the second place, the varnas have the advantage of providing a model which is both universal throughout India, and very simple compared to the proliferation of castes, subcastes, etc. Consequently it is a model which can among other things facilitate the comparison between different regions, as Srinivas has pointed out.[13] Something of the kind is found in Marx: on the one hand there is the antithesis between the bourgeoisie and the proletariat, as described in his political writings, and on the other the more complicated picture of social classes which emerges in his historical works. There is a tendency to sort the many castes in a given territory into the four classical categories (and the fifth, traditionally unnamed). However, there are regional peculiarities. Thus in the south there are scarcely any castes intermediate between Brahmans and Shudras; the warrior castes themselves are considered as part of the Shudras, and scarcely worry about this at all.

So this provides a very convenient form of classification, distinct from, or supplementary to, the criteria of purity whose complexity we have mentioned. Has its importance increased in modern times, with the improvements in transport, and, even more, with the registration of castes in the decennial censuses made by the government in the last part of the nineteenth century, and that of 1901 which sought to achieve a status ranking for each province? Srinivas thinks so. Certainly, many castes took advantage of these census reports to present claims aiming to make the public authority sanction a higher status than their real status, and these claims, sometimes vindicated in published memoranda,[14] were expressed, with greater or lesser plausibility, in terms of the varnas. Here the varnas were an instrument for mobility, but to make a claim is one thing, and for it to be accepted is another. Furthermore, the circumstances were exceptional.

Far from being completely heterogeneous, the concepts of varna and jati *have* interacted, and certain features of the osmosis between the two may be noticed. The notion of the varnas which prevails nowadays, even among anthropologists, is influenced by caste. Thus it is often said that the true Kshatriyas have been long extinct, and that the Rajputs, though having the function of Kshatriyas in modern times, are not real Kshatriyas. It is thought that in ancient India the accession to the throne, and to the dignity of Kshatriya, by dynasties of a different origin, was an irregularity. This assumes that heredity is more important than function, which is true of caste but not of the varnas. So far as the varnas are concerned, he who rules in a stable way, and places himself under the Brahman, is a Kshatriya. Moreover, these categories were not strictly endogamous either. Probably the Kshatriyas have always been rather lax in this matter. The particular place given to power in the system has had notable and lasting results; in the first place, the pattern of polygyny and meat diet, which does not correspond to the Brahmanic ideal, has been quietly preserved at this and lower levels until quite recently; in the second place, since the function is related to force,[*] it was easier to become king than Brahman: Kshatriya and Untouchable are the two levels on which it is easy to enter the caste society from outside.

Conversely, it is not enough to say that the caste system is influenced by the theory of the varnas. In the first place, the existence of the theory of the pure and the impure presupposes at least the relationship established in the varnas between priesthood and royalty. It is correct to say that the opposition between pure and impure is a religious, even a ritualistic, matter. For this ideal type of hierarchy to emerge it was necessary that the mixture of status and power ordinarily encountered (everywhere else?) should be separated, but this was not enough; for pure hierarchy to develop without hindrance it was also necessary that power should be absolutely inferior to status. These are the two conditions that we find fulfilled early on, in the relationship between Brahman and Kshatriya.

---

[*]*Force* in French, *Pouvoir*, meaning legitimate force is translated as 'power'–Translator.

In the second place, we shall maintain that the theory of castes resorts implicitly or obliquely to the varnas in order to complete its treatment of power. Indeed, in the theory of purity a vegetarian merchant ought logically to have precedence over a king who eats meat. But this is not the case, and to understand this fact it is necessary in particular to remember that the theory of the varnas, whilst it subordinates king to priest, power to status, establishes a solidarity between them which opposes them, conjointly to the other social functions. This is a subtle and important point and requires special discussion.

HIERARCHY AND POWER

Most contemporary authors see things differently. In previous generations, with the exception of the aristocratic tendency which took for granted the existence of status ranking, hierarchy was often overlooked as the central feature of the system, but the better of the materialist writers tried to explain it in terms of other features (Nesfield). Only one contemporary writer, K. Gough Aberle, has in turn taken on this thankless task.[15] Nowadays hierarchy, or rather the existence of an order of precedence, a status ranking, usually compels recognition, but it is seen only from the outside ('social stratification'), and leaves a residuum which is not reducible to the clear and supposedly basic notions of power and wealth. This unresolved duality, which has not even been properly characterised, hangs like a millstone round the neck of the contemporary literature.[16]

Usually, those who study the status ranking of the castes of a definite region distinguish between what happens 'at the extremes' and what happens in the 'middle zone' of the ranking. The extremes, where the pure and the impure are in evidence, are said to be less important than the middle zone, where the operation of power is rightly recognised. Such authors conclude, in short, that their categories are sufficient for the understanding of the system: according to them, the distribution of power (and wealth) is in the last analysis congruent with (ritual) status, except, naturally, at the 'extremes', where questions are raised by the lowly place of the Untouchable, and particularly the precedence taken by the priest over the master of the land. Emphasis is often placed on situations in which the priest is to a striking degree materially dependent on the masters of the land, but the more this is done, the more the claimed congruence is destroyed. In short it is laid down as a principle that hierarchical status is of small importance when it does not simply validate an economico-political situation. To describe this attitude is enough to pass judgement on it: it raises the question of whether our task is to provide a semblance of confirmation for our sociocentric prejudices or to do scientific work. Here is an illustration:

There was a high degree of coincidence between politico-economic rank and the ritual ranking of caste. This is a reflection of the general rule that those who achieve wealth and political power tend to rise in the ritual scheme of ranking. It is what is meant by saying that the ranking system of caste-groups was validated by differential control over the productive resources of the village. But the correlation is not perfect, since at each end of the scale there is a *peculiar rigidity* in the system of caste ... in between these two extremes, ritual rank tends to follow their economic rank in the village community.[17]

I have italicised a particularly delightful expression: here a basic feature of the caste system is reduced to a 'peculiar rigidity' at the extremities of the social order. It will be understood why we prefer another approach.

For us, on the contrary, what happens at the extremes is essential. We must free ourselves from familiar ideas; we tend to put the essential at the centre and the rest at the periphery. Here, by contrast, because it is a question of hierarchy, and more generally of ideas, and of sociology, that which encompasses is more important than that which is encompassed, just as a whole is more important than its parts, or just as a given group's place in the whole governs its own organisation. Our approach is quite unlike the preceding one and, as we have said, involves two stages: first, we shall be concerned with the ideology, which easily accounts for the overall framework; second, finding the concrete factor, power, in the 'middle zone', a factor not immediately accounted for by the theory of purity, we shall consider it in its turn.

The controversy is exemplary from the epistemological point of view, for, by keeping to the level of power, one is prevented from understanding the essential characteristic of the Indian system. This characteristic is the subordination of power, which, as we shall shortly see, is both intellectually absolute and practically limited. The alternatives must be clearly stated: one may either start from conscious ideas and move from the whole to the parts, while bringing out the important and unnoticed fact that power in India became secular at a very early date; or else one starts from behaviour, in which case one can neither account for the whole nor finally build a bridge between Indian concepts and our own.

Two approaches to the question of the relationship between hierarchy and power have just been contrasted. For us, the question only arises for the present in connection with the relationship between varna and caste. Anticipating the study of actual observable status rankings, we admit in advance that they give power a place which is not allowed for by the theoretical hierarchy of the pure and the impure. At first sight it is an example of that 'residual' component which should normally be brought out by the confrontation of ideology with observation. Then we would have to take notice of it as accurately as possible and be content with that. However, when the king or a man of royal caste, an eater of meat, takes precedence over a vegetarian merchant or farmer, it is not that the hierarchy of relative purity is simply complemented—that one could accommodate—rather, it contradicted. Must it be said that the ideology is false in the 'modern zone' of the status ladder, or should it be admitted that an extraneous factor counterbalances ideology at this point, once the extremes are located?

To start with it must be observed that, although very important hierarchy or its concrete and incomplete form, status ranking, is not everything. It leaves out power and its distribution, but given the fact that it does not attack or negate power, should it not reflect power within itself in some manner? Otherwise, and in general, the ideology provides an orientation or ordering of the datum rather than a reproduction of it, and the act of becoming conscious of something in fact always means making a choice of one dimension in preference to others—one can only see certain relationships by becoming, temporarily at least, blind to others. Then this sort of complementarity can lead to a real contradiction when it is a matter of completely ordering the datum in accordance with a single principle. In our case, power exists in society, and the Brahman who thinks in terms of hierarchy knows this perfectly well; yet hierarchy cannot give a place to power as such, without contradicting its own principle. Therefore it must give a place to power without saying so, and it is obliged to close its eyes to this point on pain of destroying itself. In other words, once the king is made subordinate to the priest, as the very existence of hierarchy presupposes, it must give him a place after the priest, and before the others, unless it is absolutely to deny his dignity and the usefulness of his function. Brahman authors have had a feeling of this sort, as can be seen from the way in which they consider royalty within the theory of the dharma. As Lingat shows in his fine work on the relationship between dharma and the law, the king tends in this tradition to appear as a quasi-providential instrument whereby the theoretical world of the dharma is linked with the real world here below. Although they lay down an absolute rule, these authors are keenly aware of its transcendent nature and of the impossibility of introducing it into the facts just as it is. Thanks to the king, and in particular to the king as the supreme judge, as the link between Brahmanic wisdom represented by his counsellors and the empirical world of men as they are, the dharma rules from on high, but does not have to govern, which would be fatal.

Thus it can be seen that there are internal reasons for the contradiction in question. The remaining task is to understand how it has been possible for this contradiction to be accepted, and it is here, in my opinion, that the theory of the varnas must be taken into consideration. Indeed, this theory from the outset sees in the first two varnas 'the two forces' which, united in their particular way, must reign over the world; in this way it enables the prince to share to some extent in the absolute dignity [of] whose servant he is. It should be observed, moreover, that there is no contradiction in the classical authors, for they speak only of the varnas, even when we may suppose that they have the caste society in mind. In this sense, it is we who distinguish a hierarchy of purity as a distinct social principle. In the minds of these authors, as soon as government or secular matters in general are involved, this view unceasingly relies for external support on the varnas. All the more reason for us to avoid incorrectly dissociating the two views, and to recognise their implicit connection as reflected in actual status rankings, when power in some way counterbalances purity *at secondary levels*, while remaining subordinate to it at the *primary* or *non-segmented level*.

As the mantle of Our Lady of Mercy shelters sinners of every kind in its voluminous folds, so the hierarchy of purity cloaks, among other differences, its own contrary. Here we have an example of the complementarity between that which encompasses and that which is encompassed, a complementarity which may seem a contradiction to the observer. Before becoming familiar with this phenomenon through concrete examples, it must be stressed that we have made a first step out of the dualism of the 'religious' and the 'politico-economic', of idealism and materialism, of form and content. Let us admit at once that the tendency we have criticised has been a considerable help to us: by its one-sided insistence on power it has made it impossible for us to overlook it.

REFERENCES

Blunt, E.A.H., *The Caste System of Northern India with Special Reference to the United Provinces of Agra and Oudh*, London: Oxford University Press, 1931.

Dumont, Louis, *Collected Papers in Indian Sociology. Religion, Politics and History in India*, The Hague: Mouton, 1971.

Evans-Pritchard, E., and M. Fortes (eds), *African Political Systems*, London: Oxford University Press, 1940.

Thurston E. and K. Rangachari, *Castes and Tribes of Southern India Madras*, 1909.

Gait, E.A., 'Caste', *Encyclopaedia of Religion and Ethics*, vol. III, 1913.

Ketkar, Shridhar V., *The History of Caste in India*, vol. I, Ithaca, New York, 1909.

Marriot, McKim, *Caste Ranking and Community Structure in Five Regions of India and Pakistan*, Poona: Deccan College, 1960.

—, (ed.), *Village India*, Chicago: The University of Chicago Press, 1955.

Mayer, Adrian C., *Caste and Kinship in Central India: A Village and Its Region*, London: Routledge, 1960.

Oldenberg, H., 'Zur Geschichte des Indien Kastenrresens', *Zeitschrift der Deutschen morgenlandischen Gesellschaft*, 51, 1897, pp. 267–90.

4

Caste Must Go*

M.K. GANDHI

My own position on the caste system may be summed up as follows:

1. I believe in Varnashrama of the Vedas which, in my opinion, is based on absolute equality of status, notwithstanding passages to the contrary in the Smritis and elsewhere.

2. Every word of the printed works passing muster as Shastras is not, in my opinion, a revelation.

3. The interpretation of accepted texts has undergone evolution and is capable of indefinite evolution, even as the human intellect and heart are.

4. Nothing in the Shastras which is manifestly contrary to universal truths and morals can stand.

5. Nothing in the Shastras which is capable of being reasoned can stand if it is in conflict with reason.

6. Varnashrama of the Shastras is today non-existent in practice.

7. The present caste system is the very antithesis of Varnashrama: the sooner public opinion abolishes it the better.

8. In Varnashrama there was and should be no prohibition of intermarriage or interdining. Prohibition there is of change of one's hereditary occupation for purposes of gain. The existing practice is therefore doubly wrong in that it has set up cruel restrictions about interdining and intermarriage and tolerates anarchy about choice of occupation.

9. Though there is in Varnashrama no prohibition against intermarriage and interdining, there can be no compulsion. It must be left to the unfettered choice of the individual as to where he or she will marry or dine. If the law of Varnashrama was observed, there would naturally be

* Extract from *Harijan*, 11 February 1933, pp. 1–2.

a tendency, so far as marriage is concerned, for people to restrict the marital relations to their own varna.

10. As I have repeatedly said there is no such thing as untouchability by birth in the Shastras. I hold the present practice to be a sin and the greatest blot on Hinduism. I feel more than ever that if untouchability lives, Hinduism dies.

11. The most effective, quickest and the most unobtrusive way to destroy caste is for reformers to begin the practice with themselves and, where necessary, take the consequences of social boycott. The reform will not come by reviling the orthodox. The change will be gradual and imperceptible. The so-called higher classes will have to descend from their pedestal before they can make any impression upon the so-called lower classes. Day-to-day experience of village work shows how difficult the task is of bridging the gulf that exists between the city-dwellers and the villagers, the higher classes and the lower classes. The two are not synonymous terms. For the class distinction exists both in the cities and the villages.

THE FOUR CASTES*

Q: You regard the four divisions of castes as based on birth. You also believe that a man's caste does not prevent him from doing the duties attaching to other castes, and that any man irrespective of his birth may have the qualities of a Brahmana or a Kshatriya or a Shudra. If this is the case, where is the use of maintaining this division, and consequently an order of superiority and inferiority? Why should the accident of birth make a man a Brahmana, or a Kshatriya or a Shudra? Why attach so much importance to birth?
A: In accepting the fourfold division, I am simply accepting the laws of Nature, taking for granted what is inherent in human nature, and the law of heredity. We are born with some of the traits of our parents.

The fact that a human being is born only in the human species shows that some characteristic, that is, caste is determined by birth. There is scope enough for freedom of the will in as much as we can to a certain extent reform some of our inherited characteristics. It is not possible in one birth entirely to undo the results of our past doings, and, in the light of it, it is in every way right and proper to regard him as a Brahmana who is born of Brahmana parents. A Brahmana may, by doing the deeds of a Shudra, become a Shudra in this very birth, but the world loses nothing in continuing to treat him as a Brahmana. Caste as it exists today is no doubt a travesty of the original fourfold division

---

* Extract from *Young India*, 21 January 1926, p. 30.

which only defined men's different callings. And this trifling with it has been its undoing. But how can I, for that reason, discard the law of Nature which I see being fulfilled at every step? I know that if I discard it, I would be rid of a lot of trouble. But that would be an idle short cut. I have declared from the housetops that a man's caste is no matter for pride, that no superiority attaches to any of the four divisions. A true Brahmana will feel it an honour to serve the lowliest of Shudras. In fact a Brahmana, to be a Brahman, should have the qualities of Kshatriya, a Vaishya and a Shudra plus his own. Only he should predominantly be a man of divine knowledge. But caste today is in the crucible and only Heaven knows, or perhaps the Brahmanas know, the final result.

5

Caste in India *

B.R. AMBEDKAR

The Hindu social order does not recognise the individual as a centre of social purpose. For the Hindu social order is based primarily on class or Varna and not on individuals. Originally and formally the Hindu social order recognised four classes: (1) Brahmins, (2) Kshatriyas, (3) Vaishyas and (4) Shudras. Today it consists of five classes, the fifth being called the Panchamas or Untouchables. The unit of Hindu society is not the individual Brahmin or the individual Kshatriya or the individual Vaishya or the individual Shudra or the individual Panchama. Even the family is not regarded by the Hindu social order as a unit of society except for the purposes of marriage and inheritance. The unit of Hindu society is the class or Varna, to use the Hindu technical name for class. In the Hindu social order, there is no room for individual merit and no consideration of individual justice. If the individual has a privilege it is not because it is due to him personally. The privilege goes with the class, and if he is found to enjoy it, it is because he belongs to that class. Contrawise, if an individual is suffering from a wrong, it is not because he by his conduct deserves it. The disability is the disability imposed upon the class and if he is found to be labouring under it, it is because he belongs to that class.

Does the Hindu social order recognise fraternity? The Hindus like the Christians and the Muslims do believe that men are created by God. But while the Christians and the Muslims accept this as the whole truth the Hindus believe that this is only part of the truth. According to them, the whole truth consists of two parts. The first part is that men are created by God. The second part is that God created different men from different parts of his divine body. The Hindus regard the second part as more important and more fundamental than the first.

* Extract from Dr Babasaheb Ambedkar, *Writings and Speeches*, vol. 3, Bombay: Government of Maharashtra, 1987, pp. 99–111.

The Hindu social order is based on the doctrine that men are created from the *different parts* of the divinity . . . The Brahmin is no brother to the Kshatriya because the former is born from the mouth of the divinity while the latter is from the arms. The Kshatriya is no brother to the Vaishya because the former is born from the arms and the latter from his thighs. As no one is a brother to the other, no one is the keeper of the other.

The doctrine that the different classes were created from different parts of the divine body has generated the belief that it must be divine will that they should remain separate and distinct. It is this which has created in the Hindu an instinct to be different, to be separate and to be distinct from the rest of his fellow Hindus.

That the principle of graded inequality is a fundamental principle is beyond controversy. The four classes are not on horizontal plane, different but equal. They are on vertical plane. Not only different but unequal in status, one standing above the other. In the scheme of Manu, the Brahmin is placed at the first in rank. Below him is the Kshatriya. Below the Kshatriya is the Vaishya. Below the Vaishya is the Shudra and below the Shudra is the Ati-shudra or the Untouchable. This order of precedence among the classes is not merely conventional. It is spiritual, moral and legal. There is no sphere of life which is not regulated by this principle of graded inequality.

The principle of graded inequality has been carried into the economic field. 'From each according to his ability; to each according t his need' is not the principle of the Hindu social order. The principle of the Hindu social order is: 'From each according to his need. To each according to his nobiligy.'[1] Supposing an officer was distributing dole to a famine-stricken people. He would be bound to give greater dole to a person of high birth than he would to a person of low birth. Supposing an officer was levying taxation. He would be bound to assess a person of high birth at a lower rate than he would to a person of low birth. The Hindu social order does not recognise equal need, equal work or equal ability as the basis of reward for labour. Its motto is that in regard to the distribution of the good things of life those who are reckoned as the highest must get the most and the best and those who are classed as the lowest must accept the least and the worst.

[1] The illustrations given above are not merely drawn from imagination. They are facts of history. The differentiation between high and low was recognised law in the time of the Peshwas. The differentiation about dole exists even no in the Bombay Presidency and was defended by a Congress Minister. *These remarks are not applicable today*—Editors.

The second principle on which the Hindu social order is founded is that of fixity of occupations for each class and continuance thereof by heredity. This is what Manu says about occupations of the four classes.

I.87. But in order to protect this universe, He, the most resplendent one, assigned separate (duties and) occupations, to those who sprang from his mouth, arms, thighs and feet.

II.88. To Brahmanas he assigned teaching and studying (the Veda) sacrificing for their own benefit and for others, giving and accepting (of alms).

III.89. The Kshatriya he commanded to protect the people, to bestow gifts to offer sacrifices to study (the Veda) and to abstain from attaching himself to sensual pleasures.

ENDOGAMY AND EXOGAMY

. . . This critical evaluation (by scholars) of the various characteristics of caste leave no doubt that prohibition, or rather the absence of intermarriage—endogamy, to be concise—is the only one that can be called the essence of caste when rightly understood. But some may deny this on abstract anthropological grounds, for there exist endogamous groups without giving rise to the problem of caste. In a general way this may be true, as endogamous societies, culturally different, making their abode in localities more or less removed, and having little to do with each other are a physical reality. . . . As pointed out before, the peoples of India form a homogeneous whole. The various races of India occupying definite territories have more or less fused into one another and do possess cultural unity, which is the only criterion of a homogeneous population. Given this homogeneity as a basis, caste becomes a problem altogether new in character and wholly absent in the situation constituted by the mere propinquity of endogamous social or tribal groups. Caste in India means an artificial chopping off of the population into fixed and definite units, each one prevented from fusing into another-through the custom of endogamy. Thus the conclusion is inevitable that *Endogamy is the only characteristic that is peculiar to caste.*

It may not also be out of place to emphasise at this moment that no civilised society of today presents more survivals of primitive times than does Indian society. Its religion is essentially primitive and its tribal code, in spite of the advance of time and civilisation, operates in all its pristine vigour even today. One of these primitive survivals, to which I wish particularly to draw your attention, is the Custom of Exogamy. The prevalence of exogamy in the primitive world is a fact too well known to need any explanation. With the growth of history, however, exogamy has lost its efficacy, and excepting the nearest blood-kins, there is usually no social bar restricting the field of marriage. But regarding the peoples of India the law of exogamy is a positive injunction even today. Indian society still savours of the clan system, even though there are no clans; and this can be easily seen from the law of matrimony which centres round the principle of exogamy, for it is not that *sapindas* (blood-kins) cannot marry, but a marriage even between *sagotras* (of the same class) is regarded as a sacrilege.

The various *gotras* of India are and have been exogamous; so are the other groups with totemic organisation. It is no exaggeration to say that with the people of India exogamy is a creed and none dare infringe it, so much so that, in spite of the endogamy of the castes within them, exogamy is strictly observed and that there are more rigorous penalties for violating exogamy than there are for violating endogamy. You will, therefore, readily see that with exogamy as the rule there could be no caste, for exogamy means fusion. But we have castes; consequently in the final analysis creation of castes, so far as India is concerned, means the superimposition of endogamy on exogamy. . . .

Hindu society, in common with other societies, was composed of classes and the earliest known are (1) the Brahmin or the priestly class; (2) the Kshatriya or the military class; (3) the Vaishya, or the merchant class, and (4) the Shudra, or the artisan and menial class. Particular attention has to be paid to the fact that this was essentially a class system, in which individuals, when qualified, could change their class, and therefore classes did change their personnel. At some time in the history of the Hindus, the priestly class socially detached itself from the rest of the body of people and through a closed-door policy became a caste by itself. The other classes being subject to the law of social division of labour underwent differentiation, some into large, others into very minute groups. The Vaishya and Shudra classes were the original inchoate plasm, which formed the sources of the numerous castes of today. As the military occupation does not very easily lend itself to very minute subdivision, the Kshatriya class could have differentiated into soldiers and administrators.

This subdivision of a society is quite natural. But the unnatural thing about these subdivisions is that they have lost the open-door character of the class system and have become self-enclosed units called castes. The question is: Were they compelled to close their doors and become endogamous, or did they close them of their own accord? I submit that there is a double line of answer: *Some closed the door; others found it closed against them.* The one is a psychological interpretation and the other is mechanistic, but they are complementary and both are necessary to explain the phenomenon of caste-formation in its entirety.

. . . Endogamy or the closed-door system, was a fashion in Hindu society, and as it had originated from the Brahmin caste it was wholeheartedly imitated by all the non-Brahmin subdivisions or classes, who, in their turn, became endogamous castes. It is 'the infection of imitation' that caught all these subdivisions on their onward march of differentiation and has turned them into castes. The propensity to imitate is a deep-seated one in the human mind and need not be deemed an inadequate explanation for the formation of the various castes in India.

In a way, but only in a way, the status of a caste in Hindu society varies directly with the extent of the observance of the customs of *sati*, enforced widowhood, and girl marriage. But observance of these customs varies directly with the *distance* (I am using the word in the Tardian sense) that separates the caste. Those castes that are nearest to the Brahmins have all the three customs and insist on the strict observance thereof. Those that are less near have imitated enforced widowhood and girl marriage; others, a little further off, have only girl marriage; and those furthest off have imitated only the belief in the caste principle. This imperfect imitation, I dare say, is due partly to what Tarde calls 'distance' and partly to the barbarous character of these customs.

. . . that *caste in the singular number is an unreality. Castes exist only in the plural number.* There is no such thing as a caste; there are always castes. To illustrate my meaning: while making themselves into a caste, the Brahmins, by virtue of this, created non-Brahmin caste[s]; or, to express it in my own way, while closing themselves in they closed others out.

. . . the 'fissiparous' character of caste, as a consequence of the virtue of self-duplication that is inherent in it. Any innovation that seriously antagonises the ethical, religious and social code of the cast is not likely to be tolerated by the caste, and the recalcitrant members of a caste are in danger of being thrown out of the caste, and left to their own fate without having the alternative of being admitted into or absorbed by other castes. Caste rules are inexorable and they do not wait to make nice distinctions between kinds of offence. Innovation may be of any kind, but all kinds will suffer the same penalty. A novel way of thinking will create a new caste for the old ones will not tolerate it. The noxious thinker respectfully called Guru (Prophet) suffers the same fate as the sinners in illegitimate love. The former creates a caste of the nature of a religious sect and the latter a type of mixed caste. Castes have no mercy for a sinner who has the courage to violate the code. The penalty is excommunication and the result is a new caste. It is not peculiar Hindu psychology that induces the excommunicated to form themselves into a caste; far from it. On the contrary, very often they have been quite willing to be humble members of so caste (higher by preference) if they could be admitted within its fold. But castes are enclosed units and it is their conspiracy with clear conscience that compels the excommunicated to make themselves into a caste. The logic of this obdurate circumstance is merciless, and it is in obedience to its force that some unfortunate groups find themselves enclosed, because others in enclosing themselves have closed them out, with the result that new groups (formed on any basis obnoxious to the caste rules) by a mechanical law are constantly being converted into castes to a bewildering multiplicity. Thus is told the second tale in the process of caste formation in India.

COMMUNAL AWARD

But it is not necessary to go to Prussia. There is evidence at home. What is the significance of the Communal Award with its allocation of political power in defined proportions to diverse classes and communities? In my view, its significance lies in this that political constitution must take note of social organisation. It shows that the politicians who denied that the social problem in India had any bearing on the political problem were forced to reckon with the social problem in devising the constitution. The Communal Award is so to say the nemesis following upon the indifference and neglect of social reform. . . . one can say that generally speaking History bears out the proposition that political revolutions have always been preceded by social and religious revolutions.

SOCIALISTS AND THE CASTE SYSTEM

Let me now turn to the Socialists. Can the Socialists ignore the problem arising out of the social order? The Socialists of India following their fellows in Europe are seeking to apply the economic interpretation of history to the facts of India. They propound that man is an economic creature, that his activities and aspirations are bound by economic facts, that property is the only source of power. They, therefore, preach that political and social reforms are but gigantic illusions and that economic reform by equalisation of property must have precedence over every other kind of reform. One may join issue on every one of these premises on which rests the Socialists' case for economic reform having priority over every other kind of reform. One may contend that economic motive is not the only motive by which man is actuated. That economic power is the only kind of power no student of human society can accept. That the social status of an individual by itself often becomes a source of power and authority is made clear by the sway which the Mahatmas have held over the common man. Why do millionaires in India obey penniless Sadhus and Fakirs? Why do, millions of paupers in India sell their trifling trinkets which constitute their only wealth and go to Benares and Mecca? That religion is the source of power is illustrated by the history of India where the priest, holds a sway over the common man often greater than the magistrate and where everything, even such things as strikes and elections, so easily take a religious turn and can so easily be given a religious twist.

The fallacy of the Socialists lies in supposing that because in present stage of European society property as a source of power predominant, that the same is true of India or that the same was true of Europe in the past. Religion, social status and property are all sources of power and authority, which one man has, to control the liberty of another. One is predominant at one stage, the other is predominant at another stage. That is the only difference. If liberty is the ideal, if liberty means the destruction of the dominion which one man holds over another then obviously it cannot be insisted upon that economic reform must be the one kind of reform worthy of pursuit. If the source of power and dominion is at any given time or in any given society social and religious then social reform and religious reform must be accepted as the necessary sort of reform.

However, what I like to ask the Socialists is this: Can you have economic reform without first bringing about a reform of the social order? The Socialists of India do not seem to have considered this question. I do not wish to do them an injustice. I give below a quotation from a letter which a prominent Socialist wrote a few days ago to a friend of mine in which he said, 'I do not believe that we can build up a free society in India so long as there is a trace of this ill-treatment and suppression of one class by another. Believing as I do in a socialist ideal, inevitably I believe in perfect equality in the treatment of various classes and groups. I think that Socialism offers the only true remedy for this as well as other problems.' Now the question that I like to ask is: Is it enough for a Socialist to say, 'I believe in perfect equality in the treatment of the various classes?' To say that such a belief is enough is to disclose a complete lack of understanding of what is involved in Socialism. If Socialism is a practical program and is not merely an ideal, distant and far off, the question for a Socialist is not whether he believes in equality. The question for him is whether he minds one class ill-treating and suppressing another class as a matter of system, as a matter of principle and thus allow tyranny and oppression to continue to divide one class from another. Let me analyse the factors that are involved in the realisation of Socialism in order to explain fully my point. Now it is obvious that the economic reform contemplated by the Socialists cannot come about unless there is a revolution resulting in the seizure of power. That seizure of power must be by a proletariat. The first question I ask is: Will the proletariat of India combine to bring about this revolution? What will move men to such an action? It seems to me that other things being equal the only thing that will move one man to take such an action is the feeling that other men with whom he is acting are actuated by feeling of equality and fraternity and above all of justice. Men will not join in a revolution for the equalisation of property unless they know that after the revolution is achieved they will be treated equally and that there will be no discrimination of caste and creed. The assurance of a socialist leading the revolution that he does not believe in caste, I am sure, will not suffice. The assurance must be the assurance proceeding from much deeper foundation, namely, the mental attitude of the compatriots towards one another in their spirit of personal equality and fraternity. Can it be said that the proletariat of India, poor as it is, recognise no distinctions except that of the rich and the poor? Can it be said that the poor in India recognise no such distinctions of caste or creed, high or low? If the fact is that they do, what unity of front can be expected from such a proletariat in its action against the rich? How can there be a revolution if the proletariat cannot present a united front? Suppose for the sake of argument that by some freak of fortune a revolution does take place and the Socialists come in power, will they not have to deal with the problems created by the particular social order prevalent in India? I can't see how a Socialist State in India can function for a second without having to grapple with the problems created by the prejudices which make Indian people observe the distinctions of high and low, clean and unclean. If Socialists are not to be content with the mouthing of fine phrases, if the Socialists wish to make Socialism a definite reality then they must recognise that the problem of social reform is fundamental and that for them there is no escape from it. That the social order prevalent in India is a matter which a Socialist must deal with, that unless he does so he cannot achieve his revolution and that if he does achieve it as a result of good fortune he will have to grapple with it if he wishes to realise his ideal, is a proposition which in my opinion is incontrovertible. He will be compelled to take account of caste after revolution if he does not take account of it before revolution. This is only another way of saying that, turn in any direction you like, caste is the monster that crosses your path. You cannot have political reform, you cannot have economic reform, unless you kill this monster.

CASTE AND DIVISION OF LABOUR

Caste System is not merely division of labour. *It is also a division of labourers.* Civilised society undoubtedly needs division of labour. But in no civilised society is division of labour accompanied by this un-natural division of labourers into water-tight compartments. Caste system is not merely a division of labourers which is quite different from division of labour—it is a hierarchy in which the divisions of labourers are graded one above the other. In no other country is the division of labour accompanied by this gradation of labourers. There is also a third point of criticism against this view of the Caste System. This division of labour is not spontaneous, it is not based on natural aptitudes. Social and individual efficiency requires us to develop the capacity of an individual to the point of competency to choose and to make his own career. This principle is violated in the Caste System in so far as it involves an attempt to appoint tasks to individuals in advance, selected not on the basis of trained original capacities, but on that of the social status of the parents. Looked at from another point of view this stratification of occupations which is the result of the Caste System is positively pernicious. Industry is never static. It undergoes rapid and abrupt changes. With such changes an individ must be free to change his occupation. Without such freedom to adjust himself to changing circumstances it would be impossible for him to gain his livelihood. Now the Caste System will not allow Hindus to take to occupations where they are wanted if they do not belong to them by heredity. If a Hindu is seen to starve rather than take to new occupations not assigned to his caste, the reason is to be found in the Caste System. By not permitting readjustment of occupations, caste becomes a direct cause of much of the unemployment we see in the country. As a form of division of labour the Caste System suffers from another serious defect. The division of labour brought about by the Caste System is not a division based on choice. Individual sentiment, individual preference has no place in it. It is based on the dogma of predestination. Considerations of social efficiency would compel us to recognise that the greatest evil in the industrial system is not so much poverty and the suffering that it involves as the fact that so many persons have callings which make no appeal to those who are engaged in them. Such callings constantly provoke one to aversion, ill-will and the desire to evade. There are many occupations in India which on account of the fact that they are regarded as degraded by the Hindus provoke those who are engaged in them to aversion. There is a constant desire to evade and escape from such occupations which arises solely because of the blighting effect which they produce upon those who follow them owing to the slight and stigma cast upon them by the Hindu religion. What efficiency can there be in a system under which neither men's hearts nor their minds are in their work? As an economic organisation caste is therefore a harmful institution, inasmuch as it involves the subordination of man's natural powers and inclinations to the exigencies of social rules.

CASTE CONSCIOUSNESS

There is no Hindu consciousness of kind. In every Hindu the consciousness that exists is the consciousness of his caste. That is the reason why the Hindus cannot be said to form a society or a nation. . . . The Caste System prevents common activity and by preventing common activity it has prevented the Hindus from becoming a society with a unified life and a consciousness of its own being.

The law of caste confines its membership to persons born in the caste. Castes are autonomous and there is no authority anywhere to compel a caste to admit a new-comer to its social life. Hindu society being a collection of castes and each caste being a close corporation there is no place for a convert. Thus it is the caste which has prevented the Hindus from expanding and from absorbing other religious communities. So long as caste remains, Hindu religion cannot be made a missionary religion and *shudhi* will be both a folly and a futility.

CASTE AND PUBLIC SPIRIT

The effect of caste on the ethics of the Hindus is simply deplorable. Caste has killed public spirit. Caste has destroyed the sense of public charity. Caste has made public opinion impossible. A Hindu's public is his caste. His responsibility is only his caste. His loyalty is restricted only to his caste. Virtue has become caste-ridden and morality has become caste-bound. There is no sympathy to the deserving. There is no appreciation of the meritorious. There is no charity to the needy. Suffering as such calls for no response. There is charity but it begins with the caste and ends with the caste. There is sympathy but not for men of other caste. Would a Hindu acknowledge and follow the leadership of a great and good man? The case of a Mahatma apart, the answer must be that, he will follow a leader if he is a man of his caste. A Brahmin will follow a leader only if he is a Brahmin, a Kshatriya if he is a Kshatriya and so on. The capacity to appreciate merits in a man apart from his caste does not exist in a Hindu. There is appreciation of virtue but only when the man is a fellow caste-man. The whole morality is as bad as tribal morality. My caste-man, right or wrong; my caste-man, good or bad. It is not a case of standing by virtue and not standing by vice. It is a case of standing or not standing by the caste. Have not Hindus committed treason against their country in the interests of their caste?

THE IDEAL SOCIAL ORDER

If you ask me, my ideal would be a society based on *Liberty, Equality and Fraternity*. And why not? What objection can there be to Fraternity. I cannot imagine any. An ideal society should be mobile, should full of channels for conveying a change taking place in one part other parts. In an Ideal society there should be many interests consciously communicated and shared. There should be varied and free points of contact with other modes of association. In other words there must be social endosmosis. This is fraternity, which is only another name for democracy. Democracy is not merely a form of Government. It is primarily a mode of associated living, of conjoint communicated experience. It is essentially an attitude of respect and reverence towards fellowmen. Any objection to Liberty? Few object to liberty in the sense of a right to free movement, in the sense of a right to life and limb. There is no objection to liberty in the sense of a right to property, tools and materials as being necessary for earning a living to keep the body in due state of health. Why not allow liberty to benefit by an effective and competent use of a person's powers? The supporters of caste who would allow liberty in the sense of a right to life, limb and property, would not readily consent to liberty in this sense, inasmuch as it involves liberty to choose one's profession. But to object to this kind of liberty is to perpetuate slavery. For slavery does not merely mean a legalised form of subjection. It means a state of society in which some men are forced to accept from others the purposes which control their conduct. This condition obtains even where there is no slavery in the legal sense. It is found where, as in the Caste System, some persons are compelled to carry on certain prescribed callings which are not of their choice. Any objection to Equality? This has obviously been the most contentious part of the slogan on the French Revolution. The objections to equality may be sound and one may have to admit that all men are not equal. But what of that? Equality may be a fiction but nonetheless one must accept it as the governing principle. A man's power is dependent upon (1) physical heredity, (2) social inheritance or endowment in the form of parental care, education, accumulation of scientific knowledge, everything which enables him to be more efficient than the savage, and finally, (3) on his own efforts. In all these three respects men are undoubtedly unequal. But the question is, shall we treat them as unequal because they are unequal? This is a question which the opponents of equality must answer. From the standpoint of the individualist it may be just to treat men unequally so far as their efforts are unequal. It may be desirable to give as much incentive as possible to the full development of everyone's powers. But what would happen if men were treated unequally as they are, in the first two respects? It is obvious that those individuals also in whose favour there is birth, education, family name, business connections and inherited wealth would be selected in the race. But selection under such circumstances would not be a selection of the able. It would be the selection of the privileged. The reason, therefore, which forces that in the third respect we should treat men unequally demands that in the first two respects we should treat men as equally as possible. On the other hand, it can be urged that if it is good for the social body to get the most out of its members, it can get most out of them only by making them equal as far as possible at the very start of the race. That is one reason why we cannot escape equality. But there is another reason why we must accept equality. A statesman is concerned with vast numbers people. He has neither the time nor the knowledge to draw fine distinctions and to treat each equitably, that is, according to need according to capacity. However desirable or reasonable an equitable treatment of men may be, humanity is not capable of assortment and classification. The statesman, therefore, must follow some rough-and-ready rule and that rough-and-ready rule is to treat all men alike not because they are alike but because classification and assortment is impossible. The doctrine of equality is glaringly fallacious but taking all in all it is the only way a statesman can proceed in politics which is a severely practical affair and which demands a severely practical test.

CHATURVARNYA

But there is a set of reformers who hold out a different ideal. They go by the name of the Arya Samajists and their ideal of social organisation is what is called Chaturvarnya or the division of society into four classes instead of the four thousand castes that we have in India. To make it more attractive and to disarm opposition the protagonists of Chaturvarnya take great care to point out that their Chaturvarnya is based not on birth but on *guna* (worth). At the outset, I must confess that notwithstanding the worth basis of this Chaturvarnya, it is an ideal to which I cannot reconcile myself. In the first place, if under the Chaturvarnya of the Arya Samajists an individual is to take his place in the Hindu society according to his worth, I do not understand why the Arya Samajists insist upon labelling men as Brahmin, Kshatriya, Vaishya and Shudra. A learned man would be honoured without his being labelled a Brahmin. A soldier would be respected without his being designated a Kshatriya. If European society honours its soldiers and its servants without giving them permanent labels, why should Hindu society find it difficult to do so is a question which Arya Samajists have not cared to consider. There is another objection. All reform consists in a change in the notions, sentiment and mental attitudes of the people towards men and things. It is common experience that certain names become associated with certain notions and sentiments, which determine a person's attitude towards men and things. The names, Brahmin, Kshatriya, Vaishya and Shudra, are names which are associated with a definite and fixed notion in the mind of every Hindu. That notion is that of a hierarchy based on birth. So long as these names continue, Hindus will continue to think of the Brahmin, Kshatriya, Vaishya and Shudra as hierarchical divisions of high and low, based on birth, and act accordingly. The Hindu must be made to unlearn all this. But how can this happen if the old labels remain and continue to recall to his mind old notions. If new notions are to be inculcated in the minds of people it is necessary to give them new names. To continue the old name is to make the reform futile. To allow this Chaturvarnya, based on worth to be designated by such stinking labels of Brahmin, Kshatriya, Vaishya, Shudra, indicative of social divisions based on birth, is a snare.

Chaturvarnya is impracticable, harmful and has turned out to be a miserable failure. From a practical point of view, the system of Chaturvarnya raises several difficulties which its protagonists do not seem to have taken into account. The principle underlying caste is fundamentally different from the principle underlying varna. Not only are they fundamentally different but they are also fundamentally opposed. The former is based on worth. How are you going to compel people who have acquired a higher status based on birth without reference to their worth to vacate that status? How are you going to compel people to recognise the status due to a man in accordance with his worth, who is occupying a lower status based on his birth? For this you must first break up the Caste System, in order to be able to establish the varna system. How are you going to reduce the four thousand castes, based on birth, to the four varnas, based on worth? This is the first difficulty which the protagonists of the Chaturvarnya must grapple with. There is a second difficulty which the protagonists of Chaturvarnya must grapple with, if they wish to make establishment of Chaturvarnya a success.

Chaturvarnya presupposes that you can classify people into four definite classes. Is this possible? In this respect, the ideal of Chaturvarnya has, as you will see, a close affinity to the Platonic ideal. To Plato, men fell by nature into three classes. In some individuals, he believed mere appetites dominated. He assigned them to the labouring and trading classes. Others revealed to him that over and above appetites, they have a courageous disposition. He classed them as defenders in war and guardians of internal peace. Others showed a capacity to grasp the universal reason underlying things. He made them the lawgivers of the people. The criticism to which Plato's *Republic* is subject, is also the criticism which must apply to the system of Chaturvarnya, in so far as it proceeds upon the possibility of an accurate classification of men into four distinct classes. The chief criticism against Plato is that his idea of lumping of individuals into a few sharply marked-off classes is a very superficial view of man and hi powers. Plato had no perception of the uniqueness of every individual of his incommensurability with others, of each individual forming class of his own. He had no recognition of the infinite diversity of active tendencies and combination of tendencies of which an individual is capable. To him, there were types of faculties or powers in the individual constitution. All this is demonstrably wrong. Modern science has shown that lumping together of individuals into a few sharply marked-off classes is a superficial view of man not worthy of serious consideration. Consequently, the utilisation of the qualities of individuals is incompatible with their stratification by classes, since the qualities of individuals are so variable. Chaturvarnya must fall for the very reason for which Plato's Republic must fail, namely, that it is not possible to pigeon men into holes, according as he belongs to one class or the other. That it is impossible to accurately classify people into four definite classes is proved by the fact that the original four classes have now become four thousand castes.

There is a third difficulty in the way of the establishment of the system of Chaturvarnya. How are you going to maintain the system of Chaturvarnya, supposing it was established? One important requirement for the successful working of Chaturvarnya is the maintenance of the penal system which could maintain it by its sanction. The system of Chaturvarnya must perpetually face the problem of the transgressor. Unless there is a penalty attached to the act of transgression, men will not keep to their respective classes. The whole system will break down, being contrary to human nature. Chaturvarnya cannot subsist by its own inherent goodness. It must be enforced by law. That, without penal sanction the ideal of Chaturvarnya cannot be realised, is proved by the story in the *Ramayana* of Rama killing Shambuka. Some people seem to blame Rama because he wantonly and without reason killed Shambuka. But to blame Rama for killing Shambuka is to misunderstand the whole situation. Ram Raj was a Raj based on Chaturvarnya. As a king, Rama was bound to maintain Chaturvarnya. It was his duty therefore to kill Shambuka, the Shudra, who had transgressed his class and wanted to be a Brahmin. This is the reason why Rama killed Shambuka. But this also shows that penal sanction is necessary for the maintenance of Chaturvarnya. Not only penal sanction is necessary, but penalty of death is necessary. That is why Rama did not inflict on Shambuka a lesser punishment. That is why *Manusmriti* prescribes such heavy sentences as cutting off the tongue or pouring of molten lead in the ears of the Shudra, who recites or hears the Veda. The supporters of Chaturvarnya must give an assurance that they could successfully classify men and they could induce modern society in the twentieth century to reforge the penal sanctions of *Manusmriti*.

The protagonists of Chaturvarnya do not seem to have considered what is to happen to women in their system. Are they also to be divided into four classes, Brahmin, Kshatriya; Vaishya and Shudra? Or are they to be allowed to take the status of their husbands. If the status of the woman is to be the consequence of marriage what becomes of the underlying principle of Chaturvarnya, namely, that the status of a person should be based upon the worth of that person? If they are to be classified according to their worth, is their classification to be nominal or real? If it is to be nominal then it is useless and then the protagonists of Chaturvarnya must admit that their system does not), apply to women. If it is real, are the protagonists of Chaturvarnya prepared to follow the logical consequences of applying it to women? They must be prepared to have women priests and women soldier. Hindu society has grown accustomed to women teachers and women barristers. It may grow accustomed to women brewers and women butchers. But he would be a bold person, who would say that it will allow women priests and women soldiers. But that will be the logical outcome of applying Chaturvarnya to women. Given these difficulties. I think no one except a congenital idiot could hope and believe in a successful regeneration of the Chaturvarnya.

Assuming that Chaturvarnya is practicable, I contend that it is the most vicious system. That the Brahmin should cultivate knowledge, that the Kshatriya should bear arms, that the Vaishya should trade and that the Shudra should serve sounds as though it was a system of division of labour. Whether the theory was intended to state that the Shudra need not or that whether it was intended to lay down that he must not, is an interesting question. The defenders of Chaturvarnya give it the first meaning . . . How many times have the Kshatriya annihilated the Brahmins! The *Mahabharata* and the Puranas are full of incidents of the strife between the Brahmins and the Kshatriyas. They even quarrelled over such petty questions as to who should salute first, as to who should give way first, the Brahmins or the Kshatriyas, when the two met in the street. Not only was the Brahmin an eyesore to the Kshatriya and the Kshatriya an eyesore to the Brahmin, it seems that the Kshatriyas had become tyrannical and the masses, disarmed as they were under the system of Chaturvarnya, were praying to Almighty God for relief from their tyranny. The *Bhagwat* tells us very definitely that Krishna had taken Avtar for one sacred purpose and that was to annihilate the Kshatriyas. With these instances of rivalry and enmity between the different varnas before us, I do not understand how anyone can hold out Chaturvarnya as an ideal to be aimed at or as a pattern on which Hindu society should be remodeled.

CASTE AMONG NON-HINDUS

. . . nowhere is human society one single whole. It is always plural. In the world of action, the individual is one limit and society the other. Between them lie all sorts of associative arrangements of lesser and larger scope, families, friendship, co-operative associations, business combines, political parties, bands of thieves and robbers. These small groups are usually firmly welded together and are often as exclusive as castes. They have a narrow and intensive code, which is often anti-social. This is true of every society, in Europe as well as in Asia. The question to be asked in determining whether a given society is an ideal society is not whether there are groups in it, because groups exist in all societies. The questions to be asked in determining what is an ideal society are: How numerous and varied are the interests which are consciously shared by the groups? How full and free is the interplay with other forms of associations? Are the forces that separate groups and classes more numerous than the forces that unite? What social significance is attached to this group life? Is its exclusiveness a matter of custom and convenience or is it a matter of religion? It is in the light of these questions that one must decide whether caste among Non-Hindus is the same as caste among Hindus. If we apply these considerations to castes among Mohammedans, Sikhs and Christians on the one hand and to castes among Hindus on the other, you will find that caste among Non-Hindus is fundamentally different from caste among Hindus. First, the ties, which consciously make the Hindus hold together, are non-existent, while among Non-Hindus there are many that hold them together. The strength of a society depends upon the presence of points of contact, possibilities of interaction between different groups which exist in it.

There may be castes among Sikhs and Mohammedans but the Sikhs and the Mohammedans will not outcast a Sikh or a Moham-medan if he broke his caste. Indeed, the very idea of excommunication is foreign to the Sikhs and Mohammedans. But with the Hindus the case is entirely different. He is sure to be outcasted if he broke caste. This shows the difference in the social significance of caste to Hindus and Non-Hindus. This is the second point of difference. But there is also a third and a more important one. Caste among the Non-Hindus has no religious consecration; but among the Hindus most decidedly it has. Among the Non-Hindus, caste is only a practice, not a sacred institution. They did not originate it. With them it is only a survival. They do not regard caste as a religious dogma. Religion compels the Hindus to treat isolation and segregation of castes as a virtue. Religion does not compel the Non-Hindus to take the same attitude towards caste. If Hindus wish to break caste, their religion will come in their way. But it will not be so in the case of Non-Hindus.

CASTE AND NATION

You cannot build anything on the foundations of caste. You cannot build up a nation, you cannot build up a morality. Anything that you will build on the foundations of caste will crack and will never be a whole.

DESTRUCTION OF CASTE

Caste is not a physical object like a wall of bricks or a line of barbed wire which prevents the Hindus from commingling and which has, therefore, to be pulled down. Caste is a notion, it is a state of the mind. The destruction of caste does not therefore mean the destruction of a physical barrier. It means a *notional* change. Caste maybe bad. Caste may lead to conduct so gross as to be called man's inhumanity to man. All the same, it must be recognised that the Hindus observe cast not because they are inhuman or wrong headed. They observe cast because they are deeply religious. People are not wrong in observing caste. In my view, what is wrong is their religion, which has inculcated this notion of caste. If this is correct, then obviously the enemy, you must grapple with, is not the people who observe caste, but the Shastras which teach them this religion of caste. Criticising and ridiculing people for not interdining or intermarrying or occasionally holding intercaste dinners and celebrating intercaste marriages, is a futile method of achieving the desired end. The real remedy is to destroy the belief in the sanctity of the Shastras. How do you expect to succeed, if you allow the Shastras to continue to mould the beliefs and opinions of the people? Not to question the authority of the Shastras, to permit the people to believe in their sanctity and their sanctions and to blame them and to criticise them for their acts as being irrational and inhuman is an incongruous way of carrying on social reform. Reformers working for the removal of untouchability including Mahatma Gandhi, do not seem to realise that the acts of the people are merely the results of their beliefs inculcated upon their minds by the Shastras and that people will not change their conduct until they cease to believe in the sanctity of the Shastras on which their conduct is founded. No wonder that such efforts have not produced any results. You also seem to be erring in the same way as the reformers working in the cause of removing untouchability. To agitate for and to organise intercaste dinners and intercaste marriages is like forced feeding brought about by artificial means. Make every man and woman free from the thraldom of the Shastras, cleanse their minds of the pernicious notions founded on the Shastras, and he or she will interdine and intermarry, without your telling him or her to do so.

It is no use telling people that the Shastras do not say what they are believed to say, grammatically read or logically interpreted. What matters is how the Shastras have been understood by the people. You must take the stand that Buddha took. You must take the stand which Guru Nanak took. You must not only discard the Shastras, you must deny their authority, as did Buddha and Nanak. You must have courage to tell the Hindus, that what is wrong with them is their religion—the religion which has produced in them this notion of the sacredness of caste. Will you show that courage?

The Hindus hold to the sacredness of the social order. Caste has a divine basis. You must therefore destroy the sacredness and divinity with which caste has become invested. In the last analysis, this means you must destroy the authority of the Shastras and the Vedas.

. . . that the Brahmins form the intellectual class of the Hindus. It is not only an intellectual class but it is a class which is held in great reverence by the rest of the Hindus. The Hindus are taught that the Brahmins are *bhudevas* (Gods on earth) वर्णानाम् ब्राह्मण गुरू …The Hindus are taught that Brahmins alone can be their teachers. Manu says, 'If it be asked how it should be with respect to points of the Dharma which have not been specially mentioned, the answer is that which Brahmins who are Shishthas propound shall doubtless have legal force.'

अनाम्नातेषु धर्मेषु स्यिद्दिति चेद्धभवेत्।

यं शिष्टा बाह्मणा ब्रूयूः स धर्मः स्यादशा ड्विकतः।

When such an intellectual class, which holds the rest of the community in its grip, is opposed to the reform of caste, the chances of success in a movement for the break-up of the Caste System appear to me very, very remote.

. . . [T]he Caste System has two aspects. In one of its aspects, it divides men into separate communities. In its second aspect, it places these communities in a graded order one above the other in social status. Each caste takes its pride and its consolation in the fact that in the scale of castes it is above some other caste. As an outward mark of this gradation, there is also a gradation of social and religious rights technically spoken of as *ashtadhikaras* and *sanskaras*. The higher the grade of a caste, the greater the number of these rights and the lower the grade, the lesser their number. Now this gradation, this scaling of castes, makes it impossible to organise a common front against the Caste System. If a caste claims the right to interdine and intermarry with another caste placed above it, it is frozen, instantly it is told by mischief-mongers, and there are many Brahmins amongst such mischief-mongers, that it will have to concede interdining and intermarriage with castes below it! All are slaves of the Caste System. But all the slaves are not equal in status. To excite the proletariat to bring about an economic revolution, Karl Marx told them: 'You have nothing to lose except your chains.' But the artful way in which the social and religious rights are distributed among the different castes whereby some have more and some have less, makes the slogan of Karl Marx quite useless to excite the Hindus against the Caste System. Castes form a graded system of sovereignties, high and low, which are jealous of their status and which know that if a general dissolution came, some of them stand to lose more of their prestige and power than others do. You cannot, therefore, have a general mobilisation of the Hindus, to use a military expression, for an attack on the Caste System.

Can you appeal to reason and ask the Hindus to discard caste as being contrary to reason? That raises the question: Is a Hindu free to follow his reason? Manu has laid down three sanctions to which every Hindu must conform in the matter of his behaviour. Here there is no place for reason to play its part. A Hindu must follow either Veda, Smriti or Sadachar. He cannot follow anything else. In the first place how are the texts of the Vedas and Smritis to be interpreted whenever any doubt arises regarding their meaning? On this important question the view of Manu is quite definite. He says:

योवव मन्येत ते मूले हेतुशास्त्राश्रयात् द्विजः।

स साधुभिर्बिहिष्कार्यौ निास्तको वेद निन्दकः।

According to this rule, rationalism as a canon of interpreting the Vedas and Smritis is absolutely condemned. It is regarded to be as wicked as atheism and the punishment provided for it is excommunication. Thus, where a matter is covered by the Veda or the Smriti, a Hindu cannot resort to rational thinking. Even when there is a conflict between Vedas and Smritis on matters on which they have given a positive injunction, the solution is not left to reason. When there is a conflict between two Shrutis, both are to be regarded as of equal authority. Either of them may be followed. No attempt is to be made to find out which of the two accords with reason. This is made clear by Manu:

श्रु तिर्द्वैधं तु यत्र स्यात्तत्र धर्माबुभौ स्मृतौ

'When there is a conflict between Shruti and Smriti, the Shruti must prevail.' But here too, no attempt must be made to find out which of the two accords with reason. This is laid down by Manu in the following Shloka:

या वेदबाहानः स्मृतयो याश्य काश्य कुद्दष्टः ।
सर्वास्ता निष्फलाः प्रेत्य तमो निष्ठा हि ताः स्मृताः ॥

So far as caste and varna are concerned, not only the Shastras do not permit the Hindu to use his reason in the decision of the question, but they have taken care to see that no occasion is left to examine in a rational way the foundations of his belief in caste and varna.

So long as people look upon it as Religion they will not be ready for a change, because the idea of Religion is generally speaking not associated with the idea of change. But the idea of law is associated with the idea of change and when people come to know that what is called Religion is really Law, old and archaic, they will be ready for a change, for people know and accept that law can be changed.

While I condemn a Religion of Rules, I must not be understood to hold the opinion that there is no necessity for a religion. On the contrary, I agree with Burke when he says that, 'True religion is the foundation of society, the basis on which all true Civil Government rests, and both their sanction.' Consequently, when I urge that these ancient rules of life be annulled, I am anxious that its place shall be taken by a Religion of Principles, which alone can lay claim to being a true Religion. Indeed, I am so convinced of the necessity of Religion that I feel I ought to tell you in outline what I regard as necessary items in this religious reform. The following in my opinion should be the cardinal items in this reform: (1) There should be one and only one standard book of Hindu Religion, acceptable to all Hindus and recognised by all Hindus. This of course means that all other books of Hindu religion such as Vedas, Shastras and Puranas, which are treated as sacred and authoritative, must by law cease to be so and the preaching of any doctrine, religious or social contained in these books should be penalised. (2) It should be better if priesthood among Hindus was abolished. But as this seems to be impossible, the priest-hood must at least cease to be hereditary. Every person who professes to be a Hindu must be eligible for being a priest. It should be provided by law that no Hindu shall be entitled to be a priest unless he has passed an examination prescribed by the State and holds a *sanad* from the State permitting him to practise. (3) No ceremony performed by a priest who does not hold a *sanad* shall be deemed to be valid in law and it should be made penal for a person who has no *sanad* to officiate as a priest. (4) A priest should be the servant of the State and should be subject to the disciplinary action by the State in the matter of his morals, beliefs, and worship, in addition to his being subject along with other citizens to the ordinary law of the land. (5) The number of priests should be limited by law according to the requirement of the State as is done in the case of the I.C.S.

Whether you do that or you do not, you must give a new doctrinal basis to your Religion—a basis that will be in consonance with Liberty, Equality and Fraternity, in short, with Democracy.

6

Ram Manohar Lohia on
Caste in Indian Politics *

D.L. Sheth

[Excerptor's note: With every election the caste and regional forces seem to acquire a firmer grip on India's representative politics. The coming elections are likely to reinforce these forces further. It is widely feared that the increasing role of caste and regional factors, particularly in parliamentary elections, may subvert the very principles of our representative system and, in the process, may even eclipse the national-secular arena of politics. Paradoxically, however, these very forces represent the democratic aspirations of the Indian masses. Thus, on the one hand the caste–religion politics seeks to link and articulate the secular interests of the numerous poor and oppressed communities, and, on the other, it pursues such exclusionary politics of 'identities' vis-à-vis each other that it inevitably prevents larger conditions of interests being formed at the macro le politics.

It was this dialectic of caste–politics interaction created by competitive politics, that is, politicisation of castes and casteisation of politics, that greatly bothered, but immensely fascinated, Ram Manohar Lohia. Much before political analysts had begun to address the caste–politics relationship some time in the late 1960s and early 1970s, Lohia was seized of the problem as early as in the late 1950s.

In his political thinking and practice, Lohia indeed revealed uncanny insights into the mobilisational potentials of castes in competitive politics, the dividends of which are being reaped in ample measure today by politicians across the party spectrum. Unlike his many followers today he, however, was acutely aware of the limitations and dangers of such politics turning into pure politics of caste, that is, politics which privileged caste as a primary social identity and a political unit in the representational system. He abhorred such politics and described it as an empty political struggle of castes, devoid of any socially transformative potential. His approach to political mobilisation was, therefore, to build a large, material interest-based political coalition

* Extracts from *Lokayan Bulletin*, September–October 1996, pp. 1–14.

which would bring together various categories of the population, all sharing common and disadvantaged social-structural locations. He believed that such a political formation, brought about through a social movement, could transform the very consciousness and forms of organisation in Indian politics which even in our democratic politics were, by and large, derived from the ideology and practices of the caste system. Lohia was at the same time apprehensive of the ideology of class, which pitted 'class' 'against 'nation', and prevented participation of the socially disadvantaged castes in secular politics. The ideology of castes, on the other hand, prevented building of the nation on the principle of equal citizenship and instead sustained the hegemonic power of the upper castes over the vast majority of the Indian masses. The numerically powerful lower castes did indeed seriously challenge this hegemony by organizing themselves in competitive politics. While Lohia welcomed this development, he ruled out the possibility of their politics producing a larger, all-India political coalition based on material interests of all oppressed groups. In so far as the backward caste politics strengthened caste consciousness and promoted caste-based political organisation of the larger castes and neglected or excluded the smaller castes, such politics, in his view, remained empty of any transformative possibility.

We reproduce below excerpts pertaining to the issue of caste-politics interaction from Lohias longer essay, 'Towards the Destruction of Castes and Classes'. Its relevance today is even greater than when it was written, in 1959.]

INTRODUCTION

British rule has ended but the caste parties that it gave birth to have continued into free India and are enjoying fresh access of strength.

The Workers and Peasants Party and the Republican Party of western India, the Dravida Munnetra Kazhagam of south India and the Jharkhand Party of eastern India alongside the Ganatantra and Janata parties are not only regional parties but also caste parties. In fact, they represent and embody regional castes. These regional castes are decisively numerous in their area. The Adivasis of Chota Nagpur are the lifeblood of the Jharkhand, the Mahars of the Republicans, the Marathas of the Workers and Peasants, the Mudaliars but also other non-Brahmins of the Dravida Munnetra.

A patriot and a progressive would look askance at the growth of parties of regional caste, even when they don a radical garb. Their capacity to disintegrate dare not be overlooked. They disintegrate the people. They disintegrate the mind. What, however, is the use of recognition by other castes of this capacity to disintegrate? The caste that becomes the instrument of such disintegration must recognise it. When can it do so? That raises the question of injury that society has done to the caste, which is in a position to hit back and does so.

The castes that went to form the Maratha, Justice or Scheduled Caste parties suffered ill-treatment from society. The British rulers made use of this sense of grievance and injury, a very bad use indeed, but they did not and could not have created it. That is why the problem has persisted. *In some cases, the caste that has suffered the injury and that which has caused it have changed places. But that does not solve the problem of injury.* Furthermore, numberless castes have yet to make themselves vocal and effective and are today content to play a passive or a subsidiary role to the contending giants. This is the chief source of injury and injustice.

The Maharashtra Scene

The political interplay of castes has unfolded itself fascinatingly in Maharashtra and the drama is not yet over. Until 1930 and a little after, the Maharashtra scene was bafflingly simple, and its backdrop was Brahmin versus the rest. The succeeding period of around twenty-five years has done nothing to diminish the amazing simplicity of the scene. Only the dominating caste has changed. The backdrop is today represented by Maratha versus the rest. The Marathas are a peculiar caste of Maharashtra, who claim to be Kshatriyas but are more like the cultivator-Sudras of north India. They have been the largest single downgraded caste of that area. Additionally, west India has few Vaishyas and Kshatriyas and the Kayasthas too are negligible, so that the Maratha was the spearhead of the revolt against the Brahmin in Maharashtra although other downgraded castes assisted him in varying degrees. The revolt was pro-British in the beginning, because the Brahmins were on the whole anti-British, but the nationalist movement proved strong enough to absorb it. The Maratha entered the party of nationalism, the Congress party, and almost took it over. *The phenomenon of caste exclusion was witnessed again, with the roles changed. On the one hand, the Brahmin began gradually to lose his monopoly of political power and, on the other, the Maratha did not share his new-found authority with the other downgraded castes.*

The Brahmin, who has increasingly been losing political power, and the downgraded castes other than the Maratha, which have felt left out, have been yearning for an opportunity to hit out. Their earlier effort to hit out on the Goa issue when the Brahmin Shaniwarpet of Poona had for a while again become the cultural capital of Maharashtra, proved a curtain-raiser to the present language effort. The Marathas have themselves to thank for this development. They proved to be as greedy for power and monopolistic as any. *They used the revolt of the downgraded castes for the assertion of their own supremacy and not for the destruction of castes as such and the injustice that goes with them. Ever and ever again, the revolt of the downgraded castes has been misused to upgrade one or another caste rather than to destroy the entire edifice of caste.*

The exclusion of the high caste from political power does not necessarily imply their exclusion from economic and other types of power. In the first place, such political exclusion has nowhere been total, not even in the south. The Brahmins have in recent years, as the sole representative of the high caste, been increasingly eliminated from legislative and administrative power in Tamilnad. Even so, they still occupy a fantastically privileged position. Although only 4 per cent of the population, their share in the gazetted services of the administration must be around 40 per cent.

The Tamilnad Situation

The Tamil situation is very intriguing. Elements of the non-Brahmin and the Dravida movements have influenced alike the Congress and the anti-Congress parties. Both the Dravida Kazhagams are openly Dravidian. So is the Congress party in a concealed and somewhat milder way. All four elements of the Dravida movement, Brahmin versus non-Brahmin, Aryan versus Dravidian, north versus south and Hindi versus Tamil are present in varying degrees alike in the Congress and the anti-Congress movements. Not being obstructed by all-India consideration unlike the Congress party, the anti-Congress Dravidian movements are fiercer in their opposition to the north, Hindi or the Brahmins as the situation demands.

A confident forecast of the future is made somewhat difficult by the absence of clearly stated economic programmes. The anti-Congress Dravidian parties are even more fuzzy than the Congress party in respect of economic programmes. Some of them have even allowed the more illusory north–south and similar prejudices to obscure and weaken the substantial caste issue. *A happy outcome would have been if both the Dravidian streams freed as they already have been of high-caste influence had increasingly rid themselves of geographical an linguistic prejudices and aimed single-mindedly at the destruction of caste and if one had tended to adopt conservative and capitalist and the other radical and socialist economic policies.*

A likelier and harmful development would be the further accumulation of prejudices. If it accepted that India's economic condition including that of the south and Tamilnad is not likely to improve in the next decade and more, the stage is set for explosively irrational politics. The people may lend their ear more and more to cries of geo graphical and linguistic oppositions. Political parties would not be human if they did not exploit such opportunities to rise to power. The likeliest development is somewhat more hopeful. It may take time to unfold itself fully. People may begin to yearn for wholesome, positive and concrete programmes. Such a programme would have to base itself on socialist principles in the economic sphere and, in the social sphere, on the total destruction of caste. *It would therefore make use of the healthier aspect of the Dravidian spirit while it would try to absorb the individual Brahmin equally with the non-Brahmin into the coming social order.* It would for some time to come have to aim at the destruction of high-caste privileges even through the award of preferential treatment to the backward castes.

Developments in Andhra Pradesh

Developments somewhat further north in the Andhra Pradesh have been, in a sense, of greater interest. The Reddys of Andhra are a cross between the Kshatriyas and the Ahirs of north India, either of whom are almost absent from the Andhra scene, and have definitely become the most influential single caste of their state. They are the ruling caste of Andhra *par excellence* but they have been elastic enough not wholly to displease the Brahmins whom they ousted from political power and have been wise enough to share their power with smaller castes like the Velmas. They have, however, been unable to make friends with the Kammas, a caste almost wholly similar to the Kurmis of north India both in respect of their appellation and their sound cultivator status. Economically somewhat enabled and politically disabled, the Kammas of Andhra have been somewhat restless in the past decade. They have almost as an entire caste sought to revenge themselves on the Reddys through the instrument of the Communist Party.

When would the Andhra political scene shift to the most numerous but the least influential castes? These are the Kapus, the Padmashalis, the Malas and Madigas, in fact, the combination which has from time to time been known as the Cherry Sangham. The Kapus are the most numerous cultivating caste, they are very poor occupancy tenants, and even poorer sharecroppers when they are not actually agricultural labourers. *In order to put energy and activity into this mass of Kapus a political party would have to arise that frees itself almost wholly from the strangle hold of the land owning Reddy and the Kamma castes.* Such a party would have to aim at the abolition of sharecropping and, as a first step, perhaps at the award of one-third or even less to the landowner and the rest to the cultivator. The Communist Party has not been such a party and perhaps can never become such. It is far too much of a landowning party, not so much the big landowners as the smaller ones. It has indeed achieved remarkable success in acquiring for itself the loyalty of the agricultural labourers, who are by and large the Harijan castes. This phenomenon of Harijan loyalty to the Communist Party prevails over all of south India. Not unless a new nucleus emerges, with wage earners' struggles, would there be any chance of enlivening the large mass of Andhra population or of causing a shift in Harijan loyalty.

The Bengal Situation

A somewhat peculiar situation obtains in an area like Bengal. It is commonly supposed that Bengal has no caste politics. What is meant is that the vast bulk of the lower castes are too unaware to speak, much less to shout. The high castes are very vocal. Furthermore, they are somewhat like the Europeans, for every single high caste has tended, at least in the towns, to acquire an individualised personality. *This silence of the lower castes and the comparative modernisation of the higher castes has obscured the true position in Bengal, the most caste-ridden portion of India.* Some day, the silence will break. That will be the time when empty struggles against caste may repeat themselves. The Mahishyas (Sudra) and the Namasudras (Harijan) are two most numerous lower castes of Bengal. They might assert themselves, not with a view to destroy caste but in order to equal or rival the Brahmin and the Kayastha. The time to prevent such empty struggles is now. A deliberate policy of uplifting all the lower castes and not merely the Namasudra or the Mahishya into positions of leadership must be followed.

The Rise of Regional Caste Parties: Politics of the Numerically Powerful Castes

The rise of regional and caste parties like the Jharkhand and Ganatantra embodies exceptionally singular phenomena. The Jharkhand has almost never fought for the rights of Adivasis or forest-dwellers nor against the vicious laws or practices that oppress them. In fact, the Socialists and similar persons have fought for them in certain areas. And yet they vote for the Jharkhand, because it lives with them, eats and dances with them, sorrows and makes merry with them and is generally apart of them. *Caste in this as in certain other cases, has driven edge between political and social kinship.* Not unless the political economic parties of national reach learn to live socially, in their births and wedding feasts and deaths, with different castes and tribes, will they be able to wrest from parties like the Jharkhand their undoubted dominion over select areas.

Among the Sudras, certain castes are numerically powerful, even overwhelming in some areas. The age of adult franchise has placed power in their hands. Some castes like the Reddys and Mudaliars of south India and the Marathas of the west have made use of it. They, and not the Dvija, are the political overlords of their areas, though, even here the high caste has strengthened its economic grip and is making most clever and deceptive efforts to stage a political comeback. This is possible chiefly because *these are empty struggles against caste. They do not change the social order in the sense of making it more just, mobile or active. They do not give power to all the lower castes, but only to the largest single section within them. They do not therefore destroy caste, but merely cause a shift in status and privileges. Some of the trappings of the high caste belonging to the Brahmin or Vaishya are stripped off them and patched on to the Maratha or the Reddy. This solves no problem. Rather, it disgusts all the other lower castes and enrages the high caste. Caste, with all its debility and some more of its irritations, remains.*

Taking the country as a whole, the Ahirs, variously known as Gvalas, Gopas, and the Chamars also known as Mahars, are the two most numerous lower castes, the former Sudra and the latter Harijan. They are the colossi of the Indian caste system, like the Brahmin and Kshatriya among the Dvija. Ahirs, Chamars, Brahmins and Kshatriyas, each comprise around two to three crores of people. Together they are roughly 10 to 12 crores of the Indian population. That still leaves a little less than three-fourths of the entire population outside their fold. Any struggles that leave unaltered their status or condition must necessarily be deemed empty. Shifts in the status and conditions of the four colossi may be of the greatest interest to them but are of little significance to society as a whole.

The Ahirs and Chamars of north India have made efforts, perhaps without much awareness, similar to those of the Reddys and the Marathas. They were bound to fail, first, because the Dvijas are far more numerous in the north and, second, because, they are not quite so numerically strong among the lower castes of the north. *Democracy is in many ways government by numbers. In a country where groups cohere through birth and long tradition, the most numerical groups tend to acquire political and economic privileges. Political parties run after them to select candidates from among them for elections to parliament and assemblies.* Additionally, their shout is the loudest for share in trade or the services. The result is most disastrous. The myriad lower castes, each of whom is numerically weak, but who together form the bulk of the population stagnate. *A war on caste must necessarily mean an elevation of all, and not merely of any one large section. A sectional elevation changes some relationships within the caste system, but it leaves the basis of castes unaltered.*

Sectional elevation is dangerous in yet another way. Those among the lower castes who rise to high positions tend to assimilate themselves to the existing high castes. In this process, they inevitably appropriate the baser qualities of the high caste. Everybody knows how the lower castes, on their rise, tend to segregate their women, which again is a quality not of the top high caste but of the medium high caste. Also the lower castes that rise begin to wear the sacred thread of the Dvija, which has so long been denied to them but which the true high caste has begun discarding. All this has an additional result of perpetuating the distinction. The risen are alienated from their own groups; instead of fermenting their own original lower groups they seek to become part of the higher castes to whose position they rise. *This process of an extremely sectional and superficial rise gives birth to another misfortune. The lever to the rise is supplied not by the cultivation of good qualities or talent but by the arousing of bitter caste jealousies and the play of intrigues.*

From Empty Politics of Castes to Politics of Social Transformation

This brings us to the (third and) true struggle against caste now on the agenda of India's history. This struggle aims to pitchfork the five downgraded groups of society, namely, women, Sudras, Harijans, Muslims and Adivasis, into positions of leadership irrespective of their merit as it stands today. What long ages of history have done must be undone by a crusade. The inclusion of all women, including Dvija women, which is but right, into the downgraded groups of society raises their proportion to the entire population to 90 per cent. This vast sea of submerged humanity, nine out of every ten of India's men and women, has doused into silence or, at best, some routine noises of seeming life. Economic and political uplift, by itself, may put some fat on their lean limbs. A restoration of self-respect through the abolition of caste, along with economic uplift, can rouse them into the activity of full men and awakened peoples. Let it not be forgotten that the high castes, Dvija, have also suffered grievously from this atrophy of the people, their education and culture hides, under the veneer of good speech and manners, the deadly poison of the lie and self-advancement through deceit. *A crusade to uplift the downgraded groups would revive also the high caste, would set right frames and values which are all today askew.* This crusade must never y be confused with the niggardly award of preferential positions to a few scores among the lower castes. It does not at all ferment the lower castes. What matters if a dozen or two of the lower castes are added to the high-caste oligarchy of several thousands in any sphere of life? There is need to add them by the hundred and the thousand. That will turn into a crusade what is today only a vote-catching, quarrel making and jealousy-inspiring device. The fact that an entrant or two from the lower castes into the higher reaches receive sharp notice, while dozens of simultaneous entrants from the higher castes are accepted in the usual course, indicates that a hot crusade would be necessary. *It must be emphasized again and again that hundreds of lower castes, who might otherwise stay unnoticed, must receive greater attention in a deliberate policy than the two colossi who would attract notice anyway.*

This policy of uplift of downgraded castes and groups is capable of yielding much poison. A first poison may come out of its immediate effects on men's minds; it may speedily antagonise the Dvija without as speedily influencing the Sudras. With his undoubted alertness to developments and his capacity to mislead, the Dvija may succeed in heaping direct or indirect discredit on the practitioners of this policy long before the Sudra wakes up to it. Second, the colossi among the lower castes like the Chamars and Ahirs may want to appropriate the fruits of this policy without sharing them with the myriad other low castes, with the result that the Brahmin and Chamar change places but caste remains intact. Third, the policy may be misused by selfish men among the lower castes for individual advancement, who may additionally use weapons of intrigue and caste jealousies. Fourth, every single case of election or selection between a Sudra and Dvija may become the occasion for acrimonious exchanges. The baser elements among the downgraded castes would use it as a constant weapon. In their overweening desire to eliminate the particular Dvija against whom they are ranged, they would in total seek to oust all Dvijas or to fill the air with darker suspicions when they fail. Fifth, economic and political issues may be obscured or relegated into the background. Reactionaries among the lower castes may misuse the anti-caste policy to serve their own ends.

Such is the poison that this policy may bring forth. Continual awareness may check it in great measure. But this should not blind us to the miraculous power of this policy to create and cure. India will know the most invigorating revolution of her history. She may also have indicated in the process a lesson or two to mankind.

With faith in the great crucible of the human race and equal faith in the vigour of all the Indian people, let the high caste choose to mingle tradition with mass. Simultaneously, a great burden rests on the youth of the lower castes. Not the aping of the high caste in all its traditions and manners, not dislike of manual. labour, not individual self-advancement, not bitter jealousy, but the staffing of the nation's leadership as though it were some sacral work should now be the supreme concern of women, Sudras, Harijans, Muslims and Adivasis.

[Excerptor's note: For more than a decade after Independence, the discourse on transformative politics survived only on the fringes of mainstream politics. It could not make a dent on the Congress-dominated politics of social consensus presided over by the political hegemony of a small elite. This paradigm ruled supreme until the mid-1960s, by which time Ram Manohar Lohia had succeeded in pushing the discourse of egalitarian politics onto the centre stage of India's mainstream institutional politics. Although his politics became something of a quick-fix 'anti-Congressism,' Lohia's political thinking as a whole constituted an enduring legacy. Lohia sought to give a direction to oppositional politics by giving it a radically different social and cultural basis in the growing democratic aspirations of the masses. For him politics, above all, was a means of social transformation and nation-building. His agenda for party politics was, therefore, to create a new political majority *by empowering and politically uniting the socially (ritually) discriminated, economically oppressed and culturally marginalized groups—all occupying similarly disadvantaged locations in the social structure.*

Left-radical politics, and the intellectual discourse on transformative politics, however, remained bogged down in the dichotomous view of caste versus class politics: 'class politics' was seen as representing forces of social change and modernisation and 'caste politics' as symbolising the atavistic ideology of the caste system which, it was believed, was rapidly losing its basis in the structure of material interests in society, surviving largely at the level of habit and sentiments. A large part of the left-radical politics was, therefore, addressed to articulating differences between economic classes. In the process, it did acquire ideological clarity and coherence, but failed to mobilise mass support for the class-based political parties.

Lohia found the unidimensional class view of politics much too simplistic and devoid of any true understanding of the Indian social reality. In his view, 'the talk of class' was often used by upper-caste, English-educated elite as a ploy to hide the caste character of the rulers of independent India. 'Caste politics' was similarly used by the numerically strong castes to paper over internal differentiations within what he called the 'caste collosi' and to establish their hegemony through the politics of numbers of the numerous but small caste groups at the still lower strata of society: the artisan and the small peasant castes, the backward among the religious minorities and women. While the former (class politics) weakened the legitimate claims of the ritually discriminated and historically deprived and oppressed groups for social justice and economic equality, the latter (caste politics) worked for establishing the hegemony of a few numerically large peasant castes from among the erstwhile Shudras. Lohia's egalitarian politics, thus, frontally attacked the caste system, its ideology and organisation, and sought to build horizontal political coalitions among all the socially discriminated, economically exploited and culturally marginalised groups. These groups could not be described in ideological terms of either 'class' or 'caste'.

In Lohia's judgement the left-radical politics as was then practised had no future in India, if it remained bogged down in the class–caste debate and ignored the dialectic of liberal democracy through which the class–caste dichotomy was getting transformed into an elite–mass relationship in politics. According to him, for left-radical politics to acquire transformative potential it had to address itself to variegated situations of inequalities ranging from gender and caste to class-based inequalities which were historically and socially manifested quite differently in India from those in western societies. The new, secular sources of these inequalities made it difficult for the micro-entities of castes to establish new social equations for themselves in politics. It became necessary for them to forge wider political categories within which they could coalesce and organise themselves for political action. Among other things, this politics gave rise to new and wider social coalitions of the castes sharing similarly disadvantaged locations in the social structure. Politics thus became an important means for upward social mobility and for improvement in economic status. As a percipient of this changed social reality, Lohia saw greater ideological and mobilisational potential in bringing about such social coalitions in politics.

Lohia therefore addressed his politics to the numerous social groups occupying the lower rungs of the social hierarchy. Although these groups were sharply distanced, socially and economically, from India's ruling elite and together they potentially shared a common secular aspiration to political power, they differed among themselves in terms of specific economic interests and the degree of social power they had in the traditional stratificatory system. This posed a serious challenge to Lohia's project of bringing them all together politically. He sought to overcome this difficulty by rejecting the caste–class dichotomy in politics and through forging interparty coalitions among the various caste–and region-based parties. He began the process at the state level, but with a clear view to expanding it to the national level. The ideological underpinning of this politics lay in his idea of achieving political integration through social transformation and his vision of nation-building as the process of creating an egalitarian social order and a democratically decentralised polity.

Lohia saw that the economic and power relations, arising through the processes of modernisation, still continued to be embedded in the antecedent system of social stratification which allocated economic activities and social power to hereditary groups in society, by ritual status. It was, however, not just the abstract ideology of the caste system that prevented the classes from acquiring political consciousness. It was the empirically emergent situation which prevented collective identification to he made in class terms. In this situation, specific castes were seeking new social and political equations and were relocating themselves in the changing social structure brought about by the processes of modernisation.

At the macro-level of society, this change had created a stratification system which, in man ways, was uniquely Indian. 'Classes' were interspersed with several social–cultural entities of castes, occupying different statuses in the traditional social hierarchy. This robbed the concept of 'class' of its ideological potential and reduced it to a characterless demographic category. Similarly the castes themselves were getting internally differentiated along the dimension of economic class, while keeping their social and cultural identities intact! By unravelling the caste character of the Indian ruling class and showing how the social and cultural barriers created by it frustrated the democratic and egalitarian aspirations of the vast majority of the population—the lower peasant and artisan castes of the Shudras, the ex-untouchables, the tribals, the backward among the religious minorities and the women—Lohia gave a new political meaning to these changes in the stratificatory system.

Lohia's distinctive contribution to Indian politics and political thinking, thus, lay in transcending the assumed class-caste dichotomy. He viewed the Indian social structure not merely in terms of a hierarchical status system of Hindu castes but also as a system of horizontal social and cultural segregations which constantly pushed not only the Hindu lower castes and the ex-untouchable castes but also the tribals, the lower strata of the religious minorities and women to the peripheries of the country's power structure. This view of the Indian social structure enabled Lohia to articulate his idea of egalitarian politics in more inclusive terms than was possible through the conventional concept either of 'class' or 'caste' politics. In the process, Lohia achieved a conceptual breakthrough in his political practice in two important respects. First, he problematised the gender issue in political terms and linked it with the other principle of segregation, that is, of caste. By using the metaphor of the Sita–Shambuk axis, Lohia suggested the possibility of political integration of the existing, gender caste *segregations in society. Two, Lohia invested the lower caste and the Dalit political discourse with counter-cultural symbolism. His signification of the ruling elite culture as representing the Vasishtha–Parashuram tradition and his identification of the counter-cultural traditions of the people with the Vishvamitra–Valmiki heritage had considerable potential, which he unfortunately did not explore or develop sufficiently to give the symbolism a political content.*

In brief, by transcending the caste–class dichotomy Lohia expanded his concept of politics of social transformation and linked it with the larger politics of nation-building. In today's context, such egalitarian politics of nation-building can effectively counter the majoritarian communal ideology of 'cultural nationalism' as well as the elitist ideology of hard-state nationalism.

Reproduced below are some excerpts from Lohia's writings around the theme of 'caste, gender and class' which are only suggestive of his political thinking on the issue and do not provide an exhaustive rendering on all the points highlighted by me in the foregoing. Two clarifications are required with regard to the following excerpts. One, all excerpts are taken verbatim from Lohia's writings, talks and correspondence collected in The Caste System *(Ram Manohar Lohia Samata Vidyalaya Nyas, Hyderabad, 1964). Since much of these materials arose from informal and context bound exchanges and are dispersed across different chapters of the book, I have reorganised them thematically and given them subtitles. Two, population and other figures reported in absolute numbers by Lohia in the course of his arguments were computed by him on the basis of statistics available to him in the 1950s and these have not been recomputed here. Emphasis in the text has been added by me.]*

THE RULING CLASS

Every country possesses a ruling class, but no country or age has ever known a ruling class so immobile and so firmly entrenched in positions of power as that in India. *Three characteristics distinguish India ruling classes; 1. High caste, 2. English education, 3. Wealth. The combination of any two of these three factors makes a person belong to the ruling classes.* One might have thought that wealth and education would be economic and cultural–social factors and therefore highly mobile phenomena. But that is not so. *The presence of the third factor of high caste freezes the whole situation into an almost impossible immobility,* for over 90 per cent of the country's ruling class belong to the high castes, and most of them possess both of the other characteristics of wealth and English education, while some possess only one or the other.

There must be something fantastic about 40 lakhs of people ruling so immobilely, so pitilessly and so completely, over 40 crores of people. How do they manage it? A known recipe of feudal, aristocratic or caste rule is the success with which a ruling class is able to distinguish itself from its own people, so that the masses themselves recognise the distinction as just and fair. This distinction pertains to speech, dress and styles of housing. Throughout the last 1500 years and perhaps even more, the ruling classes of India have spoken a speech distinct from that of the people—Sanskrit, Arabic, Persian or English. They have also sported different styles of dress. Modern India has even sought to put the government's seal on a court dress, which is the sherwani and the chudidars and, of course, the coat and tie. The ruling class modern courtier of India who wears a distinctive court dress and mouths a distinctive foreign speech has naturally also been able to usurp and monopolise modern styles of housing.

Rule over the body is made easy through successful rule over the mind, through instilling a feeling of hopeless and resigned inferiority among the ruled, the people. Distinct styles of speech, dress and housing intimidate the people and they consider themselves inferior, and those others with these distinctions as superior. The element of castes makes the whole situation almost hopelessly irredeemable. Forty centuries and more have been steadily nurturing the ruling classes by birth in this country. Certain skills of government and trade have become so specialised as to reside in certain specific castes. To these age-old traditional, routine and recognised specialisations are added the equally recognised distinctions of speech and dress and there you have the irredeemable situation of India, where 40 lakhs are alive in a selfish, elegant but barren way while 40 crores are just helpless loam and putty.

Not all the high castes belong to the ruling classes. The high castes of India would perhaps come up to a total of nine to 10 crores, but only three to four million of these belong to the ruling classes. One sees such glaring examples. The Kadua Chaubeys are each one of them the ruling class of the country, while the Mitha Chaubeys are the pandas and pilgrim-guides of Mathura. The Kashmiri Pandit who came away over 50 years ago from Kashmir to settle down in the rest of India is each one a member of the ruling class, while the Pandits who stayed back belong almost to the disabled and dispossessed classes.

Perhaps the most disastrous feature of the whole situation is the uplift of a limited section of backward and low castes into the ruling classes of the country. The Mudaliars, Nairs, Marathas and Reddys have never belonged to the backward castes of the country, except scripturally, but the recent rise of some of them to political, education or economic authority has disclosed certain disturbing features. So has the rise of individual Chamars, Momins, Ahirs, Mammas, Malas, Narnasudras and the like. These gentlemen and gentlewomen who rise from their low and backward status into positions of authority adopt the modes of distinction even more greedily than the acknowledged high castes.

I should like to conclude with a special feature that obtains within the ranks of the high castes. Some of these high castes are traditionally bureaucratic, while some others are equally traditionally industrial and trading. This physical split between the bureaucratic high caste and the trading high caste of the country sometimes creates an illusion of class conflicts and generally a situation of inefficiency and meaningless clashes. The public sector and the private sector coincide with the age-old phenomenon of castes. Their superficial conflict befools the people but nothing changes. The trading high castes have to acquire yet another skill of corrupting the bureaucratic high castes.

Politics of Social Justice

The degradation of women, Adivasis, Sudras, Harijans and backward classes among Muslims and others must be traced to the caste system. Then emerges a new sociological law that *shrinkage and contraction of opportunity and ability is a necessary accompaniment of caste.* Whatever bureaucratic ability there is in the country is to be found among Brahmins and Kayasthas, and business ability among Vaisyas, and *90 per cent of the country's population and its natural abilities in these spheres have become atrophied and paralysed. The process of shrinking of ability and opportunity once started went on indefinitely with the result that certain privileged subcastes among these Brahmins or Kayasthas acquired more privileges while the vast majority was continually deprived and becoming less able. Caste means depriving the people of their abilities and that is the most important reason why the Indian people are so backward and so often have been enslaved.*

Two outstanding facts must ever be kept in the forefront, one that 90 per cent of the population belongs to the backward sector, women, Harijans, Adivasis, Sudras and backward castes among Muslims and other religious minorities. Two, that over 90 per cent of the country's industry, government, military, free professions and almost all public existence is run and controlled and staffed, at least in its higher personnel, by high-caste men who form less than 10 per cent of the population. Long disuse of the mind over centuries by most of the Indian people has paralysed the country and also paralysed them. They can no longer run the race with the high-caste man, not even if they are properly educated, for a certain selection and cultural mutation seems to have taken place, not unless they are given preferential opportunities. Would the proposed Harijan and Adivasi assembly legislators demand for themselves and also for women, Sudras and backward Muslims and Christians for a 60 per cent reservation in all opportunities of the country be taken not as a measure of selfish advancement but as a measure of national security and advancement?

I have never been anti-Brahmin and I have almost always been anti-caste. But I made a slight mistake in imagining that the anti-Brahminism of the south could be transformed into anti-caste. The ruling elements among Reddys, Mudaliars and Nairs have in the past fifty years been anti-Brahmin only to come abreast of the Brahmins and now that they have done so, at least politically, they appear to be sated. They have given up their ideology of reservations and are now as much against the so-called communal government order as were once the Brahmins. *My hope that the south would become the leader of all India in the fight against caste is eclipsed at least for the time being. Unless the Kapus, Idavas, Mala-Madigas, Ansars, Adivasis, Avasa Christians and such like and of course the women rise and become effective electorally there is no hope.* The Reddys, Nairs and Mudaliars are not at all backward castes, and they have never been backward. They are Kshatriyas, Vaisyas and Kayasthas, of the north, with this difference that religion did not sanctify these castes. *A new ideology must be adopted, which is that abilities stem from opportunity.*

To stop talking of caste is to shut one's eyes to the most important single reality of the Indian situation. One does not end caste merely by wishing it away. A 5000-year-long selection of abilities has been taking place. Certain castes have become especially gifted. Thus, for instance, the Marwari Bania is on top with regard to industry and finance and the Saraswat Brahmin in respect of intellectual pursuits. It is absurd to talk about competing with these castes unless others are given preferential opportunities and privileges. The narrowing selection of abilities must now be broadened over the whole, and that can only be done if for two, three or four decades backward castes and groups are given preferential opportunities.

After availing this preferential opportunity for some years, traditional ability and *samskaras* will be formed among the backward classes too, and India will be strong in all its parts.

Women, Sudras, Harijans, Adivasis and the low castes among religious minorities number around 38 crores. High castes number around eight to nine crores. As a matter of policy women should not be included in high castes. High-caste males number 4½ to five crores. Therefore, in India's population there are 4½ to five crores males of high caste, and 38 crores belong to low caste.

Some change in this calculation has become necessary. The Nairs of Kerala, Mudaliars of Tamilnad, Reddys of Andhra are low castes only in the sense of sacred thread, but for all practical purposes they are equal to the Kshatriya–Vaisya of the north, perhaps even higher. The Marathas of Maharashtra, Lingayats or Vakkalingayats of Karnataka, not all but some special classes, should be considered likewise. Therefore, in a way, high-caste males number six to 6½ crores.

Low castes of the north are mistakenly thinking that their people have won in the south and now as soon as Mr Nehru leaves the scene, not only in the north but in the whole of India low castes will win and one from among them will become the prime minister. In the first place, there would be no change by merely making a low-caste person the prime minister, but by change in policy. In the second place, the Nair–Reddy and Maratha, etc., in whom low castes in the north take pride because of their self-interests and organisations, have now gone closer to Dvijas in their ways of thinking. They will be assisting the Dvija more, for they have started talking in terms of equal opportunity and have given up their 50-year-long struggle for preferential opportunity, although the fight still lingers in one form or another—be it anti-Brahmin, or anti-north or anti-Hindi.

Among high castes only fifty lakhs are rich—rich in the sense that their monthly income or expense amounts to a thousand rupees or more. This is a broad estimate giving an idea of the condition in India. It is not correct to the pie. *These three categories must be kept in mind: L Rich males of high castes, 2. Poor males of high castes and 3. Low castes.* The difference between a rich and a poor man in India is so great that the likes of it has never been nor is anywhere in the world. Such difference is perhaps not possible anywhere.

Two Segregations

The Indian people are the saddest on earth. They are so because they are also the poorest and the most diseased. Another equally important reason, however, consists in the peculiar bend their spirit has received, particularly during their recent history. They profess a philosophy of non-attachment, immaculate in its reasoning and more so in its insight, but practise the coarsest kind of attachment. They so cling to life that they prefer to live it on the lowest levels of misery rather than risk it in some great effort, and of greed of money and power, no, people on earth gives a greater exhibition.

I am convinced that the two segregations of caste and woman are primarily responsible for this decline of the spirit. These segregations have enough power to kill all capacity for adventure and joy.

All those who think that, with the removal of poverty through a modern economy, these segregations will automatically disappear make a big mistake. Poverty and these two segregations thrive on each other's arms. All war on poverty is a sham, unless it is, at the same time, a conscious and sustained war on these two segregations.

The Gender Segregation

The woman's problem is undoubtedly difficult. Her slavery to the kitchen is an abomination, and so is the stove that smokes horribly. She must be given a reasonable time-table for food and also a chimney that spirals the smoke away. She must indeed take part in the agitations against underfeeding and unemployment. But her problem also reaches beyond that.

The giving and taking of dowry must, of course, be penalised, but a change has also to take place in the mind and its values. To arrange marriages on the sight of a photograph or in the nervous atmosphere of a cup of tea brought by a shrinking phantom is any day more ridiculous than the earlier marriages through the barber or the Brahmin.

It is no responsibility of a parent to marry his or her daughter. The responsibility ends at providing a good education and good health. If a girl knocks around and elopes and mischances into illegitimacy, that is all part of the bargain to achieve normal relationships between man and woman and no stain at all.

But society is cruel. And women can be exceedingly cruel. It is annoying to see how married women behave and gossip about females, particularly if they are unmarried, who go about with different males. With such cruel minds, the segregation of man from woman will not end.

It is time that young men and women revolted against such puerilities. They should ever remember that there are only two unpardonable crimes in the code of sexual conduct—rape and the telling of lies or breach of promise. There is also a third offence—causing pain or hurt to another, which they should avoid as far as possible.

The Caste Segregation

Post-freedom India is but a strict continuance of British India in most essential ways. The Indian people continue to be disinherited. They are foreigners in their own land. Their languages are suppressed and their bread is snatched away from them. All this is done for the alleged sake of certain high principles. And these principles tie up with the system of caste, the great chasm between the few high castes and the 400 million of the lower castes. These high castes must maintain their rule, both political and economic and, of course, religious. They cannot do it alone through the gun. They must instill a sense of inferiority into those whom they seek to govern and exploit. This they can best do turning themselves into a select caste with speech, dress, manners and living of which the lower castes are incapable.

So must the high castes weave the net of illusion. This can change. In fact, this must change. The revolt against caste is the resurrection of India or, shall we say, the bringing into being of a unique and hitherto-unrealised occasion, when India shall be truly and fully alive. Is such a revolt possible? Scholars may with right deny it. Men of action will continue to affirm it. Some hope of success arises at the present time. The attack on caste is not single-barrelled.

Caste-Gender Segregations and Political Parties

Once, in the district of Ghazipur, during a meeting all eyes were turned towards the wife of Sri Sukhadeva, a depressed-class peasant, as she came smartly dressed but a bit late to the meeting. Sukhadeva is an averagely well-off farmer but is a Sudra and as such he and his relatives have often to face various injustices. Later I was told that, in a spell of frustration, Sukhadeva had been enticed by Congressmen to change over to the Congress but his wife had plainly told him that, unless the Socialist Party played foul on him, he should not give up the party he had accepted. Three years have passed since this happened but I am yet to know if Sukhadeva's wife has been given any executive position in the Mahila Panchayat or the Kisan Panchayat of Ghazipur or that a patient effort has been made to train her for any leading role. Likewise, in Kagodu in Mysore, I came across Kinchappa and Masti who, though illiterate, had more common sense and courage than many others. I do not also know of any efforts made to educate these persons to prepare them to lead the Kisan Panchayat there. Until the effort to animate the souls of Sudras and Harijans and women is pursued with relentless zeal, there is no hope of nurturing a new life in the country. The 'Dvija' tradition must combine with the vitality of the 'Sudra'. The task is by no means easy but there is no other way out.

Apart from the bitterest differences of ideology and programme, a curious but unique feature of all parties in the country, be they capitalist or socialist, is that the *leadership is* invariably held by the Dvijas. The gap between the 100 million Dvijas on the one side, and the 200 million Sudras on the other is so wide that no political party has as yet undertaken to fill it up. Political life in India is not clean. Nepotism, jobbery, opportunism, flattery, non-adherence to truth and a tendency to twist doctrines to suit particular motives are some of the traits of Dvija leadership. The traits will remain with the Dvijas unless they make a conscious effort to bridge the gulf between themselves and the Sudras. The Sudra too has his shortcomings. He has an even narrower sectarian outlook. Once in office, the Sudra tries to perpetuate himself by having recourse to dirty sectarian methods. In spite of all this, not only must the Sudras be now pushed to positions of power and leadership but sustained efforts should be made to enable them to imbibe a broad cultural outlook so that the stagnant waters of the country's social life may flow, and the Dvijas and Sudras both shed their weaknesses. *It is futile to talk of revolutionary politics unaccompanied by efforts for social change. Only that political party has a future now in the country, which would make itse6Fthe spear head of this social revolution and by its organisation herald a new dawn.*

I am certain that only that party can now make India happy, strong and truthful, which is predominated by women, Sudras, Harijans and Muslims. The old axis of Sita and Shambuk will now have to be reinforced further. Undoubtedly Dvijas will also remain in such a party. They have held the reins of leadership in the country for a long 5000 years and there certainly will be some among them who are lured by the vision of India's rejuvenation.

Political Parties and the Emerging Social Coalitions

Some political parties belong declaredly to the dispossessed and the backward classes and they are the Jharkhand of Bihar and Orissa, the Dravida Munnetra Kazhagam of Tamilnad, the Shetkari Kamgars of Maharashtra, the Republicans largely of Maharashtra. The trouble with these parties is that they have no programmes either of work or fight for four years nine months and are content to acquire such little parliamentary recognition as they possess through an electoral caste appeal of three months.

Let us contemplate a situation in which these regional parties of the backward castes and others combine to create a single exclusive party of dispossessed and disabled humanity in the country. In the first place, that would be an almost impossible undertaking, for in the moment that it begins to succeed, the high castes will siphon off its leading elements into its own ranks not necessarily openly. In the second place, it might lead to a civil strife without end and solution. Third, it might create a situation in which one group of what are today backward castes replaces the group of the current ruling castes. All these possibilities almost shut the door on the country's renewal.

Still another obstacle in the way of progress of the backward castes is the existence of a few castes among them, who constitute a decisive majority for matters like election, and so the attention is focused towards them alone and someone from them gets elected. Hundreds of other backward castes are there who, when taken separately, are not decisive for election purposes, but taken together constitute two thirds of India's population. For parliamentary elections, such backward castes should get our attention and leaders should be created from their ranks, whose voice and action may infuse and inspire satisfaction, self-respect and fearlessness among them.

Beyond the Class–Caste Dichotomy: Politics of Nation-building

Some are inclined to think that it is no use waging war against the caste system directly; destruction of the capitalist system through class struggle will automatically result in the extinction of castes. *In the first place, in a country cursed with the caste system, it is not possible to end feudal and capitalist inequalities through class struggle alone.* Moreover, why are those who view class struggle as inevitable for the establishment of a classless society so much averse towards caste struggle for the creation of a casteless society? The Socialist Party does not intend to give currency to class and caste struggles of old, dogmatic types. It aims at destroying caste and class through non-violent and peaceful means of propaganda, organisation and struggle.

It is true that the Dvijas take up the battle against caste as a matter of duty while the Sudras consider it a fight for their rights. This is an ignorant attitude, for this is a battle of rights for the Dvijas too and, after all, there is not in the long run, much to distinguish rights from duties. *By preserving this national caste system and the vast multitude of Sudras in the country, the Dvijas have made themselves the Sudras of the international caste system.* When Dvijas and Sudras line up together with the common objective of smashing the international caste system, all-around progress is bound to result. But to bring about this change, the Dvijas and Sudras are charged with responsibility in equal measure.

The educated and well-to-do amongst the Sudras are more often motivated by a sense of jealousy and the social atmosphere is such as aggravates this feeling. Some of the leaders take advantage of such a state of affairs in furthering their own political and personal ends. *It is certain that this dual role of external independence and opposition and internal co-operation will result in fatal consequences to the Sudras as well as the Dvijas.* Additionally, I want that Sudra leaders should give thought to their own sh6rtcomings also.

It is also to be remembered that generally a backward caste person would like to have connections and equality with the twice-born as against the depressed castes. This mentality is poisonous. We must now contribute to the simple mentality of a common caste of mankind. When you own this mentality, you would not say that only a Sudra can help the Sudras to rise. The Sudras and the Dvijas are both lying half dead. The Sudras should awaken the Dvijas and the Dvijas should awaken the Sudras. It may be that the application of this principle to action will be attended by a thousand difficulties but there is no other way.

The Dvija must be prepared to endure a temporary injustice so that the wrongs of several thousand years may be righted and a new era of justice and equality may begin. The proudest day for the Brahmin and the Bania would be when they end their supremacy. But there has, also, to be an awareness of the failings of the backward classes, particularly their tendency to ape the bad habits and manners of the high castes as soon as they become prosperous or powerful. Moreover, anger against the caste system and the systematic effort to destroy it should never be allowed to degenerate into bitterness against the high castes. Such bitterness would permanently enthrone mediocrity. The Sudras should not forget that the overwhelming majority of Dvijas are poor and dispossessed. The miracle of the caste system has, however, converted these eight crores and more of dispossessed humanity into upholders of the status quo. They are beggars of body, but believe themselves to be masters of the mind.

I am also fed up with Bania–Brahmin politics. It appears that this politics has resolved to finish everyone who wants to raise all the 40 crores of India. I have no enmity with thread-wearers. I want to raise them too. But I know that they can rise only when Sudra, Harijan, women and Muslims also rise. This the thread-wearers do not understand. They think that if the backward class rises, they will degrade. This ignorance is the root of evil.

It is possible that some of the Sudras may be working with the idea of vengeance against and going ahead of the thread-wearers. This is neither proper nor possible. With this mentality only those amongst the Sudras will go ahead who are double faced, or can flatter, or who are possessed with the special ability of making use of hatred. We have to produce such men who are actually capable. Only then a politics will blossom through which nomenclatures such as Dvija and Sudra will be destroyed for ever.

I want such leaders from among the backward classes who are neither flatterers nor hatred mongers and who by taking a straight and self-respecting course, become leaders of all India and all people of the country.

7

Caste, Class and Property Relations*

B.T. Ranadive

The survival of the caste system and prejudices today as well as the fight against it cannot be understood unless viewed in relation to the major political and economic developments in the country during the nineteenth and twentieth centuries.

The major political development was the rise of nationalist anti-imperialist consciousness and the rising anti-imperialist struggle accompanied by the struggles of workers and peasants which forced the British to withdraw from India.

SINGLE PROCESS

The anti-imperialist struggle, the growing sense of national unity, the anti-caste agitations and revolts, were all parts of a single process—the formation of a modern nation with its different sections demanding equality and common status in a new polity. The process was gradual and slow with different castes and subcastes expressing the urge in different ways in the beginning. Some directly addressed themselves to the fight against imperialist rule, others started awakening to their unequal status in Hindu society and embarked upon a struggle against caste inequality. At a later stage these various struggles merged to a great extent in the common struggle against imperialism, though some continued their separate existence till the end. In reality this was a process of the dissolution or, rather, undermining of the old Hindu order with its hereditary caste system. Marx underlined this process of undermining and dissolution. He said:

All the civil wars, invasions, revolutions, conquests, famines, strangely complex, rapid and destructive as their successive action in Hindustan

* *Economic and Political Weekly*, Annual Number, February 1979, pp. 337–48.

may appear, did not go deeper than its surface. England has broken down the whole framework of Indian society, without any symptoms of reconstruction yet appearing. This loss of his old world, with no gain of a new one imparts a particular kind of melancholy to the present misery of the Hindoo, and separate Hindustan, ruled by British from all its ancient traditions and from the whole of its past history.

Marx was not sorry that this old world of the Hindoo was crumbling. He knew it was based on monstrous caste distinctions and slavery. 'We must not forget that these little communities were contaminated by distinction of caste and by slavery, that they subjugated man of external circumstances instead of elevating man the sovereign of circumstances, that they transferred a self-developed social state into a natural destiny, and thus brought about a brutalising worship of nature exhibiting its degradation in the fact that man the sovereign of nature fell down on his knees in adoration before Hanuman, the monkey, and Sabala, the cow.'[1]

It was not in the interests of the colonial rule to transform Indian society. The process of changing the old society, its stratification and economic basis was slow and painful. The result was superimposition of minimum modern capitalist relations on the old feudal land relations which sustained the caste system. The exploitation interests of British colonialism required that a powerful indigenous bourgeoisie should not arise. It was interested in exploiting the Indian people on the basis of their backwardness, that is, keeping the rural land relations intact as far as possible, modifying them only to advance its own interests.

Two contradictory processes were therefore in action. The introduction of modern relations—railways, communication, telegraph, workshops and a few factories, growing commodity exch1ange, exports and imports—accentuated the tendency towards undermining the old structure, and with it the caste relations. Second, the vital interests of the colonial powers in maintaining the old land relations, in seeking political and economic support from the feudals, meant support to the fabric of caste institution.

REVIVALISM AND COMPROMISE

The leaders of the national movement, the new bourgeois intelligentsia coming from Hindu upper castes, were also interested in compromising with the caste system. One can imagine the backward economic conditions prevailing a hundred years ago. The intelligentsia just learning the alphabet of anti-imperialist struggle, without yet a solid foundation of support of the indigenous industrial bourgeoisie, stood in isolation from the downtrodden masses and was extremely afraid of hurting the religious susceptibilities of its immediate followers. Besides, the Indian nationalists, in their struggle against the British, harked back to India's past to draw sustenance for its claim to democracy and freedom. It led to revivalist thinking and ideology.

> So from the existing foul welter and decaying and corrupt metaphysics, from the broken relics of the shattered village system, from the dead remains of court splendours of a vanished civilisation, they sought to fabricate and build up and reconstitute a golden dream of Hindu culture—a 'purified' Hindu culture—which they could hold up as an ideal and a guiding light. Against the overwhelming flood of British bourgeois culture and ideology, which they saw completely conquering the Indian bourgeoisie and intelligentsia, they sought to hold forward the feeble shield of a reconstructed Hindu ideology which had no longer any natural basis for its existence in actual life conditions. All social and scientific development was condemned by the more extreme devotees of this gospel as the conquerors' culture: every form of antiquated tradition, even abuse, privilege and obscurantism, was treated with respect and veneration.[2]

The opposition to western ways was of course combined with demands for democracy and industrial advance. The revivalist bases meant defence of the caste system, its maintenance and failure to fight it. Tilak expressed his opposition to any kind of social reform including the proposal to raise the age of marriage. Tilak believed in the caste system and defended it. Even Gandhi who represented a different stage of the national movement equally relied on revivalism. During the first non-cooperation movement he carried on an open campaign against everything western, including western medicine, western education and the railways. Gandhi once declared: 'God limited man's locomotion power when he gave him two legs. But man became ambitious and built the railways.' In these days he repeatedly harped upon bringing back Ram Raj to India. No doubt in subsequent years his appeal became more modern, more 'bourgeoisfied'; but notwithstanding his onslaught against untouchability, he remained a prisoner of revivalist outlook. As early as 1921 he declared himself to be a Sanatanic Hindu.

> I call myself a Sanatanic Hindu, because (1) I believe in the Vedas, the Upanishads, the Puranas and all that goes by the name of Hindu scriptures, therefore in Avatars and rebirth. (2) I believe in Varnashrama Dharma, in a sense in my opinion strictly Vedic, but not in its present popular and crude sense. (3) I believe in the protection of the cow in its much larger sense than the popular. (4) I do not disbelieve in idol-worship.[3]

This was the ideology of the father of the nation who headed the Congress during the days of the national anti-imperialist struggle. In spite of this ideology he could move lakhs for the national struggle and make them momentarily forget their caste distinctions. It was he again who was able to bring lakhs of Muslims into the common struggle in 1920–1. But it was clear that with this revivalist outlook, with this delinking of the anti-caste struggle from the anti-imperialist struggle, caste distinctions would continue to survive. With this outlook of course it was not possible to eliminate the barriers between Hindus and Muslims.

Notwithstanding the advanced and secular views of Jawaharlal Nehru, the Gandhian outlook dominated the nationalist movement. Critics have wrongly understood this obscurantist outlook as only surrender to caste pressures and considered it as being due only to the casteism of the upper-caste national leaders. It was basically the surrender of the modern intelligentsia before the indigenous feudal land relations which sustained the caste system. Not that subjectively there was no caste consciousness, for it was inevitable if you accepted the basically unjust agrarian structure.

FEAR OF AGRARIAN REVOLUTION

Such was the double-faced intelligentsia of the earlier years. Espousing the aims and interests of the rising bourgeoisie, proclaiming new democratic values, it attacked the imperialists but at the same time allied itself with the old feudal order and institutions and explained such alliance as concentrating fire on the foreign enemy first. In Maharashtra and elsewhere its opposition to anti-moneylender bills was part of the class alliance and not just caste alliance. It defended the peasant only against government exaction and attacked land tax and other measures, but till very late in the day it refused to maintain agrarian relations in its programme. Though subsequent generations of national leaders could not maintain exactly the same position and had to manoeuvre both against caste discontent and land relations, their position essentially remained the same.

In 1920 the Congress expressed its partiality for the big landlords openly and chided the peasants for withholding the oppressive rent of the landlords. The 12 February 1922 Bardoli decision calling off the national campaign against British imperialism contained the following clauses:

> The Working Committee advises Congress workers and organisations to inform the ryots that withholding of rent payments to zamindars is contrary to the Congress resolutions and injurious to the best interests of the country. The Working Committee assures the zamindars that the Congress movement is in no way interested to attack their legal

rights, and that even when the ryots have grievances, the Committee decides that redress be sought by mutual consultations and arbitration.

This was said at a time when huge peasant masses had started moving against the landlords in the United Provinces and elsewhere.

This crude defence of landlords was not repeated in the succeeding years when the peasant masses had to be appealed to by the leaders of the Congress. The Congress began to talk about doing justice to the tenants, etc., but the opposition to agrarian resolution continued and the alliance with landlords remained. It was not for nothing that Gandhi once described the princely states as 'Indian India' and paid tributes to them and for years the Congress opposed widespread struggles in the princely states.

This fear of agrarian revolution and alliance with indigenous obscurantist forces was not fortuitous. The weak industrial bourgeoisie without the confidence of meeting the challenge of imperialism had to rely on the established propertied classes from which also came a section of the intelligentsia. Besides in the twentieth century, in the decline of capitalism the bourgeoisie was unable to play a resolutely anti-feudal role. This was noted by Marxists. In fact Lenin, noting this development, declared that the democratic revolution in Russia could be led only by the working class and working class hegemony was essential for its success. Succeeding revolutions have shown that only under the leadership of the working class anti-imperialist revolutions including the agrarian revolution have been carried out, opening the way to socialism. China, Korea, Vietnam are the recent instances. When the agrarian revolution could not be carried out, the anti-imperialist revolution got aborted, leading in some countries to fascism as in Indonesia. In the majority of underdeveloped countries where the bourgeois retained the hegemony, and sabotaged the agrarian revolution, pre-capitalist ideologies and relations continued, leading to the overthrow of democracy. Pan-Islamism, Islamic Republic, 'Guided Democracy' and many other reactionary feudal ideologies continue to dominate the minds of the people today because the soil from which they spring—the pre-capitalist or tribal relations—continues to remain fertile. Social reformers have not understood this link between the agrarian revolution in India and the retention of caste and communal inequalities, outlook and prejudices. For them casteism and communalism were just injustices unlinked with any production relation system, a prejudice to be removed by denouncing it, by asking those who practise it to reject it, and nothing more. The struggle was not to be linked with the present-day social system—its pre-capitalist and capitalist basis, its source of class exploitation. It was not to be conducted as part of the general democratic movement or modern class struggle.

THE COMMUNIST PARTY

The Communist Party was the only party which linked the struggle against untouchability and caste system with agrarian revolution and end to imperialist domination. It alone saw in agrarian revolution and class struggle the key to overcome Hindu—Muslim separateness in practice. The Platform of Action of the Communist Party of India [CPI], 1930, said:

As a result of the rule of British imperialism in our country, there are still in existence millions of slaves, and tens of millions of socially outcaste working pariahs, who are deprived of all rights. British rule, the system of landlordism, the reactionary caste system, religious deception and all the slave and serf traditions of the past throttle the Indian people and stand in the way of its emancipation. They have led to the result that in India, in the twentieth century, there are still pariahs who have no right to meet with their fellowmen, drink from common wells, study in common schools, etc.

Instead of putting an end once for all to this shameful blot on the Indian people, Gandhi and other Congress leaders call for the maintenance of the caste system which is the basis of and justification for the existence of that socially outcaste pariahs. Only the ruthless abolition of the caste system in its reformed, Gandhist variety, only the agrarian revolution and violent overthrow of British rule, will lead to the social, economic, cultural and legal emancipation of the working pariahs and slaves. The CP of India calls upon all the pariahs to join in the united revolutionary front—with all the workers of the country against British rule and landlordism.

The CP of India calls on all the pariahs not to give in to the tricks of British and reactionary agents who try to split and set one against the other the toilers of our country.

The CP of India fights for the complete abolition of slavery, the caste system and the caste inequality in all its forms (social, cultural, etc.). The CP of India fights for the complete and absolute equality of the working pariahs and all the toilers of our country.

The communists knew that in a colonial country the slow process of industrial development does not lead so much to the proletarianisation of the peasantry as to its pauperisation. Even those driven into the urban factories do not lose their rural stamp easily—as in the earlier years they retained their connection with the land and retired to the village two months in a year. Besides their ranks being daily increased with arrivals from rural areas the formation of a firm class ideology was being repeatedly distorted. It was obvious that the blow had to be given in the rural areas to the pre-capitalist land relations.

> Owing to the interference of imperialism . . . the drawing of the village into the sphere of monetary and trading economy is accompanied here by a process of pauperisation of the peasantry. . . . On the other hand the delayed industrial development in the colonies has put sharp limits to the process of proletarianisation . . . Capitalism, which has included that colonial village into its system of taxation and trade apparatus and which has converted pre-capitalist relations (for instance the destruction of the village commons) does not thereby liberate the peasants from the yoke of pre-capitalist forces of bondage and exploitation, but only gives the latter monetary expression . . . to the 'assistance' of the peasants in their miserable positions (e.g., in some localities of India and China) even creating a hereditary slavery based on their indebtedness.[4]

The CPI(M)'s memorandum on National Integration submitted in 1968 stated:

> Recently, Parliament and the whole country were rightly indignant with the ghastly burning alive of a Harijan farm-servant in open daylight in Kanchikacharia village in Andhra Pradesh. The press has been giving numerous incidents of atrocities that are being perpetrated on Scheduled Castes and Scheduled Tribes and on other backward communities. This phenomenon is not just some stray incidents confined to some particular areas or to particular states. It is a common practice, throughout the country—the legacy of the evil practice of untouchability and social oppression and brutality that persists in our rural areas, even after 20 years of independence and in spite of our laws and commission for Scheduled Castes and Tribes! It is the result of the growth of feudal and semi-feudal landlordism and of the 'new rich', on the same feudal caste and social basis, and of their grip over the village economy and life! It is a reflection of the failure of the government to liquidate the medieval feudal economic base, of its failure to abolish landlordism, give land to the tiller and assure him land and employment, fair wages, and decent living conditions (house sites, education and medical services). It is a reflection of the growing domination of the village landlords' vested interests, through the policies pursued by the Congress government in the name of community development, panchayat raj, Co-operatives, etc., all with the laudable objective of amelioration of rural masses, but which are designed to strengthen the old feudal and semi-feudal landlords

developing into a new rich and their domination over the village life. The whole state machinery, and especially the police and courts, are turned to serve this purpose. Hence, no wonder these atrocities are increasing and a terrible brutalisation of village life, negating all human values and decencies, is taking place. We need not be taken by surprise if these unfortunates, their patience exhausted, resort to desperate methods and caste riots break out on a large scale in the rural areas, which are already looming on the distant horizon. We will be having caste or race riots along with the present communal and language riots. It is only if the minimum economic living conditions are guaranteed, land and employment and social equality assured by eliminating the domination of the old-feudal and semi-feudal as well as of the new rich, this danger can be avoided. The democratic opinion and forces must-assert and force the government to give up its present policy of using the state machinery in support of the village oppressor against the rural poor, against the Harijans and backward communities but use it, use its full strength, against the vested interests and bring about radical economic and social transformation in the rural side of our country.[5]

It will be seen that the communists did not say that caste, untouchability or the communal outlook would disappear without a revolutionary struggle against the antiquated land system and British rule; or that the struggle to eradicate the caste system can be fought in isolation from the class struggle in the village and the cities, by mere denunciation of the system. They knew that this class struggle was of a people who were not yet free from caste prejudices and who therefore had to be united in the course of the struggle to discover their common identity as exploited. Real and abiding unity was to be achieved during the course of the revolutionary struggle which is fought with no holds barred.

The communists also saw that caste disintegration was taking place rapidly; in each caste, differentiation was taking place between the haves and have-nots and that the process of pauperisation was affecting all castes. Almost all peasant castes have been the victims of this process. Thus a new common bond was being created between the lower sections of all castes—a bond which had to be stressed and consolidated during the course of the common struggle. It was therefore necessary to stress this common bond while fighting against caste inequalities. Here there is no question of replacing caste by class, refusing to recognise the caste distinctions and recognising only the class distinctions. It is a question of addressing yourself to the concrete reality which combined the growing formation of an exploited class with the existence of caste distinctions—the formation process of the class. Those who did not understand this double process landed themselves into reformism.

NATIONAL UNITY AND CASTE

The expansion of the national movement inevitably led to certain changes regarding the approach to caste and communal problems. In order to forge the minimum necessary unity behind it the national bourgeois leadership had to give up its former no-change outlook in regard to caste and inequality. The necessity of appealing to the peasantry and the rural masses composed of diverse castes of the lower order forced the bourgeois intelligentsia to take a more flexible outlook towards this question, and make it consistent with the democratic claims they were putting on behalf of the people. Equality of caste was preached without its abolition. Both the problems of caste in general and untouchability in particular had to be tackled by the national leadership. In consonance with its outlook of compromise with feudal land relations the bourgeois leadership adopted a policy, which though differing in words from the earlier policy, in content remained the same. Untouchability was declared a sin by Gandhi.

> To remove untouchability is a penance that caste Hindus owe to Hinduism and to themselves. The purification required is not of 'untouchables' but of the so-called superior castes. There is no vice that is special to the untouchables, not even dirt and insanitation. It is our arrogance which blinds us, superior Hindus, to our own blemishes and which magnifies those of our downtrodden brethren whom we have suppressed and keep under suppression. And I would be content to be torn to pieces rather than disown the suppressed classes. Hindus will certainly never deserve freedom, not get it if they allow their noble religion to be disfigured by the retention of the taint of untouchability. As I love Hinduism dearer than life itself the taint has become for me an intolerable burden. Let us not deny God by denying to a fifth of our race, the right of association on an equal footing.[6]

This passionate protest leaves nothing unsaid. But the equally passionate desire to keep the landlords and Hindu religion intact reduces the protest to a formal declaration only.

Unable to think of a basic liquidation of land relations the national bourgeoisie adopted social reforms as their watchword in the struggle for national unity. Education, social mixing, intercaste dinners, statement in public meetings that 'We are Indians first and last', beyond this the class alliance of the bourgeois leaders did not permit the national movement to go.

It will be seen here that the interests of the bourgeois class operated against the unleashing of a struggle against casteism. The outlook and compromise was strengthened because almost all leaders came from the better-off castes How is it that, despite these limitations, this blatantly reactionary class policy the Congress succeeded in getting the masses and forcing the British to retreat? How is it that the vast numbers from the peasantry, consisting of diverse lower castes, joined the Congress? The appeal of nationalism and anti-imperialism attracted the peasant who found no difficulty in identifying his misery with foreign rule. This was the new class reality—the unity forged by imperialist exploitation—which the Congress fully utilised, and those who pitted themselves against it were inevitably routed. The grafting of modern imperialist exploitation on the old feudal relations led to the emergence of a sense of national unity in the midst of a hierarchical caste structure.

THE IMPERIALISTS

The British imperialists were not keeping quiet when the Congress leaders were making a bid to unite the diverse castes and communities under the national umbrella. The British countered the plan of the national bourgeoisie by offering separate electorates, reservation of jobs in government services, and educational facilities to the Muslims, backward classes and untouchables. Their aim was to raise hopes of advance in backward communities, to wean them away from the common struggle, split popular resistance and perpetuate separate caste and communal consciousness. The prevalent caste inequality, the monstrous oppression of the untouchables at the hands of the Hindus, and the communal barriers between Hindus and Muslims enabled them to play this game.

But the imperialists could not play this game for ever. They themselves firmly stood by the existing land relations, and therefore were unable to bring about any real change in the status of the untouchables or other downtrodden castes. Ambedkar himself had to warn:

> I am afraid that the British chose to advocate unfortunate conditions not with the object of removing them, but only because such a concern serves well as an excuse for retarding the political progress of India. So far as you are concerned, the British government has accepted the arrangement as it found them and has preserved them faithfully in the manner of the Chinese tailor who, when given an old coat as a pattern, produced with pride an exact replica, rents, patches and all. . . . Nobody can remove your grievances as well as you can and you cannot remove them unless you get political power in your hands. No share of this political power can come to you so long as the British government remains as it is. It is only in a Swaraj Constitution that you stand a chance of getting any political power into your own hands without which you cannot bring salvation to your people.[7]

It will be seen that three powerful class interests, the imperialists, the landlords and the bourgeois leadership, were acting as the defenders of the caste system by protecting the landlords and pre-capitalist land relations.

POST-INDEPENDENCE COMPROMISE

The story continues after Independence. The use of the administrative apparatus to offer a few concessions to the untouchables and others to raise illusory hopes is now continued by the new ruling classes. The Constitution has declared equality for all before the law, irrespective of caste; Parliament has declared untouchability a penal offence. But the basic structure of land relations overhauling of which would have given a blow to untouchability and the caste system, has not been changed. The new rulers therefore resort to the same subterfuges which the British had resorted to—reservation of jobs, reservation of seats in colleges, reservation of higher posts in government services, etc.

The land reform acts of the bourgeois landlord governments were intended only to adjust old relations to their immediate needs. Statutory landlordism was abolished but the basic structure and inequality has remained. And the acts that were passed have also not been implemented with the surplus land legislation ending in a huge farce and land concentration increasing after the Congress enactments.

Once again the full weight of the administration and class rule supports the economic structure which keeps the castes and untouchability in being. The bourgeois landlord alliance which dominates the State is incapable of doing anything else, whatever may be its pretentious claims. The miserable results of the much-advertised 20-Point Programme again prove the same truth.

In this situation it is but inevitable that the masses themselves should be victims of customs, the toilers should get divided on caste basis and forget their common bond which is being daily created. It only means that the formation of a new class of proletarians is being delayed by the retention of the land system and therefore the hold of earlier hierarchical ideology continues. The dominant class interests have after independence worked for the retention of caste inequality, untouchability and communal outlook.

THE ANTI-CASTE CURRENT

What happened to the other current which launched a direct attack on the equality of the caste system, in some places even before the advent of the Congress? Why did all these protest movements which courageously condemned the monstrous caste system produce such pitiful results? The non-Brahmin movement which at one time appeared to sweep certain parts of the country has hardly succeeded anywhere in giving quietus to the caste system. The great struggles of the untouchables notwithstanding the fact that they were led by such an outstanding leader like Ambedkar, have failed to produce the desired result of abolition of untouchability. Atrocities against the untouchables continue. Neither these struggles nor the short-cut of conversion to Buddhism have solved the problem. It is a great irony that the leaders of the neo-Buddhists have had to again demand that they should be treated as Scheduled Castes in the matter of reservation of seats, etc.

The so-called lower orders or castes of Hindu society actually form the majority; then why has not the majority succeeded in removing the stigma of caste inequality and defeat the conspiracy of a few Brahmins or upper castes? The reality is that the poison of caste division has deeply infected its victims— the masses and the lower order who further are divided into several castes and subcastes. Each recognises the injustice done to it but is not ready to remedy the injustice done to others by its own superior status. In Maharashtra you find that though the non-Brahmin movement was supposed to include all the lower orders and castes, in reality the untouchables were left to themselves. At one time Ambedkar had to say that the Marathas were bigger oppressors of the untouchables than the Brahmins.

In fact the national bourgeois leadership of the Congress could get away with its compromising policy on caste and revivalist appeal just because it could go down well among the masses.

The anti-caste leaders of the earlier days were totally different from the Congress leaders in this respect. It was inevitable that along with the rise of anti-imperialist national consciousness there should rise the democratic current attacking the caste system and untouchability. The two were parts of the same process—the process of formation of a new nation in the midst of an ocean of pre-capitalist relations.

In attacking the inequalities of the caste system and caste consciousness the anti-caste non-Brahmin leaders were attacking the ideology and the superstructure of the earlier feudal age. The ideology and consciousness had to be attacked and the superstructure had to be exposed and undermined, if society were to change. It can be nobody's argument—let the economic situation gradually change, let new economic realities and new classes emerge and the caste system and caste consciousness will automatically be eliminated.

A reactionary ideology if not fought becomes an obstacle in the way of democratic and social advance, in the way of changing the economic reality. It acts as a brake on change. In India caste domination and caste consciousness was acting as a brake and preventing the revolutionary unity of the masses. The earlier anti-caste leaders therefore did a splendid job in launching an attack against the caste system. This was all the more so because their nationalist contemporaries, coming from the upper castes, representing another section of the bourgeois intelligentsia, had not yet freed themselves from upper-caste consciousness, and some of them, like Tilak, were strong defenders of the system. Tilak, it must be remembered, opposed not only the age of the Consent Bill but a proposal for compulsory primary education also. It has already been pointed out that at the basis of this defence and, later on, compromise with the caste system lay the intelligentsia's compromise and alliance with the feudal relations. It will not be amiss in this context to treat in brief the evolution of the anti-caste movement in Maharashtra to understand the limitations and results produced by it.

JYOTIBA'S MOVEMENT

The origin of the anti-caste movement in Maharashtra is associated with the giant figure of Jyotiba Phule: Jyotiba the great secular democrat, the friend of the poor and oppressed castes never wavered in his loyalty to the downtrodden in giving priority to their interests. Whether it was widow remarriage, education, liquor shops, caste exploitation, bureaucratic oppression or usury and land alienation, the economic loot of India, the building of a new market or decorations to greet a viceroy at the expense of the people, or a dinner to a royal visitor, he defended the interests of the masses without prevarication and fears. His passion for the untouchables was unheard of and his sense of justice included every oppressed caste and he had absolutely no caste bias. He also demanded equal treatment for Muslims and Christians. No wonder the movement was originally named only as the *satyashadhak* movement—a movement against the untruth, injustice and hypocrisy of the Hindu social order dominated by Brahmin supremacy. He carried on a crusade against the Brahmins and their ideology.

A movement for equality, against caste domination, was bound to have an anti-Brahmin edge at the time, the Brahmins being the supreme caste in the Hindu hierarchy. Certain other factors added to the situation. Jyotiba's generation could not forget the nightmare of Peshwa rule under Bajirao II. Keer, the biographer of Jyotiba, quotes *Loakahitwadi* on the conditions under Bajirao II as follows: 'If the farmers failed to pay him the desired amount even during a drought or famine, he poured over their children boiling oil from the frying pan; flogging was perfected on their stooping backs, and their heads were bent over suffocating smoke. Gunpowder was blown on their navel and ears.' *Loakahitwadi* is again quoted as saying that when Baji-rao was deposed by the British, women rejoiced and said: 'We are happy that there is now no more the rule of Bajirao. The scoundrel has met the fate he deserved.' The second factor was that despite the loss of political power the Brahmins continued to dominate Hindu society, treating the non-Brahmins as inferior beings. Finally, the new intelligentsia under the British came mostly from the advanced Brahmin community, occupying strategic positions as officials, professors, lower bureaucrats, writers and editors, creating the fear of the return of the old nightmare.

Though Jyotiba inevitably directed the fire of his righteous indignation at the Brahmins, his vision was not a narrow sectarian one, but consistently democratic. That is why he was the most uncompromising opponent of Brahminism. There could be no compromise between him and his opponents, for he did not seek a place for any particular community in the Hindu hierarchy.

Jyotiba was part of the new intelligentsia. The intelligentsia and democratic trends were not arising only among the upper castes. Down below also there was ferment. Jyotiba represented the plebeian current—plebeian because it came straight from the lower order of Hindu society to which the peasant belonged. His political understanding was the same as that of the other sections of the intelligentsia. Where he sharply differed from the other sections was his uncompromising war on the Hindu social structure. *His championship of untouchables, his ruthless attack on Brahmin domination, his exposure of the origin of castes, the Aryan doctrine, his demand for complete equality. His demand for education for the lowest, and his insistence on equality between men and women, constituted a thorough declaration of war on the old hierarchical order.* This was a far more radical programme for equality and unity than the Lucknow Hindu—Muslim Pact or the Gandhian National Unity Programme. *Although the originator of the programme did not realise it, it could be achieved only by a revolutionary liquidation of the feudal land relations in India and colonial rule.* He considered that the main instruments of realising the programme were the spread of education and enlightenment, the anti-caste consciousness and the fight against Brahmin domination and against the upper-caste monopoly of advance under British rule. It was not accidental that the later-day non-Brahmin leaders lost their fervour for the programme, because further advance was possible only by attacking the land monopoly of the dominant castes and classes in the villages which included non-Brahmins also.

Ideologically, Jyotiba's programme was a consistent application of democratic values to Hindu society. In other words, it was an uncompromising attack on the ancient and feudal superstructure based on feudal land relations. Here was the big contrast between the upper-caste intelligentsia and Jyotiba—the former allied itself with indigenous reaction and its feudal base and superstructure while attacking the British; the latter took an uncompromising stand against the superstructure and demanded its demolition. In somewhat more favourable circumstances, this would have led the latter to challenge the basic agrarian relations.

OPPORTUNISM IN ANTI-CASTE MOVEMENT

With the passing away of Jyotiba the movement lost its all-embracing character which was highlighted by the fact that it was now headed by the Maharaja of Kolhapur, a feudal prince. His demand that he should be treated as a Kshatriya marked a new compromising stage of the movement. Jyotiba died in 1896; and within ten years of his passing away the new leader started fighting for Vedokta rights (to be recognised as Kshatriya) for the Marathas and in another two decades the movement had turned full circle—only the Brahmins were to be replaced by the Kshatriyas. A new opportunism to seek favourable place for his own community, especially the Maratha community, in the Hindu hierarchy and later on in the struggle for office and patronage under British rule, now overwhelmed the movement.[8]

With this change in outlook anti-Brahmin oratory became merely anti-Brahmin and did not represent anti-Brahminism. It represented more an effort to secure positions in the new society for the new intelligentsia rising from the lower order. This led to relying on the British for the anti-Brahmin struggle. In reality this led to the non-Brahmin leadership ranging itself against the first wave of the anti-imperialist resistance of the 1920s. The result was that when huge numbers in cities and villages were boiling with indignation over the Jallianwalla Bagh massacre, when the working class of Bombay was engaged in angry demonstrations against the visit of the Prince of Wales, the Maharaja of Kolhapur succeeded in drawing a large number of peasants to Poona to greet the British Prince of Wales, who was given the honour of laying the foundation stone of the Shivaji Memorial.

But, obviously, this divorcement from the anti-imperialist struggle could not last long. There was enough vitality in the movement to overcome this degradation, the more so that it was linked with the peasant mass; and the peasant mass of India after 1920 was a different one from that in the previous years. By 1920, when the new Congress movement began to reach the peasantry, the radical and fighting elements in the non-Brahmin movement overcame their separation from the national movement, joined it, and the movement merged in the Congress.

But though this was far better than waiting on the British, or remaining in opposition to the national movement led by the Congress, this was certainly not a fitting sequel to the all-round rebellion which Jyotiba tried to unleash. His programme of a total annihilation of the Hindu hierarchical system could have been carried out only by combining it with a programme for the destruction of feudal and semi-feudal relations and for political power in the hands of the democratic masses, in short, a programme for the completion of the democratic revolution. Neither the compromising leadership of the Congress, nor the new patriotic leadership of the non-Brahmin movement was capable of this, because both belonged to the same class. The result was a retreat on all fronts, helping the bourgeois leaders to gather the masses behind them. The hope of an independent revolutionary mobilisation of the people raised by the pioneer disappeared. A movement which could have independently mobilised the peasantry for a revolutionary onslaught went under the leadership of the bourgeoisie.

LANDED INTERESTS AGAIN

What were the reasons for the non-Brahmin movement merging with the Congress? There were two reasons. One, the leadership connected with the peasantry felt the anti-imperialist national urge. It had to give up its earlier isolation from the national struggle with the peasant masses participating in it. Second, the movement could have struck an independent path only if it had dared attack the basic pre-capitalist land relations, the source of peasant exploitation and caste inequality. Like the Congress intelligentsia the non-Brahmin intelligentsia was not prepared to do it.

Here, the caste distinction disappears. The intelligentsia nurtured among the non-Brahmins, the product of western education and bourgeois conditions, gives exact weight, acts as a compromising bourgeois intelligentsia, gives up the pioneer's uncompromising principles, merges inside the Congress later on to head its ministries, suppresses the people and keeps the castes in existence. Once again we see that whatever may be one's anti-caste pretensions, the bourgeois class outlook with its compromise with land interests vetoes any radical reform or eliminations. Post-independence experience shows that the ministries composed mostly of non-Brahmin intelligentsia with a sprinkling of untouchable leaders have kept the earlier Congress traditions and hardly done anything in the way of eradication of the caste system. The oppression, especially of the untouchables, is not less in Maharashtra and elsewhere.

When the anti-caste movement gets divorced from agrarian revolution, when it further gets divorced from the anti-imperialist movement, what happens to it can be seen from the life of the great anti-caste warrior, Periyar E.V. Ramaswamy.

Ramaswamy was first connected with the Congress and campaigned for independence. But he turned with revulsion against the Congress because of the caste prejudices of the leadership. Having lost his contact with the anti-imperialist struggle, he strayed far away from it, only momentarily coming to the fight against the agrarian relations and again relapsing into alliances and ways which were not to lead to the desired goal. In his review of Marguerite Ross Barnett's 'The Politics of Cultural Nationalism in South India', N. Ram sums up Periyar's quest for caste abolition as follows:

As a youth boldly violating caste-based rules of social behaviour; as a
young man who sought and failed to find the personal and social
answers he was looking for in sanyasihood and religion; as an ardent
Congressman who campaigned wholeheartedly for independence and
social reform and spent a personal fortune as part of his commitment
to the freedom movement and to social reform; as a Congressman
alienated by the high-caste prejudice and social obscurantism of the
Congress upholding the banner of social reform and, following a visit
to the Soviet Union, campaigning with short-lived enthusiasm in
support of communism and organising conference against landlordism;
as a leader of the Self-Respect League falling, tragically, into the trap
of collaboration with the anti-national justice Party; as the leader and
publicist of a separatist movement demanding Dravida Nadu and
campaigning against northern domination and the imposition of Hindi;
as the leader of a Justice Party completely discredited among the people;
as the founder leader of the Dravida Kazhagam collaborating with
British imperialism against the freedom movement; as a tragic figure
railing against the transfer of power, characterising Independence Day
as a 'Day of Mourning' and demanding' freedom from Brahmin Raj';
as a supporter of the newly formed Dravida Munnetra Kazhagam and
an enemy of the Congress Ministry headed by C. Rajagopalachari; as
a supporter of the 'Kamaraj Congress' seen as representing the interests
of 'real Tamilians'; as a supporter of the DMK in power; as an idol-
breaker who, towards the end of his long life, polemicised against and
rejected the Tamil language and Tamil culture set up as idols; as a
militant propagandist of social reform divorced from class analysis and
from a scientific theory of economic and political change . . .[9]

Periyar did succeed in creating a great feeling against caste, and did raise
his voice to overcome untouchability. But for obvious reasons the task could
not be achieved. The latest evidence has been the cruel Villupuram riots in
which several untouchables have been killed. It may be mentioned here that
it was under the DMK government that the rapacious Thanjavoor landlords'
agents set fire to Harijan agricultural workers' houses and burnt alive more
than seventy women and children. Those charged -with this gruesome mass
murder were acquitted.

AMBEDKAR

The monstrous atrocities against the untouchables under the present and
the previous regimes reveal how the old tyrannies and injustices operated after
three decades of freedom. In the earlier years Ambedkar, the most outstanding

and tireless fighter on behalf of the untouchables, exposed the upper-caste hypocrisies, lambasted the Congress and later on demanded land and separate colonies for the untouchables. This of course could not have been achieved without an agrarian revolution. But the idea of land distribution to all the untouchables to escape serf dependence on other castes was a very correct idea. It at the same time could have been achieved only through the common struggle of all the landless.

Later on he asked his followers to embrace Buddhism to escape the injustices of Hindu society. But the grim social reality based on iniquitous land relations did not change because of changeover to Buddhism. The quest for love and *samata* has not succeeded as recent atrocities have shown. The tragedy of the situation has been that the intelligentsia springing from the most oppressed communities also could not ideologically look beyond formal declaration of equality, more jobs, reservation of seats, education facilities, etc. Smashing the present socio-economic system was not part of its consciousness. The fight against land relations which also meant a common fight along with others, escaped them. The intelligentsia from these communities sooner or later accepted the framework of bourgeois democracy and satisfied itself with a general declaration of democratic rights without touching the present property relations in land and industry.

No one directed more concentrated fire against the Congress leaders and their hypocrisy than Ambedkar. And yet he was one of the main architects of the Indian Constitution hailed by the Congress till recently as the last word in democracy, and under which the untouchables' houses are burnt, their houses are pillaged, their wives raped and they are murdered. No wonder Ambedkar felt himself cheated.

THE WORKING CLASS

The rise of the working class and trade union movement and the communist propaganda against caste and communalism had minimal effect under the circumstances. The kisan movement headed by the communists has been weak and is weak today compared with the requirements of an agrarian revolution. The basis for smashing caste distinctions, for developing caste equality can arise only in the course of widest and intense struggles against the common oppressor. Such unity was achieved on a wide scale during the armed Telangana struggle when the Harijan agricultural workers and caste peasants fought together. The communist insistence on agrarian revolution is at the same time directed to storm the basis and fortress of casteism.

The working class which was still largely connected with land could not completely act as a modern class. It has been in the stage of formation. Nevertheless it showed great capacity to organise itself as a class in its daily struggles with all castes and communities, participating in strikes. The class instinct has repeatedly foiled attempts to organise trade unions on caste or communal lines. The communist propaganda both against caste and communalism since the earlier years has helped in this class solidarity.

REFORMIST INFLUENCE

Nonetheless caste and communal distinctions remain and are capable of being exploited for reactionary purposes.

Apart from this the slow progress in cities and among the workers has other reasons. A substantial, even a major part of the working class has been under the ideological influence of the national bourgeoisie and their supporters. In carrying out strikes and struggles they take particular care to conceal the class relations in society, the class character of the State and the government and reduce the joint struggles to sheer economism. This together with the total absence of all reference to the conditions of the peasants and the downtrodden castes obstructs the release of the working class from caste influence.

However, it has to be admitted that there has been a certain neglect in the ideological struggles against caste and communalism and the CPI(M) for its part has decided in its recent Plenum to resume a widespread struggle against feudal and semi-feudal ideologies. The common consciousness generated through the economic struggle cannot be pushed forward without such struggle and direct intervention of the movement on caste oppression. And the ideological struggle is not only to be linked with the necessity of changing the present social order in toto including the land relations; it cannot be successful unless the socio-economic role of the Hindu religion, and religion in general, is properly put before the working class. The question of eliminating the caste system can no longer be presented as a question of Hindu social reform and in isolation from the main struggle of our times—the struggle for agrarian revolution, the struggle for ending the domination of monopolies and imperialist exploitation, the struggle for a state of People's Democracy leading to socialism.

All variants which sought to fight the anti-caste struggle in isolation from the main class struggles of our times have failed and produced pitiful results. It has been again proved that the anti-caste struggle cannot be fought in isolation, that it must be fought as part of the contemporary democratic and class struggle. The caste inequality and injustice have become an integral part of all modern class injustices. To remove them requires the common struggle of all the exploited strata to whichever caste they belong.

Initially this may appear difficult because the untouchable who is supposed to join hands with the non-untouchable poor peasant often faces him as an attacker on behalf of the landlord or his caste. Herein comes the vital role of the kisan movement which must put together the untouchable, the agricultural worker, the poor peasant against the common exploiters, the landlords, etc. The caste barriers have to be broken in the course of the struggle aided by anti-caste propaganda and education of the peasantry.

NEW SITUATION

The three decades of independence and Congress rule have created a new situation which openly announces the intensification of class struggle in the countryside which the landlords and their henchmen, and the bourgeois-landlord government seek to convert into struggle between the castes.

The three decades of independence have, under the capitalist path, seen an extreme deepening of poverty and unemployment in rural and urban areas alike. Irrespective of their caste status millions are being pauperised while land and capital gets concentrated in a few hands. After thirty years of Congress land reforms and mass evictions there are huge sections of landless besides the untouchables. 'According to Reserve Bank Data the concentration ratio of assets (mainly agricultural land) owned by rural households was 0.65 in 1960–1 and increased to 0.66 in 1971–2. The poorest 10 per cent of the rural households owned only 0.1 per cent and the richest 10 per cent owned more than half of total assets in 1971–2 as well as in 1961–2.'[10] This concentration has meant mass evictions of peasants of all castes apart from the loss of land to the tribals and untouchables wherever they had land.

The process of robbing the small people of their means of production which is the hallmark of the capitalist path is again throwing thousands on the streets.

> Less than full employment of the rural labour force is attributable . . . to the progressive displacement of craftsmen and artisans by competitive modern industry. Urban unemployment, likewise, concerns not only workers laid off by declining industries, new entrants to the labour force and migrant workers from the surrounding rural areas, but a whole mass of self-employed persons and casual workers in the 'informal sector' eking out a precarious livelihood. . . . Attempts have been made to measure the extent of poverty in India, and depending on the terms used, the 40–60 per cent of the population is below the minimum acceptable standard. According to recent estimates using norms of calorie consumption, the percentage of population below the poverty line in 1977–8 may be projected at 48 per cent in rural areas and 41 per cent in urban areas. The total number of the poor so defined would be about 290 million.[11]

In reality the total number of poor is much above the estimated figure, as the estimate is based on an arbitrary definition of the poverty line. And finally unemployment in cities and rural areas has already reached staggering dimensions. The registered unemployment in cities has exceeded 10 million while the total unemployment is estimated to have reached more than 40 million. (Official figures try to underplay the extent of unemployment, and the Planning document estimates it as 4 million of wholly unemployed persons in 1973. Taking into consideration those who find casual employment it estimates the figure at 18.6 million.)

The concentration of land and capital is taking place at one end; the concentration of economic poverty and unemployment is taking place at the other end. This is the class reality that has developed rapidly during the last three decades.

Notwithstanding the existence of social discrimination etc., the problem of castes and subcastes of untouchables and toilers is now inextricably connected with the problem of general landlessness and joblessness—the problem of growing expropriation of all sections under the capitalist path. This reality could not be understood in the earlier years. It is now becoming too palpable to be ignored.

The redistribution of land, the break up of the land monopoly of the landlords—most of them from the upper castes—is the common need of all landless and jobless.

LAGGING CONSCIOUSNESS

The consciousness of the sufferers is however lagging behind this reality. Instead of a common struggle it appears as if the caste struggles are reaching a new crescendo, castes appear to be pitted against each other as never before, and civil strife seems to be the order of the day. Witness the agitations leading to sabotage, burning of vehicles, uprooting of railway lines following reservation of jobs for backward classes in Bihar and Uttar Pradesh. These protests from certain upper castes reached their climax during the Samastipur election when the bureaucracy almost exclusively recruited from the upper castes not only helped the Congress (I) candidate (upper caste) but threatened to arrest a minister of the Janata government.

Official policies are definitely contributing towards diverting the common struggle into caste conflicts—the bourgeois-landlord way of serving its class rule. The competition for land, for jobs, for official concessions, for loans and educational opportunities has immensely intensified, leading to easy diversion into casteist channels. The problems of backward castes, of reservation of jobs for untouchables and tribals, of reservation of promotions and eliminating the backlog in promotions, are leading to inner conflicts among the toilers, enabling the vested interests to split their unity as an oppressed class.

Tied to the landed and monopolist interests the bourgeois-landlord government seeks to divert the challenge of unemployment and poverty by offering petty measures of relief to sections of downtrodden castes—reservation of jobs in government services, seats in colleges, facilities for education, talk of reservation of promotions.

In the very nature of things these palliatives will neither solve the problem of poverty and unemployment, nor change the condition of untouchables and other downtrodden castes. They will certainly offer some relief, to individuals from these communities, enhance their confidence in their advance, but not change their status. For the ruling classes these concessions play an important role. In the first place in the general competition for jobs, etc., they pit one section of toilers against another. Second, they create an impression among some sections that government is their real friend and they should confine the struggle within the framework of the bourgeois system. Thus a basic challenge to the present socio-economic system from the most downtrodden sections is prevented.

FIGHT THE SOCIO-ECONOMIC SYSTEM

It is obvious that in the present situation when untouchables and certain other sections are openly discriminated against, the democratic and working class movement cannot object to reservations of jobs and other concessions. They have to be supported to cement the unity of the toilers.

At the same time all sections of toilers from all castes have to be educated that these palliatives do not solve a single problem; they neither alleviate the conditions of the downtrodden sections nor solve their job problem. They only serve to divert attention from the main enemy—the landlord and monopolists. The common class struggle in the present favourable situation can be waged only if the working class, the democratic movement and the kisan sabhas carry on an incessant ideological propaganda against caste domination and actively intervene on the question of caste oppression.

The class struggle is already unleashing itself in the rural areas. A large number of the attacks on untouchables originate because they refuse to work as former serfs, and want to work as modern labourers on settled conditions about their work. The mobility of labour, higher wages, freedom to move and cultivate the land-these form the content of a number of disputes leading to atrocities against the untouchables. They reveal the real economic basis behind untouchability. These struggles constitute an integral part of the peasants' struggle and have to be fought unitedly.

The advanced trade union movement will have to discharge its responsibility in overcoming its weakness on this question. It is being faced with a new problem regarding promotions and arrears of promotion. And it must solve it keeping the spirit of class solidarity intact.

The new situation calls for giving up the tradition of fighting caste battles in isolation from other toilers. It was inevitable that in the earlier years the movement of the downtrodden castes should be conducted on the basis of caste versus caste. It was all the more inevitable in the case of the untouchables who were denied human existence. This tradition has led to an exclusiveness which refuses to consider that there are toiling sections in the other castes who have to be detached from their caste leadership and to be brought face to face with the common oppressor. The vested and opportunist interests in some downtrodden castes seek to keep their followers away from the common struggle so that they can continue to have their hold on them. All this must change; and without lowering the banner against caste oppression, every effort should be made by them to join the common struggle for democracy and social advance.

For it has to be realised that the present socio-economic system is based on property relations which sustain both caste and class oppression. It is sheer deception to think of abolishing untouchability or caste with the landlords and monopolists dominating the economy and bourgeois-landlord government in power. The caste problem is inevitably merged with the problem of ending the rule of the bourgeois-landlord class and moving forward to socialism.

Part II

The Diffusion of Power

Introduction

With the accelerated growth of the capitalist mode of production, accompanied by agrarian reforms, a greater penetration of market industrialisation, and of centralised administrative systems and competitive politics, traditional authority structures have changed hugely during the last five decades. A diffusion of authority has replaced overly centralised power. Caste has acquired a new role via this diffusion. Three essays examine these changes.

In 'The Transformation of Authority in Rural India' Oliver Mendelsohn argues that the agrarian structure has undergone much change in rural India: land and authority have been delinked. Traditional sources of power have declined and the void filled by the state. He joins issue with Dumont and Srinivas on the issue of the basis of power in Indian society. Empirical data collected from Rajasthan, Mendelsohn argues, shows that the Brahmin, the ritually highest caste, is not necessarily a dominant caste. Land, and not ritual status, delivers economic and political power. Villages are now closely integrated into larger economic and political units. In other words, the quality and sources of dominance have changed considerably. Traditionally low castes are now asserting their rights and dignity, which they were not able to do in the past.

Most sociological village studies and 'textbook' scriptures give an impression that jati is a homogeneous social and economic entity: all members of the caste follow the same occupation and have a more or less similar economic status. Even if this was true for the pre-colonial and colonial periods, it is no longer true. D.L. Sheth argues that ideological and structural transformations of caste have led to stratification within most castes, more so among the low castes. The composition of the middle class has also changed and with all this the nexus of caste and ritual status has broken down.

The formation of caste associations among various jatis of the same, or even of different ritual ranking, was a development in the colonial period. This has accelerated within competitive electoral politics. Some caste associations get involved in political processes by mobilising caste members in politics, functioning as pressure groups for protecting and asserting their interests (as perceived by their leaders) with government and political parties. The Gujarat Kshatriya Sabha is one of them. Rajni Kothari and Rushikesh Maru examine the role of caste associations in the state politics. They argue that caste associations have augmented the process of democratisation and secularisation. In the process, the traditional functioning of caste and its unity have weakened.

8

The Transformation of Authority in Rural India *

OLIVER MENDELSOHN

Who or what constitutes the dominant power and/or authority in village India today? This sort of question is hardly ever amenable to any generally agreed answer for any society, and the Indian case is no exception. But to say this is already to have made a comment on the main stream of post-independence scholarship on agrarian India. Very soon after independence an academic orthodoxy hardened as to the character of agrarian social structure and power. The argument of this essay is that this orthodoxy is no longer valid and that it obscures what is a profound transformation in the character of agrarian India.

For a period of roughly a generation during from the early 1950s, scholars drawn from both India and abroad set about providing a new picture of social life in rural India. Like earlier accounts of the British period, these post-independence studies were preoccupied with the phenomenon of caste. But there were also important departures, on both methodological and substantive levels. The new methodology consisted simply in systematic fieldwork conducted by live-in professional anthropologists, as opposed to the less rigorously empirical style of British, other European and Indian scholarship in earlier periods. The fruit of this empiricism was what seemed to be a substantially fresh account of the structure of rural society.

*A number of bodies have supported the research on which this work is based. My major institutional debt is to La Trobe University for the requisite leave and some travel assistance. The people who have helped in village-level research are too many to mention. When I began this work I was helped greatly by P.C. Mathur of the University of Rajasthan.

* Taken from *Modern Asian Studies*, 27, 4 (1993), pp. 805–42.

In Behror D.P. Sharma and the late Rang Bahadur Mathur, among many others, gave me invaluable assistance.

The image of village India to emerge from the new anthropology was one of systematic domination and subordination that had little to do with the great books of Hinduism. Agrarian society was now seen to be organised according to a predominant formula whereby a single caste was in effective control of a village or cluster of villages. This idea of the 'dominant' caste was first expressed by M.N. Srinivas in 1955 and it seemed to epitomise agrarian structure to many of the new generation of fieldworkers and their readers. Srinivas defined the dominant caste thus: 'A caste may be said to be "dominant" when it preponderates numerically over the other castes, and when it wields preponderant economic and political power. A large and powerful caste group can more easily be dominant if its position in the local caste hierarchy is not too low.'[1] Four years later he qualified the definition in several ways that are not relevant here, stripping away some of its precision while increasing the likelihood of its fit to diverse village situations.[2] But later Louis Dumont more than restored the original sharpness by insisting that dominance consists solely in economic power rather than factors like numerical preponderance, and that this power flows exclusively from control of land.[3]

The concept of the dominant caste was subjected to vigorous criticism in the years after it was propounded, and manifestly there are problems with it. just one difficulty is the assumption of a single corporate interest in the dominant caste. The presence of factions, let alone different class elements, within any caste grouping tends in practice to falsify this assumption. At best dominance could be expressed only through certain men (not women) drawn from but not, necessarily representing the landowning caste.[4] A more fundamental limitation is the observation that some villages do not possess even a presumptive dominant caste; power is seen to be shared.[5] Despite these problems and the undeniable limitations of the concept, it has proved remarkably resilient and perhaps still represents something of an orthodoxy. This vitality owes much to the rise and fall of intellectual styles (chiefly Marxist-inspired class analysis) in more recent years, and thus the absence of any simple analytical substitute. Inasmuch as caste is obviously still an important aspect of agrarian social structure, so the idea of the 'dominant' caste has continued to exert some influence on social analysis.

My own view is that despite major methodological and practical problems, the concept of the dominant caste did refer to a central reality of village life. Perhaps Srinivas was not saying very much more than that village life in India tended to revolve around a single strong caste in the village or wider locality. But this was a particularly important thing to say at the time, since he was showing that the varna system was not descriptive of contemporary life in the villages. At a behavioural as opposed to ideological level, caste was demonstrated to be a local and not an all-India form of organisation. The hierarchy of the varna system was not necessarily the local hierarchy in practice—neither the Brahmin nor the Kshatriya necessarily reigned supreme at the level of the village or somewhat wider locality. At the same time but in a different intellectual direction, Srinivas's account undercut romantic nineteenth-century British views of the village as-a kind of self-sufficient, yeoman republic.[6] The later nationalist Indian version of this myth took the form of nostalgia for a supposed village panchayat or deliberative body in which everybody (or at least all men) took part. In the hands of Srinivas and other anthropologists of the mid1950s, the villages took shape as a far more hierarchical world.

The argument here is that by now the concept of the dominant caste obscures more than it illuminates agrarian social structure in India. *The contrary argument of this essay is that land and authority have been delinked in village India and that this amounts to a historic, if non-revolutionary, transformation.* I do not mean to say that land no longer delivers economic, social and political power in India-clearly it does. The proposition is that this power is not nearly so overwhelming as it once was and that it fails to provide a base for the kind of authority which the local dominants once tended to possess. This is particularly notable in the field of juridical authority or dispute settlement, which is the major empirical focus of this essay. The change has seemingly been working itself through over a period of many years, but the pace has greatly quickened since independence. *So the suggestion is not that Srinivas was wrong when he articulated the idea of the dominant caste in 1955, but rather that he was identifying something at the very historical moment when it was disappearing or at least be coming less significant.*

The departure from the order depicted by Srinivas and Dumont has not entailed a radical redistribution of property and power—it has been too gradual and partial to amount to this. Precisely because of its non-revolutionary character, the transformation has tended to be downplayed or not even recognised. The changes are as much cultural and political as economic, and they are difficult to sum up in phrases drawn from a scholarship which inevitably reflects modern western experience. Indeed, it may be still too soon to be able to sum up the transformation at all. But it is at least possible to identify the past, and the argument here is that *the dominant caste* belongs to that past. Everyone in village India knows this instinctively, as it were, but social science has been painfully slow to recognise it. This is partly because we are programmed to see another kind of transformation on the basis of class, which has not taken place—at least not so as to erase I traditional' Indian structures like caste. A second reason is that very few researchers are nowadays doing sustained village studies.

A simple but important example can identify the suggested transformation. It must strike any careful observer that low-caste and even untouchable villagers are now less beholden to their economic and ritual superiors than is suggested in order accounts.[7] It is only the degree and therefore significance of the change that can be in question. For example, for many years now there have been suggestions that untouchable women are less at the sexual beck and call of local magnates than they used to be. Whatever the deeper origins of this change, its immediate cause has been the resolve of untouchable communities to end a degrading practice. They have felt sufficiently emboldened relative to the high castes to assert their will in this matter, whereas in an earlier era they would have been frightened to do so. Similarly, untouchable boys who leave the village to study at college report that they no longer accord high-caste men the same deference they were taught to practise—they are unlikely to squat in the dust while a high-caste man perches on a *charpai*. These sometimes subtle changes in the attitudes and behaviour of those at the very bottom of the hierarchy illustrate a developing cultural transformation. At the same time, of course, the fact there are still magnates and untouchables also exemplifies the awesome inequality that persists in India. Whether one stresses the persistence or the change is a matter of context.

If there has been a significant stiffening of resistance on the part of untouchables as a general phenomenon throughout India, then this can only reflect a major change in the structure of authority. This is because the untouchables have been almost by definition the most subordinated group in the Indian countryside. In pointing to this change I am not making the mistake of assuming that untouchables were ever totally compliant and never resisted their masters with the aid of what James Scott has called 'the weapons of the weak'.[8] But what is at issue is a resistance which is both more resolute and more open than can generally have been the case before the suggested change.

THE STRUCTURE OF JURIDICAL AUTHORITY IN VILLAGE INDIA

The Scheme According to Srinivas and Dumont

Srinivas, Dumont and a number of other anthropologists have tended to identify dominance chiefly by reference to a capacity to exercise *juridical authority*, do *justice* or bring about *dispute settlement*—the terms vary with the author. In his initial article on the subject Srinivas notes in passing that 'members of the non-dominant castes may be abused, beaten, grossly underpaid, or their women required to gratify the sexual desires of the powerful men in the dominant caste'.[9] But for the rest, he concentrates almost exclusively on the matter of the dominant caste's role in dispute settlement.

Just why is there so much attention paid to a matter which is undeniably important but at the same time seemingly not a primary constitutive force in agrarian society? Certainly the focus must appear unsound to a Marxist trained to look first to the mode of production. The answer may be partly evidentiary or methodological in nature and partly more substantial. As to the first, moments of conflict and stress might be thought to reveal an underlying structure of control/order/power which is ordinarily not so visible. On this view, the disposition of problem cases provides the otherwise elusive evidence of patterns of dominance.

The more substantial reason for concentrating on disputes, formal processes like panchayats, and 'juridical authority', is that the capacity to impose one's will in situations of conflict is taken to represent the pinnacle of social dominance. Probably both these evidentiary and more substantial propositions are accepted by the writers examined here. What Dumont and the others seem to be identifying in the dominants is a capacity to make *law*, though they shrink from using this term. And presumably they regard this capacity as a property of only the most highly developed social authority. But while they seem to have an unspoken model of law in mind, they also seem to be identifying the source of *order* in the countryside. Now, *law* and *order* are not the same conceptual thing—it is possible to have law without order, and vice versa—though empirically it may sometimes be difficult to distinguish them.[10] But in the case of Srinivas, Dumont, Cohn and others, the implicit suggestion seems to be that there was/is a moral economy in which the source of order is a caste whose authority is ultimately legal or 'juridical' in its depth of dominance. In short, the two concepts are not adequately distinguished in this writing.

Srinivas claims that the dominant caste (i) characteristically settles disputes where both parties are from non-dominant castes; and (ii) even frequently settles disputes where both parties are from one (non-dominant) caste, despite the seemingly orthodox procedure whereby a caste panchayat has authority to settle disputes internal to its own caste. Only the untouchables can be seen to make an effort to settle their disputes among themselves.[11] A similar view is painted by Cohn at about the same time.[12]

Dumont sets about creating a larger analytical scheme into which the authority of the dominant caste can be fitted: 'Contemporary observation shows that there are three main organs of justice: the caste panchayat, the panchayat of the dominant caste, and the official courts.'[13] So Dumont is suggesting that 'justice' is dispensed by two kinds of caste organisation and also the courts of the state. He wants to argue further that the same three sources supplied justice in the pre-British era too: 'The continuity between former royal justice and today's official justice should be pointed out. Whatever novelties were introduced by British justice, it was no novelty in so far as b1eing official justice. . . .'[14]

The dominant caste may not be, and usually will not be, the Brahmin or ritually highest caste. It is only where the Brahmins happen to control the land that this occurs. Land delivers economic and political power. And power yields authority too: 'Just as the Brahmans have authority in religious matters, so the dominants have authority in judicial matters.'[15] Dumont does not elaborate on the translation of 'power' into 'authority, being content to note that the dominated recognise the authority of the dominants to the extent of having recourse to them to settle internal disputes.[16]

The link between the village and the wider world in the pre-British era is through the dominant caste: 'The dominant caste to a greater or lesser extent reproduces the royal function on a smaller territorial scale. . . .'[17] So the court of the king becomes, at the village level, the 'panchayat of the dominant caste'—there is often an institutional connection between the two. Royal justice is thus organically linked to the justice of the dominant caste.

The third source of justice is the panchayat of individual castes, a body which has jurisdiction only over the members of the particular caste. The most notable penalty imposed by such panchayats is out-casting or excommunication for wrongdoing which damages the reputation of the caste. But apart from this penal justice which looks outwards to the reputation of the caste as a whole, the caste panchayat will also dispense another kind of inward-looking justice by conciliation and arbitration. The panchayat does this in order to 're-establish harmony within the group and to maintain the authority of the panchayat'.[18]

Thus in Dumont's scheme caste authority operates both vertically or hierarchically and also horizontally among equals. Within any one village all but the dominant caste will be subject to twofold authority—that of the dominants and that of their caste fellows. The dominants will be subject to only one authority, that of their caste fellows. Both groups will be subject to a third authority outside the village, that of the king and now the law of the state. And beyond this authority structure lies a parallel scheme of religious authority in which the Brahmin is supreme but does not necessarily hold sway in the world of affairs. The principal difference that the British arrival made to this structure was to substitute their official courts for the juridical authority of the king.

From what has already been said it will be apparent that these accounts of juridical authority are not accepted here. The basis of my position is fieldwork extending over almost 20 years in Behror, a village (now township) in Alwar district of Rajasthan, together with less intensive inquiries in various parts of India. These sources suggest quite a different picture of the structure of authority than the one presented by Srinivas, Dumont or a number of other anthropologists of the same generation. But first, it will be helpful to look at a couple of earlier case studies of a less theoretical nature than Dumont's work.

Two Village Studies—Devisar and Madhopur

(a) Devisar. The first of these studies is Chakravarti's account of a village in Jaipur district, published in 1975 and based on fieldwork done a decade earlier in 1964–5; this may be one of the very last whole village studies undertaken by an anthropologist.[19] Chakravarti's study is somewhat different from earlier village studies in its single-minded interest in the matter of changing authority relations within the village of Devisar. His effort is to show that the Rajput *phase* of Devisar is now in the past, replaced by more competitive political relations, within the village. The watershed was the year 1954, when *jagirdari* abolition deprived the Rajputs of much of their land. Prior to this event, the concept of dominant caste was an 'adequate frame of reference' for understanding relations between dominant and non-dominant castes in the village, though it did not comprehend the totality of relations of power in Devisar. But after 1954 the concept is no longer a sufficient guide to the constitution of the village.

Jagirdari abolition in 1954 accomplished two things in Devisar. First, it redistributed landholding in the village. Prior to the redistribution the Rajputs owned over 84 per cent of the village land but they now own only slightly more than 29 per cent—they had lost over half the village, mainly to the cultivating castes of Jats, Kumavats and Ahirs.[20] Second, and increasingly over time, *Jagirdari* abolition combined with the new statutory panchayat scheme to delegitimate the *traditional* authority of the Rajputs and pave the way for acceptance of the legal authority of the Administration.[21] The greatest engine of change was the new, anti-traditional (and therefore anti-Rajput) political environment in Rajasthan which in effect forced itself upon the village of Devisar. This change in the external environment was amplified by certain local factors of leadership, thereby hastening the demise of Rajput power in the village.

Chakravarti does not seem to regard the actual loss of land by the Rajputs of Devisar as the primary condition for the destruction of their dominant status. What is emphasised far more than questions of local land structure, is the ideological and general political environment outside the village and also leadership factors internal to the village.

Chakravarti is able to give a number of examples of Rajput authority during the period of their dominance prior to 1954; indeed, this work is richer in case studies of disputes or conflict than any of the other field studies. A number of the examples are of the Rajput landholders or Bhomias 'upholding the traditional social order'.[22] In about 1928, for example, the Rajputs were successfully able to intervene in a dispute arising from the sexual liaison between a Brahmin widow and a Mahajan man.[23] Both had been excommunicated by their caste but the assistance of the Bhomias was enlisted to bring about a resolution of the matter. In consultation with elders of both castes, the two paid a fine of Rs 151 and were readmitted to their caste. What was novel about this—though Chakravarti does not take it up—is that one might expect this problem to have been handled exclusively by the Brahmin and Mahajan caste panchayats sitting separately. After all, it was their members involved in a breach of caste rules. But apparently the authority of the Rajput Bhomias was such that their help could be enlisted in what was conceivably a delicate set of negotiations involving two twice-born castes. Both Srinivas and Dumont have noted the occurrence of this sort of involvement of the dominants.

Chakravarti gives several other examples of this maintenance of 'the traditional order' by the Rajputs. In about 1924 an altercation arose out of a calf straying into fields where it did not belong, and it culminated in a blow to a Rajput struck by a 14-year-old Ahir. All of the Bhomias met soon afterwards and some suggested that a fine of Rs 101 belevied on the miscreant for having dared to raise a hand against a Bhomia. But in response to pleas about the youth of the offender, the matter was dropped. But the case shows that 'the beating of a Bhomia by a non-Rajput was a serious enough issue to merit the consideration of all the Bhomias'.[24] The second case in about 1954 was similar, except that it involved an untouchable. The dispute arose over the illicit milking of a couple of goats that belonged to a Raegar.[25] During the altercation a Rajput man lost his temper and struck one of the Raegars with a rake, whereupon the Raegar responded with a blow of his own. All the Raegars of the village were required to bow down in symbolic submission and apology before the father of the Rajput who had been slapped, and the father of the offending youth was fined Rs 11. In a third case, in 1952 a Raegar was beaten and ultimately forced to remove the carcass of an animal belonging to a Brahmin for whom the Raegar traditionally performed this task.[26] The Raegar was following a resolution of his community in refusing to perform the task but it was not for some years that the Raegars were able to make their resolution stick.

At this point we can interpolate a case collected by Kathleen Gough and reproduced by Cohn.[27] Cohn cites as an example of what he calls juridical *authority* this case wherein Brahmins castrated, beat to death and then hung a cowherd who had been for some time cohabiting with the young wife of an old and bedridden Brahmin. The violence was apparently precipitated by the cowherd having compounded his sin by using the front door of the Brahmin's house, contrary to caste rules. The killers were father and son neighbours of the wronged husband and there was further Brahmin involvement in the successful cover-up. Cohn is -not explicit as to why he chooses to call this action juridical but the use seems to arise from the ritual aspect of the violence. The affair was a right-minded punishment for wrongs done to the whole dominant Brahmin community. What makes the term juridical stand out is that it would not ordinarily be applied to an angry and violent act entered into without deliberation of any formal kind and where the juridical authority is a party to the dispute rather than a third party. But clearly Cohn is trying to find language appropriate to describe the awful and self-righteous execution of their inferior by the dominant Brahmins.

If we return to Chakravarti's cases, we can see a similar problem of categorisation. It may be true that the four cases are examples of the Rajput Bhomias 'upholding the traditional social order'. But they can also be categorised in a different way. Thus cases two and three (the beatings) are of the same type if not the same seriousness as Kathleen Gough's case, namely, members of the dominant and ritually purer caste angrily handing out punishment to a subordinate who has defied and hence defiled them. The far stronger reaction to the untouchable presumably reflects the greater insult in being beaten by such a person—bad enough from an Ahir, far worse from an untouchable. In the fourth case the dominants may be less immediately interested in the outcome, since they are protecting the interest of a Brahmin rather than one of their own number. At the same time, the Rajputs must have been able to see that their own interests would be immediately infringed if the Raegars were allowed to stop their polluting work of removing dead animals. So arguably this case also concerns the interest—albeit the economic interest rather than the status—of the dominant Rajputs. And all three cases are analytically distinct from the first case, where the Rajputs are an invited third-party authority in a dispute between two other castes.

Chakravarti is concentrating in these examples on the immense power of the Rajputs in old Devisar. This concentration has led him to ignore an obvious distinction between an authority voluntarily accepted and one that is imposed by physical force or other compulsion. Perhaps Chakravarti is assuming that in the old order in Devisar there was no meaningful distinction between direct force on the part of the Rajputs and seeming acceptance of their superior role by the subordinates. The argument might be that concepts of willingness or acceptance have no real meaning in an order built on local force which is in turn buttressed by a shared Hindu ideology of hierarchy. Such an approach is essentially Weberian in its conception of the nature of traditional authority. It is also the general line taken by Dumont. While the view has considerable plausibility, its weakness is that it tends to pass over the outlook of the subordinates as opposed to the dominants. The Ahir and the Raegars were punished precisely because they returned blows or, in the carcass case, refused to do a polluting job which traditionally fell to them. In short, they were *resisting, rebelling,* or *challenging* the authority of the Rajputs.

Similarly in relation to the case described by Gough, we can agree with Cohn that through their gruesome violence the Brahmins were trying to affirm a traditional order in which they were supreme in a moral as well as political sense. But it is precisely this moral claim that the cowherd adulterer was denying when he came in by the front door of his Brahmin lover's house. He may not have been part of any organised resistance but he was clearly asserting a claim to some kind of social equality. *Authority* is a relational concept which seems to entail some underlying acceptance. It therefore seems one-sided to call the castration and murder an act of juridical authority. At the other extreme, Chakravarti's example of the Rajputs being invited to resolve the dispute between the Mahajans and Brahmins is a case where the term juridical authority appears appropriate. The middle position may be seen as those cases perhaps typical of the *jajmani* relationship, where the subordinate is obliged to attend to his/her patron's wants but where the compulsions fall short of, or are at least not invariably, gross physical force.

The foregoing discussion may seem artificial in its attempt to slice up and assign to different pigeon-holes the various relationships typical of agrarian life. But I am not trying to make some neat linguistic point. Today, throughout India, there are still cases of the kind cited, by Gough and Chakravarti, whereby ritually inferior, most frequently untouchable, persons, are violently or humiliatingly subdued for daring to stand up to their superiors. What is now extremely difficult to find, however, is an example like Chakravarti's case of the Brahmin and Mahajan freely tolerating and perhaps inviting the authoritative intervention of their Rajput masters. Nor would one easily find example such as that of the whole Raegar community agreeing without the production of naked force to bow down in symbolic submission and expiation for the (retaliatory) blow of an individual Raegar youth. These events depended on a pool of tradition which is no longer available to the dominants.

The *ancien régime* has died without a revolution because there was always rather less acceptance and more resistance than accounts like those of Dumont and Srinivas depicted. On the surface the principal change sometimes seems to lie in the psychology of the subordinates, the untouchables above all, and undoubtedly there have been important changes. But it is easy to exaggerate the degree of psychological subordination before the transformation. It is certain external changes which have intruded themselves and enabled significant breaks with the past.

The passage from dominance to post-dominance has been a gradual process, and this is the major difficulty with Chakravarti's work. It is simply implausible that Rajput dominance was perfectly intact until 1954, when it was suddenly destroyed by land reform and the injection of competitive politics. Chakravarti seems too wedded to a Weberian approach in which he is looking for a change from traditional authority to the authority of the state. In his telling, this transition did not take place until the integration of Jaipur State with the rest of independent India. He concedes that 'by the time of the abolition of *jagirs* in 1954 the village had already become in some degree integrated into the wider political society. But this did not result in any major change in the authority wielded by the Bhomias *because both their authority and that of the princely state were traditional* (emphasis added).'[28]

This argument is implausible for two reasons. First, it is artificial to distinguish the character of Jaipur State from that of British India on the ground that the former was traditional (because it was run by Rajput princes, presumably). Jaipur State was deeply penetrated by the British Raj, to the extent that the basic nature of the bureaucratic apparatus was the same. And second, the incursion into the power of the dominant Rajputs is unlikely to have been simply and neatly a matter of power being taken up by the state.

(b) Madhopur. Among a number of Bernard Cohn's articles derived from his 1952–3 fieldwork in Madhopur, a village near Banaras, is a work on the changing status of Chamars.[29] Cohn's contention is that these untouchable labourers were no longer quite so beholden to their Thakur masters as they once had been. The relationship between the two castes is an important test case, since the Rajputs' authority over the lowly untouchables exceeded their authority over any other caste. If that authority was slipping here, then *a fortiori* it was slipping in relation to all other castes.

Cohn fails to sum up the change in any simple way but I understand its essence to consist in a decline in the moral authority of the Thakurs, such that the Chamars are now increasingly concerned to govern themselves and raise their own status. So the relationship between the two groups is now weaker than it was previously. The change has been subtle rather than dramatic and the causes far from clear—factors of identification and cause are run together. What does stand out is that the Chamars have come to depend somewhat less on the Thakurs, particularly in an economic sense, while Thakur solidarity has simultaneously declined. Through moving out of the village for work, the Chamars have increasingly (though still only to a limited extent) been integrated into the wider economy. This temporary migration is not new— it has been going on for 100 and even 200 years—but during and after the Second World War the numbers have grown more rapidly. Their participation in various local and national elections since the 1920s has fed their political consciousness and made them more intolerant of their subordinate status. Ritually, they have been concerned to rid themselves of polluting and demeaning tasks and emulate the religious customs of higher castes. And they have been anxious to settle disputes among their number internally, without resort to the Thakurs.

On the side of the Thakurs, their capacity to impose their will on the non-dominants including the Chamars can be seen to have declined over a long period. The elaborate and formal Thakur panchayat for the taluka has disintegrated. Up to the nineteenth century this structure was crucial in dispensing authority in problem cases but thereafter it appears to have crumbled under the impact of competitive and otherwise destructive forces. One of the competing structures was the administrative hierarchy established by the British revenue administration and an overlapping police hierarchy. There was also an abortive early-twentieth-century attempt to set up a statutory village panchayat system. And, of course, there were the courts established by the British; the first 'plague of lawsuits' began only in 1906: 'When people learned that there were outside legal agencies to which they could turn and which could enforce decisions through the official revenue and police administration, the traditional panchayats of the village and of the taluka began to wither.'[30] But Cohn is able to note that despite all of the signs of a weakening of Thakur control, 'most [Chamars] continue to identify their own interests closely with those of their Lords and of the Thakurs of Madhopur in general'.[31]

There is obviously considerable convergence between the observations of Cohn and Chakravarti. Both of them are writing about a decline in power of the Rajputs, traditionally the most powerful caste of north India. Where the accounts differ most clearly, is in the relevant time-frame. Cohn studied Madhopur before *jagirdari* abolition had made a substantial difference to Rajput landholding in Madhopur and amidst an early collapse in low-caste solidarity in the new statutory panchayats. But he was already able to discern a substantial diminution in Rajput power which had been working itself through since at least the nineteenth century. It was in the earlier period that the Rajputs' solidarity started breaking down and rather later that the low castes began to take steps to increase their own power.

Cohn's approach is convincing, despite his sketchy evidence for long-term Rajput decline in Madhopur. But while Chakravarti appears to have posited too sudden a collapse of the *ancien régime* of Devisar, he is no doubt right to have discerned a very sharp difference in social life after *jagirdari* abolition and the introduction of *panchayat raj*. Even where land reform did not entail the radical redistribution that it did in Devisar, post-independence social developments have generally been dramatic relative to change in the nineteenth or first half of the twentieth centuries. A number of institutions and facilities have played their part in this—the spread of schools, for example—but surely the single most important factor has been the rapid penetration of electoral politics. The moral economy of the old order was nothing less than delegitimated by the individualist ideology of representative democracy. Just how this has worked itself through has obviously varied but the direction of change has been the same.

The Ahirs of Behror as a Non-Dominant Caste

In the village of Behror and over much of the whole block, the dominant landholding caste is the Ahir. M.F. O'Dwyer's Settlement of 1901 makes clear that this pattern has prevailed for at least the last 150 years, and conceivably it could be many centuries older.[32] The Ahirs are now the proprietary tenants, in effect owners, of the great majority of lands under the village, though redistributive measures since independence have invested people from various other communities with small plots. But to know the land structure of Behror is not simultaneously to discover its political nature or its pattern of authority. The Ahirs do not control the village of Behror—it is comparatively easy to show this. What is far more difficult to develop is an alternative framework that makes sense of the social structure and process of Behror today. The reason is that Behror does not have any simple essence, just as a small contemporary township in America or England is unlikely to have such an essence. Behror has become too complex to be crystallised with a simple analytical formula.

Behror is not an ideal example in an argument about the demise of old-style dominance, since there is no evidence to show that the Ahirs ever possessed the degree of dominance identified by Srinivas or Dumont.[33] While this may limit the utility of this village study in an argument about change, my own understanding from many visits to other villages in the area is that the present condition of Behror broadly conforms to the situation of those villages which did once approximate to the Srinivas/Dumont model. Behror can thus be used as an example to make some broader remarks about the structure of authority in village India today, and just how it differs from earlier periods. Moreover, the study of Behror was undertaken in terms not merely of its internal processes but also of the relation of those internal processes to the institutions of the state—chiefly, the courts and statutory panchayats. I will take up this perspective later in the essay.

It may be helpful to begin by specifying as a counter-factual, the kind of power that could be expected if the Ahirs of Behror were in fact dominant. First, individual Ahirs would presumably have power over the lives of their immediate retainers. This could be predicted to arise through patron–client ties, whereby the patron is entitled to goods and services in return for allowing the subordinate a designated share of the produce of his land. Second, there could be agreed policies among the Ahirs as to how to treat the other castes in particular matters. This could take the form of agreements or customs as to the entitlements of their dependent clients, and general policies calculated to entrench and ramify their superior status in relation to all the other castes of the village. And third, the Ahirs might conceivably be the authority for subordinate castes when the latter are unable to resolve problems either within a single caste or between two or more castes. This situation is the distinctive form of triadic authority which Srinivas, Dumont, Cohn and the other anthropologists take to represent a particularly advanced dominant status.

Today, and as early as 1971 when I first encountered the village, the Ahirs of Behror do not possess any of this hypothetical power. Two interconnected explanations are offered here for the comparative weakness of the Ahirs relative to the model of the dominant caste. First, they lack the coherence and will to pretend to such status. Second, and more important, the social structure of the village has developed to a point where it would be impossible for the Ahirs to embody old-style authority even if they had a mind to. This second aspect will be examined first.

The most basic constraint on the Ahirs is their lack of sufficient economic power to make the rest of the village inescapably dependent on them. There are two aspects to the economic question. First, the apparently traditional system of patron–client relations, usually called *jajmani*, cannot be seen at work in contemporary Behror. This system was first identified in the literature of social science by the Wisers' book in 1930,[34] and has very widely been seen to have been the basis of the non-monetary economy of the village whereby goods and services were exchanged between different castes. Although a *jajman* or patron was not necessarily a landholder—the Brahmin priest might serve the lowly barber in return for services provided by the barber—it was the dominant landholders who are said to have commanded the widest and most intense array of services within the village.[35] In Behror today, the landed Ahirs still receive goods and services from other castes in return for an annual share of the crop from their land. But such arrangements are no more than marginal to the overall economy of the village. Most economic relationships between the Ahirs and other villagers are strictly monetary in nature.

Second, and parallel to this, the villagers of Behror are now so extensively engaged in economic activity outside the village that there is no longer a discrete village economy remaining. A great many of the workers of Behror are not now dependent on the Ahirs who control the land because they find employment outside the village or even within the village but not from the Ahirs. And without solid economic domination built on the basis of land control, possession of authority sufficient to resolve the disputes of subordinate castes is scarcely conceivable.

Again, it has to be conceded that Behror is not typical in the degree of its economic integration with the larger regional economy. The settlement stands adjacent to the national highway linking Delhi and Jaipur and, subsequent to my initial stay there, has developed a tourist stop and major regional bus interchange. Even before this, it was a trading centre with a *kasbah*. Moreover, the reason I chose to study Behror was its position as the subdivision centre and seat of magistrates' courts. All of this brought a flow of outsiders and economic opportunities to the people of Behror; it was never a backwater village. At the same time, Behror is not so much exceptional as more developed along a continuum that is characteristic of the whole surrounding region of north-eastern Rajasthan and Haryana. The region is a 'green revolution' area which has seen the expansion of grain output, establishment of stone quarries, brick kilns, and small workshops of various kinds.

Every community has been affected by the rapid economic growth over the last quarter century but this has no more than built on a foundation that was already well advanced. Take the Bhangis, for example, who are ritually the lowest community in Behror. In 1985 all but five of the sixty houses in the Bhangi colony were *pukka*—made out of brick and stone—whereas twenty years ago there was only one such house. This first brick house was built by a tailor, then the one Bhangi to have made a break with the traditional occupation of sweeping. By now the Bhangis have a long tradition of working outside the village. In 1985, thirty-two men were working outside the village—twenty in Pune, five in Ambala, three in Delhi, two in Bombay, and two in Darjeeling. Some of the men had been working in Pune for more than thirty years. With the development of the bus stand the Bhangis have become local rickshaw-pullers too; in 1985, fifteen men were carting goods and people to and from the stand.

Another untouchable community, the Dhanaks, had become so progressive by 1985 that all their men and most of their women had resolved to perform no more agricultural work, not even the financially rewarding task of harvesting. The reason is simply that such work is regarded as menial and beneath the dignity of a community bent on progress through education and the acquisition of 'service' positions. Only a small proportion of the community is currently employed in these desirable positions—in 1985 there were two teachers, two policemen, an office orderly and a *patwari*. Most of the Dhanak men are either skilled or unskilled construction workers. This manual employment is not necessarily more lucrative than field labouring; indeed, at harvest the returns can be higher in the field. But there are perceived status distinctions which make construction a better option in lieu of the most preferred service positions.

A lessening of dependence on agricultural labour among many communities in Behror has gone hand in hand with a reduced need for such labour among the landholding castes. Nowadays non-family labour is sometimes needed only for the harvest. Ploughing tends to be done by tractor and is likely to be performed from within even a prosperous landholding family. So the retention of field-servants is now very rare among the Ahirs of Behror. If they need a labourer they will usually hire him or her on a daily basis.

At the higher end of the social scale in Behror, employment outside the village is even more marked and has a longer history. For example, the Brahmins have long ago moved out in large numbers into accountancy, clerical and teaching positions and into other 'respectable' occupations such as that of a medical orderly in the army. The Brahmins of Behror have not on the whole been a wealthy community and their livelihood depends absolutely on achieving 'service' positions in the wider economy. They have tended to lose most of the usually quite small parcels of land they formerly controlled and therefore have nothing to fall back on.

The Ahirs too have long since raised their sights outside the village. As individuals and as a community, the Ahirs are becoming more ambitious all the time. Their sons and to a lesser extent their daughters too are expected to study, many of them at the tertiary level. Professional, government, military or business occupations are almost a universal ambition and have already been taken up by many of the sons of the village. The community is fast erasing the gap between its own sophistication and that of the Brahmins, Banias and Kayasthas. There are now a number of Ahir commercial entrepreneurs operating trucking and bus lines, brick kilns, stone quarries and even a synthetic yarn mill. Most of these enterprises are centred on Behror and the area nearby but one family, for example, operates a trucking business in and out of Kathmandu. Poorer Ahirs have worked for at least a generation in the grain *mandis* of Punjab. The rate of pay for this work has always been relatively good but, just as important, the venue is far away from the village; for reasons of status, none but the most desperate Ahir will work in a paid labouring situation in the vicinity of Behror.

The connection between Behror and the district town of Alwar has become increasingly close over the years. Daily bus, truck and even private vehicle traffic between the two settlements is intense. Many of the leading figures of Behror and the surrounding villages have established households in Alwar as a support for their increasingly urban ambitions. One step down from this urbanisation, Behror itself has attracted a number of the Ahirs from smaller villages in the block. This is particularly true for Ahir lawyers practising in Behror; they have found it convenient and politically useful—they often have political ambitions—to establish a household in the subdistrict headquarters. All of this functional migration and urbanisation is typical of many areas of India today, and again serves to blur the boundaries of 'the village'.

Nonetheless, it is still possible to find persisting examples of what looks like the 'traditional' economic life of Behror. There are still some more-or-less permanent relationships between individuals from service castes in Behror and their 'patrons'. Barbers will cut the hair and shave the beards of men in particular Ahir families and they will tend to be paid in kind for these services. Potters, too, tend to supply pots on a regular basis to particular families and this is sometimes done on an annual-exchange basis rather than by monetary charge for individual transactions. On the other hand, the carpenters of Behror seem to operate in an ordinary contractual way. And in the case of the barbers and potters, their arrangements are not always limited to the Ahirs. The barbers in particular seem prepared to enter into permanent arrangements with any comparatively well-to-do family in Behror—Brahmins and Bamas, for example. So the persistence of such arrangements is not really evidence of the continuing hold of *jajmani* relationships so much as the persistence of a mutually convenient alternative to charging and paying for individual services. Moreover, the two styles of doing business in fact coexist—the potters of Behror supply pots to individuals within Behror and also a number of surrounding villages on the basis of a charge per item too.

Even where something like the old *jajmani* relationship seems to persist, it has now diminished in intensity and is increasingly strained. Thus the barbers of Behror do not enjoy an easy relationship with their Ahir employers—they complain that the Ahirs are active in preventing them getting ahead. There is probably nothing new in this but the difference is that the barbers are now prepared to talk freely about it and even to act against their employers' interests. Thus the barbers have drawn back by refusing to perform the ritually polluting task of removing the dirty plates at their employers' banquets. This ban is not special to the barbers of Behror but was enacted more than a quarter of a century ago at what was said to be an all-India meeting of barbers. The penalty for breaching the ban or for having contact with someone who has breached it, is outcasting. And some years prior to my stay in Behror one of the barbers of the village had in fact been outcasted by his fellows for having had contact with a man in the nearby town of Rewari, Haryana, who had himself been outcasted for performing the polluting task of cleaning plates. What all of this tends to show is that the old relationship between the barbers and their patrons is increasingly fragile. Manifestly the Ahirs are not able to dominate their barbers in any thoroughgoing way.

All of the activity directed outside the village has had the effect of stripping away much of the old significance of village affairs to the more enterprising people in Behror. Among the Ahirs, their leading figures now display little interest in village issues. But the less than wholehearted concern to dominate the village arises not merely from a lack of interest but also from a lack of coherence in the community. While the caste in Behror and more generally throughout north India has been highly ambitious and successful in the post-independence period, success has brought with it the atomisation that now affects all the high-caste communities of Behror and indeed India in general. On an everyday level there now seems very little point to caste solidarity. Factionalism was once believed to be the principal impediment to achievement of one-caste village dominance, but it now seems that a pragmatic individualism or at least family-centredness may be a still more fundamental barrier.

This lack of coherence can be seen partly in the fact that the Ahirs never meet as a community and no one I spoke to was able to recall any such meeting in the past. Of course, many of them gather for weddings and funerals but unlike some other castes, these occasions are not routinely used to hammer out agreements in disputes internal to the community. The only meetings attended by the Ahirs of Behror were whole district affairs held many years ago in the town of Alwar, for the purpose of encouraging social advancement through ritual emulation of the high castes (sanskritisation) and education. On a day-to-day basis, the Ahirs do not behave as a community and, even more, do not have any obvious community of interest. They behave as large, medium or small peasants, as small-to-medium commercial entrepreneurs, as teachers or army officers. It is too early to talk of *class* among the Ahirs of Behror but there is already considerable inequality based on occupational differentiation. Of course, it would be foolish to understate the importance of their personal identity as Ahirs. This caste identity remains fundamental to their being and is sustained by rules of endogamy and a myriad of cultural traditions. At the same time, it now appears unwarranted to treat this culture and psychology as dictating all the important associations and life choices of the Ahirs of Behror. Certainly, there is a decreasing willingness to accept authority in the person of elders of their caste community. A young man who has been educated to tertiary standard, for example, is now going to care little for the so-called authority of an elder who may be illiterate.

In these characteristics the Ahirs of Behror are scarcely unique, since all the high castes of the village are also similarly fragmented. The Brahmins, for example, never meet as a community. The last time they did meet was more than forty years ago, to consider the affront of one of their men cohabiting with a Chamar woman. The man was duly outcasted and it was decreed that no Brahmin sit with him, that he not be invited to community functions, and that his children be denied marriage within the community. This state lasted some ten years, after which time the man finally made apology and was readmitted to the community. Nowadays, a similar transgression could not be confronted in this same resolute way. The energies of the Brahmins have been directed away from the world of the village and also away from orthodoxy.

Another way of calling attention to the erosion of authority in the high-caste, Ahir and some low-caste communities is to talk in terms of a decline and subsequent disappearance of the caste panchayat. This second of Dumont's three sources of justice now fails to exist in any recognisable form for these communities. By contrast, they continue to play a role of some significance in a number of the low and particularly untouchable castes of Behror. By far the tightest and most active caste panchayat is that of the Bhangis. But the Bhangi tailor who is his community's most respected figure, can foresee that increased prosperity will soon erode the community's solidarity.

To return to the Ahirs, it can be seen that they lack solidarity sufficient to want or be able to resolve conflicts within their own community through any formal mechanism. Clearly, this says something about the coherence of the community, though not sufficient to conclude that they totally lack the will to dominate others. But it has also been established that the capacity to dominate is now reduced by the development of a progressively more open and outward-looking economy, rather than the prevalence of patron–client, non-market relations. It is now quite beyond possibility that the Ahirs could act as arbitral authority in a dispute internal to or between members of other castes. All the time people are busy intervening in other people's disputes in Behror—sometimes even by invitation—but the Ahirs have no special status in such matters. Someone from a prosperous group who is at the same time generally regarded as a fair person, may possess unusual influence and may sometimes be approached as a third party in other people's disputes. In the nature of things, such a person might well be an Ahir—I came across one case where the Ahir MLA for Behror was drafted into such a role. But the third party in such a case is clearly something of a mediator rather than the judge of anthropological literature. And he will not necessarily be an Ahir.

It might be thought that the Ahirs would always have been a weak candidate for dominance, by virtue of their relatively low ritual status. Most of the examples of dominant castes in the literature are twice-born—Rajputs are the favourite example for north India. But Kessinger[36] has demonstrated a high degree of control in the hands of a Jar community in Punjab, and it is doubtful that the Ahirs are 'too low', in Srinivas's language, to acquire dominance. Moreover, in the immediate vicinity of Behror those villages that did once conform to the Srinivas model can be seen to have moved in the same direction as has Behror.

The village of Tasing, some seven miles from Behror, is a good example. Tasing was the seat of four small *jagirs* covering some twelve villages prior to independence. The *jagirdars* were Rajputs of a different clan from that of the ruling clan of the state but the four families appear to have acquired effectively permanent tenure of the *jagirs*. The *jagirdars* are generally conceded to have exercised very considerable personal power over the villagers within their small *jagir* prior to independence, seemingly greater power than that of any Ahir in Behror. As usual their power appears to have been greatest in relation to the invariably landless untouchables.

Jagirdari abolition stripped the Tasing Rajputs of much of their land and delivered it to Ahirs and other cultivating castes of the area. Loss of power in village affairs followed. In 1972 Rajput power in Tasing was very far from the model of the *ancien régime*, though still closer to that model than Ahir power in Behror. It was still possible to find some residual Rajput involvement in the disputes of subordinates. Thus, like their caste fellows in Behror, the Bhangis of Tasing tried to contain internal disputes within their community. But if this, proved impossible or if one of the parties to the dispute was from another caste, they were apparently still prepared in 1972 to seek the intervention of their old *jagirdar*. It so happened, however, that the figure they sought out was by then *sarpanch* of the *gram panchayat*—he was thus part of the modern as well as the old order. And his personal power was far greater than that of the other ex-*jagirdars*—one of these complained loudly and openly that nowadays he possessed no power: 'Not only do people not consult me about disputes. The even call me a fool!' In the case of the *sarpanch*, his traditional status was clearly an additional source of power. But without his statutory position, it seemed doubtful that much of his old power would remain. I have not visited Tasing since 1972 but there can be no doubt that the vestiges of the old order have further eroded in the intervening years. The reason is simple: there is no longer any structural basis for Rajput dominance in Tasing.

If the landowning Ahirs of Behror lack the quality of power suggested by the literature of 'the dominant caste', just what is their position relative to the other castes of the village/township? To answer this question one needs evidence of common action and, except during elections, such evidence is difficult to find. I came across the odd assertion that Ahirs sought to impose their corporate will over others in the village; for example, claims about suppression of the barbers are reported above. And there is some evidence that the Ahirs as a group of landholders have been active in seeking to prevent the redistribution of government-owned lands to landless persons, usually untouchables. But these examples are not really central.

What is of central importance to the village is the common interest that many of the Ahirs have as farmers and employers. But these interests look more like class than caste interests. Clearly, the category of employer is far wider than the boundaries of the Ahir caste in the context of an outward-looking economy. And conversely, the Ahirs are far from homogeneous—there are both employers and employed persons among them. Even if it is appropriate to see the Ahirs as having a largely common interest in keeping wages as low as possible, the Ahir employers of Behror are only a fragment of a much larger labour market. The wage rates in Behror reflect rates prevailing in the larger region.

Beyond the common pursuit of cultural norms, caste consciousness and collective action are least ambiguously seen among the Ahirs during elections. Statutory panchayat, state assembly and Lok Sabha elections bring caste tensions and even violence to Behror. In the words of a Brahmin 'social worker' (that is, politician) of the village, the Ahirs want to win every seat that is open to them and this causes ill-feeling. The apparent contradiction of this ambition coexisting with an increasingly westernised, secular, even individualistic outlook demands explanation. What must be avoided is the assumption that there is a simple material interest of the caste at stake in elections. Often the only interest is in the sheer victory of their caste fellow. Whereas daily life makes no claim on caste solidarity because there are seldom any corporate caste interests, an election provides a competitive format which readily lends itself to caste rivalry of an almost atavistic kind. Every Ahir can feel personally gratified by the success of a caste fellow against an outsider—an election reproduces the competition that is part of the overall caste order.

The major political groupings have long since realised the advantages of fielding an Ahir candidate in the Rajasthan assembly seat of Behror. Congress has been represented by an Ahir candidate in every assembly election since its inception after independence. With the exception of 1985, they have won the seat every time. Since the early 1970s a grouping with some roots in the Lohia socialists of the 1950s has developed into a credible opposition force in the area, and its most successful representative has been an Ahir resident (though not native) of Behror. When Ramjilal Yadav stands in an election and the Congress is represented by another Ahir, the caste factor is effectively neutralised. But he is powerless to deliver the Ahir votes which he can command for himself to a non-Ahir candidate he is supporting. Thus in the assembly election of 1985 Ramjilal acted as a loyal Janata Party member and threw his support behind the Brahmin candidate of the party. His Ahir followers refused to follow him. It was too much to vote for a Brahmin against a fellow Ahir turning out for Congress. Questions of ideology or personal faction gave way to straightforward caste feeling.

During its existence (ended by the advent of the municipality), the Ahirs did not dominate Behror's *gram panchayat*. In 1974 the caste composition of *panch* elected from the fourteen wards of the panchayat was Ahir six, Brahmin four, Bania two and Chamar two. So the Ahirs just failed to constitute a majority, an outcome which closely parallels their share in the population of Behror. More important, the directly elected *sarpanch* or head of the Behror panchayat was never an Ahir. The man who made this position almost a career was a Bania. He was able to take advantage of the fact that whatever the differences among them, the non-Ahirs are almost united in their opposition to the Ahirs in local elections.

The basis of this opposition varies to some extent with the different communities. The high-caste Brahmins, Banias and Kayasthas tend to look down on the Ahirs as peasants who have pretensions above their true status and deserts. The attitude of low-caste and untouchable people is more complicated. Basically, they have nothing to gain from the ascendancy of the Ahirs and possibly something to lose. Their general perception is that the Ahirs are happy to block improvements in their own position. And some of them look back to an earlier era of unpleasant domination by the Ahirs, though this is never well documented. The Ahirs of Behror are unlike many of their caste fellows across north India, in that they were not the subordinate tenants of high-caste proprietors. But they still have much in common with Ahirs elsewhere. They represent a predominantly middle-to-poor peasantry—in Bihar, for example, there are a great many poor Ahirs—who have been rising fast in the post-independence period. Their ambitions have tended to engender tensions among both those above and those beneath them in the rural hierarchy. Some of the political alignments hostile to the Ahirs of Behror reflect these same tensions.

This lengthy discussion of the character of Behror will scarcely be novel to those who are familiar with contemporary village India. Some of the tendencies which are now more mature in Behror were described as early as the mid-1950s in the works of Cohn, F.G. Bailey and, somewhat later, Andre Béteille[37] to name several. But since more recent village accounts are rare, I have thought it useful to describe a village at a later stage of this process of change. What emerges from this discussion is a village where the landowning and most numerous caste is the principal political power without being dominant as this is understood in the literature of the dominant caste. It is my understanding that this is a very common situation throughout India, whatever the past character of the village.

The particular focus of this essay has been on what Dumont calls the system of 'justice', and clearly there is nothing like the 'panchayat of the dominant caste' to be discerned in Behror today. Nor is it possible to sustain the more general proposition implicit in Dumont, Srinivas and others that the landowning caste is the source of *order* in the village; the political power of the Ahirs falls far short of this. The more limited justice dispensed by individual caste panchayats can still be found in Behror and sometimes it retains substantial importance for particular castes. But caste panchayats are confined to untouchables and a few other low castes, and they make little overall impact on village life.

Dominance in the Wider Context

If authority arising from sources outside the state has declined in Behror and elsewhere, then logically it would seem to follow that the void will have been filled by the state. There is indeed a good deal of evidence that this is the case. Certainly, the state is a much larger presence in Behror than it was during the British period, and the same can be said generally throughout India. The welfare and development activities of the post-independence state have connected government officials and villagers in a far closer way than occurred during the British era. Statutory panchayats have been established to promote local development activities and to act as a form of local government in the physical settlement of the village. Other specifically judicial panchayats, often called nyaya panchayats, were established in order to provide the accessible and affordable justice which the regular courts were believed not to provide. And the intense world of electoral politics is obviously part of the apparatus of the state. Moreover, the police, as principal enforcement agency of the state, have been greatly strengthened following independence. All these developments have been part of the closer integration of village life into a larger political and administrative construct.

But we also need to be cautious about conceiving of the change as a transfer of authority from social formations outside the state to the institutions of the state. Despite the erosion of local authority, the state still exerts a relatively light presence in Behror. The courts, in particular, have declined rather than grown more formidable as a presence in Behror and generally throughout India. Put simply, there is a declining case-load. So there is no question of Dumont's third source of 'justice' picking up the slack created by the decline of village dominance.

This is not the place for any extended analysis of the sociology of the Indian court system, but a little needs to be said about the perhaps counter-intuitive decline of lawyer's law in village India. From their inception the courts were dominated by disputes over land, and a larger proportion of these were an artefact of the distinctive British interventions in land administration. Post-independence changes including *jagirdari* abolition have served to reduce the number of disputes arising directly from land administration. To give only one example, rent suits in Bengal fell from an annual figure of over half a million in the 1940s to zero with *jagirdari* abolition after independence. These rent suits were simply part of the zamindars' tactics to extract rent from their tenants, a portion of which was then passed on to the state as land revenue. When the state abolished the structure of revenue intermediaries, it took away the whole rationale of the rent suit: now the state collects the revenue directly from every landholder.[38]

In Behror there has not been the same decline in court usage, since there was never as high a resort to litigation in the first place: the region was settled on the more direct lines of Punjab rather than on the eastern zamindari model. But in Behror, too, the structure of landholding is now more settled than it has been since the intrusion of the British in the latter part of the nineteenth century, indeed probably more than it has ever been. So litigation and also criminal prosecution arising from disputes over land have declined. And there is no major new source of litigation in the countryside, in contradistinction to the cities. The ever-growing bar of lawyers in Behror has to share a steadily declining quantum of litigation. Nor has judicial business been transferred to the statutory nyaya panchayats; in Behror and more widely, these have tended to fall into desuetude.[39] The courts and quasi-judicial institutions of the state can thus be said to represent a diminished rather than an enhanced presence at the very same time that the authority of the dominants has been declining.

Further, it is easy to exaggerate the separation between state and society. Locally powerful communities and persons can shape, sometimes dictate, the performance of institutions of the state. So the Ahirs of Behror and their counterparts throughout India have scarcely been displaced in any systematic way by the expansion of state institutions in the post-independence period. To give a simple example, the size and power of the police establishment have greatly increased over the last half century; logically, this must have worked to increase state power at the expense of village autonomy. But notoriously in regions like Bihar and universally throughout India (indeed virtually anywhere in the world), the behaviour of the police proceeds in an intensely political context. Often the caste composition of the police force will reflect regional patterns of caste power, and this composition is bound to have some effect on police behaviour. So powerful caste communities have been able to adapt to the loss of local autonomy by influencing institutional behaviour at local or higher levels.

Beyond these questions of the nature and impact of the state apparatus, it is clearly a major distortion to think of the changes to agrarian structure only in narrowly institutional or even political terms. A major fault of much of the anthropological literature—this applies strongly to Dumont, for example—is that it fails to attend sufficiently to the structural impact of new economic forces. The discussion of employment in Behror together with a wealth of other writing shows that the force pushing/pulling people out of the village has frequently been the developing capitalist market. This force has proceeded under the umbrella of the modern state but it would be absurd to reduce it to the status of some kind of element of the state. Again, the precise impact of developing capitalist relations on agrarian structure is an empirical question. But clearly one effect has been to create a wider field of vision for both dominants and subordinates. In the case of Behror I have tried to show that the Ahirs have a dwindling interest in the affairs of the village, since their ambitions are now directed to advancement in the modern, urban sector and to political representation at levels higher than the councils of the village. On the other side, the subordinates have escaped some of the rigours of the old order by taking advantage of new economic opportunities outside the village.

If dominance at the village level has clearly waned in India, the leading castes have not so clearly lost their power at the state and even national levels. In many of the states of India it is possible to locate one or sometimes several castes which tend to dominate politics and administration. The Lingayats and Vokkaligas of Karnataka fall into this category; so do the Nayars and, to some extent, the Ezhavas of Kerala; the Rajputs, Brahmins, Bhumihars and Kayasthas of Bihar; the Jats of Rajasthan and also Haryana; the Reddys and the Kammas of Andhra; and so on.[40] The nature of this new-style dominance and its relation to older forms needs to be clarified. Clearly, there is a connection between the two, since many of the castes which are now most prominent in state politics are the same castes which earlier exercised dominant power in many of the particular region's villages and which still own a high proportion of lands. But not all the castes named above were in this category: the Ezhavas, for example, can lay claim to have once been ritually untouchable, and certainly they were a poor community at the turn of the twentieth century. The Ezhavas prospered socially and later politically by virtue of their large numbers and an early attachment to advancement through modern education, rather than from a base in landholding.

The Jats of Rajasthan, Punjab, Haryana and Uttar Pradesh represent a different case. In Rajasthan, Jars were very often the subordinate cultivators of Rajputs during the princely period but after *jagirdari* abolition their economic position has improved greatly and they have become the state's most successful caste in terms of political representation. In Punjab, Haryana and western Uttar Pradesh, the Jars' post-independence success has been built on what was already a stronger base than was prevalent in Rajasthan. In these regions Jat cultivators tend to have been recognised by the colonial authorities as proprietors rather than subordinate tenants under the intermediary system. In some instances their power was sufficient to qualify them as 'dominant caste' within Srinivas's or Dumont's specifications.[41] Overall, their position can be seen as broadly comparable with that of the Ahirs of Behror.

In the small state of Haryana, Jats have come to dominate recent politics. But the more interesting case is that of the largest state of Uttar Pradesh. The greatest population of this state is located in the eastern regions, where the two traditionally most powerful castes are the Thakurs (Rajputs) and the Brahmins. These castes dominated Congress governments from 1952 to 1967.[42] But since 1967 a grouping of so-called backward castes led for many years by Charan Singh, has been an alternative and sometimes governing political coalition. This grouping is more socially heterogeneous than its mixture of Gandhian and socialist ideology would sometimes suggest. The most powerful group within what became the Janata coalition in 1977 was Charan Singh's own Jat community, which is neither high caste nor backward. Their occasional position as the principal political power of the state has by no means converted the Jats to the status of the dominant caste of Uttar Pradesh. The Thakurs and Brahmins are still far more powerful by virtue of their landholding—there are still very large individual parcels of land—and increasingly because of their position in the bureaucracy, the professions and business. Especially during the early days of independence but persisting to the present, they have won political representation disproportionate to their numbers. But equally, their position is now far less dominant than it was during the zamindari period, since they have had to make a good deal of room for the Jats and some of the backward castes.

The great variety of caste relations in the various states makes generalisation difficult. But the Uttar Pradesh example is more generally instructive in suggesting that once caste dominance has been lost at the village level, it cannot functionally be replaced at a higher political level. The Thakurs of Uttar Pradesh turned in the 1950s to the new electoral politics of India at the very time that they were losing control of village affairs. For a time the Thakurs and the Brahmins were able to exert a high level of dominance of the ruling Congress party. But the period since 1967 has seen intense electoral competition among different parties drawing on different caste communities. The neighbouring state of Bihar has undergone a similar political transformation over a slightly later time-frame, with an increasingly powerful opposition based on the so-called backward classes in continuous competition with the high-caste-dominated Congress party. So while the once-dominant local fragments of castes have adapted to the world of electoral politics through a process of aggregation on a whole state or even multistate basis, their opposition has been doing the same thing.

This competition between drawing on different castes is not the only state pattern of politics—it does not adequately sum up the contemporary politics of Tamil Nadu, for example. What it also masks is the increasing power of commercial, industrial and administrative elites based in the cities of India and indeed internationally. These have social connections with caste groupings in the various regions but analytically they are increasingly distinct from them. The development of these urban elites has the effect of making the intense competition for resources between caste-based groupings at the state level seem of less central importance. Given the economic power, wealth and desired lifestyles being built in the large centres, regional and village power tends to lose its attraction to those who can aspire to these. Attitudinal shifts of this kind have taken place first among the traditionally best-educated and most mobile high-caste communities but have quickly spread to the other communities. There can be no doubt that Indian life decreasingly revolves around the concerns of the agrarian scene, despite the continuing concentration of population there. And one of the effects of this development is to make the categories of class rather than caste increasingly relevant in social analysis.

To sum up, the decline of the dominant caste at the village level has been part of an economic, social and political integration of villages into larger units under the aegis of the modern state. This has not yet resulted in any tidy pattern of power or authority throughout India as a whole—the institutions of the state have not simply succeeded to functions previously discharged by the dominant caste. Nor can it be said that the apparatus of the state has been perfectly captured by the castes which were once dominant in the villages. It is true that these castes have often successfully organised at territorially more inclusive levels over the period since independence, but their success in the face of stiff competition has been far from invariable. They have had to compete with other caste coalitions while the competition itself has been downgraded by the increasing significance of the commercial, industrial and bureaucratic establishments. The once-dominant castes supply many of the personnel for these modern organisations but the latter have taken on a life of their own in the context of world economic developments.

Juridical Authority in Historical Perspective

This essay is essentially about change and it therefore rests on the identification of states before and after the change. Earlier the idea of the dominant caste was endorsed as a general guide to the structure of power and/or authority in village India before the historical change, but no substantial evidence was offered in support of this endorsement. This was not an oversight but rather a postponement of what is a difficult exercise. Conclusive evidence of the decline of local and regional authority would need to include field observations across time and region. Even for the post-independence period such material is scanty, and there are only fragments available for earlier periods. Instead, for the pre-British period we have to make inferences from documentary and epigraphical material. If we read this material in the light of observations of the recent past made by Srinivas and others, it tends very broadly to confirm the dominant-caste thesis.

Some of the most significant confirmation for the pre-British period comes from writing on the Mughal regime. The literature on Mughal administration suggests by way of negative inference that imperial reach into the villages was largely indirect. Moreland[43] is probably correct in his claim that the Mughal administration was overwhelmingly directed to the production of revenue and the maintenance of military security. A study of administrative and judicial officials—particularly the amil, qazi, faujdar and kotwal—leads to the conclusion that there was no systematic judicial presence in the countryside as opposed to the towns of Mughal India.[44] The qazi, in particular, fails to emerge as the free-ranging judge he is sometimes supposed to have been. Certainly, there was no regular bureaucratic hierarchy of courts during Mughal times. There was considerable judicial activity in the cities and at least occasional such action in serious criminal matters throughout the rural areas controlled by the Mughals. Disputes surrounding revenue collection seem to have frequently been addressed by revenue officials of the central authorities, but these interventions were never inflated into a great judicial enterprise. Unlike the British, the Mughals did not conflate the administrative problem of maximising revenue with conceptual enquiries into the true and/or proper basis of landownership in India.

The administrative picture of Mughal India needs to be set beside the view of agrarian life to be gained from accounts like those of Irfan Habib and Nurul Hasan.[45] These establish quite convincingly that local and regional power was concentrated in what Habib calls 'primary' zamindars (the village zamindars of the early British administration), who were marked by two characteristics: first, they tended to be drawn from particular castes or clans, such that there was often a monopoly of that caste/clan in a particular region. And second, they often possessed great military strength, which arose independent of the Mughal regime. So in the context of a minimalist central Mughal power, the idea of village control in the hands of the dominant caste becomes plausible. At the same time, this concept lacks the detail to be a model of a working system.

Cohn developed a somewhat parallel idea in his argument that the Banaras region was organised in the eighteenth century on the basis of 'the little kingdom' and that the operative unit for governance in the kingdom was generally the taluka. These talukas were constituted as revenue units of the larger administration of the Raja of Banaras but they were built on the basis of a unit of sociological significance: the taluka was in the control of a particular, usually Rajput, lineage, which had absolute control of land revenue assessment, taxation, police and judicial functions. Cohn's account is emphatic about the high degree of autonomy of the taluka.[46]

While this formulation has greater specificity than a blanket claim about control by the dominant caste, it, too, lacks empirical detail. One of its problems is an assumption that there is a single corporate body within the taluka, whereas in practice there are likely to have been serious and endemic structural tensions between different levels of the controlling clan.[47] The clan members resident in a particular village may have had different histories and different interests than non-residents at structurally higher levels. Just who controlled the village and dispensed 'justice'—the resident Thakurs or the more powerful clansmen resident at sometimes distant centres? Questions like this demonstrate the deep imprecision of accounts such as that of Cohn. And even if Cohn's account is accurate in a schematic sense for Banaras, generalisation from the Banaras model is hazardous.

Despite these various limitations of the material on agrarian authority in the Mughal and interregnum periods, the accounts are convincing as to the primarily local or regional character of this authority. Certainly, it is no refutation to point to the many instances of intervention in village affairs, particularly about revenue matters, by officers of the imperial authorities. The argument about localism is one about broad tendencies, not invariability.

Some of the most illuminating recent writing on the pre-British period has concentrated on south India.[48] This work suggests that earlier historical accounts may be flawed. Thus Dirks conceives of his work as an engagement with Dumont, whose work is seen to be flawed by a profound orientalism. Specifically Dirks objects to Dumont's emphasis on Brahminism, and hence 'religion', within the caste order, at the expense of the political power of the king. Dirks wants to substitute a view of India which is less sacred and oriental, more down to earth:

> It is my contention . . . that until the emergence of British colonial rule in southern India the crown was not so hollow as it has generally been made out to be. Kings were not inferior to Brahmans; the political domain was not encompassed by a religious domain. State forms, while not fully assimilable to western categories of the state, were powerful components in Indian Civilisation. Indian society, indeed caste itself, was shaped by political struggles and processes.[49]

This debate is no doubt an important one but it exists alongside, rather than cuts across, the concerns of the present essay. Both Dirks and Ludden provide a wealth of material to illustrate the fundamental importance, of caste in general and the dominant caste in particular, in the ordering of pre-British south India. Thus Ludden talks about 'dominant caste domains' based on 'status, power and interests in land'.[50] The conception of 'dominant caste' employed by these writers is by and large the standard one that has so preoccupied thinking about India for almost forty years now. Moreover, both these accounts are consciously built on the foundation of Cohn's concept of 'the little kingdom', a concept we have seen to be enmeshed with the idea of the dominant caste. So whatever challenge to orthodoxies the new history of the south represents, it builds on rather than challenges the idea of dominant caste as a crucial part of the Indian past.

If one follows Srinivas and Dumont, nothing much seems to have changed in the basic constitution of authority since Mughal times or the periods and regions discussed by Dirks and Ludden. Of the anthropologists who have concerned themselves with agrarian authority, only Cohn has sought to develop a historical perspective which points to a long-term erosion of local authority. But Cohn's fieldwork was done immediately after independence, at a time when he was no more than tentative about the decline of the local dominants. His remarks about the agents of change are only impressionistic and conjectural.

Over the succeeding decades the surprising tenacity of the idea of the dominant caste and also the persistence of an opposition view that the concept never referred to a solid phenomenon, have inhibited work on historical change in patterns of agrarian authority.

Two historical dividing lines can be seen to stand out in the decline of dominance: the arrival of the British and then the coming of independence in 1947. As to the first, the British eventually built a state apparatus that was both more extensive in its geographical reach and more intensive in its bureaucratic form than its predecessor regimes. In the context of the wider economic and social impact which gathered force from late in the nineteenth century, this state apparatus represented a threat to entrenched village power. Thus the establishment by the Anglo-Indian state of a much-used judicial apparatus must have worked against the authority of local dominants. This is not as self-evident as it may seem, since the new courts of the Raj did not compete directly with village dominants in most matters that came to their attention. The courts were overwhelmingly preoccupied with land matters, which had sometimes occupied the central authorities even during the Mughal period. But the institutional presence of the collector in his administrative and judicial roles and the progressive expansion of the court system from the late nineteenth century, can only have represented a challenge to local authority. The pacification of the countryside through the superiority of British arms and, mainly in the twentieth century, the development of a police force, were a straightforward downgrading of local authority.

The indirect impact of the Raj may have been scarcely less important in destabilising local authority than the institutions of the state. The gradual blurring of the boundaries of the village economy; the nationalist movement against British rule; the campaigns for social reforms, including the abolition of untouchability; the tentative steps towards electoral participation; the building of railways, roads and cities; these were some of the developments during the colonial period which helped break down local isolation. Indeed, it is less the decline than the persistence of local autonomy and dominance that demands explanation. So-called traditional life carried on largely because of limited British ambitions: the Raj may not have been so minimalist as the Mughals, but its aims and institutional apparatus were far more modest than those of a modern European state or of post-Independence India. Mass education, for example, was never an accomplishment or even an aim of the Anglo-Indian state. For many villages, contact with *sarkar* must have been minimal even at the end of the Raj; this was particularly true in the zamindari areas, where land revenue collection was not a direct function of the state. The chief government presence in the districts was the collector, a combined revenue, general administrative and judicial figure. The legendary power and status of the collector no doubt reflected the authoritarian nature of the Raj, but it also said something about his institutional isolation out there in the district.

The pace of change has speeded up enormously since independence, the second of our two dividing lines. If the argument of this essay is accepted, then Srinivas identified the phenomenon of the dominant caste on the eve of its disintegration. That disintegration has been proceeding with remarkable speed, measured against the weight of history and tradition that kept the old order in place. Among the engines of change, central place must go to the competitive electoral process which has reached maturity in the post-independence period. The phenomenon of the dominant caste can scarcely coexist with serious elections premised on the concept of individualism. But there has also been the profoundly important impingement of capitalist relations onto the agrarian scene; the phenomenon of temporary migration to employment centres; the liberating force of education; the impact of radical ideology; and so on. Whatever the continuing force of purely ritual hierarchy, the old secular hierarchy of village power has not been able to withstand such erosion of its ground.

CONCLUSION

This essay has sought to identify some important changes in the n the structure of agrarian life which have been too little recognised in the literature of social science. In a word, the power of landholders has fallen quite dramatically relative to historical models and even relative to life in the early 1950s. Villages are now more closely integrated into larger economic and political units, and the quality of domination that was possible in an isolated village is not replicable in the wider world. This change has tended to strip power from groupings which are portrayed in influential anthropological literature as examples of a special category called the dominant caste. No such special category is now useful in agrarian analysis. The change has many of the outward characteristics of the European transition from feudalism to capitalism, though the difficulties with this analogy are such that it is not defended here. But even mention of the European parallel helps make the crucial observation that the collapse of the *ancien régime* of village India has not ushered in an era of equality. The reduction of local tyrannies does not necessarily entail the emergence of a whole social and political order significantly more attuned to the interests of the most subordinated Indians.

9

Caste and Class: Social Reality and Political Representations*

D.L. Sheth [†]

My purpose in this essay is to assess the nature of changes that have occur red in the caste system in modern times and to examine their implications for the growth of a new type of stratificatory system in Indian society. A perspective that has for long dominated the sociological discourse on the caste system in India emphasises the cultural and structural continuities manifested by the system. It views changes either as endogenous to the system itself or as representing such exogenous elements which the self-perpetuating system of castes selectively incorporates and recasts in its own mage—for its survival and maintenance. The continued predominance of such a perspective in the field of sociology has prevented recognition not only of some important aspects of the traditional system itself, but more particularly of the changes which are qualitatively different from those that occurred in pre-modern times and have severely undermined the system's governing principle, that is, of ritual hierarchy. The first part of the essay provides an overview of changes that have occurred in the caste system in modern times which, I argue, have resulted in the ideological and structural transformation of the caste system. In the second section I show how these changes in the stratificatory system of society have been embodied by the institutions of competitive representational politics which, in turn, have given rise to new socio-political identities in society. The third and last section empirically examines how the changes in the caste structure and ideology have opened up new spaces in the macro-system of stratification, in which the hierarchical order of castes is being stretched horizontally, causing the collapse of several castes occupying different high and low locations in the antecedent ritual hierarchy, into a new stratificatory category I call the middle class.

* Extract from *Contemporary India*, ed. Pai Panandikar and Ashis Nandy, Delhi: Tata McGraw Hill, 1999, pp. 331–56.

[†] In writing this essay I have benefited immensely from discussions with my colleagues, Giri Deshingkar and V.B. Singh.

CHANGES

Significant changes had taken place in the caste system during the colonial period, when the interrelated forces of modernisation, secularisation and urbanisation began to have their impact on Indian society. Alongside the historical forces, the policies of the colonial rulers, aimed primarily at delegitimising the power of the then existing social elite and creating support for their own rule, produced some specific and far-reaching changes in India's stratificatory system.[1]

The most important among the changes was, in my view, the formation of a new, translocal identity among the lower castes, collectively (as a people) oppressed by the traditional system of hierarchy. The discourse on rights, until then quite alien to the concepts governing ritual hierarchy, made its first appearance in the context of the caste system. New ideological categories like social justice began to interrogate the idea of ritual purity or impurity according to which the traditional stratificatory system endowed entitlements and disprivileges to hereditary statuses. The established categories of ritual hierarchy began to be confronted with new categories like 'depressed' and 'oppressed' castes.[2]

Second, the colonial state, by using the traditional status categories for classifying the population in the censuses, acquired an agency, even a legitimate authority, to arbitrate and fix the status claims made or contested by various castes about their locations in the traditional ritual hierarchy. At the same time, the enumeration of castes and their ethnographic descriptions compiled by the state highlighted how the social and economic advantages accrued to some castes and not to others in the ritual hierarchy. This led to demands among many castes for special recognition by the state for receiving educational and occupational benefits as well as for political representation.[3] The colonial state was only too willing to concede these 'demands', for the idea itself was mooted by its rulers in the first place.

Third, the colonial state, by playing the dual role of a super Brahmin who located and relocated disputed statuses of castes in the traditional hierarchy and of a just and modern ruler who wished to 'recognise' rights and aspirations of his weak and poor subjects, albeit as social collectivities, sought to secure the colonial political economy from incursions of the emerging nationalist politics. This, among other things, induced people to organise and represent their interests in politics in terms of caste identities and participate in the economy on the terms and through mechanisms set by the colonial regime. But all this also required that castes, as they entered the new arena of politics, were freed from their statuses in the ritual hierarchy. This resulted in making the hierarchical order of castes increasingly subject to horizontal political competition and conflict among castes. In the process, while caste *qua* caste became a recognised and legitimate category for political representation and for administering the social and welfare policies of the state, the principle of ritual hierarchy began to lose its ideological legitimacy.

Fourth, several castes occupying more or less similar locations in different local hierarchies began to organise themselves horizontally into regional–and national-level associations and federations, as it became increasingly necessary for them to negotiate with the state and in the process project their larger social identity and numerical strength.[4]

Fifth, movements of the lower castes for upward social mobility, which were not new in the history of the caste system, acquired a qualitatively new dimension as they began to attack the very ideological foundations of the ritual hierarchy of castes, in terms not internal to the system (as was the case with the Buddhist and Bhakti movements), but in the modern ideological terms of justice and equality.

Such changes have not only intensified during the fifty years after decolonisation, but with India establishing a liberal democratic state and the institutions of competitive, representational democracy, they have acquired still newer dimensions and a greater transformative edge, producing some fundamental structural and systemic changes in the traditional stratificatory system.[5] The hierarchically ordered strata of the traditional caste system now increasingly function as horizontal groups, competing and co-operating with one another for the new economic and political power released in society through the process of modernisation of its economy and democratisation of its political institutions.

Alongside this change in the organisational structure, that is, its horizontalisation, the form of consciousness is also changing. The consciousness of members belonging to a caste is increasingly felt subjectively in terms of community consciousness and is often expressed as caste chauvinism. The sense of belonging to a high or a low status in the ritual hierarchy is gradually fading away; in any case, it is less and less accepted by concerned actors in the system as a good enough argument to justify status claims.

The traditional status system is now thickly overlaid by the new power system created by elections, political parties and, above all, by social policies—such as of affirmative action—of the state on the one hand and, on the other, by changes in the occupational structure of society which has not only created vast numbers of non-traditional occupations not bound to caste but has also given rise to new types of social relations even among the groups following traditional occupations.[6]

The nexus between hereditary ritual status and occupations which constituted one of the caste system's defining features is progressively breaking down. It is becoming increasingly unnecessary to justify the occupation one follows in terms of its correlation with the ritual purity or impurity of one's inherited status. The traditional ritualistic idea of cleanliness or otherwise of the occupation one follows has become unimportant if that brings a good income to the individual. A Brahmin dealing in leather or an ex-untouchable dealing in diamonds is no longer looked upon as deviant behaviour; that the former is more a frequent occurrence than the latter has only to do with the resources at one's command and not with observance of any ritual prohibitions attached to the statuses involved. In any event, the cleanliness or otherwise of an occupation is increasingly seen in a physical and biological sense than in ritual or moral terms.[7]

Significant internal differentiations have taken place within every caste. Traditionally, an individual caste, whether located on the upper or lower rungs of the hierarchy, functioned internally as a truly egalitarian community, both in terms of rights and obligations of members vis-à-vis each other and of lifestyle, that is, the food they ate, the clothes they wore, the houses they lived in, etc. Some differences in wealth and status (of clans) that existed among households within the same caste were rarely expressed in power terms. Today, members of a single caste are becoming increasingly differentiated among themselves in terms of their occupations, educational and income levels and lifestyles.

The castes which occupied a similar ritual status in the traditional hierarchy, but were divided among themselves into subcastes and sub-subcastes by rules of endogamy, are now reaching out increasingly into larger endogamous circles, in some cases their boundaries coterminate with those of the respective varna in a region to which they supposedly belong. Marriage alliances across different strata of the 'upper castes', even crossing the self-acknowledged varna boundaries, are no longer very uncommon; they may either be arranged by parents or blessed by them when self-arranged by the prospective spouses. In fact, the category of upper castes now includes in several regions of India, the upwardly mobile, dominant castes of the erstwhile Shudras. Instead of the ritual status of the particular castes involved in a marriage alliance, the criteria of education, wealth, profession and social power of the brides/grooms and/or their parents have become important for such marriage alliances. They more often represent what may be called intercaste marriages within a group of castes or a class. The only 'traditional' consideration that enters such cases of intercaste marriages among upper castes is the vegetarian–meat-eating divide which is also becoming somewhat fuzzy. Although, statistically, the incidence of intercaste marriages is not yet significant, what is significant is the trend they represent. A more important point is that when such marriages take place they attract little, if any, censure within their respective castes, perhaps just some raising of eyebrows. In fact, in many an upper caste the mechanisms through which castes used to exercise such censorial authority have either disappeared or have become defunct.

The caste rules of commensality have largely become inoperative outside one's household. Even within the household, observance of such rules has become quite relaxed. In caste dinners too, friends and well-wishers of the host, belonging to strata ritually lower as well as higher than that of the host, are invited and are seated, fed and served together, with the members of the caste hosting the dinner. The caste panchayats, if they exist, show increasingly less concern in invoking any sanctions in such situations.

Summing up, today, both the ideology and organisation of the traditional caste system have become vastly eroded.[8] As may be expected, such erosion has taken place to a much greater extent and degree in the urban areas and at the macro-system level of social stratification. But the local hierarchies of castes in the rural areas are also being progressively subjected to the same process.[9] In the villages too, the traditional social relationships are being redefined in economic terms. This is so, because in the last three decades, particularly after the 'green revolution' and with the increasing role of the state and other outside agencies in the food production and distribution system of a village, the social organisation of the village has substantively changed. From the kind of social system the Indian village was (a system of ritual status hierarchy), it is increasingly becoming an economic organisation. The priestly, trading and service castes, that is, social groups not directly related to agricultural operations, are leaving villages, or serving them from nearby towns if and when such services are still required. The socio-religious content of economic relationships is reduced; they have become more contractual and almost totally monetised. The traditional *jajmani* relationships, which regulated economic transactions in socio-religious terms, have been replaced by, relationships of employer and employee, of capital and wage labour. When social and religious aspects of economic relationships are insisted upon by any caste, such as traditional obligations of one status group to another, it often leads to intercaste conflicts and violence in the villages. In brief, the pattern of relations, sustained by the internal system of food production of a village and the conformity of status groups to their assigned roles in the system, is fast disintegrating.

The stratificatory system as it functions in India today, can, therefore, no longer be characterised as a hierarchy of ritual statuses. Put in stronger terms, the Indian caste system, for long conceived of as a ritual status system has disintegrated, although castes as individual self-conscious communities continue to survive. But by organising themselves horizontally into larger conglomerates and coalitions, they are now entering new social formations which have emerged in India's stratificatory system.

POLITICAL REPRESENTATIONS

For about two decades after independence the political discourse on castes was dominated by the left-radical parties and liberal modernist intellectuals who saw, somewhat naively, changes in the caste system as suggesting its transformation into a system of polarised economic classes. Consequently, the discourse remained bogged down in the dichotomous debate on caste versus class politics. 'Class politics', that is, the strategy of mobilising popular support on political issues along class lines, was seen as the only rational/scientific way of representing forces of social change and modernisation in society. Caste politics, on the other hand, symbolised the 'atavistic' ideology of the caste system which, it was believed, was rapidly losing its basis in the structure of material interests in society; it survived largely at the level of habit and sentiments. In effect, the class view of castes ignored the community identities and status resources attached to the different castes which were supposed to belong to a similar 'class'. Hence, the left parties, both of the communist and the socialist varieties, by and large, sought to articulate political issues and devise strategies of mobilising electoral support in terms of assumed common economic interests of social groups, which in their view constituted a sufficient basis to form a single class.[10] In the event, although these parties could credibly claim to represent the poorer strata and even occupied some significant political spaces in opposition to the Congress party at the time of independence, they failed to expand their electoral support in any significant measure for decades after independence. The binary opposition of caste and class continued to get sharpened in the ideological debates but the actual politics of elections and parties persisted in adapting itself to the social reality of intercaste competition.

The actors in competitive politics with their ear to the ground, whether of the left or the right, could not afford, for too long, to take a pure ideological view of castes. While the ideologues of the left parties continued to emphasise the view that the upper and lower castes were divided by their economic interests and could hence be mobilised in politics in terms of polarised classes, their electoral strategists and the rank and file saw the grey area in between and in effect devised their electoral strategies taking into account what they called the caste factor. The parties of the right, like the Swatantra Party and the Jan Sangh, did not take an open ideological position in favour of the ritual hierarchy of castes but in their politics they sought to make use of the existing vertical linkages of castes, such as between the landowning and the service castes dependent on them, in harnessing their electoral bases.[11] Such linkages, however, did not survive once competitive politics became full blown, with the result that the parties of the right could not retain their support bases from one election to the next.

The process of politicisation of castes acquired a great deal of sophistication in the politics of the Congress party, which scrupulously avoided taking any theoretical-ideological position on the issue of caste versus class. It saw caste as a socio-economic entity, one which linked different interests through expansion of its identity for political gains. The Congress party was politically aware of the change in the agrarian context; the agricultural castes particularly, were now seeking new (non-ritual) identities through politics. Thus by relying on the caste calculus for its electoral politics and, at the same time, articulating political issues in terms of national economic development and integration, the Congress was able to evolve durable electoral bases across castes—almost in proportion to the size of the castes in the population—and to maintain its image as the only and truly national party. This winning combination of caste politics and nationalist ideology secured for the Congress party a dominant position in Indian politics, for nearly four decades after independence.[12] The Congress party rarely used such dichotomies as upper castes versus lower castes or the capitalists versus the working class in its political discourse. Instead, the operative categories for the Congress party were the middle class, and the lower castes. Its politics was largely addressed to link vertically middle-class rule to lower-caste support. And the ideology used for, legitimation of this vertical social linkage in politics was neither class ideology nor caste ideology; it was the ideology of 'nation-building'.

The politics and programmes of the Congress party at the national level were thus projected as representing 'national aspirations' of the Indian people, albeit as articulated by the homogeneous middle class or the new power elite that played the leadership role at the time of independence. Its homogeneity lay in the fact that it was almost entirely constituted of the upper castes. At the regional levels, however, the party consolidated its social base by endorsing the power of the numerically strong and traditionally dominant intermediate castes of landowning peasants, for example, the Marathas in Maharashtra, the Reddys in Andhra, the Patidars in Gujarat, the Jats in Uttar Pradesh and so on. In the process, it created patron–client type of relationships in electoral politics, relationships of unequal but reliable exchanges between political patrons, that is, the upper and intermediate castes, and the numerous lower-caste communities of voters, popularly known as 'vote-banks' of the Congress party. Thus, in the initial two decades after independence, the changing power relations in society were processed politically through elections. This ensured for the Congress a social consensus across castes, despite the fact that it was presided over by the political hegemony of a small upper-caste, English-educated elite in collaboration with the regional social elites belonging, by and large, to the dominant castes of landed peasants. The latter were seen by their collaborating patrons, who saw themselves as the modernist 'national elite', as representing the parochial, traditionalist elements in society.

This collaboration between the two types of elites, although unequal in the mould of patron—client relationship, not only linked castes vertically in political relationship to national or central governance but also aligned different sectors—the urban-industrial with the rural-agrarian. Thanks to the complexity of democratic politics and the radical changes that had already occurred in the occupational structure of Indian society, the rule of this elite at the national level could not be typified as the rule of the upper castes. The ruling national elite did have their origins in upper castes-but they had become detached from their traditional ritual functions. They had acquired new interests and lifestyles which came through modern education, non-traditional occupations, and a degree of westernisation in their thinking and lifestyle. Thus, the upper castes, constituted as a middle class, no longer discharged the functions required of their status in the ritual hierarchy. They could afford this, as the status associated with traditional functions of castes had already declined in the changed occupational structure. At the same time, their caste identities *qua* upper castes were far from dissolved. They could comfortably own both the upper-caste and middle-class identity as both categories were then concomitant with each other. More importantly, even while they had, by and large, ceased to perform functions associated with their ritual status, they continued to benefit from the enormous resources that their traditional high status brought to them while operating in the modern system of power in which they were already ensconced. In fact, they were the natural first entrants to this new power system as their status in the traditional hierarchy afforded them to take quickly to modern education and professions and also to convert whenever necessary their inherited wealth into new means for acquiring elite positions of power. In the formation and functioning of this, what can broadly be described as the new elites or the middle class, their castes had indeed fused with the class, and the status dimension had acquired a power dimension. But in so far as this process of converting traditional status into new power was restricted only to the upper castes, they sought to use that power in establishing their own caste-like hegemony over the rest of society. In effect, the modernised, urban section of the upper castes functioned as a power group of elites. It is this nexus between traditional status and new power that severely inhibited the transformative potentials of both modernisation and democracy in India.

The emergent relationship between the traditional status system and the new power system worked quite differently for the numerous, *non-dwija*, lower castes. In negotiating their way in the new power system, their traditional low status, contrary to what it did for the upper castes, worked as a liability. The functions attached to their traditional low statuses had lost relevance or were devaluated in the modern occupational system. Moreover, since formal education was not mandated for them in the traditional status system, they were handicapped in their effort to acquire modern education. Nor did they have the advantage of inherited wealth as their status in the traditional. hierarchy had tied them to subsistence livelihood patterns.

In brief, for the lower castes of peasants, artisans, the ex-untouchables and the numerous tribal communities, their low statuses in the traditional hierarchy worked negatively for their entry into the modern sector. Whatever social capital and economic security they had in the traditional status system was wiped out through the modernisation process; they no longer enjoyed the protection that they had in the traditional status system against the arbitrary use of hierarchical power by the upper castes. On top of that, they had no means or resources to enter the modern sector in any significant way, except becoming its underclass. They remained at the bottom rung of both the hierarchies, the sacred and the secular, of caste and class.

This did objectively create an elite–mass kind of division in politics, but it still did not produce any awareness of polarisation of economic *classes* in society. In any event, it did not create any space for class-based politics. In fact, all attempts of the left parties at political mobilisation of the numerous lower castes as a *class* of proletarians or as a working class did not achieve any significant results either for their electoral or revolutionary politics. Nor did their politics, focused as it was on class ideology, make much of a dent on Congress-dominated politics, for it had established the political hegemony of the upper-caste-oriented middle class with the electoral consent of the lower castes. It was a very peculiar caste–class situation in which the upper castes functioned in politics with the self-identity of a class ('ruling' or middle) and the lower castes with the consciousness of their separate caste identities. The latter were linked to the former in a vertical system of political exchange through the Congress party, rather than horizontally with one another.

It took some three decades after independence for the lower castes of peasants, artisans, the ex-untouchables and the tribals to express in politics their resentment about the patron–client relationship that had politically bound them to the Congress party. With a growing awareness of their numerical strength and the role it could play in achieving their share in political power, their resentment took the form of political action. The awareness among the lower castes about using political means for upward social mobility and for staking claims as social collectivities for a share in political power had arisen during the colonial period, but it remained contained, if not subdued, for almost three decades after independence, under the influence of caste-based nationalist politics of the ruling Congress party. But the long-term consequences of the policy of affirmative action for various categories of lower castes and tribals, which had been in operation in one form or another since colonial times, also became visible after independence. Towards the end of the 1960s, despite tardy implementation, affirmative policies had created a small but significant section of individuals in almost every lower-caste group, who, by acquiring modern education, had entered the bureaucracy and other non-traditional occupations. This gave rise to a new political leadership among backward castes in different regions of the country.

By the mid-1970s these developments had resulted in radically altering the social bases of politics in India.[13] First, the Congress party-dominated politics of social consensus, presided over by the hegemony of an upper-caste, English-educated elite, began to crumble. The Congress organisation could no longer function as the system of vertical management of region–caste factions. The elite at the top could not accommodate the ever-increasing claims and pressures from below, by different sections of the lower castes, for their share in power. Between the mid-1970s and the 1980s, large sections of the lower strata of social groups abandoned the Congress. By the end of the 1980s many of them had constituted themselves into shifting alliances of their own separate political parties. The vertical arrangement of the region–caste factions that the Congress had perfected, just collapsed. Not only the Congress, but every other national party had to now negotiate for political support directly with different social–political collectivities of the lower castes or with the regional caste parties constituted by them.

The lower castes, now operating through larger social collectivities, were not content with proxy representations by the upper-caste, middle-class elite; they wanted political power for themselves. Politics became for them a contest for representation, in which they operated as horizontal power groups vis-à-vis the upper castes. The lower-caste groups, instead of functioning as factions within a larger party, preferred to bargain independently as distinct interest groups or to form their own new parties. Whatever had survived of the hierarchical dimension of the traditional stratificatory system in politics was now effectively horizontalised.[14]

Second, competitive politics made it difficult to view caste either as a pure category of 'interest' or of 'identity'. Its involvement in politics fused the dimensions of interest and identity in such a manner that a number of castes could now share common interests and identity through larger conglomerates of which they had become parts. The process itself was of politicisation, but it had ramified in the macro-system of social stratification, such that the elements of both hierarchy and separation among castes were being reorganised and recast in larger social collectivities such as the Dalits, the tribals, the backward castes and the forward or the upper castes.[15] Significantly, in this process, the ritually lower non-*dwija* castes of rich farmers (for example Reddys in Andhra Pradesh or Patidars in Gujarat) also began to be viewed in many regions as constituting parts of the larger collectivity called the upper castes. These new collectivities did not resemble either the old varna categories or anything like a polarised class structure in politics. In some cases, an enlarged identity shared by many castes, for example of Dalits which comprised various castes of the ex-untouchables, acquired what can be described, for lack of a more appropriate term, as an ethno-political identity.

Third, the horizontalisation of castes in the political arena dovetailed with other ethno-religious communities such as the Muslims and the Christians on the one hand, and at once prevented the Hindu lower castes from joining the bandwagaon of cultural nationalism or Hindutva on the other. The Hindutva movement, led by the Bharatiya Janata Party (BJP), thus could not fill the void created by the collapse of the Congress caste–class combine. The BJP's strategy of political mobilisation of all Hindus could not succeed, in any significant measure, in mobilising electoral support among the lower castes. Its appeal of Hindutva failed to override, except temporarily when emotive issues like the mosque versus the temple were raised, the fear of the lower castes that the BJP represented a Congress-like caste hierarchy in its political organisation and generally in politics. The BJP, despite its Hindutva politics, thus could not incorporate these groups on a durable basis either in its organisation or support structure in any significant proportions, for the BJP's politics of Hindutva appeared to large sections of these groups as the ploy of an upper-caste minority to acquire an electoral majority. In the appeal for religious unity of all Hindus, the lower-cast Hindus did not find any reflection of their interests or aspirations. Like any other party today, the BJP must now negotiate with these Hindu groups separately as horizontal power groups. This, in fact, compelled the BJP to dilute its Hindutva image and enter into coalitions and alliances with several caste-based regional parties and even with a non-Hindu ethno-religious party, namely, the Shiromani Akali Dal.

Fourth, in the emergent context of the caste–and region-based political coalitions competing for power, the politics of class polarisation, which in fact never took off, seems to remain grounded. The left parties, probably due to their experience of coalitional politics, have, but only lately, come to realise how the linkages between socio-cultural identities and economic interests work in Indian politics. So, they have changed their strategies of electoral and political mobilisation of the 'masses'; they now increasingly address their politics to specific groups of the oppressed and deprived sections, often identified in caste terms, than to a generalised class of the proletariat. But they still do not see the caste dimension in the making of a ruling class in India.

This new horizontal politics of caste coalitions, in its alignment with the politics of affirmative action, has far-reaching implications for changing the opportunity structure in Indian society.[16] The old middle class that was almost coterminous with upper castes at the time of independence, is now making spaces, even if slowly, for different sections of the lower castes. And the lower castes, while forming coalitions in politics, compete intensely among themselves at the social level for an entry into the growing middle class. It is this aspiration among the lower castes to enter the middle class, and the possibility of its realisation for quite a few among them, which seems to have prevented their political organisation as one single class of the oppressed proletarians. In any event, far from creating a polarised structure of economic classes, the process of politicisation of caste is working towards opening spaces in the middle class for sections of the lower castes and, in the process, the middle class is not only growing in size, but is changing both its character and composition. Put in a nutshell, with increasing modernisation of the economy and democratisation of political Institutions in India, its stratificatory system is enlarging the middle.

THE MAKING OF A MIDDLE CLASS

The macro-stratificatory system of traditional Indian society, which did not have a centralised polity, functioned superstructurally as an ideology of varna hierarchy. Thus, it supplied a common social language and categories of legitimation of statuses to various local hierarchies of jatis.[17] But after India became a pan-Indian political entity governed by a liberal democratic state, new social formations, each comprising a number of jatis—often across the ritual hierarchy and religious communities—have emerged at the regional and all-India levels and these formations have given structural substantiality to the macro-stratificatory system of a kind it did not have in the past. The nomenclature that has stuck to these formations is the one that was devised by the state in the course of implementing its social and cultural policies—especially of affirmative action (reservations). As such, the new formations are identified as: the forward or the upper castes, the Other Backward Castes (OBCs), the Dalits or Scheduled Castes (SCs) and the tribals or the Scheduled Tribes (STs). Over the years, these categories have acquired a strong social and political content, each category providing a collective self-identification to its members.

Unlike the closed status groups of the caste system, the new soc.al formations function as relatively loose and open-ended entities, competing with each other for political power and control over economic and cultural resources. In this competition for power and status in the new macro-stratificatory system, members of the upper-caste formation have the resources of their erstwhile traditional higher status and those of lower-caste formations have the advantages accruing to them from the state's policy of affirmative action, as also from their large numbers, both of which they use politically as well as collectively for upward social mobility. Thus, the new emergent stratificatory system represents a kind of fusion between the old status system and the new power system. Put differently, the ritual hierarchy of closed status groups is being transformed a relatively more open and fluid hierarchy among the new social groups.

The advantages, secured collectively by castes in the political arena, are used by members of each formation, competing intensely among themselves and with those of the other formations, for entry into yet another new generic social category, namely, the 'middle class'. This has lately become a salient category in India's macro-stratificatory system. The politicisation of castes and their progressive detachment from the ritual hierarchy have contributed to the emergence and growth of this class. Its membership is associated with new lifestyles (modern consumption patterns), ownership of certain economic assets and the self-consciousness of belonging to the middle class. The ritual purity or impurity of statuses held by its members in the traditional status system has, for the most part, ceased to be a criterion for their recognition or otherwise, as members of the middle class. As such, it is open to members of different castes and communities—who have acquired modern education, taken to non-traditional occupations and/or command higher income and the political power—to enter the middle class.

And yet, the Indian middle class cannot be seen as constituting a pure class category—a construct which, in fact, is a theoretical fiction. It is important to recognise that the Indian middle class carries within it some elements of the antecedent status hierarchy and ethnic divisions that exist in the larger society. Further, for the larger part, entry to this class is dependent on traditional status resources at one's disposal (as in the case of upper-caste members) or on such modern legal provisions like affirmative action (as in the case of the lower castes). So, it seems the Indian middle class will continue to have a caste element to the extent that modern status aspirations are pursued, and the possibility of their realisation is seen by individuals in terms of the castes to which they belong. But crucial to the formation of the middle class in India is not just the fact that members of lower castes are entering it in increasing numbers but that the nature of their pursuit for upward mobility has radically changed. Their quest is for acquiring modern education, white-collar jobs, wealth, political power and such other means of modern status, rather than registering higher ritual status.

Thus viewed, the middle class in India today is not a simple demographic category comprising sections of different castes and communities. It is a socio-cultural formation in which the caste identities of its members survive, but their ritual hierarchical statuses have lost relevance. Individuals from different castes and communities, as they enter this middle class, acquire not only economic interests and modern lifestyles but also a new self-image and a social identity as members of a middle class.

The process of middle-class formation in India is empirically illustrated by the findings of a recent all-India sample survey. The survey, based on a stratified random sample (probability proportionate to size) of 9457 Indian citizens drawn from all the Indian states, excluding the state of Jammu & Kashmir, was conducted by the Centre for the Study of Developing Societies (CSDS), Delhi, in June–July 1996. I present below some preliminary findings of the survey which show how different social formations are constituted and to what extent they are represented in various middle-class positions (see Table 9.1).

The sample population is classified into five social formations:
1. *Upper castes*: This social formation comprises castes with high ritual status (*dwija*) in the varna hierarchy as well as some upwardly mobile dominant castes of rich farmers, traditionally identified with a low varna status that is, Shudra. The castes included in this category are not entitled to benefits of affirmative action (24.8 per cent in the sample).
2. *Backward castes*: These include Hindu castes of lower peasantry and of artisans traditionally identified with the lowest varna category of Shudras as well as the lower peasant and artisan communities belonging to other non-Hindu religious groups (non-Hindus also have caste-like formations). Castes and communities comprising this category are entitled to the benefits of affirmative action (39.3 per cent in the sample).
3. *Dalits*: These include castes and communities of ex-untouchables belonging to different religious groups, receiving benefits of affirmative action (19.7 per cent in the sample).
4. *Tribals*: These communities belonging to different religious faiths, tribal and the mainstream, but entitled to affirmative action benefits (9.7 per cent in the sample).
5. *Muslims*: This category excludes those Muslim communities that are classified as backward and as such are included among backward castes. It includes only the upper strata of Muslims not entitled to affirmative action benefits (6.5 per cent in the sample).

The table shows distribution of the above five social formations in different middle-class positions. Five separate indicators are used for identifying middle-class positions: (a) education: those with education above the high school level; (b) occupation: those in white-collar occupations; (c) housing: those living in *pucca* houses, that is, houses constructed of brick and lime or cement; (d) ownership of assets: those owning three or more assets among the following: (i) a car/jeep/tractor (ii) a scooter/motorbike (iii) water-pumping set (iv) house/flat (v) television; (e) self-identification as members of the 'middle class': respondents who reject working class identity and choose for themselves the middle-class identity.

Table 9.1: Representation of Social Formations in Different Middle-class Positions

Social formation	Number and per-centage in sample	Education above high school	Occupation white collar	Housing brick and cement	Ownership of assets	Middle-class self-identification
Upper castes	2345	1057	873	1369	1112	1229
	(24.8)	(44.1)	(53.3)	(45.2)	(49.6)	(43.8)
Backward castes	3716	829	435	946	719	1001
	(39.3)	(34.6)	(26.6)	(31.3)	(32.0)	(35.7)
Dalits	1863	281	151	373	196	254
	(19.7)	(11.7)	(9.2)	(12.3)	(8.7)	(9.0)
Tribals	917	95	56	158	91	146
	(9.7)	(4.0)	(3.4)	(5.2)	(4.1)	(5.2)
Muslims	616	134	123	181	126	177
	(6.5)	(5.6)	(7.5)	(6.0)	(5.6)	(6.3)
Total	9457	2396	1638	3027	2244	2807
	(100.0)	(100.0)	(100.0)	(100.0)	(100.0)	(100.0)

The main findings of this study are:[18]

1. The middle class which was almost exclusively constituted by members of the upper castes, who had ceased to perform their traditional ritual roles vis-à-vis other castes and had taken to modern education and non-traditional professions, has now structurally expanded to include members of the lower castes and of religious minorities.

2. However, even today the upper castes dominate the Indian 'middle class'. While the upper-caste formation accounts for about a quarter of our sample population, it constitutes nearly half of this middle class. For example, 24.8 per cent of our respondents belong to upper castes but their representation in the two crucial middle-class categories, that is, white-collar occupations and ownership of assets, is over 53 per cent and about 50 per cent, respectively. This also means that in relative terms the proportion of upper castes in the 'middle class' has been reduced over the last 50 years; first because the size of the 'middle class' has grown substantially since independence, and second, because members of different lower castes have been able to avail of the new openings in this class. Despite this development, compared to every other formation, members of the upper castes in our sample are consistently over represented in all the five categories of the middle class.

3. The lower-caste social formations, that is, the Dalits (SCs), the tribals (STs) and the backward communities of peasants and artisans (OBCs) are, in different degrees, underrepresented in the present middle class compared to their size in the population. But all categories of the lower castes and those of the Muslims, which taken together constitute 75 per cent of the sample population, show a total representation of about 56 per cent among high school educated, about 47 per cent among the white-collar workers and over 50 per cent among the asset owners. Seen in the context of their inherited lower ritual status in the traditional hierarchy, this is a significant development. Even more significant is the fact that when members of the lower castes acquire modern means of social mobility, that is, education, wealth, political power, etc., their low ritual status does not come in the way of acquiring consciousness of being members of the middle class. A total of 56 per cent non-upper-caste population in our sample show self-identification as members of the middle class. On the whole, it can be inferred from the data that members of non-upper-caste formations who constitute three-fourths of the sample population, account for about half of the middle class.

4. The Dalits or the castes of ex-untouchables, which constituted the underclass of the ritual status system, have also begun to enter this

middle class. While it is true that the proportion of Dalits in the middle class is lower than that of the other lower-caste categories, the data suggest that significant numbers among them have been able to acquire education, white-collar jobs and assets. Compared to their 19.7 per cent strength in our sample population, the Dalit representation among the high school educated is about 12 per cent and about 9 per cent each in the categories of white-collar workers and asset owners. This, of course, indicates a very low level of their representation in the middle class. But it is quite significant in terms of the trend it suggests. It seems that some castes among the Dalits, through political awareness, organisation and movements of self-upliftment, have been able to take advantage of the state's policy of affirmative action and have been able to enter the middle class. But the rest still survive as the underclass of the modern system. The most significant change, however, is in the nature of consciousness among Dalits. The data show that after acquiring objective middle-class characteristics, the Dalits, like members of the other lower-caste formations, also develop subjective identification as members of the middle class. Their lowest traditional ritual status does not come in the way of such identification.

5. The backward castes who occupied the lowest (but higher than the Dalits') status in the varna hierarchy constitute the largest and a relatively more heterogeneous social formation of them all. As such, the representation of this social formation is not consistent across all middle-class locations. On the whole, compared to their proportion in the population (39.3 per cent), they are underrepresented in all categories of the middle class. They still remain, by and large, bound to their traditional occupations. Note that their representation in the white-collar category is only 26.6 per cent, which is about 13 percentage points less than their proportion in the sample. Thus, the OBC representation in white-collar jobs is the lowest compared to all other social formations. Compared to the Dalits and the tribals, a greater number among the backward castes, however, exhibit middle-class identification, which, in proportion to their size in the sample, is only 3 percentage points less. But compared to the upper castes, the OBCs remain severely underrepresented in every category of the middle class, including ownership of assets.

6. The tribals, who constitute 9.7 per cent of the sample, are represented by about 4 to 5 per cent in the middle-class positions. But they are relatively more underrepresented in white-collar occupations. Like the Dalits and the backward castes, the tribals also acquire middle-class identification, with a rise in education levels, in ownership of assets, and acquisition of white-collar jobs.

7. The Muslims occupy middle-class positions approximately in proportion to their size in the population, which is much lower compared to the upper castes, but higher than the OBCs, the Dalits and the tribals whose representation in every middleclass position is much lower than their respective size in the population. It needs, However, to be repeated that the category of Muslims here does not include all Muslims in the sample; it precludes about 4 per cent of Muslims belonging to communities entitled to reservation and are, as such, included in the category of backward castes. Their proportion in the middle class will dwindle if computed on the basis of the total Muslim population in the sample, which is 10.7 per cent.

In sum, the data suggest two important points about middle-class formation in India. First, the possibility of acquiring new means of upward mobility have opened up for the traditional low castes, with the result that significant numbers from among them have entered the middle class. More importantly, in this process, their lower ritual status does not come in the way of acquiring middle-class identification. Second, despite this development, the middle class still remains dominated by the upper castes who had more resources of traditional status at their disposal while entering the middle class.

To conclude, the nexus of caste and ritual status has broken down. The erosion of the ritual status hierarchy, however, does not mean that castes, *qua* communities, are disappearing or will disappear in the foreseeable future. They continue to exist, but as socio-cultural entities detached from the traditional hierarchy of ritual statuses. By forming themselves into larger horizontal, not vertically hierarchical, social groups, their members now increasingly compete for entry into the middle class. This has changed the character and composition of the old, pre-independence, middle class which was constituted almost entirely of the upper castes. Nearly 50 per cent members of today's middle class come from the lower strata of the traditional social hierarchy. The preliminary analysis of data on middle-class formation presented here does not allow us to answer an important question about the political and cultural orientations of members of the new middle class. But they do suggest at least a plausible hypothesis which may be explored in the future analysis of CSDS survey data, which is that members of the new middle class are likely to acquire common political and cultural orientations, distinct from those of their caste/community compatriots.

10

Federating for Political Interests: The Kshatriyas of Gujarat *

Rajni Kothari and Rushikesh Maru

The impact of modernisation processes on indigenous social structures has been a subject of much recent discussion on the new nations. The crucial question in this respect relates to the extent to which violent upheavals can be avoided in the processes of adjusting time-honoured institutions to the exigencies of modern times. In so far as such an adjustment is to take a permanent and legitimised form, it would depend upon two things. It would depend upon the ability of the indigenous system to absorb new changes and adapt its own structures and values accordingly. It would also depend upon the ability of the new institutions and leadership to take into confidence the inherited authority structures and media of communication and identification. Evidence suggests that such a process of mutual exposure and functional interaction will succeed better in a country where neither existing pluralities nor newly emerging differentiations are suppressed for the exclusive preservation of either the traditional or the modern sectors of society. It follows that where this happens what emerges out of this interaction is neither mainly traditional nor mainly modern.

A study of the interactions between the caste system and political democracy in India rejects the familiar dichotomy between a traditional society and a modern polity. On the contrary, it underlines the functional relevance of indigenous patterns of communication and differentiation in modernising a new nation. Much, of course, depends on the developmental potentiality of a particular social system. Where a relatively open society, by an act of conscious

* Extract from *Caste in Indian Politics*, ed. Rajni Kothari, Delhi: Orient Longman, 1970, pp. 70–101. An earlier and shorter version of this essay was published as 'Caste and Secularism in India: Case Study of a Caste Federation', in *The Journal of Asian Studies*, vol. XXV, no. 1, November 1965.

preference, resolves to undertake the task of building a modern nation through a democratic polity, the result is a purposive fusion of various elements. In India, under the impacts of western education, the nationalist movement, and adult franchise, the traditional community structure has undergone continuous change and adaptation. What is important is the mutual exposure and adaptation of traditional and modern authority structures, communication media, and identification symbols. The new institutions have established their hegemony precisely by taking into confidence the pluralities of the antecedent culture. Caste has been politicised but in the process it has provided to Indian politics processes and symbols of political articulation.

The process of articulation has taken many forms. In places where a large and homogeneous 'dominant caste' prevails, rival factions within the dominant caste led by individual leaders tend to draw their additional political support from adjacent and non-adjacent caste groups. This makes for competing alignments in which personal networks of influence and power both run along and cut across caste networks, thus giving rise to cross-cutting loyalties within the broad framework of a dominant caste.[1] In a multicaste situation made up of three or four castes, each fairly large but none in a position to acquire a place of dominance, the alignments take the form of coalitions of castes and subcastes struggling for power. There are many variations of both these types. In all cases other solidarities besides caste enter in the process. And in all cases it is the secular potential of caste that is brought out by its adopting an associational form of organisation and then functioning in an interactional framework. Reinforcing as well as cutting across changes in the status system brought about by other factors both internal to the system (such as emulation of 'sanskritised' practices) and external to the system (such as land legislation), is this changing orientation of caste organisation for participating in the secular political process.

A clear instance of the secular orientation of caste organisation is provided by the political articulation of the 'lower castes' in India. These are found to federate together into a common organisation and then press for their demands. Instances of such an upsurge are to be found all over the country. In what follows we provide an illustrative case study of such a movement in the state of Gujarat. It is a movement that has gained in importance over the years in the mobilisation of mass political support in the state. The study shows how once a caste organisation (in this case a caste federation) acquires a position of strength through numerical power and organisational cohesion, it can not only devise strategies with reference to political parties, but also feel confident enough to bargain with a more powerful caste group which has been its age-old rival and of which it had for a long time felt apprehensive. It also shows how such a process of secularisation brings about great shifts in the structure, policy priorities and leadership of the several castes and, in consequence, allows both the caste system and the political system to gain in sophistication and adaptability. The study is based on published and unpublished records and on interviews, and has been brought up to the third general election in 1962.

The concept of caste federation refers to a grouping together of a number of distinct endogamous groups into a single organisation for common objectives, the realisation of which calls for a pooling together of resources or numbers, or both. By and large, the objectives pursued are secular and associational, although the employment of traditional symbols for evoking a sense of solidarity and loyalty towards the new form is not uncommon. The traditional distinctions between the federating groups are on the whole retained, but the search for a new organisational identity and the pursuit of political objectives gradually lead to a shift in group orientations. A caste federation is, therefore, to be distinguished from a caste association both because of the range of social reality that it covers, and because of its search for an inclusive rather than a 'functional' identity. The former often takes a class or varna form and cuts across the ascriptive identity of caste in its jati form.[2] The caste federation is thus no mere agency of an endogamous group or groups set up for undertaking a specific task. Rather, it represents a new notion of caste organisation, is based on real or supposed sharing of interests and status attributes, and gives rise to its own symbolism.

The Gujarat Kshatriya Sabha is a caste federation, representing many castes and lineage groups, most of them drawn from the economically depressed communities of cultivators. The sabha is largely responsible for spreading the 'Kshatriya' label, and the consciousness that goes with it, to many caste groups ranging all the way from Rajputs who are highest in the Kshatriya hierarchy, to Bhils who are semi-tribal, with Bariyas (a Koli caste) middle of the way. Socially, there is great distance among the various caste and lineage groups in the Kshatriya hierarchy, although Rajput hypergamy does permit the daughters of Bariya chiefs to be married into some Rajput families. Economically, barring the well-placed Rajput nobles, most of these castes are poor and landless, some of the Rajput families as destitute as the Bariyas, if not worse. It is common economic interest and a growing secular identity born partly out of folklore but more out of common resentment against the well-to-do castes that have brought these different castes together in a broader organisation. On the other hand, barring a few exceptions, the more aristocratic Kshatriyas from the former ruling families have in the past generally kept away from the sabha.

In this process of assimilation, still going on, the economic factor was supplemented by the Kshatriya Sabha's constant efforts to upgrade the position of the lower castes in the social hierarchy of Gujarat. This was in fact a strong uniting force in the Kshatriya organisation. The process was one of group enfranchisement whereby entire castes and caste groups were 'accepted back' into the Kshatriya fold.[3] There was a conscious and deliberate attempt on the part of the leaders of the movement to break the shackles of tradition. Symbols of caste pollution were deliberately done away with. One of the first to go was the eating restriction: high and low were made to sit together in common feasts. More gestures followed. Thus an incident when progressive rulers, including the Maharaja of Baroda, were made to sit on the floor with other Kshatriyas in one of the annual conventions of the sabha has been proudly chronicled. The Kshatriya Sabha has proved to be the great levelling force for its various constituents.

Alongside emulation of higher castes (sanskritisation) and social and educational reform (westernisation),[4] such an urge to come together in a larger association (secularisation) is an important factor in social mobility, one that is likely to gain in importance under universal franchise and democratic politics. While it partly derives from 'sanskritised' attitudes of the lower castes, it also derives from the 'westernised' egalitarian attitudes of the upper caste. Cutting across both these orientations, however, is the association-federal urge motivated by the need to mobilise adequate support in order to function in a competitive polity. The search for status takes on a more complex character, composed of both conflicting and emulative components. Social emulation, a continuous process in any society, will now relate to the politicised attitudes and ideas of the upper castes. The stage of Brahminic adaptation is likely to be skipped or will take on a totally different connotation. Secularisation, while thus narrowing wide social distances between castes, is also narrowing the gulf between the reformist and the orthodox sections within the upper castes created by 'westernisation'. It is a mechanism of caste integration that is more powerful than any of the other influences discussed in the literature on caste.[5] The critical point about such a process of secularisation is that it is based on an identification that is known and understood and one that raises rather than dampens consciousness of social being. At the same time, such a consciousness also becomes a basis for change and serves as an adaptive mechanism in a changing society.

In the case of the Kshatriyas in Gujarat, the initiative for such a process of secularisation came from upper-caste, well-to-do Rajputs. In December 1946, Narendrasinh Mahida, a western-educated noble of high standing, launched the publication of *Rajput Bandhu*, a community mouthpiece with the object of propagating social reforms and liberal-democratic ideas among the Kshatriya community. He was inspired by his elder brother Motisinh's career as a writer and social reformer. Motisinh died young and Narendrasinh carried on his work. At the same time, Natvarsinh Solanki, another educated Rajput, a talukdar[6] of Kaira district, a skilful organiser and one with bitter experience of the politically dominant Patidars, was running an association called the

Charotar Kshatriya Samaj.[7] He joined Mahida as co-editor of *Rajput Bandhu*. Mahida and Solanki were to be the two major influences in the course that the Kshatriya movement took in the next fifteen years, Mahida providing the movement with an ideological sweep and a dominating personality, and Solanki skilfully building up organisational support and the allegiance of locally influential community leaders. There were also other prominent Rajput leaders who especially felt the need of promoting educational activities among the Kshatriyas. With a donation from Mahida, they started an educational society called the Gujarat Rajput Kelavani Mandal,[8] with Mahida as president and Solanki as secretary, respectively. The Mandal, which was started in December 1946, was at first conceived of as an educational institution. Gradually, however, it developed into a broader social organisation.

It was soon discovered by the leaders of the Mandal that it was not enough to collect a few thousand rupees and distribute scholarships. The need was to create a social consciousness among the fragmented and disorganised mass of Kshatriyas. In order to do this, Mahida suggested that the leaders and workers should tour villages on foot, an idea he got from Gandhi's *padyatra* in riot-stricken Bengal. A meeting of Kshatriya workers was held on 24 April 1947 to chalk out the details of a programme. The meeting was presided over by Ravishankar Maharaj, a saintly and devout Gandhian and the foremost 'constructive' worker of Gujarat, whose influence on the Kshatriya movement has been remarkable.[9]

At this meeting of April 1947 it was decided that the Mandal should send batches of workers into the villages, each batch to be composed of 22 Kshatriya youths in traditional Kshatriya uniform.[10] The main purpose of the *padyatra* was fourfold: the enlistment of members, propagation of abstinence from drink, emphasis on education, and mobilisation of support for the removal of restriction on arms, especially the wearing of the sword.[11] The mixture of reformist and traditionalist appeals should again be noted. The burden of the effort, however, was directed to the removal of drinking habits and the conscious promotion of a civilised way of life that would bring the community out of its lowly existence and enable its members to stand as equals with others. Attempts were also made to change traditional customs and introduce reforms such as abolition of marriage dowries. The enthusiasm was kept by organising in each village that was covered a non-official militia which emphasised the martial tradition of the Kshatriya and sought to instil a sense of organisation and discipline in the Kshatriyas, an otherwise inchoate and apathetic mass. Seemingly revivalist, the idea was to unite these various caste groups by making them conscious of their common 'Kshatriya' heritage. The *Rajput Bandhu* was refashioned to become the mouthpiece of the Mandal from July 1947.

The *padyatra* was a great success. The Kshatriya leaders, some of them from highly placed families, toured from village to village, covering entire districts.[12]

The impact of this was considerable. Several drinking houses were closed down and vows of abstinence taken. People were persuaded to send their children to school, a general fund was collected and reform activities were launched. For the village masses, this was a new experience altogether.

In 1948, after Gandhi's assassination, the government introduced measures to curb 'communal' movements. The Kshatriya militia was banned. The district magistrate of Kaira ordered suspension of the programme of *padyatras*. After a time, they were allowed to be revived, but without the uniform and the sword.

Thus what had started as an educational fund soon developed into a social movement based on a subtle combination of the Gandhian technique and Kshatriya symbols. The technique of *padyatra* which had a mass appeal made the Kshatriya castes conscious of their corporate strength. It is this consciousness which led them at a later date to assert themselves in the political sphere in the form of a populous and powerful caste federation.[13]

The extent of response evoked by the *padyatras* was realised when a convention of the Mandal was held in Nadiad on 11 January 1948. About 50,000 people turned up from all parts of Gujarat. There were also some from the adjoining territory of Saurashtra who were attracted by the movement launched in Gujarat. It was proposed at this meeting to enlarge the area of operation so as to include Saurashtra and Kutch where too there was a large Kshatriya population.[14] There were already Rajput organisations in these areas; what was proposed was an integration of these into a larger organisation. It is interesting to look at this attempt at integration of a region whose economic and social structure differed widely from that of Gujarat, as it brings out the sort of conditions that promote or retard the growth of a caste federation.

In Gujarat, the *ryotwari* system of land rights, direct revenue administration under the British, and increasing fragmentation of the few *jagirdari* estates were factors that militated against concentration of landownership. Under these conditions, it was the peasant-proprietor caste of Patidars, who treated land as a basis of prosperity and power rather than as a hereditary title, that came to own the bulk of the land. The majority of the Kshatriyas, including high-caste Rajputs, were gradually turned into tenants and labourers. In Saurashtra and Kutch, on the other hand, ownership rights were vested in the princely and *girasdari* families. Here the Rajputs were the landowning class and the Patidars and other lower castes their tillers.[15] This difference in the economic structure led to a different composition of the Kshatriya community in the two regions. Common economic interests helped to narrow down the social distance between different layers of the Kshatriyas in Gujarat. One of the main purposes of the Kshatriya movement in Gujarat was to reform and upgrade the Bariyas, Thakardars and Bhils, the lower castes in the Kshatriya hierarchy.[16] In this the Rajputs themselves took the lead. Such a process of assimilation led to two important results. First, the lower castes felt upgraded and readily accepted Rajput leadership of the movement. Second, a common lack of economic and political power forced upon these various caste groups the need to depend upon numerical strength as the only effective weapon in pressing their demands. In contrast to this, the Rajputs of Saurashtra and Kutch did not recognise the claims of the lower castes such as Kolis, Kathis and Mers, to be accepted into the Kshatriya fold. And this was the direct result of the wide gap that existed between the economic conditions and political status of the Rajputs as compared to the other caste groups.

Gujarat and Saurashtra differed also in the response evoked by land reforms from the various Kshatriya communities. While the Saurashtra Rajputs opposed these measures as they impinged upon their economic power, the Rajputs in Gujarat, being cultivators, welcomed them. These divergences in the approach to social and economic reform introduced from the very beginning a discordant note in the attempt at bringing the Kshatriyas of these regions into a common organisation under Rajput leadership.

In spite of these differences, however, the effort to integrate Kshatriyas of the different regions was undertaken, motivated partly by zeal for reform and partly by discontent with the administration. In Saurashtra, a Girasdar Association composed of landowning and high-caste Rajputs was already functioning. In Kutch also, there was an organisation of high-caste Rajputs known as the Kutch Rajput Sabha. The leaders of these organisations were contacted and an informal meeting of the concerned leaders was held at Dhrol on 15 November 1947. At this meeting it was decided to make necessary changes in the constitution of the Gujarat organisation and to rename it as the Kutch–Kathiawar*–Gujarat Kshatriya Sabha. The decision was ratified at the Nadiad convention referred to above. Narendrasinh Mahida continued to be the president and three joint secretaries, one from each of the three regions, were elected. It was decided that the *Rajput Bandhu* would now be published as the mouthpiece of the new organisation.

The new organisation was beset with difficulties inherent in the situation. The divergence in social composition and economic interests discussed above got articulated in the form of conflicting attitudes to land rights and the reforms introduced by the Congress government. While the Girasdars of Saurashtra and Kutch fought bitterly against the legislation which impinged upon their economic rights, the Kshatriyas in Gujarat, being tenant-cultivators, readily took to the legislation which, among other things, bestowed ownership rights on the tenants and threatened the absentee landowners among the Patidars.

The differences on land reforms also led to divergent attitudes to the Congress. At the time of the elections to the Interim Legislative Assembly in Saurashtra held in 1948, some of the Girasdar leaders pressed the Congress to

---

* 'Kathiawar' is another name for Saurashtra.

give a balanced representation to different 'interests' in the state. When the demand was rejected, a concerted move was made by the Girasdar Association to put up candidates against the Congress. Nothing much came out of the move. The rift with the Congress widened further when the demand for retention of a portion of the land by the landlords was also rejected. The situation in Gujarat was totally different and the Kshatriyas there did not share the anti-Congress attitude of Saurashtra leaders. Foremost among the believers in the Congress was Mahida.

Mahida as president of the Kshatriya Sabha, and having access to well-placed Congress leaders, made efforts to bring about a rapprochement between the Kshatriyas and the Congress in Saurashtra. Himself a staunch supporter of the Congress, Mahida emphasised that the Congress was the only party capable of representing all sections of society. 'The structure of Congress will be broadened day by day and all different interests in society will have to be merged in it.' Moreover, being the party in power, the Congress alone could help the Kshatriyas in meeting their economic and political demands. 'We should not forget that Congress is an unparalleled institution of our nation. We also should not forget that Congress has brought us independence through great struggle. We must strengthen the Congress by accepting her ideals. This is the only way in which we can convince the people that we are not reactionaries in our thinking, but are as progressive and democratic as any Congressman.'[17]

Amidst the storm of conflict in Saurashtra, Mahida and his lieutenants in Gujarat openly advocated an alliance with the Congress. 'In the present age, even social and educational activities cannot strengthen themselves without gaining some political colour. This becomes more emphatic in times of elections. All our fellow Kshatriyas shall have to use their right of vote in the next elections. This has necessitated a rapid solution of the problem.'[18] Such an awareness of the role of political activity in strengthening social organisation was, in a sense, the result of the experience in Saurashtra where the Kshatriyas were found alienated. Mahida put forward his alliance plan in a letter addressed to all the important Congress leaders of Gujarat, the leaders of the Kshatriya movement and prominent social workers. Many welcomed the plan. The Saurashtra leaders, on the other hand, strongly opposed it. An unofficial meeting of Kshatriya leaders and workers was held at Ahmedabad in November 1949 to decide on the issue. It was resolved at this meeting that the Kshatriya Sabha should adopt the 'Sarvodaya' policy of the Congress in the political field and advise the Kshatriya population to follow the same.[19] Upon this the Saurashtra Kshatriyas demanded withdrawal from the organisation. The demand was finally conceded at the Ahmedabad convention of the Kshatriya Sabha held on 28 May 1950 and inaugurated by Morarji Desai. It was decided at the convention to split the Kutch–Kathiawar–Gujarat Kshatriya Sabha and to make the *Rajput Bandhu* the exclusive mouth-piece of the Gujarat Kshatriya Sabha.[20] Thus came to an end the short-lived experiment of a statewide association. Lacking a basic identity of interests, the ideological appeal of Mahida to support the Congress created a crisis in the organisation, and led finally to a split. In the process, of course, the Gujarat Kshatriyas moved closer to the Congress.

During this same period the work of the Kshatriya Sabha in Gujarat gained further momentum. The same convention at Ahmedabad also discussed the problem of 'forced labour' in Banaskantha, a backward district in the north of Gujarat. In this district, nearly 8000 to 9000 Rajputs had been subjected to forced labour since the beginning of the rule of the Muslim state of Palanpur. They were allowed to till some land without payment in exchange for which they were obliged to give their free services in guarding the border areas. With the passage of time this was exploited and they were virtually turned into forced labour. Now with the new consciousness of social justice that came with the Kshatriya movement, the Rajputs opposed such a system of forced labour. Upon this, the government—now the Congress government— threatened to take away the land from them. This gave rise to a protracted struggle and finally resulted in the Rajputs resorting to non-violent resistance under the banner of the Kshatriya Sabha and the leadership of Ravishankar Maharaj. They claimed that the land had been in their possession for the last 700 years. The government, on the other hand, took the position that the Nawab of Palanpur had given this land to Rajputs in the past in exchange for their free services and that accordingly they must either resume their duty or surrender the land. Morarji Desai, in his inaugural speech to the sabha's convention, referred to this problem. He reiterated the stand of the government. The convention, in the presence of Morarji Desai, resolved that 'the views expressed by Shri Morarjibhai are devoid of real facts. These units of landholding are in the possession of Rajputs since last 700 years. Their claim must be viewed with the right attitude.'[21] This resolution reflects an important priority of motives. In spite of their acceptance of the Congress ideology, the Kshatriyas were not ready to compromise in a matter which affected their vital interests. The incident also highlights the importance of conflict with the government machinery in raising the level of political awakening. Finally, it throws interesting light on the developing relationships between caste and politics. The Kshatriya community had in the past enjoyed certain privileges as a caste. With changes taking place in the social and economic organisation, these privileges were infringed at some stage. And this, in turn, led to a rallying together for the preservation of privileges and interests in a deliberate and organised manner. Ascriptive status is here turned into a symbol of mobilisation for building up an interest organisation. With this takes place a marked shift in both the nature of the caste organisation and its idiom of communication.

The short-lived attempt at building up a larger organisation for the Kshatriyas covering divergent interests not only underlined the important fact that a viable caste federation could be created only on the basis of an identity of social and economic interests but also brought to the surface pertinent problems of political articulation that the Gujarat Kshatriya Sabha was to face in the coming years. The problems were also of immediate relevance. To what extent should the sabha take an active interest in politics? And to the extent it did, how far should it identify itself with the Congress? As we shall see, both these issues were to crop up again and again giving rise to a controversy between those who emphasised political action and those who urged staying away from politics and concentrating on education and reform activities. The controversy will be highlighted in the pages that follow.

During the first general elections in 1952, specific directives were given to the Kshatriyas of Gujarat by their leaders to vote for the Congress. A few of these leaders were themselves elected on Congress nomination. Social and educational activities suffered during this period of involvement in politics. After the elections, an annual convention of the Kshatriya Sabha was held on 13 April 1952, where it was demanded that the government should classify the Kshatriyas under the category of 'backward classes', and make them eligible for the benefits that went with such a classification. The reasons urged were poverty and backwardness of the majority of the Kshatriyas.[22] The demand was rejected by the government.

In November 1952, Mahida resigned as president because of bad health and was replaced by Bhagvansinh Chhasatia, an active leader of the movement but not as highly placed as Mahida.[23] With this change, and with greater freedom from political activities, many leaders felt the necessity of reviewing the social programme of the Kshatriya Sabha initiated during the *padyatras*. The unit of operation was decentralised and each unit allotted to one batch of workers. Training camps were also organised for these workers, and Congress leaders were invited to lecture at these camps on important problems of social policy and implementation. These trained workers were to be responsible for the execution of social reform measures and educational activities initiated by the sabha.

While the sabha was engaged in defining a social programme for the Kshatriyas, the Congress party resolved at its Avadi session in 1955 that no active member of the Congress could hold simultaneous membership of any caste or communal organisation. While this created a stir among the politically inclined Kshatriyas, it confirmed those that emphasised the social programme of the sabha. In December 1955, the executive committee of the sabha considered the implications of the Congress resolution and decided that the organisation should confine itself to its social activities. In the annual convention held in May 1956, no politicians were invited, and a deliberate attempt was made to emphasise the sabha's 'non-political' character. Although prompted by the Avadi resolution, the convention also underlined the sabha's growing disillusionment with politics and especially with the Congress.

Events, however, were soon to overshadow such a mood of the Kshatriyas. The aspiration for a separate linguistic state had not materialised in Gujarat which continued to be part of the bilingual Bombay state even after most of the states were reorganised on the basis of language. A powerful agitation for a separate state of Gujarat was launched in 1956, in which all the opposition parties and a number of independent and non-political groups joined together under the banner of the 'Mahagujarat Janata Parishad'. The Congress opposed the move. For the Kshatriya Sabha, the agitation was important in that its leadership was faced with divided loyalties, one towards the Congress and the other towards their own people within the sabha who had spontaneously joined the 'Mahagujarat' upsurge. The upsurge took on the character of a mass movement based on solidarities that cut across both party and caste. As so many of the workers of the sabha joined the movement, the leadership found itself in a great dilemma.

As always happened with this extremely active organisation, a general meeting of all Kshatriya leaders was called in December 1956 to take a decision on the sabha's stand in the 1967 elections, especially in the context of the Mahagujarat issue. Most of the speakers advocated support for the demand of linguistic autonomy. This made the leaders uneasy as the Congress, whom they had considered their naturalally, stood against such a demand. It found a way out by leaving the decision to 'individual discretion'. No specific directions were given. A resolution was adopted which reflected this indecision. Apart from its indecisive character, the resolution was important in voicing the sabha's disillusionment with the Congress for not taking any interest in the development of the community. The resolution took note of 'the painful fact that the different political parties of Gujarat have taken practically no interest in the overall development of the backward Kshatriya population'. Though it refers generally to the indifference o all political parties, it is clear that it was at the Congress that the criticism was directed. Moreover, it was in this convention that Mahida for the first time openly confessed his failure to get any co-operation from the Congress. 'I cannot ask you', he said, 'to support the Congress because they have neglected you throughout these years. You are all free to decide according to your own discretion.'

On the other hand, Mahida's lasting contribution to the ideology of the Kshatriya Sabha was made in these circumstances of great strain, when he

exerted himself desperately in finding some way of reconciling his great failure
in serving the Kshatriya cause with his still-unshaken faith in the Congress.
The second general elections in 1957, fought on the issue of Mahagujarat,
divided the Kshatriyas politically. Mahida attributed these divisions to the
lack of a common political ideology for the whole community. He based his
thesis on the premise that to have an integrated approach towards social
problems, unanimity on political matters was essential.[24] With great eloquence
and incessant logic, he pressed his viewpoint on other Kshatriya leaders who,
though they were reluctant to agree that it should be the Congress ideology
that they should adopt, had no alternative to offer, and owing to the great
veneration in which they held their leader, a resolution was passed at the
convention held in April 1958 at Dakor which pledged the sabha's support for
the Congress. The sabha's constitution was amended to incorporate this
change.[25] K.K. Shah, a prominent Congress leader, attended the convention
as its chief guest and assured the gathering that their interests would be
safeguarded by the Congress. With this the sabha entered a new phase in its
development, the phase of direct participation in politics.

The Kshatriya leaders made earnest efforts to implement the Dakor
resolution. Taluka and village tours were undertaken and attempts were made
to enroll Congress members from the community. Training camps for workers
were held, and lectures on social and economic development and the ideology
of the Congress were organised. Congress policies were popularised through
the *Kshatriya Bandhu*. But the response of the Congress was poor. It took no
step whatsoever towards accommodating and recognising the sabha as it did
for other backward, tribal and Harijan organisations, nor did it even take
important Kshatriya leaders into positions in the Congress. The end, however,
came abruptly when Mahida took up the matter personally with Morarji Desai
and was told that the sabha, being a communal organisation, could not be
recognised by the Congress.

Such an outcome deeply humiliated the Kshatriya leaders and aggravated
the already growing trend of anti-Congress feeling. After this, through a rapid
succession of events, the political complexion of the sabha underwent a
complete reversal. A powerful group of Kshatriyas led by Natvarsinh Solanki,
the sabha's secretary and the organisational brain behind the Kshatriya
movement, called for a reversal of the Dakor decision. This was done at the
thirteenth convention of the Kshatriya Sabha, held at Bayad on 25 March
1961. Mahida did not attend the meeting. The convention re-amended the
sabha's constitution, deleting the portion relating to the strengthening, of the
Congress and allegiance to it.

The Bayad resolution of 1961 should not be thought of as a sudden reversal
of the Kshatriya Sabha's political positions. In fact, a careful scrutiny of the

sabha's deliberations brings out the gradual development after 1953 of a trend towards increasing unwillingness of the Kshatriyas to involve the sabha too closely in the politics of the Congress party. The Avadi resolution against communal bodies, and the indifference of Congress leaders at district and state levels to the Kshatriya leadership, contributed to this. The trend away from the Congress was accentuated during the Mahagujarat movement, and the 1957 general elections. The resolution at the Dakor convention of April 1958 to affiliate the sabha to the Congress came against the run of this developing trend and can only be explained by reference to Mahida's tremendous power over the Kshatriyas. The reversal of this decision that came at the Bayad convention, though it made explicit the alienation of the sabha from the Congress, was something to be expected. To fully grasp the change from the sabha's close association with the Congress to its final departure, one must turn to the personality factor in the development of the Kshatriya Sabha, and the shift in leadership that took place in it.

From the very inception of the Kshatriya movement, two persons, Narendrasinh Mahida and Natvarsinh Solanki, provided its leadership. Though widely differing in their approach towards practical problems of politics, a common social purpose kept these two men united in the sabha. Mahida, a Rajput of high standing, was moved by a high idealism which was the product of the simultaneous impact of western higher education and Gandhian ideology. Solanki, on the other hand, a graduate of an Indian university, had as a small talukdar to contend for status and power with the powerful Patidars of Kaira district, and had thus learnt his first lessons of politics in the field. Mahida's appeal to the masses flowed from his liberal idealism and urban orientation. His ideological flair, high social status, and his sacrifice of prosperous landlordism and a budding career in Bombay, made him an idol of the Kshatriya masses. He was deified by his followers, and his power in the Kshatriya organisation derived from his mass appeal. Solanki, on the other hand, was a hard-headed organiser and wielded power in the sabha through his command over the organisation. Mahida's link with his followers was direct and he did not need an elaborate organisation to perpetuate his following. Solanki depended almost wholly on the organisation for his strength. 'When the two worked in the same institution, it was natural that Mahida occupied the president's chair, a position which associated him with the masses and yet enabled him to keep above the mundane routine of the party organisation, while Solanki was the secretary, attending to every detail, being in constant touch with the field, and closely controlling the organisation and the men. In reality, Solanki knew the Kshatriya masses better, perfectly followed their idiom of communication, and knew what motivated them to action. But he was not their idol, which Mahida was beyond any doubt.[26]

Natvarsinh Solanki did not share the devout enthusiasm of Mahida for the Congress, still less for its ideology. If he went with the Congress up to a point, it was no more than a strategy to countercheck the power of the Patidar group. To belong to Congress gave him no sense of fulfilment as it did to Mahida. It was not an end, only a means to the strengthening of Kshatriya power. Mahida, on the contrary, was so overwhelmed by the Congress posture of righteousness that he did not hesitate to use the Kshatriya Sabha as a means of strengthening the Congress. Solanki, as soon as he discovered that there was no longer any elbow room left within the Congress, turned hostile to it. Mahida, on the other hand, strained hard to make a virtue of his disappointments, still hoping that the Congress would come to his rescue. His was a tragic plight in politics.

The root of Solanki's attitude to the Congress can be traced back to the Patidar–Kshatriya cleavage in Kaira district. Both the landowning Rajputs, and the evicted Bariya tenants suffered from the tenancy legislation, which benefited the peasant-proprietor class of Patidars. On the other hand, the Patidar leaders of the Kaira Congress organisation early realised the potentialities of a 'Kshatriya' alliance between the Rajputs; and the Bariyas under the leadership of the former. They tried to curb the power of men like Solanki and gave them no place in the Congress.

In 1952, however, the Congress faced a challenge from the 'Khedut Sangh' movement, an anti-Congress peasant organisation born out of resistance to the Land Tenancy Act. The movement was led by Bhailalbhai Patel, a dynamic and powerful person who was himself a Patidar. Architect of the rural University of Vallabh Vidyanagar in Kaira, a man of tremendous drive and power, an outstanding Patidar and a known protagonist of the late Sardar Patel, 'Bhaikaka' posed the first major threat to the Congress in Kaira. He himself stood against the Congress in the first general election. Such a powerful Patidar candidate could only be countered by putting up someone like Solanki who commanded the votes of the numerous Kshatriya population. Though the Patidars of Kaira were reluctant, Morarji Desai invited him and gave him the responsibility of defeating Patel. At the same time, as if being given a bargain, he was also given the responsibility of winning another seat in a neighbouring constituency which had a large Kshatriya vote for a Muslim candidate of the Congress. The task appeared difficult. Solanki, however, took up the challenge and won both the seats for the Congress.

On joining the Congress, Solanki found the Patidar leadership of the party cold-shouldering the question of sharing power with the Kshatriyas. He decided not to suffer this. Thus in 1957, when he was not consulted in the nomination of the Congress candidates in Kshatriya-dominated constituencies, he protested strongly, and in public. His position was that if the Kshatriyas were not given the recognition òf a special interest within the party, there was no sense in continuing with the Congress. Other leaders of the sabha agreed with him.[27] The calculated indifference shown to the Kshatriyas by the leaders of the Congress organisation gave an edge to the unpopularity of the party caused by the Mahagujarat issue. Even when Mahida's appeal for affiliation to the Congress was accepted, it was done in the teeth of severe opposition and was considered by many as an imposition from above. In one of our interviews with him, Mahida admitted that he had to exert his personal influence in getting the resolution passed.

The resolution stands as a testimony to the respect and affection in which the Kshatriya masses held Mahida. Soon afterwards, however, his failure to get recognition for the sabha from the Congress shook their faith in him. It was the defeat of a leader who had failed to lead the masses towards the promised goal. It was exactly at this moment that Solanki took the initiative in leading the Kshatriyas out of the Congress, in the process also weaning them away from the influence of Mahida. The prevailing anti-Congress feeling created an atmosphere in which Solanki's action found the approval of the rank and file. It facilitated the shift in leadership.

The fact was that Mahida's indifference to problems of organisation left him a mass leader without a base. At a time when the Congress let him down so completely, his sudden dissociation from the sabha rendered him powerless. It was now his turn to follow the masses. For a time he stood away but was soon forced to return to the Kshatriya fold. The lesson is important. Mahida realised that his importance in the political field derived from his command over the Kshatriya masses. His return was not dictated by any caste considerations but followed inevitably from the nature of his position in politics. At the same time, it is important to realise the personality dimension of this relationship. Mahida's influence on the masses was out of the ordinary. He had been the unifying symbol of the sabha for such a long time that his departure created a void in its organisation. His self-imposed isolation from the sabha appeared unnatural to the Kshatriyas who had made him their idol for so long: the concern to bring him back in their fold was expressed again and again. Solanki and other leaders sensed this feeling; they also realised that for mass appeal there was no substitute for Mahida. He was subjected to intense pressure, including pressure from very close kinsmen of his, before which he at last gave way. He contested against the Congress during the 1962 general elections and was elected with great public backing. For Mahida, however, it was both a victory and a defeat. The event broke his confidence in politics and in himself, and he found solace only by returning to the Congress shortly after the elections.

With all their differences, both Mahida and Solanki shared one basic approach. They were both proponents of a political solution of the Kshatriya problem, of course with the vital difference that whereas for Mahida ideology constituted the core of politics, for Solanki politics was a serious and sustained struggle for power. There were others in the Kshatriya fold who wanted the sabha to keep aloof from politics. These were, however, largely ineffective. Although lip-service was paid to their sentiments, and although Solanki sought their support in his conflict against Mahida, for all practical purposes the Kshatriya Sabha, at first under Mahida and later under Solanki, established itself as a political organisation of a larger and hitherto-submerged section of Gujarat society.

The rapprochement with Mahida was followed by another remarkable rapprochement in the politics of Gujarat (and of Kaira in particular). Old Bhailalbhai Patel, doyen among the anti-Congress forces in Gujarat and one-time rival of Natvarsinh Solanki, was the key figure in the newly formed Gujarat Swatantra Party. He tried to persuade Solanki to put up a common front against the Congress. His argument was based on the numerical strength that could be mobilised if the Kshatriya and Patidar communities in Gujarat joined hands. A Patidar–Kshatriya alliance would indeed provide a formidable opposition to the Congress. Such a prospect attracted the Kshatriyas whose dominant motive at the time was to demonstrate their strength to the Congress. Under the impact of politics, the traditional Kshatriya hostility to Patidars turned into hostility to Congress Patidars only. As evidently the Congress was losing its grip on sections of the Patidar community, it was natural for the Kshatriyas to join hands with the latter. It was this alliance that became the basis of the Swatantra Party in Gujarat. In turn, the alliance was also to create problems for the new party, as we shall presently see.

The choice of the Swatantra Party as compared to any other opposition party or group in Gujarat—with many of whom the Kshatriya leaders were in negotiation—was conditioned by two other considerations. First, being in its formative period, the Swatantra. Party provided an opportunity for the Kshatriyas to capture important positions in the party organisation. The sabha's bitter experience with the Congress had made this a prime consideration for its leaders. Second, the new party provided financial and other resources necessary to build the organisation and to mobilise the large mass of Kshatriyas spread over a large area. The antagonism to the Congress had made the Kshatriyas more conscious than ever before of the need to build an organised mass base through politics. The Swatantra Party offer provided them with the wherewithal to launch such an offensive.

There followed a period of intense negotiations with the Swatantra Party. The Kshatriyas squarely put forward their demands. These demands were accepted, although not without opposition from the orthodox Patidar elements in the party. Accordingly, a reshuffle of the party executive was made to accommodate the Kshatriya leaders in the organisation. A similar accommodation was made in the allocation of party nominations for the 1962 elections. Natvarsinh Solanki was given the charge of organising elections on behalf of the Swatantra Party in the whole of Gujarat. Kshatriya candidates were also financed and given vehicles to organise their election campaigns.

Such a sudden reshuffle of power created a sense of dissatisfaction amongst the established group in the party. Most of them were Patidars. The feeling of newcomers taking away power from old workers revived the historical Patidar–Kshatriya antagonism. Although the top leadership fought hard to counter this, there is no doubt that the Swatantra Party started its career in Gujarat divided into two factions based on caste. It was a case of politics bringing together traditionally rival castes into an alliance based on a new identity of interest, and then once the alliance took the form of a single organisation, the traditional groups reasserting themselves. These factions substantially influenced the outcome of the elections. Kshatriyas being the most numerous caste and Kshatriya workers aspiring for power everywhere, they demanded seats in each district, which it was not possible to give without alienating substantial local leaders from the Patidar community.[28] Thus the formula of a Kshatriya–Patidar alliance against the Congress could not work at all places. Where it worked, it brought handsome rewards to the Swatantra Party whose impressive success in some parts of the state (for example, Kaira) in its very first and hurriedly organised attempt owed much to this alliance. Elsewhere, however, the very attempt at forcing an alliance between the two castes turned the party into a divided house (for example, Ahmedabad and Mehsana districts).

The Congress too had not completely lost its hold over the Kshatriya voters. In quite a few places it also managed to put up Kshatriya candidates, some of them with a good standing in the locality. The outstanding example, of course, was the Prince of Baroda who not only bagged practically all the seats in Baroda district for the Congress but also obliged the Kshatriya Sabha, to whose activities he had generously donated in the past, to lie low as far as Baroda. was concerned. Thus political divisions within the Kshatriyas helped the Congress. So did political divisions within the Patidars. To cite again an example from Baroda district, the Congress there has been controlled for a long time by a Patidar group. But there also emerged in 1962 in the city of Baroda a powerful group of Patidar industrialists against the Congress. This group was with the Swatantra Party. The Patidar leaders of the District Congress, however, used the influence of the Prince of Baroda on the Kshatriya Sabha which did not allow the rival Patidar group to gain control of the District Swatantra Party and secure nominations from it. In this the Patidar leaders at the state level were also made to concur through the persuasion of Solanki and Mahida. Here is a truly subtle case of the interaction between different levels and forms of political power. Both caste groups and political groups were divided, resulting in caste factions within parties and party factions within castes,[29] providing the cross-cutting nature of loyalties which politicisation brings in its wake. The Swatantra Party in Gujarat, even before it had consolidated its power, became a base for such a process of factional interactions which characterises Indian politics everywhere.

We have examined the impact of the Kshatriya Sabha's alliance on the internal structure of the Swatantra Party. What was the effect of the sabha's alliance with the Swatantra, Party on its own organisational structure and leadership?

The new relationship with the Swatantra Party crystallised the already increasing politicisation of the sabha's activities. As we have seen, even before 1962 there had taken place in this respect a noticeable shift in the character of the sabha. Although the social programme of the sabha and the political involvement of its leaders always exerted competing pulls on its organisation, the emphasis on the political side kept increasing, with Mahida driving the organisation towards the Congress. Even when frustration with the Congress began to mount, Mahida's remedy was not less but more involvement in politics: he advocated complete identification with the Congress. Indeed to some extent Mahida was able to drive the Kshatriyas along his way precisely because of the absence of a political alternative to the course proposed by him. As for those of his critics who emphasised the sabha's social function at the expense of politics, he silenced them by demonstrating that an apolitical sabha would only become the scene of factionalism as happened under the Mahagujarat movement.

Despite Mahida's naive faith in the unifying role of politics, there is also no doubt that a compartmentalisation of the sabha's work into the social and political was also misleading. The two were closely interrelated. It was the awareness of strength that came out of the movement for social integration and reform that had made the leadership conscious of its power. In turn, political power opened up new vistas for the Kshatriya masses and gave them a sense of unity and strength that they had never before possessed. With this there also took place a shift from voluntary effort to demands for state protection and political placement as-a means to the welfare of the community. Finally, with the departure from the Congress, the alliance with the Swatantra Party, and the acceptance-by the leading Kshatriya leaders of formal positions in the Swatantra organisation. have crystallised the sabha's political identity more clearly than at any time in the past. To that extent, the alliance has hastened the process of politicisation.

With the direct entry of the Kshatriyas into politics, the sabha has also begun to extend its area of operation. In Gujarat itself the mobilisation of Kshatriyas under a common leadership has been spreading to districts which could not hitherto be properly attended to. In the process, new leaders with considerable regional hold have been brought into the organisation in formal positions. Of more interest is the change that is coming in Saurashtra where earlier the sabha had completely failed, first on account of different social conditions and the land issue, and second because of the pro-Congress leanings of the leadership in Gujarat. Here two developments are important. In Saurashtra during the 1962 elections, Rajput leaders from former princely families contested against the Congress and won in a few places.[30] In order to win, however, they had to mobilise support from the lower strata of the population. The princes and *girasdars* in Saurashtra have since realised the advantage of bringing together the lower castes such as Kathis, Kolis and Mers into a single organisation of 'Kshatriyas'. They have seen that the basis of power has shifted from hereditary rights in land to organisation of political support. A gradual integration may thus follow on the lines of Gujarat, although it will take time and will perhaps come through a more directly political process of mobilisation.

With these developments in Saurashtra, efforts at a statewide integration of the Kshatriyas have been revived. A committee consisting of Kshatriya representatives from Gujarat, Saurashtra and Kutch has been formed. It is important to note that the Prince of Jasdan, a representative of the Kathis, a low-placed Kshatriya caste in Saurashtra, is a prominent member of this committee: politics has again worked as a cementing force. The result has been rewarding. For it was the Jasdan prince who was one of the important factors in defeating the Congress in the 1963 parliamentary by election in Rajkot where the Swatantra leader M.R. Masani was elected. Rajkot has been a stronghold of the Congress for the last thirty years and had returned U.N. Dhebar, former Congress president, with a large majority in the 1962 elections only a year earlier.[31]

The other development has been on the side of the Gujarat Kshatriya leadership which has also turned hostile to the Congress. This has narrowed the differences amongst Kshatriya leaders and has opened the way to expansion of the Kshatriya base of the Swatantra. Party in the state as a whole. During the 1962 general elections, the Swatantra Party could not gain substantially in Saurashtra. There was a general lack of organisation and mobilisation of significant leaders from relevant social strata—strata that have been neglected or taken for granted by the Congress. This is precisely what the Swatantra Party accomplished in Gujarat and failed to accomplish in Saurashtra in 1962. But the Rajkot by election has shown the way to such mobilisation in Saurashtra too. The Swatantra. Party has made overtures to the Rajputs, Kathis, Mers and other Kshatriyas in Saurashtra, and the latter have responded favourably.[32] All these trends point to the possibility of some form of integration of the

Kshatriya organisation in the three regions that could be effected by a political party. What could not be achieved socially may be achieved politically.

It has been argued that 'the appeal of India's relatively weakly articulated voluntary associations is confined to the urban educated who are more or less attuned to the modern political culture. Caste, however, provides channels of communication and bases of leadership and organisation which enable those still submerged in the traditional society and culture to transcend the technical political illiteracy which would otherwise handicap their ability to participate in democratic politics.'[33] An examination of the history of the Kshatriya Sabha bears out this general contention but leads to a different emphasis. It is found that caste provides not only channels of communication and leadership support for 'submerged' sections of society but also an important basis for joint and 'voluntary' action in the organisation of which the urban-educated take the initiative. The urban-rural dichotomy is in fact misleading. Caste federations, for instance, are conscious creations of the urban-educated political elite seeking institutional bases and numerical strength for their support. The absence of highly developed interest organisations of the western form is being filled in India by the federal form that caste is taking, thus abridging hierarchical rigidities and adapting the indigenous social structure to the exigencies of democratic political institutions. Caste is thus found not only performing *functions* performed by voluntary organisations elsewhere, but also assuming forms that are comparable to the latter.

The difference in India between western-type voluntary organisations and castes underlines the crucial role of the latter. Here voluntary organisations as commonly understood have to a considerable extent been fed on external stimuli, either sponsored or triggered by the government. They do not have the character of self-governing associations found in some other countries. In India, the castes display an autonomy of their own with a distinctive way of life and corporate strength found in voluntary associations in the early development of western societies.[34] They play an important role in absorbing substantial changes in the balance of social power and adapting a traditional culture to modern impacts and are a vital factor in avoiding the traumas of an uprooted 'mass' society.

On the other hand, caste besides being a system of segmental differentiations ('jatis'), is also a system defining status, possesses a secular character, and is endowed with a class symbolism in the form of 'varnas'. With these latter aspects gaining in function and importance, caste is shedding some of its old-time character and is acquiring a new emphasis and orientation. While still retaining a good part of the traditional modes of integration, it has entered a phase of competitive adjustment in the allocation and reallocation of functions and power among various social groups. The institution of caste association and caste federation are the media through which such an adaptation in roles is taking place.

The important thing is the motivation that lies behind such a process of group assertion. Here caste consciousness no doubt plays an important part in mobilising and consolidating group positions. But the motivation behind it indicates an important shift in emphasis from the preservation of caste traditions and customs to their transformation through political power. It is essentially a secular motivation in which mobilisation of group support follows rather than precedes individual competition for power. Caste always had a political aspect to it but now the political aspect is gaining in emphasis more than ever before, especially in regard to individualised rather than group orientations to power. The network of kin and caste relationships is by stages drawn into personal networks of influence and power, and in the process greatly politicised. To this extent, caste identification and caste consciousness become means in the power struggle, the latter also influencing the normative orientation of such consciousness. Even social motivations such as the anxiety of the groups higher up to preserve their positions, and of the lower groups to rise in status through identification with some higher groups become fused with political considerations. With individuals in the upper castes keen on building numerical strength and those in lower castes agreeing to give such support provided the former comply with the new rules of the game, the status overtones in the original motivations become blurred. In the process, intergroup orientations undergo a radical change. Although the lower castes still grant the privilege of one or more upper castes to govern and rule, such deference is increasingly conditioned by norms of accountability and notions of interest and right.

Leadership struggles within either the same caste or caste federation, or between castes, tend to follow from political differences and the competition for power. The new divisions very often take the line of horizontal and regional divisions and cut across vertical divisions. The disparities (social and economic) of the latter are now countered by disparities (political) of the former in which the low-placed caste groups gain an advantage.[35] The change involved is towards cross-cutting interactions and identities in the communication between society and politics. It is the essence of secularisation in a caste society.

It is impossible to say whether politics divides or unites castes, for it appears to do both. The political technique consists of articulating existing and potential divisions, fostering new alignments and loyalties, and giving rise to a structure of interests and identifications based on its own standards. If it appears to bring certain proximate strata together, it is only part of a more organised process of division and confrontation in the context of a new awareness of interests and loyalties. In this process some of die traditional loyalties and identities may be allowed to persist, be reinforced, or simply disintegrate, depending upon how functional or functionless they have become to the political society.

On the whole, however, the following can be said. A strong caste solidarity is conducive to political strength and power, but the possession of power tends to weaken the solidarity by creating internal competition. Such competition may be mitigated in an organisation with a strong authoritarian structure and orientation (such as was the case with the Kshatriya Sabha until 1958), but participation in democratic processes and spread of egalitarian values undermines such authoritarianism, gives rise to competition, and leads to new alignments that cut across solidarities and commitments which initially brought power.

The usual dichotomy between caste and politics is misleading and what is called for is a more systematic examination of the changing form that a caste society assumes under the impact of new and dynamic forces of change. One such force comes from the diffusion of new cultural values as expressed in the sanskritisation–westernisation syndrome. Another comes from technological impact and takes the form of economic individualism and territorial expansion.[36] Both these impacts are further conditioned by the operation of a new scheme of allocating influence and power in society. Politicisation of power relationships has thus brought about a striking shift in the pre-occupation of a caste society already under the impact of social and economic transformation. The shift consists in activising the secular and mobilisation aspects of caste at the expense of other aspects, and making secularisation the dominant theme in the ordering of caste relationships. The phenomenon of caste federation discussed in this essay is one form that such a shift in orientation takes.[37] A highly diffuse and plural society is here found to come to terms with the centralising tendencies of a modern polity. By inducing diverse social strata to enter into larger identifications and by providing to political leaders significant communication channels and a relatively stable loyalty structure, such a reorientation of the caste system fills an important place in the emerging infrastructure of modern India.

Part III

Caste and Political Processes

Introduction

This section presents the role of caste in political processes at the state level. There are different kinds of caste alliances in India's states. For want of space, we take three states in different parts of the country and focus on different aspects of the caste-politics relationship. These states are Karnataka, Gujarat and Bihar. (Frankel and Rao's multi-volume *Dominance and State Power in Modern India: Decline of a Social Order* [1989] seeks to understand the nature of the caste and politics relationship in several more states.) The fourth essay in this part examines electoral behaviour among the Scheduled Castes, that is, Dalits, using all-India data.

James Manor analyses the pragmatic and progressive politics of Devraj Urs in Karnataka's politics. Urs was chief minister for nearly seven years, between 1973 and 1980, during which period he built a broad alliance of deprived groups. He broke the dominance of the landowning strata of the Lingayats and Vokkaligas by enacting and implementing land reforms. He also carried out certain welfare programmes relating to education and employment which assisted certain backward castes and minorities.

Sanjay Kumar examines the new phase of Bihar politics which began in the 1990s. The process of realignment of social forces began in Bihar in the 1970s, prompted by the aspirations of middle castes for a share in political office. This process was most evident in the first half of 1990. The changing social composition of political representation today is a clear indicator that these caste groups have come to play a major role in state politics.

Gujarat is one of the strongholds of Hindutva politics. The BJP captured power there in the 1998 elections. Ghanshyam Shah analyses how Hindutva politics—the BJP, the Sangh Parivar, and other religious organisations and leaders—has mobilised various backward and Dalit castes against the 'others', that is, Muslims, and won elections.

Pushpendra analyses the voting behaviour of Dalits. He argues that they assert their political strength through elections. They change parties, or form their own political parties to find their political space. At the same time, there was been an erosion of their confidence in political parties.

11

Pragmatic Progressives in Regional Politics: The Case of Devraj Urs *

JAMES MANOR

I

Can the liberal parliamentary model deliver social and economic justice by humane political means in the non-western and less developed countries? The case of India is central to any discussion of this question because of its size and its use of that model, at least until the end of the 1970s; and if we try to identify the most promising development to flow from this model at the regional level up to the end of the 1970s, where do we look?

Let us first be rather arbitrary and eliminate from consideration the various communist and Left Front governments that have existed in Kerala and West Bengal. The achievements of the better of these governments, particularly the present regime in West Bengal, appear easily to exceed those of non-communist regional governments.[1] But we exclude them for two reasons. First, in terms of cultural, social and economic history, Kerala and West Bengal seem to stand at one remove from the rest of India, from what we might call mainstream India. The left parties' lack of success at penetrating other regions to any substantial degree bears witness to this. Second, since the commitment of these parties to the liberal parliamentary model is open to serious doubt, it hardly seems fair to attribute to that model the achievements of groups who are so deeply sceptical of it.

The most promising non-communist regional experiment to develop in this period seems (to this writer at least) to be that of D. Devraj Urs in Karnataka which ran for roughly seven and a half years until his resignation as chief

* *Economic and Political Weekly*, 15 (5–7), Annual Number, 1980, pp. 201–13.

minister in the first week of January 1980. In assessing the historical importance of the Urs experiment we must arrive, as far as possible, at conclusions on several key issues. We need to know whether he has proved that it is possible to break the control of dominant landed groups over regional politics. We need to know' how successful his various programmes for reform have been in politicising the weaker sections of society at whom they were aimed. We need to know how much these programmes have given poor people new economic and political resources, so that they may begin to fend for themselves and the programmes may begin to take on a life of their own, even in the absence of a government to promote them. We need to know how successful Urs has been at generating broad popular support for his experiment and, specifically, how well he has done at building bridges between less prosperous caste Hindus and two other groups from whom they are often divided—Muslims and Scheduled Castes (Scheduled Tribes being a very small group in Karnataka). We also need to know whether any of Urs's programmes is likely in the long run to prove counterproductive and, if so, whether the experiment as a whole can bear the strain.

Three other issues, which are raised by Urs's going but which can only be settled on the basis of evidence from several different regions of India, need to be borne in mind. First, to what extent must regional governments that expect to survive re-election campaigns include at least a significant proportion of the weaker sections of society within their circle of allies receiving spoils—substantive spoils at that, not just tokenism? Second, does Devraj Urs, a patently self-interested and pragmatic man, signify not only that it is possible for a chief minister to become something of a progressive in his own interest, but that it is becoming necessary for pragmatists to turn progressive? And finally, what parallels are there between the Urs phenomenon and recent developments in other regions? Is he the wave of the future in mainstream India or simply an accident—an eccentric product of circumstance, of his own considerable talents and of the peculiarly favourable social, economic and political conditions in Karnataka?

II

One potential misunderstanding needs to be disposed of straightaway. The result of the 1980 Lok Sabha poll did not represent a negative popular verdict on the Urs regime. This must sound odd since the Urs Congress did not just lose the election in Karnataka, it was buried. The Congress (I) won 27 of the 28 seats (losing the last narrowly to Janata), 23 of which were won by an absolute majority. The Urs Congress came third, behind Janata, in 18 seats and nowhere was it close to victory. Nevertheless, this result should be read as a perverse endorsement of Urs's achievements. Voters believed that Indira

Gandhi was the source of the post-1972 reforms and that Urs was merely her instrument. Urs himself had helped to create this impression, mainly because such slavish loyalty to Indira Gandhi was necessary to avoid the kind of irrational intrusions from the high command which had wrecked promising leaders and programmes in other states. The truth of the matter, however, is that Urs was principally responsible for the changes in Karnataka and—especially after 1974—he had accomplished these things not because of Indira Gandhi but in spite of her. He had also largely protected Karnataka from the distasteful aspects of the Emergency despite great pressure from the Sanjay caucus.[2]

The Lok Sabha result in Karnataka was thus a case of mistaken identity. The break between Urs and Indira Gandhi occurred in June 1979. The main cause of this, according to extremely reliable neutral observers, was the intense pressure that was being brought upon Urs by Sanjay Gandhi. When the break came, Urs believed that he had at least two years before the next election to establish in the voters' minds an identity distinct from that of Indira Gandhi. At the time, this was a reasonable assumption. But within a few weeks, the bizarre machinations of politicians in New Delhi had plunged the country into a parliamentary election. Urs had too little time to carve out a separate identity for himself, hampered as he was by illness and the need to spend time outside the state. Voters generally had one of two reactions. Most were confused, not fully grasping that a split between Urs and Indira Gandhi had occurred; accounts have been obtained of thirty-eight occasions on which Urs's election rallies closed with cheers for both him and Indira Gandhi. The second reaction was anger at Urs for his bad grace in attacking a woman and a person whom he had recently lauded. Even many Congress (I) workers in the state concede that Urs's record won Indira Gandhi the election. She polled many votes from those who opposed Urs, but her majorities were predominantly based upon the coalition of interests which Urs had constructed. One of the main aims behind Urs's unforced resignation as chief minister when the election trends became clear was to dramatise to voters that he and Indira Gandhi were now in opposite camps.[3] The widespread reports of shock among Karnataka villagers that their votes for Indira Gandhi and the hand symbol had caused Urs to resign lend credence to the view that most votes were not cast against Urs.

There can be no doubt that Urs has demonstrated that it is possible to break the control of dominant landed groups over state-level politics in Karnataka. A detailed account of this has already appeared in I these pages.[4] Put briefly, Urs became chief minister in 1972 after a quarter century of Lingayat–Vokkaliga ascendancy in state politics. He was from a tiny jati that had no link to either of these groups. So in the interest of his own survival, he had to mobilise support among the less powerful sections of society who formed well over 60 per cent of the state's population. Both his selection and his survival during his early months in office owed much to the support of Indira Gandhi. But before long Urs had developed a broad range of reform and social welfare programmes which—together with his extraordinary talent as a political operator—had won him broad support not only among the groups who had suffered the dominance of Lingayats and Vokkaligas, but also among poorer elements within those two groups. His programmes hastened the erosion of vote-banks which was already occurring as a result of socio-economic change and growing political awareness.[5] Urs's new alliance of the weaker sections of society provided a firm base for election victories in 1977, 1978 and, ironically, in 1980.

LAND REFORM

Let us begin by considering the most central of the Urs programmes, land reform. In 1955, when Daniel Thorner delivered what have become five classic lectures on agrarian India, he rightly included Mysore among the 'areas of least change' since independence. Most of the other areas which came together the following year to form the composite state of Mysore (now Karnataka) witnessed 'some perceptible change'. But neither the anticipation nor the enforcement of land reform laws, nor any other factor had altered to any significant extent the old agrarian structure.[6] In old Mysore, the inertia which prevailed was partly explained by the low incidence of gross inequalities in the distribution of land; the state had one of the highest proportions of owner-cultivators and lowest incidences of landlessness in the subcontinent. More important, however, was the pre-eminence enjoyed in state politics by representatives of the two dominant landowning groups, the Vokkaligas and the Lingayats.

In 1961, the legislature of the enlarged state of Mysore (now Karnataka) passed a new Land Reforms Act. It created a common framework for the whole state, the constituent parts of which had previously been under five separate administrative authorities with rather varied land laws. The driving force behind the act (which came into effect in 1965) was the revenue minister Kadidal Manjappa (a Vokkaliga), an idealist who had vivid memories from his youth of sufferings experienced by land-poor and landless relatives and neighbours. On paper, the act banned leases (with minor, insignificant exceptions) and gave tenants considerable security against takeovers by landowners of the plots which they worked. It fixed a ceiling on holdings—with the excess to be distributed among the poor—banned the acquisition of land by anyone except cultivators and agricultural labourers, unless a buyer planned to take up cultivation.

It was, however, a failure. Exemptions for co-operatives, sugar mills, joint farming societies and the like created loopholes which allowed many to escape the net of land ceilings which in any case were set rather high. The claims of tenants had to be dealt with by tribunals whose procedures were cumbersome and easily circumvented and, after 1968, by officials who were overburdened with other work and intimidated by politicians representing vested interests. Certain provisions of the new law were used by landlords to resume control of lands from tenants in ways and to a degree unintended by the framers of the act. There was also a failure of political will by politicians at the state level—excluding Manjappa and a few others—who depended on vote-banks of landed groups.[7]

Under Devraj Urs, a new and substantially different Land Reforms Act was passed in 1973 and came into force on 1 March 1974. Under the act, the only persons eligible to hold land are those engaged in personal cultivation, with the sole exception of soldiers and sailors who are a tiny minority in Karnataka. Even widows, minors and disabled persons are barred from leasing and Sharecropping is similarly abolished. The use of hired labour remains legal, but only through payment of wages (in cash or kind) and not in a share of the crop. Violators of the ban on the leasing of land are punished severely with, among other things, loss of the land to the government. Before 1974, landlords had the right—subject to certain restrictions—to resume control of tenanted land. The new act forbids this. Where the old law merely strengthened the tenants' right to occupy the land that they worked, the 1974 act gives the government ownership of all tenanted lands. The government is then to confer ownership of these lands to the tenants who work them.[8]

Tenants obtain land by making application to land tribunals, of which there are now 193 across the state, with at least one per taluk, varying according to the volume of applications. (There are 176 taluks.) Tribunals consist of an official as chairman and four non-officials including by law at least one member of the Scheduled Castes or Scheduled Tribes and usually a member of the legislative assembly. The tribunals are the pivotal element in the whole land reform process since their actions are not subject to prior approval by a higher authority or to subsequent appeal. Urs put his revenue minister, B. Basavalingappa—himself a Scheduled Caste man—in charge of the composition of the tribunals. He packed them with persons who supported both the Urs government and the land reform programme. In 1975, tribunals were further armed with special powers to vest land with tenants while cases awaited their attention, without prejudice to final decisions. The act also gives an agricultural labourer living in a house on land not belonging to him the right to own the house and 1/20 of an acre of land surrounding it. In theory, he can obtain this through application to the tribunal.

The government is committed to paying the landlord at a moderate level for lands taken from him by a tribunal. All former tenants who become owners are required to pay the government twenty times the annual income in the case of dry lands or fifteen times the annual income in the case of irrigated lands. But payments are spread over a period of twenty years at low interest after a down payment of Rs 2000, for which bank finance can be obtained.[9]

The 1974 act also contains a marginal change in land ceiling rules. There is controversy over whether in practice this increases or decreases ceilings, but in either case the change is slight. Procedures for the declaration of ceilings have been simplified and punishments for refusal enhanced in order to make ceiling regulations easier to implement. Surplus lands gained from the imposition of ceilings are, it is said, intended for distribution among the landless, with 50 per cent being reserved for the Scheduled Castes and Scheduled Tribes. Plantation lands are exempted because of their importance to the state economy.[10]

How well has the 1974 act worked? The preceding discussion may have suggested that tenancies and not landlessness were the main target. Let us then first assess its impact upon tenancies. At the end of November 1979, 798,582 applications had been received from people claiming to be tenants who qualified for ownership of the lands they worked. Of these applications, 530,441 had been dealt with by land tribunals, 319,909 or 60.3 per cent of these cases had been decided in favour of tenants, with 1,249,174 acres being thus distributed. When we consider that the 1971 census stated that there were only 397,042 tenanted holdings in Karnataka, totalling 2,063,654 acres, these figures appear impressive.[11]

This is particularly true when we note that tribunals have processed only 66.4 per cent of the applications that have reached them. Indeed, if things continue at this rate, the tenancies awarded will easily exceed the total of tenancies in the census. There are at least three explanations for this, all of which are probably partly true. First, the census may have underestimated the number of tenancies (which may also have grown since 1971). Tribunals, which in a clear majority of cases are reliably reported to be pro-tenant, are in some cases awarding lands which are not true tenancies to people falsely claiming to be tenants, to the chagrin of landlords. And finally, tribunals are awarding tenancies to false claimants who have been set up by landlords to help them bypass the ceiling law. It is impossible to determine on present evidence the relative importance of these explanations.

At first glance, the average size of tenancies awarded in different districts suggests that the act has been implemented rather unevenly. In the northern districts of Bijapur, Bidar and Gulbarga, the average sizes of awards to tenants are respectively 11.3, 10.9 and 10.3 acres. This is a far cry from Uttar Kannada, Mandya and Hassan where the average awards are 1.8, 1.8 and 1.5 acres respectively. But as Table 11.1 indicates, these figures are reasonably consistent with the average size of tenancy per district.[12]

Table 11.1: Size of Tenancy in Karnataka

District	Average tenancy	Average award
Bijapur	12.1	11.3
Gulbarga	12.1	10.3
Bidar	9.4	10.9
Raichur	9.4	8.9
Dharwad	8.2	7.5
Bellary	7.9	5.5
Chitradurga	6.4	6.7
Belgaum	5.9	5.4
Kodagu	4.0	3.3
Tumkur	3.7	2.5
Shimoga	3.5	3.5
Chikmagalur	3.2	2.8
Dakshina Kannada	3.0	2.3
Bangalore	2.7	1.9
Mysore	2.5	1.9
Uttar Kannada	2.2	1.8
Mandya	2.2	1.8
Hassan	2.2	1.5
All districts	**5.19**	**4.75**

Not surprisingly, the act has had its most profound impact in the two coastal districts of Dakshina Kannada and Uttar Kannada which together account for over one-third of the applications in the entire state[13] (Table 11.2). Indeed, the incidence of tenancies outside these two districts is so low that official documents concede that 'the impact of land reform through tenancy abolition was of substantial significance in these two districts mainly'.[14] One corroboration of this is the absence of any interruption in growth in the agrarian sector during the land reform years.

The large number of cases decided in favour of tenants is impressive when set alongside the number of tenants in the state. But we should also take note of reports from the field which indicate that in a very small number of areas, the act is not penetrating, in others relatives or allies of landlords are sometimes wrongly gaining land, weak tenants without links to powerful people are failing to gain land due to them (although there is no evidence of evictions on a massive scale), and tenants receiving lands sometimes remain under the control of landlords because of a continuing imbalance of resources. Many land

Table 11.2: Land Tribunals in Karnataka

District	Applications	Decisions favouring tenants (%)	Land under tenancy (%)
Dakshina Kannada	173,241	84.0	54.4
Uttar Kannada	95,697	83.6	68.2
Belgaum	69,512	73.5	15.9
Gulbarga	61,370	14.4	10.6
Dharwad	61,116	64.3	18.2
Shimoga	59,345	56.9	21.5
Bangalore	46,142	41.2	5.1
Bijapur	41,037	62.9	9.8
Mysore	35,741	57.3	3.6
Hassan	25,312	46.6	3.5
Kolar	24,393	49.0	6.2
Raichur	21,642	19.3	3.7
Chikmagalur	18,993	58.8	8.2
Bellary	18,974	31.0	5.9
Mandya	14,440	54.0	2.0
Tumkur	14,129	33.2	1.7
Chitradurga	7733	35.3	1.5
Bidar	6052	26.4	2.8
Kodagu	3773	29.0	1.4
Total	**798,582**	**60.3**	**11.2**

tribunals (estimates range from 25 per cent to 35 per cent) are corrupt. Their decisions, especially in coastal districts, are often greeted with violent resistance which sometimes succeeds.[15] But having said all of this, nearly all sources indicate that very substantial gains have been made in the assault on tenancy.

What has been the impact of the act upon the problem of landlessness? Earlier we stated that the incidence of landlessness in old princely Mysore, roughly the southern half of Karnataka, was comparatively low. But in the two northern districts of old Mysore (Shimoga and Chitradurga) and further north in the inland districts of Bombay, Hyderabad and Karnataka, the problem is quite serious. in these districts, an average of 49 per cent of the active population in agriculture were landless labourers in 1971. In Dakshina Kannada district, on the coast the figure was 45.8 per cent and in the state as a whole, it was 40 per cent. The state had 2,717,537 landless agricultural labourers in 1971.[16]

The land reforms have had little impact on this problem. By the end of November 1979, only 37,812 acres of surplus land had been distributed among 7127 landless people which is less than 0.3 per cent of the landless population.[17] Only 1509 applications have been filed by landless agricultural labourers for ownership of houses they occupy on others' lands, and of these a mere forty-seven have been processed by land tribunals—as opposed to over half a million tenants' petitions processed.[18] In aiding the landless, the Land Reforms Act is an abject failure.

High officials in Karnataka who were involved in the creation of the act have plainly stated that it was never intended to aid the landless.[19] Both they and Urs recognised that the act was inadequate, that it could only be a first step in a longer and more radical process. But they believed that it was necessary to end tenancies first—a step which they rightly claim is in important respects an advance over the West Bengal legislation involving 'bargas'—to consolidate the government's base before proceeding to a marked lowering of ceilings and an assault on landlessness.

If we translate this into political terms, it gains considerable credence. Who would be most threatened if a vigorous assault were made upon landlessness? The answer is: the landowning, cultivating sections of the Lingayats in the northern districts of the state where landlessness; is most pronounced.[20] It is at this point that the problem of land reform becomes entangled with another important policy of the Urs years—that of preferment for the 'backward classes' In education and government employment and promotion. The people who lost (and stand to lose) by far the most from this policy of preferment are the Lingayats. (The Vokkaligas, the other group formerly dominant in state politics, are included in the list of 'backward classes', partly because they are less educationally advanced than Lingayats and partly because it would be politically risky to alienate them thoroughly.) But to say merely that 'Lingayats' will lose is to be far too unspecific. The Lingayats are a huge category spread over most of northern and western Karnataka and divided into various jatis and occupational groups which are often in conflict with one another. The most marked of the conflicts—which has often become quite bitter—is that between the large 'Sadar' group whose main occupation is cultivating and the 'Banajigas' who are traditionally merchants and traders.

Who among Lingayats gained most in education and government employment before the arrival of Devraj Urs as chief minister? In proportion to their total numbers, the small 'Jangama' (priestly) group and the Banajigas— both traditionally urban and literate—did far better than any of the cultivating groups, including the Sadars. One prominent Lingayat leader (from a neutral group) stated in 1971 that major gains among the Sadars in education and employment were limited to 'a few families' which he proceeded to name.

When his remarks were checked with others, they proved to be only a slight understatement. This uneven distribution of preferment added heat to the traditional conflict between Sadars and Banajigas and caused resentment among other cultivating groups as well. They had been promised a great deal by Lingayat politicians—not least by the presiding genius over the entire Lingayat political enterprise, S. Nijalingappa, a Banajiga. Those promises led many to perceive themselves as Lingayats first and as other things second, and they evoked intense Lingayat chauvinism similar to that recently displayed by Jats in Haryana and western Uttar Pradesh. But during the Lingayat heyday in state politics (1956–71), the actual gains in education and jobs for the numerically powerful but educationally less advanced Lingayat cultivating groups were disappointing. One of the principal reasons for the surprising ease with which Urs broke and replaced Lingayat–Vokkaliga dominance in Karnataka was this estrangement between the urban Banajigas and the Jangamas and the cultivating Lingayats with their great numerical and economic strength. The latter were partially neutralised as a result of their estrangement.

Urs knew that this was a crucial factor in his favour and he was understandably reluctant to take any action which would drive the landed and the urban Lingayats together. A land reform programme which mainly attacked *tenancy* posed no serious threat to any major group outside the two coastal districts which are of marginal importance in the arithmetic of state politics. Indeed, it would help many poorer Lingayats in rural parts. A policy of preferment for 'backward classes' in education would mainly hurt the elite urban Lingayat groups who were the only Lingayats who still harboured high expectations in this area. And predictably, it is from this quarter that the main protests against 'backward class' preferment have come—led by a retired Jangama civil servant. But an assault on landlessness was quite another matter. It would have threatened the prosperity of Lingayat cultivators in the inland districts of northern Karnataka and could easily have revived their alliance with urban Lingayats. It is principally for this reason that no attack on landlessness was made in the 1974 Land Reforms Act. Urs and his closest advisers intended such an attack, but they preferred to solidify their support among ex-tenants before proceeding to that stage.

PREFERMENT FOR 'BACKWARD CLASSES'

There is a lesson in the Lingayats' experience with promises of preferment in education and government jobs for anyone who considers making such promises. They are an effective way of crystallising the political consciousness of a group whose support a politician needs. For a certain period, they can be used to sustain the solidarity of the politicised groups. But in the long term, the expectations such promises generate cannot be fulfilled and disillusionment and anger are bound to follow. There are simply not enough government jobs to satisfy the aspirations of any sizeable group—and it is always to large groups that such promises are made. There may be enough reserved seats in primary and secondary schools and even in undergraduate colleges to satisfy such groups, but there are seldom enough seats in the elite professional colleges to which so many aspire. Nor is there sufficient employment to assuage the appetites of those emerging from secondary and higher studies. The policy of preferment is a double-edged sword offering only temporary advantage.

Devraj Urs knows this. It is no accident that he announced his acceptance of a report advocating reservations in schools and government service for Karnataka's 'backward classes' during the run-up to the 1977 Lok Sabha elections. He chose that moment because he realised that the main result of such programmes is not the transformation of the lot of the 'backward classes' but rather a temporary surge in their political consciousness which he needed at that election.

The timing of this announcement is significant in one other way. It was made fully five years after he had taken office, after his various programmes for reform and social welfare had had time to make an impression, and fully three years after the main element of his programme, the Land Reforms Act, had taken effect. In other words by the time he announced his programme of preferment, he had already demonstrated, by substantive action rather than mere rhetoric, that he was the champion of the groups which had previously been dominated by Lingayats and Vokkaligas. Because he had demonstrated this, he mortgaged far less of his prestige to the ultimately risky promises of preferment than those who *begin* their drive for power with such promises. If (when) 'backward class' people found that the promises could not be fulfilled, their frustration would be tempered by the knowledge that they had gained from Urs in other ways.

This point about the timing of promises is important in discussing the analogies which are often rather loosely drawn between Urs's doings and those of Karpoori Thakur in Bihar. Thakur proclaimed his policy of preferment for the 'backward classes' soon after taking office. He did so in order to signify 'that the Backwards had displaced the Forwards as the dominant force in Bihar politics, that the old days of dominance in public affairs from village to Vidhan Sabha by the "twice-born" were gone forever'.[21] But he made this announcement before he had either consolidated 'backward class' control in the state-level political arena or developed programmes to provide 'backward class' people with new economic and political resources in the form of substantive patronage from government. His early offer of preferment inflamed feelings among both forward castes and Scheduled Castes who felt threatened by it and led to the collapse of his government before it had time to achieve its major goals. It was replaced by a government which is dominated by 'Forwards and Jana Sanghis'[22] In the words of Devraj Urs, 'Karpoori climbed into the ring before he learned how to box'.[23]

Comparisons are also drawn between Urs's doings and the endeavours of Charan Singh to cultivate 'backward class' support, mainly in Bihar, Uttar Pradesh and Haryana. (Rajasthan is a different matter.) There are some parallels between them. Several of the occupational groups which Charan Singh (and Karpoori Thakur) sought to help were also among Urs's constituents, notably poorer cultivators, some artisans and service castes and people engaged in animal husbandry. Many, probably most, of these people are economically weak. Charan Singh (and Karpoori Thakur) sought to create programmes to aid these groups educationally, politically and economically. It would thus be wrong to overstate the contrasts between Charan Singh and Devraj Urs.[24]

Nevertheless, important contrasts exist which cannot be ignored. A great many of Charan Singh's supporters are cultivators who have, over the last decade or so, made significant economic gains. (We are badly in need of hard evidence on the proportions of the prosperous and the underprivileged among Charan Singh's supporters.) Thus in addition to uplifting certain economically weak groups, Charan Singh is also proposing to use state power to further bolster the position of economically strong groups. (One also suspects that, when the time came to divide the spoils among Charan Singh's supporters, the strong would receive a disproportionate share.) Urs is engaged in something quite different and less ambiguous. His followers are overwhelmingly drawn from economically weak groups. Although Vokkaligas who formerly enjoyed political dominance are listed among: Karnataka's 'backward classes', the criteria for the allotment of preferment (which, in addition to caste, give preference to the poor and to rural dwellers) favour the underprivileged among them. Urs is thus using state power to strengthen economically weak groups and to forge them into an alliance that can maintain political ascendancy over more prosperous elements.[25]

BASES OF SUPPORT

There is one other important contrast between Urs and the north Indian leaders. Urs has maintained a firm alliance between less prosperous caste Hindus, the Scheduled Castes and the Muslims. This is not the case in north India. Karpoori Thakur's government fell in part because of Scheduled Caste fears about the 'backward class' movement. Perhaps the more enlightened elements in Charan Singh's camp desire an alliance between the 'backward classes' and the Scheduled Castes. But such sentiments are outweighed by the post-Emergency violence against the Scheduled Castes in the Hindi areas. Raj Narain's outbursts against reservations for Scheduled Castes and the blatant and widespread intimidation of Scheduled Caste voters in the 1980 Lok Sabha poll by Jats and others in Haryana, western Uttar Pradesh and—by others and perhaps less widely—in Bihar.[26] Urs's careful cultivation of Muslim support through generous patronage to Muslim groups and waqf boards stands in stark contrast to the rancid anti-Muslim diatribe that this writer had to listen to from high Lok Dal officials in the party's headquarters on the eve of the 1980 elections. In north India, Madhu Limaye had developed a strategy inclusive of Muslims and some Muslim farmers appear to have backed the Lok Dal,[27] but most of their votes were lost.

The only genuine parallel in north India to the experiment in Karnataka, as Urs himself emphasises, is the Shekhawat government in Rajasthan.[28] But it has not had time to develop its programmes fully and since it is a Janata Party enterprise, its days seem numbered in the wake of the Congress (I) victory in the Lok Sabha elections.

One further question is pertinent in the light of the failure of land reforms in Karnataka to assist landless people who are very often members of Scheduled Castes. If preferment programmes in north India have been seen as threats by the Scheduled Castes, how did Urs maintain an alliance between the 'backward classes' and the Scheduled Castes? He did so through a combination of symbolism and substantive action. On a symbolic level, he kept the Scheduled Caste leader, B. Basavalingappa, in the prominent role of revenue minister, more than doubled Scheduled Caste representation in the cabinet (with important portfolios) and had the assembly speaker chosen from among their number. Urs also sought—largely successfully, by all accounts—to reassure the Scheduled Castes that reservations for 'backward classes' meant no diminution of their statutory quotas. He drove the point home by energetic efforts to see that Scheduled Caste quotas which had never been adequately filled in the higher ranks of government service were more fully met during his tenure and went to the extent of increasing representation over the statutory level to compensate for previous shortfalls. He did this despite considerable resistance from caste Hindu officials.[29] This was an area in which he showed particular determination and satisfaction in reviewing his time in office after his resignation.[30]

On a more substantive level, the Urs government sought to compensate for inaction on behalf of the landless by promoting social welfare programmes for the Scheduled Castes. Such programmes were not as alarming to cultivating Lingayats in northern districts as an assault on landlessness would have been. Among the more important of these were schemes to aid small and marginal farmers, to grant house sites on unoccupied land, to build houses for the poor and to increase scholarships and places in hostels for Scheduled Caste students. In urban areas, slum clearance boards often gave Scheduled Castes first access to houses. Child development programmes extending from anti-natal care to school-going age have often been aimed in large measure at the Scheduled Castes and located in areas where they are found in large numbers. Old age pensions have also reached some of them. The government acted firmly in many parts of the state in an effort to get primary education to all children, and brought pressure upon teachers to ensure this. Government vigilance and pressure upon employers brought for the first time some substantial compliance with minimum wages laws in 1977 and after. Some significant inroads were made on the practice of bonded labour for the first time. A law passed in 1976 liquidating rural debt and allowing former debtors to redeem pledged property made a tangible difference to the Scheduled Castes, although government schemes to make alternative credit available were slow in making an impact. Urs, who had concentrated several key portfolios and enormous power in his own hands, maintained considerable pressure on officials to show greater sympathy to Scheduled Caste people. To assist him in this, he appointed Scheduled Caste officials to the crucial post of deputy commissioner in several districts. The degrading practice of carrying night-soil on the head was banned and evidently widely abandoned after a campaign against it by B. Basavalingappa and others.[31]

Most of this information comes from Mumtaz Ali Khan, a longtime specialist in and advocate of Scheduled Caste interests who has been a frequent critic of government in the past. His surveys of Scheduled Caste villages in every taluk of Bangalore district (which contains both backward and developed areas) in 1970 and 1977 uncovered considerable gains for Scheduled Caste people in the struggle against the practice of untouchability. He also found them much more willing in 1977 to place cases of discrimination before the police (partly because under Urs the police were fairer in their treatment of the Scheduled Castes), demonstrably less afraid of once-dominant landed castes and far more outspoken about their attitudes to political parties and candidates.[32] It must however be emphasised that these government initiatives failed to penetrate in many places, particularly in more backward rural areas;[33] and the change is far from revolutionary. The story of Karnataka's Scheduled Castes in the 1970s is of a transition, for some, from wretched to slightly less wretched conditions and, for others, of no transition at all. It is impossible on present evidence to quantify either the size of these categories or the extent of transition. But serious efforts have been made on their behalf and despite the Urs government's timidity on landlessness, which afflicts so many of the Scheduled Castes, its record is on balance quite enlightened and reasonably effective.

III

We have already noted that Devraj Urs has demonstrated that it is possible to break the control of dominant landed groups over state-level politics and to replace it with a solid alliance including most of the less powerful groups in society. He sustained this for seven and a half years and his resignation was not caused by any fracturing of this alliance. How durable will it prove in his absence?

Nearly all of the programmes and reforms enumerated in the discussion above of Scheduled Castes also aided less prosperous caste Hindus (and, in many areas, Muslims). These programmes, taken together, form on paper an impressive range of initiatives. Others can be added to the list—bank finance to artisans (a traditionally deprived section in Karnataka), special programmes to assist handloom weavers, free legal aid, a restructuring of co-operative societies to break the dominance over them of small groups of rich people, the 'socialisation' of some urban land, nutritional schemes for children, a programme (which pre-dated the Centre's Food-for-Work programme) to provide up to 100 days' employment for seasonal labourers, an effort to provide villages with drinking water and another to supply electricity in underserved rural areas.[34]

Serious reservations must be registered about some of these programmes. Some were conceived too late to have any substantive impact and in any case were implemented only in limited portions of the state. The rural electrification drive, the creation of agricultural estates to rehabilitate bonded labourers and the scheme for seasonal labour (in its application rather than its conception) are examples. At least two other initiatives—one to provide several thousand auto-rickshaw drivers with funds to purchase their vehicles from their present wealthy owners (developed independently of similar Congress[I] promises) and another to allow the rural poor to purchase tracts of land for a nominal payment of Rs 100—appeared so late as to be little more than election promises.

Those programmes which were in operation for longer periods must also be regarded with some reservation. With most of them, there were problems in securing their penetration to the local level. There were many reasons for this. Some assembly members who might have played a major role in promoting these schemes allowed themselves to be bought off by wealthy interests in their constituencies. Within the bureaucracy, particularly among minor officials in the mofussil (many of whom are drawn from groups threatened by the reforms), there was considerable foot-dragging. To combat this, higher civil servants organised special one-day camps in many local areas where villagers were granted rights to land, old age pensions and access to other benefits very expeditiously and without recourse to local officials or middlemen. But such exercises could only reach a very small portion of the rural population.

The widespread erosion of vote-banks has not been accompanied by an equally rapid erosion of poor (especially illiterate) people's dependence on intermediaries for their dealings with government bureaucracy. A man who votes according to his own preference may still find it necessary to go to a village accountant or a notable in a neighbouring town to enquire into the documentation needed to obtain a piece of land, a pension or a concession to which he is entitled. These intermediaries often exploit and deceive those who come to them and thereby thwart the penetration of reforms and social services.[35] High civil servants concede that this has impaired and even vitiated the effectiveness of many programmes and has prevented the kind of important, if hardly revolutionary, changes which they might have wrought in the socio-economic framework. And yet in a great many areas some of these programmes are getting through, particularly those most energetically stressed by Urs on his frequent tours—land reforms, pensions for needy people over sixty (Rs 40 per month), sites and houses for the poor and, to a lesser extent, the restructuring of co-operatives.

It is impossible to quantify the extent to which the programmes have penetrated to the villages. In these matters, we see through a glass darkly. It is thus impossible to say with any assurance to what extent Urs's programmes have wrought changes that will permanently alter the logic of politics. In some areas this has certainly not occurred. In many, and probably most, a substantial beginning appears to have been made. In other places, that would be an understatement.

Urs himself believes that to ensure the durability of both his coalition of less prosperous groups and the socio-economic changes he envisions, he needed another three years in power. This man, who began as a pragmatist sensing that his interest lay in progressive policies but dependent on advisers for guidance, is now clearly in advance of them on one crucial issue. They tend to speak of the government's policies in terms of 'doing good for the poor', in well-intentioned but faintly patronising terms. Urs, however, has sufficient political sensitivity to see that the great weakness of his efforts so far is their failure to foster the *organisation* of the weaker sections of society for their own defence. He understands that politicisation, which is clearly widespread, is inadequate without organisation.[36] Whether he will have another opportunity to act on this insight remains an open question.

Other important questions remain. Will preferment for the 'backward classes' come to be seen as a threat by Scheduled Caste people without the reassuring figures of Urs and his Scheduled Caste lieutenants in power? Will the failure of land reforms to aid the landless become a grievance among the Scheduled Castes and others who are similarly deprived? And—a closely related question—will the transformation of many former tenants into small landholders alter the agrarian structure to the disadvantage of the landless labourers and possibly deprive them of much-needed work?

In winding up this assessment of the Urs years, we must also take note of the large-scale corruption which has marked his regime from early days. Urs has developed 'fund-raising' in the state to something of a science and is responsible for a huge increase over previous regimes in the role of money in politics. To say this, however, is to be so imprecise as to mislead. It must be emphasised that the money which was raised ('extorted' would perhaps be a more accurate word) came not from the weaker sections of society whom Urs seeks to help but rather from large industrial, planting and urban interests and from predominantly lower-middle-class seekers of favours and promotions from government. This is not to say that Urs is a Robin Hood. A great deal of the money obtained ended up in the pockets of supporters. A great deal more ended up in the coffers of Indira Gandhi's party at the national level until Urs broke with her. But much of this 'fund-raising' was forced upon Urs by the Congress(I) high command and his success at this game bought Karnataka freedom from disruptive interference from above.

It must also be emphasised that the money Urs raised, like the many key portfolios he rather undemocratically kept for himself, gave him extra political powers which in many cases were necessary to see that reforms were at least partially implemented. The single most striking change that this writer noticed, returning to Bangalore after two and a half years, was in the views of several reliable and well-placed sources on this matter. They had earlier reacted with disgust to the money game and were bitterly negative in their view of Urs. But in the intervening period they had become extremely sympathetic, annoyed by the corruption but seeing much of it as an element in Urs's remarkably successful campaign ' to force through reforms which are beginning to have a substantial impact in Karnataka.

It is a measure of this impact that Urs's successors cannot afford to change his policies to any significant extent. The entire front rank of Congress(I) leaders are—like Urs—from small, non-dominant groups. They may ease somewhat the burden on the urban middle class who have been squeezed to fund the reforms.[37] But they cannot seek to reconstruct some variant of the old system in which Lingayats and Vokkaligas dominated. They cannot do so for two reasons. First and most obviously, they and others from similar social backgrounds could be swept aside in the process. But second and more importantly, they could not hope to retain support among the less prosperous groups whom Urs has brought together if they attempted an accommodation with the Lingayats or Vokkaligas. The idea of the new alliance of weaker groups has taken root and will not be easily abandoned. The great question hanging over Urs's successors—and over the Congress(I) across the nation—is whether they are competent to manage an Increasingly complex policy with skill and sensitivity. If they are not, the ensuing muddle could wreck the achievements of recent years or open the way for Urs to return.

IV

Before we can judge the historical importance of the Urs experiment, we will need to know not only how things go in Karnataka and India over the months and years ahead, but also how things have gone already in other regions of the subcontinent. Detailed studies of other regions may suggest that such reforming regimes can only be built and sustained by politicians possessing both an acute intelligence and an aggressive, audacious temperament. Urs has both, but most leaders do not. More to the point, only leaders who do not have such gifts are likely to be given the opportunity to wield power in the regions Linder Indira Gandhi. It may also be true that such an experiment can succeed only in a state with officials of high calibre in the upper and middle echelons of the bureaucracy, a productive agrarian sector, a well-developed technological infrastructure, and which is also relatively free of destructive intercommunal and interregional strife. Most crucially, perhaps this sort of experiment can succeed only in a state where traditional disparities between rich and poor are comparatively less acute. Perhaps Urs and Karnataka are as much cases apart from mainstream India as are Kerala and West Bengal. Only time and research on other regions can answer these questions. But for the moment, this writer holds that Karnataka is not as eccentric as all that. The Shekhawat government in Rajasthan—surely one of the last places one might have expected a reformist government to appear, let alone succeed—suggests that conditions at large may soon be right for the emergence of pragmatic Progressives at the state level.

12

The BJP and Backward Castes in Gujarat *

GHANSHYAM SHAH

The Bharatiya Janata Party's (BJP's) perspectives on the economy notwithstanding, it comes nowhere near questioning the sanctity of private property. The BJP solidly supports the economic status quo in favour of the propertied, inclusive of class divisions and hierarchised distribution of economic production. Simultaneously, it also strives to create a Hindu *rashtra*. That does not necessarily mean a *de jure* theocratic state. In practice it is an attempt at reinforcing the dominance of the majority Hindu community in social and cultural spheres. Unity among Hindus vis-à-vis 'others' is a necessary condition for such a project. For that, and to win elections the party has developed strategies to appease the backward castes. It manipulates the social and economic interests of various strata of society and creates new alliances among different classes and/or castes among Hindus. The party constructs and reconstructs certain values and institutions as cultural heritage and redefines the Hindu social order, Hinduism and 'others' (non-Hindus). This particular construction of the social order wishes away hierarchical relationships and uneven distribution of resources among various social strata. Such a scheme of unity is fragile. It is pivoted more around emotions and sentiments than the material interests of those who are at the bottom of the hierarchy.

However, the BJP and Rashtriya Swayamsevak Sangh (RSS) leaders assert in the post-Babri Masjid demolition phase that the emerging Hindu identity has considerably reduced caste, sect, language and regional differences among the Hindus. H.V. Seshadri, the RSS chief, argues that united Hinduism would eradicate caste-based differentiation.[1] Such an assertion is, of course, debatable. But it is certainly true that consciousness of Hindu identity has spread in all castes including backward or low castes (including tribals). The latter join hands with the upper castes against Muslims. What makes backward castes

* *South Asia Bulletin*, 14 (1), 1994, pp. 57–65.

forge unity with upper castes? Does it mean that consciousness of being Hindu also amounts to unity of interests with upper castes and acceptance of their hegemony? The present essay seeks to examine BJP strategies to win the support of the low castes. We shall also probe possible explanations for favourable backward caste responses to BJP—as an electoral party and as a purveyor of the ideology promoting a unified Hindu identity.

BACKWARD CASTES

In the traditional caste hierarchy, Sudras and Ati-Sudras are considered low castes. But in present-day Gujarat all Sudras are not treated as such. Patidars or Kanbis, for example, for all practical purposes have allied with Brahmins and Vanias in the socio-cultural and economic spheres. They have successfully acquired the status of upper castes. This is also the case with some artisan castes such as Suthar, Bhavsar, and Khatri. On the other hand, Adivasis or tribals who had traditionally not been part of the *chaturvarna* system, now call themselves Hind They are largely considered by upper-caste Hindus as Ati-Sudras along with Dalits or Scheduled Castes (SCs). Scheduled Tribes (STs) constitute 14 per cent of the population, Scheduled Castes 7 per cent and other backward castes (OBCs) around 40 per cent. Thus, backward castes altogether constitute nearly 61 per cent of the population.

The SCs, STs, and OBCs are divided into a number of endogamous jatis. Among the SCs there is also an hierarchical order based on pollution and purity. The STs, however, are by and large free of rigid caste hierarchy, but status differentiations exist.

Many other backward castes are localised, confined to a taluka or district. Castes such as Bafans, Madaris and Vadis are economically very poor and less than 5 per cent of them are literate. They are practically landless and earn their living by selling their labour power. Many of these castes are so small and scattered that they have virtually no political significance in local or state elections. Wherever some low castes—for example, Machchi, Mar and Rabari in Saurashtra, Waghari in central Gujarat, Machhi or Kharava, Ganchi and Gola-Rana in south Gujarat—have significant numerical strength in some talukas or districts, it provides them with political clout in elections.

The Kolis constitute the largest caste-cluster comprising 24 per cent of the population of Gujarat. They are spread throughout the state. Major jatis of the Kolis are: Chunavaliya, Khant, Patanvadiya, Bareeya, Thakarada or Thakor, Talabda, Dharala, Matia, Gulam. Some of them use the term Koli as a suffix such as Matia Koli or Gulam Koli, whereas others do not use the term Koli at all. In fact the Bareeyas and Patanvadiyas of Kheda and Vadodara districts, and Dharalas, Khants and Thakors of the Panchmahals, Mehsana, Ahmedabad and Sabarkantha districts find it degrading to be called Kolis, preferring to be referred to as Kshatriyas. The Kolis of south Gujarat introduce themselves as Koli-Patel whereas those of Saurashtra call themselves just Koli. It is a generic term used for poor cultivators and labourers. The British census officers clubbed them together for census purposes to differentiate them from the Patidar or the Kanbi on the one hand and the aboriginal on the other. Later, political aspirants and social reformers of these castes created legends of 'oneness' and formed organisations to unite various castes having nearly similar social status. But so far, there is no organisation uniting all Kolis.

The backward castes are on the whole economically poor, that is, they do not own enough resources to generate sufficient income to meet their basic needs. Most of them are small and marginal farmers and landless agricultural labourers in rural areas. But there are a few exceptions to this pattern. A small section of different backward castes own sufficient means of production to employ labourers and expropriate the surplus. Eleven per cent of the Kolis, 10 per cent of OBCs and 5 per cent of SCs cultivate more than 15 acres of land. Two per cent of the heads of households are engaged in white-collar jobs. A few are lawyers, medical doctors or engineers.[2]

Gujarat has not witnessed an anti-Brahmin or backward caste movement as in south India. Some religious sects mobilised backward castes with a view to sanskritising social customs. While doing so, they reinforced over time the caste system and the dominance of upper castes. For example, the Swaminarayan sect established in the early nineteenth century attracted a large number of followers from backward and middle castes as well as from upper castes. The sect had an ambivalent attitude towards caste status. Though it did not advocate continuation of the caste system, restrictions on interdining and intermarriage not only continued but basic caste duties were reaffirmed.[3] Gandhi took up the problem of untouchability and Gandhians worked among OBCs and tribals for their betterment. Though the attitude of Gandhians to the caste system was also ambivalent, the 'improved' social lifestyle that they asked the low castes to follow was Brahminical.

Some members of low castes, who have improved their material conditions as they have availed themselves of new opportunities in agricultural, trade and white-collar sectors, strive for higher status and a new identity. In the past, many OBCs followed the path of sanskritisation by imitating upper-caste lifestyles and rituals. This process had been encouraged, facilitated and legitimised not only by the British colonial rulers, but also by social and religious reformers and liberal leaders. It has continued in post-independence India with some differences. It is no longer sanskritisation as in the past. Their quest is for 'modernisation' with idioms of sanskritisation, the paradigm formulated by the ruling class. In this process, the Kolis do not find it beneath their dignity to be called Koli. What they now want is respect and dignity, without challenging the caste framework. They want equality with those who are above them in the hierarchical order. At the same time they would like to keep some groups below them. Besides the nature of capitalist economic development and modern ethos, electoral politics played in important role in reinforcing such aspirations. Caste associations of upper as well as backward castes have been formed to mobilise caste members in elections, and to undertake secular functions such as education, health and income generating programmes to meet the changing needs of the members. In the process, caste as well as Hindu consciousness is invoked. Symbols like the sword, *trishul* and swastika are deployed to rally members not only around caste but also simultaneously around Hinduism. A section of the upwardly mobile backward castes perceive these as emblematic of their new identity.

NEW MEANING OF HINDUISM

Like all religions, Hinduism has, from time to time, been reinterpreted by Hindu theologians. One of the main agendas of the many Hindu reformers since the early nineteenth century has been to reformulate and rejuvenate Hinduism as they believe it to have existed during the Vedic period. At the same time, to counter Islam and Christianity, emphasis was placed on instituting ecclesiastical religious organisation. The central plank of this agenda is forging unity among Hindus. The meaning of Hindu unity varies from school to school. All those who believe in Hindu unity are not anti non-Hindus, nor are they champions of the superiority of Hinduism or the Hindu social system over others. They also do not interpret Indian culture as Hindu culture. But this is not the case with the Vishwa Hindu Parishad (VHP), RSS, BJP, not to mention many others who are not part of the Sangh Parivar, whose reconstruction of Hinduism is not just religious. It is *essentially political*, centred on the notion of Hindu rashtra vis-à-vis others who are depicted as competitors or enemies.

In contemporary Gujarat, a number of organised efforts are afoot by social and religious 'reformers' or founders of various sects to build unity across sects and castes within Hinduism. Though some of them favour the caste system, they are critical of untouchability. All of them advocate Hindu *qaum*, that is, community, as Hindu *rashtra*, invoke communal categories vis-à-vis non-Hindus, and the spirit of nationalism and glorification of the nation.

Sachchidanand, one of the radical *sants* and *swamis* to have made a mark on the politics of Gujarat, has been acclaimed as Narmad, the father of the Gujarati 'renaissance', for his social reform and literary work. He regularly writes a social commentary in a widely circulated regional newspaper, and lectures at colleges and universities. Political leaders of the Congress and the

BJP adore him. His mission is to rejuvenate Hinduism and nationalism. Towards that end, he works for the eradication of the degraded status of backward and Scheduled Castes. Being a strong critic of caste, the varna system and untouchability, he asks, 'How can varna-based *Sanskriti*, that is, culture and heritage, be beneficial to all—Sudras, Ati-Sudras, untouchables and women?'[4] The varna system which was once created on the basis of *gun-karma*, that is, virtues and skill, is now a degenerate system. That system cannot be called 'good which created the *Kshatriyas, six* per cent of the population brave and remaining population docile . . . The foreign aggressors knew our weakness, that they had to fight with only six per cent (and not the whole population). . . .'[5] The caste system created internal rivalries and competition which benefited others (Muslims). Though tolerance is a virtue, it also has limits. He asserts that the tolerance of Prithvi Raj for Shahbuddin made the nation a slave (of Muslims).[6]

According to Sachchidanand, the word 'Hindu' is used differently in three different contexts: constitutional, religious and social. Hindu is primarily used in a social rather than religious context. It includes several dharma, sects, subsects, social groups whose national interests are the same. Their places of worship are respected by each other, and *roti–beti vyavahar* relations are possible among them.[7] However, Hindus are dispersed, narrow minded, meek, docile, and have a tendency to be reduced to insignificance. (The Muslims, on the other hand, though small in number are stronger than the Hindus in many ways. The Muslims in India are not as nationalist as they were in 1947. They set off fire-crackers when the Pakistan team wins at cricket. They like India's defeat. Those who like India's defeat in a thing like a cricket match, what would their attitude to India's death be in other matters? This is obvious.[8] If India had not been partitioned, the Muslims would have ruled this country. In such a situation, Sachchidanand pleads for unity among Hindus, and that requires not only abolition of the caste system but also positive measures for ameliorating the condition of the Sudras and Ati-Sudras, that is, backward and Scheduled Castes.

Pandurang Athavale, addressed with reverence as Dada, that is, grandfather, by his followers is another popular religious leader. The architect of the Swadhyay sect from Maharashtra has a large following among traditionally low castes such as Machchis, Kharvas, Kolis, Vagharis, Harijans and Adivasis in Gujarat. He refers to Machchis and Kharvas, traditionally fisherfolk and sailors, as Sagarputra. (sons of the sea), Adivasis or tribals as Vanvasi (forest-dwellers), and diamond cutters as Ratnakar (jewellers). Incidentally, the BJP also refers to tribals as Vanvasi. A number of judges, doctors, professors, journalists, engineers and other members of elite sections of society are also his followers. One university invited him to give a convocation address, honouring him as a distinguished figure. Athavale's birthday is celebrated as *manav gaurav*, that is, human dignity day. In 1992, his birthday celebrations on the beach at Umargaon, south Gujarat drew over one million devotees who participated in the function with remarkable discipline. Congress and BJP leaders also attended the function, though Dada did not give much importance to them.

This sect had its origins in the mid-1950s in Bombay. The Swadhyayis initially used to go to villages, much like Christian missionaries, every week or fortnight with their own bedding and food and talked to people in general and deprived groups in particular about the *Gita*, man–God relationship and human dignity. According to the organisation, 'The Swadhyayis go from house to house, village to village with their hearts overflowing with love to kindle, augment and protect the fast-disappearing feeling of love and tenderness.'[9] The Swadhyay also sponsors economic and social welfare programmes such as co-operative farming, forestry and fishing. The devotees also give a certain proportion of their income to the collective to sustain the weak without hurting their dignity. The sect runs residential schools and postgraduate centres. There are regular weekly study groups in which Athavale's discourses on the *Gita* are viewed and listened to on video or read. Examinations are conducted on Swadhyay philosophy which emphasise Indian culture and heritage. In 1992, around 49,000 candidates appeared in the examination.[10] Some activities of the Swadhyay are well depicted in the film *Antarnad*, directed by Shyam Benegal.

The Swadhyay repeatedly emphasises self-dignity, dignity of labour, individual identity, culture and devotion. It is claimed,

> By the medium of Swadhyay, 'we shall create a society which self-disciplined, has faith in God, is adventurous and brave, loves culture and the holy scriptures, is truly democratic and is filled with devotion. In this society, greater importance will be given to right attitude rather than to action, thoughts will be valued more than things, feelings more than employment, self-surrender more than selfishness, group more than the individual, culture more than manners, efforts more than results, goodness more than strength, truth more than logic, and righteousness more than wealth.[11]

Like Sachchidanand, Athavale is also a strong critic of superstitions and 'irrational' rituals prevailing in various sects. The Swadhyay tries to resolve sectarian disputes between Vaishnavites and Shaivites. Icons of Shiva as well as Vishnu have been installed in Swadhyay temples. These temples are open to all and meant for large gatherings, thus 'striving to make the temple a centre of socio-economic and cultural life'.[12]

The Swadhyay opposes the caste system but not the *chaturvarna* system. According to Athavale, the *chaturvarna* system created by Sri Krishna has no hierarchical differences of low and high. It is a materialist arrangement for distribution of occupations so that people need not have to worry about their food and shelter. Rigid status differentiation of touchability and untouchability is a degeneration of the system. Athavale repeatedly emphasises that 'no man born on this earth is lowly and degraded'.[13] Distinctions on the basis of caste, creed and class are not recognised. All are children of the same lord. Individual dignity and identity are highlighted. At the same time, the chaturvarna system makes arrangement for *roti* (bread) and *beti* (daughter, exchange of girl in marriage), which enables human beings to develop and become prosperous.[14]

According to Swadhyay, the concepts of nation and patriotism are enshrined in the Vedas which call for loyalty to the land. This is *yagna bhumi*, the holy and great land. It has a great and glorious history. The Aryans who created the Vedas are a great race. The local non-Aryans were not converted. They first learned the Vedas and understood them and then of their choice got assimilated with 'us'. The Aryans had only two instruments: 'great ideas and loving relationships'. Bharatiya (that is, Hindu) tradition is a great tradition. Bharatiya is one who accepts the Hindu philosophical traditions. This is the holy land of Sri Ram and the Raghuvansh clan. The philosophy and the principles of the Raghuvansh kings were relevant not only for their time but for all time and all human society. They are above space and time. A true nationalist is one who is filled with love for one's land and towns created and protected by God. 'Bharat is a nation, therefore it has a great and unique tradition, unique ideology, unique vision, unique spiritual way and unique religious way—one who remembers all this is truly national.' Nationalism respects Dwarka of Sri Krishna, Ayodhya of Sri Ram, our holy Jyotilinga (Shiva's temple in four parts of the country), the holy rivers flowing in our country, the great *rishis*. Athavale denigrates Muslim invaders and Muslim rulers for destroying temples and converting 'our people'. This was possible primarily because Hindus lost their ethos. Athavale argues, 'People of other religions have destroyed our temples, burnt the Vedas; not only that, but they also urinate on the places of our faith and ideals for which people were once ready to shed their blood, yet there is nobody to counter them!'[15]

Morari Bapu, another religious figure, is one of the most popular kathakars (religious storytellers) of the Ramayana. He began public narration of Ram Katha in 1966 and had till 1998 presented more than 400 *katha* sessions, each of eight and sometimes even ten days. Morari Bapu declares that the *Ramayana* was not meant for this or that varna; it was meant for *manav* (human beings), for all, irrespective of sect or religion. It is a matter of faith for the devotees to listen to the *Ramayana* with devotion and follow its teachings. Morari Bapu says that the story of the *Ramayana* is well known; however, its relevance to modern life needs elucidation. Without posing as a social reformer, he asserts that Ram Rajya can only be established when the Dalits get equal status with others. Like Athavale, he strongly condemns sectarian attitudes among Hindus. Instead of constructing many temples, there should be a few large temples where people could get together. Like Sachchidanand and Athavale, Morari Bapu insists that Indian culture is Hindu culture that has a glorious past going back to Vedic times, whereafter, *kaliyug* set in. Muslim rule, according to him, is responsible for the destruction of Hindu, that is, Indian tradition.

Morari Bapu's *kathas* attract a cross-section of society though a large majority are from upper and middle castes. Upwardly mobile sections of the OBCs also participate. The social and political elite, too, attend the *kathas* and compete with each other for the blessings of Moran Bapu. The *nouveau riche* patronise these programmes. Collections from the *kathas*, often running into several lakhs of rupees, are used for charitable activities—relief for drought, flood and fire victims, construction of temples, hospitals and schools. One of the leading universities in Gujarat organised his *katha* to collect funds for the university and the vice-chancellor at the time, an internationally renowned scholar, attended the function as a *bhakta* (devotee). Such programmes not only legitimise Morari Bapu's teachings but also add to his stature.

Sachchidanand and Athavale have not supported the Sangh Parivar campaign for the construction of the Ram temple in Ayodhya. But they have not opposed it either. Morari Bapu, on the other hand, openly supported the campaign and participated in the functions organised by the BJP and Sangh Parivar. On the occasion of *paduka pujan*, that is, worship of Ram's slippers, in 1992, Morari Bapu said:

> We [he includes himself] organised Sri Ram *rath* [led by Advani], did *shilanyas* [Sri Ram temple foundation stone ceremony] and worshipped Ram *paduka*—three *satyas* [truths] have been completed. But the government has not responded to this positively. This is a cruel joke upon the *satyas*. And when truth has been made a mockery of, it is necessary to use the fourth *satya*—*shakti* [power] . . . It is now time for the youth of this country to do *kesaria*, i.e., accept martyrdom, by fighting till the last for the construction of the Shri Ram *mandir*... Time demands that Hindus get united.[16]

For VHP, 'Hindu' refers to nationality; it is not a *mazhab* (note that the VHP does not used the word dharma), sect or opinion. 'Those who believe themselves to be Hindus are also Hindus.' The word Hindu unites four varnas and several castes, and a number of sects, dialects and languages. The theme of unity among the Hindus is repeatedly found in *Vishwa Hindu Parishad*, the organ of the VHP edited by K.K. Shastry, an ex-president of the Gujarati Sahitya Parishad, who received the title of Vidya Vachaspati (a pre-eminent learned person). The journal often exhorts its readers: 'All Hindus should unite against *vidharmis* [people of other religions, obviously a reference to Muslims]. Outmoded feudal values still prevail in our villages which have kept the caste pollution intact and thus resulted in friction within the Hindu fold. . . . Savarna Hindus should now become alert and not widen the gap between the castes, must compromise with Dalits and not continue to remain selfish.'[17]

The Bharat Sevashram (BS) and Hindu Milan Mandir (HMM), all-Indian organisations started in the 1920s, have been active in Gujarat since the early 1970s. Besides undertaking activities to unite various sects and organising Ganesh festivals, they carry out welfare and relief measures among the backward castes. Though they invite political leaders of all parties to their functions, they have become very close to the BJP over the past five years. They shared a platform with the BJP on the issue of the Ram Mandir. The leaders of these organisations issued a public appeal to Hindus to vote for that party which works to protect Hindu interests. The main thrust of these organisations is to build unity and harmony among upper and lower-caste Hindus. They reject the notion that Sudras occupy an inferior and degraded position, though they do not reject the caste system. Co-operation and unity of the upper and lower castes for protection of Hindu dharma and Hindu *samaj* is called for. Hindutva consciousness and Hindu inspiration are the starting point for realisation of the power necessary for self-protection of the Hindus. According to these organisations, low-caste Hindus are the most hardworking and strong and able to bear much suffering. 'Because of their numerical strength, they are truly the spinal cord of Hindu jati [race]. Lakhs and crores of these people are getting dissociated from Hindu *samaj* because they are humiliated and looked down upon. As a result, Hindu jati is becoming weak and powerless.'[18] They are the real Kshatriyas, that is, warriors, who protected the Hindu *samaj* in the ancient period against all calamities, aggressions and shocks. The Hindu jati can become strong only by uplifting the lower castes and not without them. They could be brought forward by imparting knowledge to them in ethics, good behaviour, education and other fields. 'They have to be made human beings in the true sense of the term.'[19]

The BS and HMM argue that despite the fact that the Hindu *samaj* is several times more powerful in many ways than that of the Muslims, it suffers humiliation and discredit because of a lack of internal cohesion, community feeling and faith in religion among members. The Hindus and the Muslims can work on an equal footing, and friendship between the two can develop only when the Hindu samaj becomes as strong, powerful and united as that of the Muslims. This calls for a sense of power among Hindus. The Hindus are reminded that they are apostles (*upasak*) of Shakti—the worshippers of Mahashakti. A *trishul* in the hands of Shiva, *sudarshan* in the hands of Krishna, bow and arrow in the hands of Ram, *khadag* with blood in the hands of Kali and different instruments in the ten arms of the goddess Durga are important symbols of the Hindu heritage. 'Hindus! If you want to preserve your existence, you should arm yourself with different weapons dear to Gods and Goddesses.'[20] Hindus are exhorted that they should not hesitate to take up arms when needed. They must understand that weakness, timidity, unmanliness are great sins and bravery and masculinity are great *punya*, that is, virtues.[21]

The RSS has floated the organisation Samajik Samrasata Manch (SSM), that is, Social Assimilation Platform, to attract Ambedkarists and other Dalits for the purpose of developing Hindu unity. The organisation was launched on 14 April 1983, birthday of Dr Ambedkar and Dr Hedgewar (the latter the founder of the RSS). Dr Hedgewar, according to the proponents of the SSM, did not support caste and class divisions. Caste-based divisions should be given up or ignored: 'We are one.' He emphasised: 'We all are Hindus, where is untouchability? For us all are Hindus and nothing else. . . . There is no varna of the *chaturvarna* or of caste. Today we have only one varna and jati, that is Hindu.' He lays stress on the inculcation of brotherhood among all Hindus. Society survives on the basis of a person-to-person bond and their collective participation.[22]

According to the proponents of the SSM, the central thrust of Ambedkar's ideology is dharma. He was a strong critic of the Brahmin caste which exploited society in the name of religion. But that was, according to RSS leader Dattopant Dhengadi, the fault of Brahmins and not of religion. Giving a twist to Ambedkar's decision to adopt Buddhism, it was asserted that Ambedkar did not accept Islam or Christianity because he feared those religions would make people anti-national.[23] With such assertions, the RSS supports its position that the Indian nationalist is one whose *punya bhumi* is India. And, to strengthen its position further, the RSS 'quotes' Ambedkar, thus: 'I would support a movement for the saffron flag.'[24] In order to legitimise their position, they highlight Ambedkar's 'Thoughts on Pakistan'.[25] According to the RSS interpretation, Ambedkar believed that so long as a Muslim believes he is a Muslim, he cannot become an integral part of Hindustan. Aggressiveness is part and parcel of Muslims who misuse the weakness of the Hindu *samaj*. Therefore, it is an objective of the SSM to assimilate Dalits with the mainstream and strengthen Hindu society and the nation.

BJP's STRATEGIES

Elsewhere I have analysed the Congress's policy and approach to the caste system and its strategies to win over backward castes in electoral politics.[26]

Suffice it to mention here that the Gujarat Congress succumbed to the pressure of some caste associations and distributed party positions on a caste basis. It has openly taken a pro-backward caste stand since the late 1960s. In its 1971 manifesto the party pledged 'to promote with special care the educational, employment and economic interests of the weaker sections of the people particularly the Scheduled Castes, the Scheduled Tribes and the backward classes'. The party gave more tickets to OBCs in elections and party positions. In Gujarat it concentrated on SCs, STs, and Kolis more than on OBCs whose numerical strength at the state level is not as significant, though some of them enjoy significant strength in assembly constituencies. The Congress supported, and later enhanced, reservations for OBCs in government jobs and educational institutions. And, there are a few Congress leaders who openly and unequivocally stand for backward castes and oppose upper castes in the distribution of divisible and indivisible benefits within the given political framework. They have set up educational and other institutions for carrying out welfare programmes for these communities. As a result, they often become the target of the wrath of the upper castes. Two anti-reservation agitations in the 1980s dominated by upper castes were against the reservation policy of the Congress.

The Jana Sangh, the forerunner of the BJP came into existence in the early 1950s, though its electoral visibility in the state is a recent phenomenon. But the penetration of Hindutva ideology is neither recent nor sudden. Various caste and religious organisations, often under the patronage of the Congress, reformulated and legitimised Hindutva ideology. And, there has been no ideological counter to it. A series of communal riots which began in Gujarat in the aftermath of the Indo-Pakistan war of 1965 have contributed to the strengthening of Hindu consciousness and militancy. In many riots, besides poor and middle-class Muslims, OBCs were also victims.

Ideologically, the BJP is against the caste system, mainly high–low status differentiation based on birth. But like the RSS, it believes in ignoring caste differentiations. Hindu unity, it is hoped, will wipe out differentiations. Unlike a section of the Congress, the party believes that upper castes are not responsible for degrading the condition of OBCs. They could improve their position by education, and inculcation of 'good' values and behaviour. The conflicts between castes today, according to the BJP, have been created mainly by the Congress for the purposes of electoral gains. They are 'political' and artificial. Therefore, the party has not been enthusiastically in favour of reservation for SCs, STs and OBCs. For political exigency it did not oppose it either. But no BJP state-level leader opposed the anti-reservation agitation by mobilising its cadre. In fact, many of its supporters were actively involved in the agitation.

Soon after the anti-reservation agitation, the party, in its 1985 election manifesto, mentioned welfare programmes for certain STs called Vanvasi, but failed even to take cognisance of the problems of SCs and OBCs who were the main victims of the agitation.[27] At the same time the 'party supported reservation for OBCs and promised to take special measures for the uplift of SCs, STs and OBCs. But it was more political rhetoric than commitment. This is evident from the 1991 survey in which 46 per cent of the state-level and 77 per cent of district-level leaders expressed the opinion that they were not in favour of the existing reservation system.[28] Their arguments are more or less the same even today as those of anti-reservationists. The majority of them are in favour of providing similar benefits to the poor of the upper castes. Those who are not against reservation believe that though OBCs should be given this facility, it should not be at the cost of meritorious upper-caste persons. Upper-caste BJP members, like their caste fellows outside the BJP, complained about the Congress giving 'too much importance and favour' to SCs, STs and OBCs. In informal conversations they look down upon backward castes. Though they do not blame them for their ascribed status, they do find fault with their values and lifestyle. One of the strong supporters of Hindutva and BJP said that besides the Muslims, backwards were responsible for most of the present-day problems of our society.[29] These views are shared by many upper-caste members.

Upper–and middle-caste members control the party. In 1991, as many as 63 per cent of the state-level and district-level leaders were from upper or middle castes—Brahmin, Vania, Patidar or Rajput. At the state level, 14 per cent together were SC of STs, but their proportion was only 6 per cent at the local level. Leaders from the ranks of OBCs were 17 and 30 per cent at the state and district levels respectively.

Many backward castes, as mentioned above, are not homogeneous. Economic differentiations among them have sharpened in the last four decades. With electoral politics, political aspirants, particularly those who have improved their economic condition, have multiplied. They want *swaman*, that is, self-respect, status and recognition not only from caste brethren but also from others. Though the Congress has given a larger number of party and government positions to backward caste members in recent years than in the past, all those who aspire for positions could not be accommodated. Not only members of the upper and middle castes but also early entrants from backward castes act as barriers to the entry of the aspirants. Such dissatisfied politicians find the BJP an alternative avenue to move up the political ladder. Realising the importance of their numerical strength, the BJP accommodated a few of them. One Dalit leader, though he claims to be 'radical' in his ideology, told us in 1991: 'The BJP subscribes to Brahminical ideology, but the Congress in practice is in no way different. Moreover, I worked in the Congress for more than ten years but I did not get a position whereas the BJP has given me a party position.' However, his day-to-day confrontations with party leaders on Dalit and tribal problems caused him to resign from the party in 1991.

The present president and vice-president of the state party belong to backward castes from south and north Gujarat respectively. The earl let president was also from a backward caste in north Gujarat. In the last assembly elections (1990), the party gave tickets to forty-three candidates belonging to OBCs, as against fifty-eight candidates of the Congress. However, the party did not put up candidates in seven ST–and four SC-reserved constituencies. This was part of an electoral alliance with the Gujarat Janata Dal.

In order to make inroads into the ranks of Kshatriya—Bareeya, Thakor, Patanwadia of central and north Gujarat—voters, BJP leaders organised a Kshatriya Sabha in the early 1980s as an alternative to the Congress-dominated Kshatriya Sabha. Like the Congress, it also extended support to various backward caste associations and used their platforms to appeal to voters during elections. The party formed Harijan and Adivasi cells in 1980 to take up the problems of these groups. Occasionally the party also protested against atrocities on SCs and STs particularly in cases in which either Congress lead s or the government had been involved. For instance, in 1989 the BJP was the first political party to support the protest of the Dalits of Sambarda village in north Gujarat against atrocities by upper-caste Hindus. The village Dalits who improved their economic condition and wan their *swaman* migrated *en masse* from the village to protest against the arrogance and harassment of the upper castes. It may be noted that the Congress member of Parliament and minister at that time belonged to an upper caste of the same village; and he lent tacit support to his caste brethren against the Dalits. The pro-Dalit faction of the Congress was upset and agitated about the episode but could not actively show support for the Dalits because of the minister's clout with the party high comamnd.[30] Similarly, in 1992 the BJP supported the demand to give away government land to tribals in the Dangs. The CPI(ML) mobilised the tribals and also organised demonstration in 1982 and 1991 in several district headquarters demanding protection for Harijans. The party organised a *nyaya yatra* (march for justice) in 1985–6. The *yatra* began on Ambedkar's birthday— 6 December—and ended on Vivekananda's birthday—12 January. It toured 118 talukas and fifteen districts covering 26,000 km in thirty-eight days.[30] Recently, the party launched a campaign, headed by Dalit leaders, to enroll 25,000 Dalits as party members.

The BJP and the Sangh Parivar mobilised backward castes in, various programmes related to the issue of Ramjanmabhumi. Special efforts were made to collect bricks and token cash contribution from tribals and OBCs. In the tribal areas of Bharuch district, for instance, a campaign was started to collect Rs 1.25 per household in big villages, a token contribution for construction of the Ram temple in Ayodhya. The tribals were asked, 'Are you Hindus? If you are, then prove it by contributing Rs 1.25 for *Ramshila pujan* [worship of bricks to be used in construction of Ram temple in Ayodhya]. If you do not contribute that would prove you are from a Muslim womb!'[32] It may be mentioned that among the tribals, those who have somewhat improved their economic condition follow the practices of caste Hindus. This process is more than a century old. Thus, to be Hindus and get recognised as such is recognition of a higher status. A similar campaign was launched for Ram *paduka* in 1992. The BJP claims that 380 *paduka yatras* were organised in different parts of the state, which covered a large number of villages. We do not know what part backward caste members played in *paduka puja* at the village level. However, the BJP specially recruited *kar sevaks* from different castes and more so from backward castes for the December 1992 Ayodhya event. The BJP and Sangh Parivar sought the support of *sants* and swamis of different sects for the brick collection, *paduka puja* and *kar seva*. One of these, the Swaminarayan sect, has many devotees among OBCs and tribals. These *sants* and *swamis* issued an appeal during the 1990 assembly elections and 1991 parliamentary elections to vote for the party that was serious about protecting Hindu interests. They said: 'The present awakening for Hindutva is an inevitable consequence of larger changes. . . . For rejuvenation of Hindu culture, the voters should vote for BJP candidates.'[33] Morari Bapu issued an appeal exhorting people to vote for those supporting the following issues of national importance: (i) construction of the Ramjanmabhumi temples; (ii) deletion of Article 370 which separates Kashmir from the rest of the country; and (iii) ban on cow-slaughter. 'Vote only for patriots . . . Let the martyrdom of those innocent Ram *kar sevaks* not be in vain.' The communal riots following the demolition of the Babri Masjid aroused communal passions and a militant communal consciousness. The communal hurricane did not spare Dalits, tribals or OBCs, many of whom have become anti-Muslim.

OVERVIEW

On the electoral front, the BJP made its first significant show in four major municipal corporation elections—Ahmedabad, Baroda, Rajkot and Surat—in 1989. It then captured 67 out of 187 state assembly seats with 27 per cent of the votes polled in 1990. Next year, the party swept the Lok Sabha poll by winning 20 out of 25 seats from the state. This obviously would not have been possible without the support of SCs, OBCs and STs. The BJP has made a more significant dent in OBC support for the Congress than either SC or ST support. The Congress retained two ST-reserved seats in the 1991 Lok Sabha poll. The majority of the Dalits are still not supporters of the BJP. They either continue to vote for the Congress or have become ambivalent.

Left parties, the Republican Party and the Bahujan Samaj Party are almost absent in Gujarat. The Janata Dal is insignificant. And the Congress is in bad shape. It is not only faction-ridden but its pro-backward caste leaders are marginalised. Upper-caste leaders rule the Congress with a vengeance. However, it would be simplistic to say that OBC and Dalit support for the BJP means their acceptance of Brahminical dominance and adherence to the project of rejuvenating Vedic *sanskriti*. They are aware of the oppression of the upper castes. And this awareness has already created subterranean tensions within the BJP that will inevitably be sharpened if and when the party comes to power. Today, it is part of the electoral game that meets the needs of the upwardly mobile aspirants of backward castes to some extent. But the BJP is unlikely to get their support, *en bloc*.

13

New Phase in Backward Caste Politics in Bihar, 1990–2000 *

SANJAY KUMAR

INTRODUCTION

Bihar, economically, educationally and socially one of the most backward states of India, is also politically one of the most important. This is not only because this state accounts for 54 Lok Sabha seats, but also because the long process of democratisation has inculcated a sense of empowerment among the people. The backward castes started sensing this empowerment as early as in the mid-1970s—a feeling which, in a way, fully bloomed fully in the early 1990s when Laloo Yadav became chief minister of Bihar. With his implementation of welfare programmes for the lower sections of society, especially the Dalits, they too began sensing the change in the mid-1990s.

THE PROCESS OF EMPOWERMENT IN BIHAR

Empowerment of the marginalised sections of society is nothing new. Though it emerged suddenly in the 1970s and then in the 1990s, it was actually the culmination of long-drawn political movements dating back to the pre-independence period.

With nearly 80 per cent of the population depending upon it for their livelihood, agriculture formed the mainstay of Bihar's economy. But agricultural land remained monopolised by the three upper castes—the Rajputs, the Bhumihars and the Brahmins. The upper layer of the backward castes, namely, the Yadavs, the Kurmis and the Koeris, were left with very little land. But for

* *Economic and Political Weekly,* 34 (34–5), August 1999, pp. 2472–80.

some exception other lower castes were largely landless. During the pre-independent period, the state witnessed strong movement for land reforms, which continued for a long time. The movement was led by leaders of the Kisan Sabha formed in the year 1920. The movement was led by Swami Bidyanand, Swami Sahajanand Saraswati and Karyanand Sharma mainly in the north Bihar region. The leaders of the Kisan Sabha demanded minimum wages for agricultural labour, abolition of the zamindari system, licensing of moneylenders' security to the tenant cultivator and other reforms. Since it was mainly the upper castes who owned land and wielded social and political power, such movements inevitably got directed towards them. On the other hand it was primarily the backward castes owning some land who formed the backbone of the movement, as they perceived a direct benefit from such reforms. Though it could not achieve the desired results, redistribution of land as a result of the Bhoodan movement led to the breaking of the hold of the upper castes over the land to a great extent.

With a bit of land and with the diversification of their occupation, these backward castes were able to improve their economic status and emerged as a newly rich rural agrarian class, popularly known as 'kulaks', and started to play an important role in the social and political, spheres. On the other hand, this struggle also sowed the seeds of a sense of empowerment among them.

This assertiveness kept growing with various social and political movements, but took on a particularly intense form in the mid-1970s with the movement led by Jaiprakash Narayan in which, though it was an all-India movement, Bihar played a leading role. This movement ultimately led to a change of guard at the centre.

The social struggle in the mid-1980s and 1990s, particularly in central Bihar, certainly inculcated a sense of empowerment among the deprived people actively associated with it though it could not bring about major changes in the social, political and economic spheres. The growing number of contestants in the successive Vidhan Sabha and Lok Sabha elections, and the increasing turnout over the period 1952–2000, bears testimony to this. From 1602 contestants in, the 1952 Vidhan Sabha elections the number went up to 8463 in 1995. Similarly, from 198 contestants in the 1952 Lok Sabha elections, the number went up to 1448 in 1996. However, their numbers declined to 451 in 1998 because of certain restrictions imposed for contesting the election. The turnout of voters also increased phenomenally during this period. From 39.7 per cent in the 1952 Vidhan Sabha elections, the turnout went up to 61.8 per cent in 1995. The 1998 Lok Sabha elections witnessed a 64.6 per cent turnout as compared to 59.5 per cent in 1996. (Table 13.1). With only a 39.7 per cent turnout in the 1952 Lok Sabha elections, the state had certainly moved ahead in the process of democratisation.

Table 13.1: Candidates, Increasing Number and Performance: Assembly Elections, 1952–2000

Year	Total number of candidates	Average number of candidates per constituency	Candidates forfeited deposit (%)
1952	1602	5.0	53.3
1957	1394	4.3	46.9
1962	1529	4.8	53.0
1967	2025	6.3	64.5
1969	2154	6.7	63.4
1972	1982	6.2	62.9
1977	2973	9.1	73.7
1980	2959	9.1	74.6
1985	4238	13.0	83.2
1990	6439	19.8	91.5
1995	8410	26.0	91.8
2000	3934	12.1	–

Source: Up to 1985, V.B. Singh and Shankar Bose, *Elections in India*, Delhi: Sage Publications, 1988; *Statistical Report on the General Elections to the Legislative Assemblies 1989–90*, vol. I, Election Commission of India, New Delhi; 1995; *Statistical Report on the General Elections to the Legislative Assembly of Bihar*, Election Commission of India, New Delhi.

Though the country started witnessing political change as early as in the mid-1960s, with various non-Congress governments coming to power in different states in 1967 (Bihar being one of them), it was in 1977 that it witnessed a major political change for the first time.

Not only was the monopoly of the Congress party broken at the centre and the Janata Party came to power, but in a large number of states non-Congress governments were installed with thumping majorities. This central government did not last long and the Congress returned to power in 1980. It was only nine years later that once again a new formation in the shape of the Janata Dal came to power at the centre. Bihar played a major role in the formation of both these non-Congress governments, returning a large number of non-Congress representatives to Parliament in the 1977 and 1989 Lok Sabha elections. The Congress drew a blank and its votes went down to 22.9 per cent in the 1977 Lok Sabha elections as compared to 39 seats won and 40.1 per cent votes polled in the 1971 elections. In the Vidhan Sabha elections of 1977, Congress seats were reduced to only 57 as compared to 168 seats won in

Table 13.2: Candidates, Increasing Number and Performance: Lok Sabha
Elections 1952–1999

Year	Total number of candidates	Candidates candidates per constituency	Average number of forfeited deposit (%)
1952	198	3.6	33.8
1957	189	3.5	40.2
1962	233	4.3	46.3
1967	315	5.9	61.2
1971	421	7.9	71.0
1977	340	6.2	70.2
1980	594	11.0	76.9
1984	676	12.5	82.9
1989	711	13.1	81.0
1991	1246	23.0	90.3
1996	1448	26.8	91.5
1998	451	8.5	72.2
1999	497	9.2	76.2

Source: Up to 1984, V.B. Singh and Shankar Bose, *Elections in India,* Delhi: Sage
Publications, 1986; 1989–1991, V.B. Singh, *Elections in India, 1994–1996; Statistical
Report on the General Elections to the Eleventh Lok Sabha Election, 1996; 1998,
Statistical Report on the General Twelfth Lok Sabha Elections, 1998; Statistical Report
on the General Elections to the Thirteenth Lok Sabha Elections, 1999,* Election
Commission of India, New Delhi.

the 1972 Vidhan Sabha elections. The Congress lost nearly 10 per cent votes
in these two elections as its votes went down to 23.6 per cent in 1977 as
compared to 33.1 per cent in 1972. The Congress regained much of the lost
ground in the 1980s but again suffered a major setback in the 1989 Lok Sabha
elections. As compared to 48 seats and 51.8 per cent votes in 1984, the party
managed to win only four Lok Sabha seats and its votes went down to 28.1 per
cent during the 1989 Lok Sabha elections, while the Janata Dal won 31 seats
with 36.4 per cent votes and the Communist Party of India (CPI) and
Communist Party of India (Marxist) (CPM) won four seats respectively with
7.9 and 1.4 per cent votes.

Traditionally a Congress stronghold, the success of a larger number of
non-Congress representatives in the state was primarily on account of the
realignment of the backward castes who had generally voted against the
Congress in both the 1977 and 1989 Lok Sabha elections. So the process of
realignment of the backward castes which started in the mid-1970s and took

full shape in the early 1990s gave way to a process of de-alignment, with the consolidated backward castes further breaking apart and a section of them aligning with the upper castes to put up a challenge to the dominance of one section of backward castes represented by the Yadavs.

BIHAR ASSEMBLY ELECTIONS, 1995: ASSERTION OF THE 'BACKWARD CLASSES'

Though the change in Bihar politics started as early as 1990, the real *shift* in the political sphere was reflected in the outcome of the 1995 Vidhan Sabha polls. The state witnessed the assertion of backward caste politics which ushered in a scenario that may stay for some time to come. The state went to the polls in a unique polarised situation. The polarisation was not only among the upper and backward castes, but even the backward castes were divided. Laloo Yadav after completing his term in office even with a minority government went to polls in the midst of an anti-incumbency wave that was sweeping the country. The consolidated backward castes had fragmented into two blocs, one comprising the Yadav represented by the Janata Dal and the other the Kurmis and Koeris represented by the Samata Party. For the first time, the upper castes felt totally marginalised in the state's politics since the support base of their natural ally, the Congress, had been completely eroded, while the BJP was unable to make much inroads among the voters.

The Janata Dal contested the elections with its traditional alliance partners, the CPI, CPM and Jharkhand Mukti Morcha (JMM), whereas the Bharatiya Janata Party (BJP), Congress and Bihar Peoples Party (BPP) contested alone, leaving only the Samata Party and the Communist Party of India Marxist-Leninist (CPI-ML) to enter into an alliance. The results of the 1995 Vidhan Sabha elections came as a surprise to many. Belying expectations, the Janata Dal returned to power with an absolute majority, winning 166 of the total of 324 seats with 27.9 per cent votes, with its alliance partner CPI getting 26 seats with 4.8 per cent votes, CPM getting six seats with 1.3 per cent votes and JMM (S) capturing 16 seats with 3.7 per cent votes. Further, the BJP won 41 seats with 12.9 per cent votes, acquiring the position of the opposition party and relegating the Congress to third position. The Congress could manage to win only 29 seats with 16.4 per cent votes.

The Janata Dal's performance was an all-round success. Except for some poor performance in the south where it could manage to win just 13 seats with 14.8 per cent votes, its performance in north and central Bihar was spectacular. Of the total 138 seats in north Bihar, the Janata Dal won 97 seats with 34.9 per cent votes. In central Bihar, it won 54 seats with 20.1 per cent votes, out of a total of 92 seats. The BJP did well in south Bihar, winning 21 of the total 94 seats with 18.3 per cent votes. The performance of the Congress was bad throughout the state.

The success of the Janata Dal and its allies was due to the fact that the alliance drew a large measure of support from the numerically strong, poor and deprived sections of society. A survey conducted by the Centre for the Study of Developing Societies (CSDS), in a representative sample of 16 assembly constituencies spread across all three regions of Bihar, reveals that there was massive support for the Janata Dal and its allies specially among the Dalits, the backward castes, the Muslims, the illiterate, and landless agricultural labourers. Nearly 48.7 per cent of the Dalits, 49.8 per cent of the backward castes, and about 57.3 per cent of the Muslims voted for the Janata Dal and its allies. It remained the most popular party among the Illiterate as 47.3 per cent of them voted for it; 43.8 per cent of the landless agricultural labourers also voted for it. The support base of the Congress had eroded in general, but it still appeared to be a popular party among the upper castes. Of the upper caste voters, 39.1 per cent voted for the Congress while only 20.9 per cent voted for the Janata Dal. Though the BJP managed to win 41 Vidhan Sabha seats, it still lacked a broad support base in Bihar. Except for 19 per cent votes among the tribals, 16.5 per cent among the upper castes and 18.3 per cent among the middle class, its support base among the other sections continued to remain very low.

The biggest surprise was that despite being constantly blamed for neglecting developmental work, Laloo Yadav drew large support from the largest sections of society. If one takes a deeper look into the functioning of the Laloo government, during the period 1990–5, one can understand why the poor and the Dalits voted for the Janata Dal. Although nothing much was done for them besides constructing some houses under the Indira Awas Yojana for the Musahars, the poorest among the poor Dalits, the very fact that most of them were being allowed to vote freely gave them a sense of empowerment.

The backward castes, particularly the Yadavs, had reason to vote for Laloo: they did not want to let the power they had gained after a long struggle slip from their hands. Though during the 1995 Vidhan Sabha elections the two dominant backward castes, the Kurmis and Yadavs, contested the electoral battle against each other, the Samata Party was blamed for fighting a proxy war for the upper castes in the name of the casteist politics of Laloo Yadav. This feeling consolidated the other backward castes, besides the Kurmis and Koeris, behind the Janata Dal.

The Muslims, except for a few instances where personal affiliation with the candidate or his otherwise clean image mattered, voted largely for the Janata Dal. The Bhagalpur riots were still fresh in the minds of the Muslims. Further, the arrest of the BJP leader L.K. Advani at Samastipur during his Rath Yatra made Laloo Yadav a great hero among them. Besides, in the aftermath of the demolition of the Babri Masjid, when the country was reeling under communal violence, and a large number of people were killed in riots which continued unabated for almost five days, it was Laloo Yadav who stood for the protection of the Muslims in his state. There were no instances of riots or violence in Bihar. The protection given to Muslims during Laloo's regime was unprecedented, and ever since then the Muslims clearly identify themselves with the Janata Dal.

The results of the 1995 assembly elections in Bihar set the trend for backward caste politics for the next few years. It was the first time backward castes fought among themselves and the upper castes remained at the margins of the political struggle. The backwards managed to have a firm control over political power.

One of the major achievements this time was that the majority of the most deprived sections, the Dalits, were allowed to vote. For the first time, they had a sense that they mattered in electoral politics. Though the Yadavs took the driver's seat in the matter of governing the state, the other backward castes and the Dalits remained aligned with the Janata Dal. They felt that they did have a share in the political power in the state. During the Congress regime, power remained monopolised by the upper castes and no serious attempt was made to incorporate the aspirations and demands of the Dalits and backward castes into governance of the state.

LOK SABHA ELECTIONS, 1996: BJP ON THE RISE

As stated earlier, the rapid de-alignment of electoral force led to a major shift in the politics of the state. The results of the 1996 Lok Sabha elections demonstrate that a new beginning was made in the politics of Bihar. The Janata Dal and its allies suffered major setback in these elections which provides more than one signal. First and foremost, the election results clearly pointed to the limitations of sectional politics. Further, they demonstrated the constraints of the ruling party in a multiparty democracy, when most of the opposition parties united against the ruling party while contesting elections. In a multiparty democracy, where a political party captures political power with barely 30 per cent votes, it is exposed to severe limitations once the divided opposition, unites against the ruling party.

The results of these elections clearly followed from such a scenario.

During the Vidhan Sabha elections in 1995, the Janata Dal and its allies CPI, CPM and JMM (Soren—S), fought a badly divided opposition. Though the Samata Party had some understanding with the CPI (ML), it was the BJP, the BPP, the Congress and a few other smaller parties that opposed the Janata Dal and its allies separately. The net result was that with just 27.9 per cent votes, the Janata Dal managed to get an absolute majority with 166 seats, and its allies CPI, CPM and JMM (S) won 26, six and 16 seats respectively with merely 4.8, 1.3 and 3.7 per cent votes. Many people had great faith in the Samata. Party, formed or, the eve of the elections, and thought that it may provide an alternative to the ruling Janata Dal. A party formed mainly by the defectors of the Janata Dal and with Nitish Kumar as its leader, it was expected to draw large support from the Kurmis and Koeris. But the party performed well, winning only seven seats with 6.9 per cent votes. The Congress with the support of just the upper castes, went down to a mere 29 seats with 16.4 per cent votes. The BJP, though it managed to improve its tally, winning 41 seats with 12.9 per cent votes, did not come much closer to realising its dream of calling the shots in Bihar.

After the success in the Vidhan Sabha elections it seemed as if the Janata Dal had become an invincible party in Bihar. The political parties opposing it realised their weaknesses and shortly after the elections and several rounds of talks, the Samata Party and the BJP entered into an alliance, where BJP contested 32 seats leaving 22 seats for the Samata Party. Leaders of both the parties welcomed this alliance. However, the leaders of the Samata Party, particularly George Fernandes and Nitish Kumar who swore by the socialist tradition, came under severe criticism on account of their alliance with a communal party. These leaders termed it a special arrangement needed for a special time in a special state, 'the need of the hour' to challenge the casteist politics of Laloo Yadav. The Bihar People's Party (BPP), which had been completely routed in the Vidhan Sabha elections, merged with the Samata Party. Since it drew some support from upper-caste Rajputs, it was perceived that this alliance may broaden the base of the Samata Party much beyond the support of only the backward castes. Entering into an alliance with the BJP was certainly a step towards forming a front against the Janata Dal. The other opposition party, the Congress, marginalised to a great extent, contested the election alone, like the splinter groups of the JMM parties. The Janata Dal on the other hand contested along with its traditional partners CPI and CPM. But as compared to earlier elections, the only change was in terms of seat sharing, as Laloo completely, dominated over his alliance partners, the CPI and CPM. Of the total, Janata Dal contested 44 seats, leaving only eight for the CPI and two for the CPM.

Though Laloo Yadav seemed confident of winning most of the seats in Bihar, he was put on the defensive by the opposition parties which launched a virulent campaign against the fodder scam unearthed during the tenure of the Janata Dal government. On the other hand, the Janata Dal championed the cause of uplift of the backwards and the poor from the platform of social justice. It called upon the people to vote for the Janata Dal and its allies and to save Bihar from the threat of the communal party, namely, the BJP. On the other hand, the BJP and Samata combine attacked Laloo Yadav for perpetuating casteist politics in Bihar in the name of social justice. They blamed the government for the fodder and other scams that occurred during his regime. Though the *hawala* issue could not make a dent as an election issue among the poor rural masses of Bihar, the fodder scam—popularly termed the 'Gawala' scam—got wide publicity. In the beginning it seemed as if this scam would have little bearing on public opinion and may not affect the electoral prospects of the parties. Two rounds of pre-election surveys conducted by CSDS made it amply clear that the Janata Dal still remained the most popular party. Of the total respondents, 32.9 and 40.3 per cent intended voting for the Janata Dal in the first and second round, respectively, whereas the support base for the BJP was 7.9 and 9.9 per cent only.

But things changed rapidly as the elections drew closer. The virulent attack on the Janata Dal and its policies by the BJP and its alliance parties led to a last-minute change in the mood of the people at large. The Kurmis and Koeris had already reposed full faith in the BJP–Samata alliance, but the Brahmins and other upper castes, which traditionally used to vote for the Congress, shifted their support to the BJP–Samata alliance as well. This led to some surprise results.

The party which had won an absolute majority in the Vidhan Sabha elections barely a year ago was cut down to size, even though its leaders had been confident it would win all the seats. The Janata Dal managed to win only 22 seats as compared to 33 seats in the 1991 Lok Sabha elections. Its vote went down by nearly 2.2 per cent as it could get just 31.9 per cent votes as compared to 34.1 per cent in the 1991 Lok Sabha elections. Its alliance partners, the CPI and CPM, also suffered major losses. The CPI lost more than half the seats and won only three Lok Sabha seats as compared to eight in the 1991 elections. Its votes were drastically reduced from 7.6 per cent to 5.1 per cent in 1996. The CPM could not even retain the lone seat it had won in the 1991 Lok Sabha elections.

The BJP, in alliance with the Samata Party, became the major gainer. It won 18 Lok Sabha seats with 20.5 per cent votes as compared to five seats won in the 1991 elections with 15.9 per cent votes. But actually the increase in the BJP votes was much higher than it appeared, for in the 1996 Lok Sabha elections it contested only 32 Lok Sabha seats as compared to 51 seats in the 1991 elections. The Samata Party won six Lok Sabha seats contesting 22 seats and its vote went up by nearly 7.6 per cent as compared to its votes in the 1995 assembly elections. Though the Congress doubled its tally from one to two, its vote went down from 24.2 per cent in 1991 to 13 per cent in 1996. The JMM, which won six seats in the 1991 Lok Sabha elections, suffered a major loss. The party not only lost much ground in its traditional tribal belt of south

Bihar, it also suffered a loss because its various factions fought amongst each other, which resulted in the split of votes. The JMM (S) managed to win only one Lok Sabha seat, and that too with a slender margin of 5000 votes.

LOK SABHA ELECTIONS, 1998: EMERGENCE OF RJD

The premature dissolution of the Lok Sabha pushed the country towards another Lok Sabha election much sooner than expected. Even in this short duration, the political scenario in Bihar had taken a major turn. There was mounting pressure on Laloo Yadav, from the left parties and even from within his own party, to step down from the post of party president and as chief minister of the state. This resulted in a split in the Janata Dal and the formation of the Rashtriya Janata Dal (RJD) by Laloo Yadav before the 1998 Lok Sabha elections. The formation of the new party opened up the possibility of a fresh, realignment among various competing political parties.

Though there was no major shift in the already existing alliance among the dominant political parties, the BJP maintained its alliance with the Samata Party and the Janata Dal still retained its alliance with the CPI and CPM. The Congress, which had performed badly in the past few elections, was desperately looking for ways of revival. Though Laloo Yadav showed confidence about achieving big success in the election, he knew that it was not going to be easy this time. Three major factors seemed to be working against him. First, he feared a division in the Yadav vote, which could indirectly help BJP in winning more seats; second, he knew it would not be not easy to make people familiar with the new symbol of the 'lamp' allotted to RJD; third, he realised that the absence of a party organisation at the local level may add to the problems for his new party. In view of these constraints, Laloo Yadav was looking for an alliance to at least minimise the split of vote. He allied with the Congress, which was also in search of an alliance partner. The JMM, a party that was very strong in south Bihar in the 1991 Lok Sabha elections, but performed badly in the 1996 elections because of division in the party, was also searching for an alliance. Laloo Yadav knew his party had very little presence in south Bihar and so he wisely entered into an alliance with the JMM.

With the alliance pattern, Bihar seemed to be heading towards a three-cornered contest. With the split in the party, the Janata Dal was put to a severe test. It was widely believed that the split in the Janata Dal would lead to division of votes between the Janata Dal and the RJD and cause major loss to the party. It was primarily Laloo Yadav, leader of the RJD, who would be tested for his personal charisma. Many believed that the RJD may not be successful as Laloo Yadav after his involvement in the fodder scam had become a spent force in the state's politics and it would be hard for the party to win seats. In alliance with the Congress and the JMM, Laloo Yadav hoped to put up a strong contest in north Bihar on account of the shift of the traditional Congress voters still with the party towards the RJD. With 12.2 per cent votes polled by JMM and 16 per cent by the Congress in south Bihar in the 1996 Lok Sabha elections, the alliance hoped to put up a formidable contest there too. The BJP–Samata combine, on the other hand, expected that it would gain most from the three-cornered contest.

What followed came as a major surprise for political speculators. The Bihar elections actually turned out to be a direct contest between the RJD and the BJP–Samata combine, with the Janata Dal and its allies putting up no contest at all. The results, however, revealed that the 1998 Lok Sabha elections more keenly contested were than the past few elections. The previous three Lok Sabha elections in the state had witnessed a narrowing of the victory margin in a large number of constituencies. As compared to only six and 10 constituencies where the victory margin was less than 5 per cent in 1991 and 1996, in the 1998 elections the victory margin was less than 5 per cent in as many as 18 constituencies and between 5 and 10 percent in another six. The narrowing of the victory margin in the 1998 Lok Sabha elections clearly indicates that the state witnessed more competitive politics as compared to the past few elections.

The 1998 Lok Sabha elections virtually saw the end of the Janata Dal in the state. Ram Vilas Paswan was the only Janata Dal candidate who won from the Hajipur Lok Sabha constituency. The party managed to get only 8.3 per cent votes compared to the 31.9 per cent it polled in the 1996 elections. Its alliance partner, the CPI and CPM, could not win a seat and polled as low as 3.1 and 2.1 per cent votes respectively. Belying popular expectations, the RJD won 17 seats and, polling 25.2 per cent votes, still emerged as the largest party in terms of votes. Though the Congress got only 7.2 per cent votes, nearly 6 per cent less than it polled in the 1996 elections, it managed to win five seats and regain some lost ground. The fewer votes for the party was largely attributed to its contesting fewer seats on account of the alliance with the RJD. In spite of the triangular alliance, the JMM could not open its account and polled 3 per cent votes. As an alliance, the BJP–Samata combine turned out to be the major gainer in the 1998 Lok Sabha elections. With the BJP getting 19 seats with 23.1 per cent votes and the Samata Party winning 10 seats with 15.8 per cent votes, the alliance won 29 seats, improving its tally of 24 in the 1996 Lok Sabha elections.

LOK SABHA ELECTIONS, 1999: SETBACK FOR RJD

The joining together of the anti-Laloo forces, a process which began just before the 1996 Lok Sabha elections, went a step forward. The Samata Party merged with the Janata Dal to form the Janata Dal–(United—U) which decided to contest the 1999 elections in alliance with the BJP. The BPP also decided to contest the election in alliance with the BJP–Janata Dal (U) combine. So with Congress forming an alliance with the RJD it was going to be a strait bipolar contest.

In this contest the BJP and its ally the Janata Dal (U) won 41 seats and polled 45.5 per cent of the votes, while the RJD–Congress combine won only 11 seats and polled 37.1 per cent votes. One set each was won by the CPI and the BPP. If winning seats is the only indicator of a party's success, then one can assume that the BJP–Janata Dal (U) registered a massive victory over the RJD–Congress combine, in what seems like a one-sided affair.

But if one looks at the margins of victory, of the past three Lok Sabha elections this was certainly the most keenly contested election. The difference in vote share between the two alliances was 8.4 per cent. Of the 54 seats, the results in 23 Lok Sabha constituencies showed a less than 5 per cent victory margin, while in 1998 there had been only 17 constituencies with a victory margin this small.

Compared to its tally in 1998, the RJD–Congress alliance suffered a major loss, dropping 11 seats. However, it is worth noting that in terms of votes, the RJD remained the single largest party in the state. In fact, the vote share of the RJD increased by a little over three percentage points in the 1998 Lok Sabha elections.

The success of the BJP–Samata alliance cannot be attributed to the rise of the BJP in the state. Although it increased its seat tally by three seats, it lost nearly one percentage point in vote share; this, of course, might have been due to it contesting fewer seats. To a greater extent the success of the alliance can be credited to the merger of the Samata Party and the Janata Dal into the Janata Dal (U) and the working out of a formidable alliance between the BJP, the Janata Dal (U) and the BPP. This led to a strong consolidation of the anti-Laloo Yadav vote in the state. Though the Janata Dal (U)'s vote share fell by nearly three percentage points (if compared with the combined vote for the Samata Party and Janata Dal in 1998), it managed to increase its joint tally by six seats.

LOK SABHA ELECTIONS, 1991–1999: REGION-WISE ANALYSIS

The overall results of the Lok Sabha elections held in 1996, 1998 and 1999 indicate that the Janata Dal (RJD since the 1998 Lok Sabha elections) which had witnessed a decline over the past few elections, was nearly wiped out in the 1999 Lok Sabha elections. The BJP–Samata alliance (BJP–Janata Dal [U] in 1999 with the merger of the Janata Dal) became stronger and stronger over the Lok Sabha elections of 1998 and 1999. In order to assess the strength of these parties it is better to look at the performance of different parties in the three distinct geographical regions of Bihar, that is north, central and south.

The poverty-stricken, flood-prone terrain of north Bihar, accounting for 26 Lok Sabha seats, is politically the most important region of Bihar. It had been a stronghold of the Janata Dal during the elections held after 1990. In the 1991 elections, the Janata Dal won 22 seats from this region with 48.3 per cent votes, and with the CPI winning three seats, the combined tally for the alliance was 25 seats. But in the 1996 elections, the Janata Dal lost six seats in this region. It won only 16 seats with 40.3 per cent votes. The CPI won two seats, bringing the combined tally to a total of 18 seats. The BJP, which had drawn a blank here in the 1991 elections, managed to win six seats with 33.8 per cent votes with its alliance partner, the Samata Party. The 1998 elections witnessed further gain for the BJP–Samata combine in the region where it managed to win eight seats and polled 35 per cent votes. The Janata Dal and allies overall performed badly in the state, but could still manage to save face in north Bihar, polling 18.3 per cent votes and winning a lone seat from this region. The RJD virtually swept the polls here, winning 14 seats and polling 29.4 per cent votes (Table 13.3).

In the 1999 elections, the BJP and its allies registered an Impressive victory in north Bihar. The allies won 20 seats and polled 46.2 per cent votes. The RJD suffered a major loss of 10 seats as compared to its tally in the 1998 elections. This loss does not indicate that the party was losing support in this region. In terms of votes polled, the RJD increased its votes by nearly 5.4 per cent as compared to the 1998 elections. However, despite the increased support base, the party lost a large number of seats mainly due to the consolidation of the anti-Laloo vote. With the merger of the Janata Dal and the Samata Party a large number of the anti-Laloo votes polled by the Janata Dal in the 1998 elections consolidated with the BJP and its allies (see Table 13.3).

This gives a clear indication that Laloo Yadav remained a major force in the politics of the state. The RJD had a strong presence in north Bihar and a minor division among the anti-Laloo votes in this region could lead to a thumping victory for the party in this region.

The BJP had a strong presence in the mineral-rich hilly terrain of south Bihar, accounting for 14 Lok Sabha seats. The BJP had not only remained the most dominant party in south Bihar, but it virtually swept the polls in the entire region in the Lok Sabha elections held in 1996, 1998 and 1999. As compared to the five seats it won in the 1991 elections, the BJP managed to win 12 of the 14 seats from this region both in 1996 and 1998 and 11 seats in 1999. An equal number of seats for the party in the three Lok Sabha elections (1996, 1998 and 1999) does not indicate that there was no change for BJP in

Table 13.3: Electoral Performance in North Bihar: Lok Sabha Elections, 1991–1999, Total seats 26

Year	Turn-out (%)	Congress			BJP +			JD +			RJD		
		Con-tested	Won	Vote (%)	Con-tested	Won	Vote (%)	Con-tested	Won	Vote (%)	Con-tested	Won	Vote (%)
1991	64.4	25	0	22.8	24	0	13.0	25	25	53.9	–	–	–
1996	61.0	26	1	12.1	24	6	33.8	27	18	45.4	–	–	–
1998	66.6	10	2	5.5	25	8	35.0	28	1	18.3	20	14	29.4
1999	66.1	3	0	3.9	26	20	46.2	–	–	–	21	4	34.8

Source: CSDS Data Unit, Delhi.

south Bihar. Though the vote for the party remained more or less the same in the elections held in 1998 and 1999, the BJP increased its support base enormously in this region between 1996 and 1998. As compared to 34 per cent votes in the 1996 Lok Sabha elections, the party polled 45.55 per cent votes in the 1998 elections.

The Janata Dal had registered some success in this region in the early 1990s, winning three seats in the 1991 Lok Sabha elections. In the 1996 elections, the Janata Dal polled 24.5 per cent votes, though it failed to win a seat. But after the elections in 1991 and 1996, the Janata Dal has never been a strong party of popular support in this region. Besides, the BJP, the Congress and the JMM had some presence in this region. Just before the 1998 elections, the RJD entered into an alliance with the Congress and the JMM. Though expected to spring a few surprises in this region, the alliance could hardly make its presence left. The JMM, which had won the lone Dumka seat in 1996, where the party president Shibu Soren won by a slender margin of about 5000 votes, drew a blank in both 1998 and 1999 and its votes also went down from 12.2 per cent in 1996 to 10.5 per cent in 1998 and further down to 9.2 per cent in 1999. It was the Congress which registered some gain in this region. It con tested all 14 seats, but won only one and polled 16 per cent votes in the 1996 elections. The Congress contested for only seven seats in the 1998 elections, but managed to win two seats and polled 15.7 per cent votes. Though in 1999 it could not increase its tally of seats, the Congress polled nearly 8 per cent more votes as compared to the 199 Lok Sabha elections (see Table 13.4).

The agriculturally rich central Bihar, accounting for 14 Lok Sabha seats, witnessed numerous agrarian struggles after independence. These struggles of the farmers were mainly led by various factions of the left parties. The Janata Dal and other left parties were particularly strong in this region. Though the Janata Dal remained the dominant party in this region, it faced a stiff challenge from the BJP–Samata combine during the 1996 Lok Sabha elections. The Janata Dal and its allies won 13 of the total of 14 seats from this region in 1991 Lok Sabha elections, but suffered a major loss as the alliance got only seven seats (Janata Dal six, CPI one) in 1996, with the Janata Dal getting 25.1 per cent and the left parties 10.6 per cent votes. In the 1998 elections, the Janata Dal and its allies lost heavily even in the traditional stronghold of the left. The alliance not only drew a blank but its votes also went down to only 8 per cent. The newly formed RJD could not perform well in this region and won only three seats but polled 35.9 per cent votes. The RJD did, however, put up a strong contest in this region and polled 32.4 per cent votes in the 1999 elections, but could manage to win only two seats. The BJP–Samata alliance remained the biggest gainer even in this region in the Lok Sabha elections of 1996, 1998 and 1999. The BJP, which had drawn a blank in 1991, in alliance

Table 13.4: Electoral Performance in South Bihar: Lok Sabha Elections, 1991–1999, Total seats 14

Year	Turn-out (%)	Congress Con-tested	Won	Vote (%)	BJP+ Con-tested	Won	Vote (%)	JD+ Con-tested	Won	Vote (%)	RJD Con-tested	Won	Vote (%)
1991	49.9	14	0	17.9	14	5	32.9	7	3	12.5	8	6	21.4
1996	54.8	14	1	16.0	14	12	34.0	14	0	24.3	14	1	12.2
1998	59.7	7	2	15.7	14	12	45.5	10	0	6.2	8	0	10.5
1999	48.5	11	2	23.8	14	11	45.5	–	–	–	12	0	9.2

Source: CSDS Data Unit, Delhi.

with the Samata Party managed to win six seats with 37.9 per cent votes in 1996. The alliance further improved its tally to nine seats and its votes increased to 42.8 per cent in the 1998 elections. With the merger of the Janata Dal and the Samata Party in 1999, the BJP and its allies further consolidated their position in central Bihar. The allies won 10 seats and polled 44.2 per cent votes. The Congress won both the seats it contested from this region (Table 13.5).

VIDHAN SABHA ELECTIONS, 2000: RE-EMERGENCE OF RJD

The assembly elections in Bihar were held soon after the ruling RJD was badly defeated in the 1999 Lok Sabha elections. The results of the 1999 Lok Sabha elections gave an indication that the assembly elections were going to be tough for the RJD: the party may face defeat and pave the way for formation of the BJP–Janata Dal (U) government in the state.

The leaders of the Congress party were not happy about the alliance with the RJD. The state leadership was opposed to it even before the Lok Sabha elections, but it was the central leadership which was in favour of contesting the Lok Sabha elections in alliance with the RJD. The central leaders of the party had expected to gain much from, this alliance, but there was very little success for the party in the 1999 Lok Sabha elections. As a result, the Congress decided to contest the assembly elections on its own, breaking the alliance with the RJD. The RJD found CPM and the MCOR as its new allies.

Cracks started appearing in the BJP–Janata Dal (U) alliance on the issue of ticket distribution and leadership as all the alliance partners had a stake in the state. This eventually led to the breaking up of the Samata Party–Janata Dal (U) alliance, but both parties decided to contest the election with a seat-sharing arrangement. The issue of ticket distribution, however, could not be fully resolved as the three alliance partners put up claims to contest more and more seats. Eventually they contested the elections against each other in several constituencies.

The electoral outcome of the assembly elections in the state was a setback both for the National Democratic Alliance (NDA) and the RJD. The setback was more apparent for the NDA, for its central and state leadership had built high hopes of a decisive and runaway victory. The NDA had registered an impressive victory in the 1999 Lok Sabha elections, winning 41 out of 54 parliamentary seats and leading in 199 of the 324 assembly segments. Throughout the campaign and till a day before counting, NDA leaders were confident about securing 170–180 seats. The final tally of 125 seats (including four unofficial candidates who won elections outside the NDA seat-sharing arrangement) fell way below this expectation. But what was worse, it fell behind the final tally of 126 for the RJD and the CPI (M). With 124 seats and 28.2 per

Table 13.5: Electoral Performance in Central Bihar: Lok Sabha Elections, 1991–1999, Total seats 14

Year	Turn-out (%)	Congress			BJP+			JD+			RJD		
		Con-tested	Won	Vote (%)	Con-tested	Won	Vote (%)	Con-tested	Won	Vote (%)	Con-tested	Won	Vote (%)
1991	62.9	13	1	31.5	13	0	8.4	14	13	46.5	–	–	–
1996	61.1	14	0	12.1	14	6	37.9	13	7	35.8	–	–	–
1998	68.1	4	1	3.5	13	9	42.8	15	0	8.0	12	3	35.9
1999	63.6	2	2	6.4	15	10	44.2	–	–	–	11	2	32.4

Source: CSDS Data Unit, Delhi.

cent of the popular vote, the RJD emerged as the largest party in the state while the BJP finished way behind with 66 seats and 14.5 per cent votes.

If the election results did not appear as a setback for the RJD it was largely because of the bleak picture painted by the media, which was to a great extent ignorant of the ground-level polarisations in Bihar. Against this background, the RJD's defeat appeared like a victory. Laloo Prasad Yadav presided over a historic shift in the social balance of political power in 1990, a shift that was reaffirmed in the subsequent verdicts of the Lok Sabha elections in 1991 and Vidhan Sabha elections in 1995. But the 2000 assembly elections and the Lok Sabha elections in 1998 and 1999 showed his inability to consolidate the social shift into an enduring political regime of the kind the Left Front established in West Bengal. The loss of 43 seats in the 2000 elections as compared to the 1995 elections is a verdict of misgovernance. In fact, the RJD could have ended up behind the NDA's combined strength but for a strange coincidence. The party won five out of the seven seats, which were decided by less than 500 votes and another four of 12 seats, which were decided by a margin of between 500 and 1000 votes. The NDA, however, alleged that this was no coincidence and that pressure on administrative officials affected the counting.

Regional Pattern

An analysis of the pattern of the results points to the relative strength of the various parties in the three regions of Bihar. The BJP and the Samata Party had contested the 1995 assembly elections against each other. As compared with the assembly elections held in 1995, the NDA made gains in all three regions of the state, in terms of both votes and seats. The gain in terms of seats was more or less proportional to the total number of seats in the region, but in terms of vote share, the alliance performed much better in south Bihar as compared to central and north Bihar. Yet it failed to sweep the Jharkhand region. It is clear now that if a separate legislature were to be carved out for Jharkhand from the present assembly, that would also be a 'hung' house, like its parent assembly. The RJD, which had swept practically all of north Bihar except the eastern pocket last time, lost the maximum number of seats from this region. But such was its dominance then that despite losing heavily it performed best in the region, winning 74 of its 124 seats there. In central Bihar, though it lost seven seats, the RJD increased its vote by nearly 6 per cent. This was largely because the RJD did not have a poll pact with the CPI and contested most of the seats on its own. It came as no surprise that the party did not perform well in south Bihar (Table 13.6).

The Congress went to the polls alone in the 2000 assembly elections and was hoping for a recovery as in Uttar Pradesh. The final results were disappointing. It could not stage a comeback and won only 24 seats and polled 11.1 per cent votes.

The Congress did not lose seats in the north but its vote went down by 7 per cent despite contesting a much larger number of seats. In the south, however, the party lost two seats as compared to the 1995 assembly elections but increased its vote marginally. The Congress remained a force in the south, but clearly no more in the north (see Table 13.6).

The results were a setback for the left parties as well. All the left parties combined (CPI, CPI [M], CPI [ML] and MCOR) had won 40 seats in the 1995 assembly elections. In the 2000 assembly elections, they managed to win only 13 seats. Both the CPI and CPI (M) faced an overall decline. It was a long time since the CPI had contested elections without a mainstream party as its ally. The invisible decline of the party in this period came to the surface, as it finished behind the CPI (ML). The party won only five seats, a loss of 21 seats as compared to the previous assembly elections. It lost its position as the dominant left party in the state with the CPI (ML) one seat ahead of it despite contesting fewer seats. Though the CPI(M) contested the 2000 assembly elections in alliance with the RJD, it also suffered a loss of four seats as compared to the 1995 elections. But its support base remained intact in terms of per cent of votes polled. A.K. Roy's Marxist Coordination Committee (MCOR), which had won two seats in the 1995 assembly elections, could not even open its account (see Table 13.6).

Comparative Performance of Alliance Partners: BJP, Samata and Janata Dal (U)

The BJP performed much better as compared to the Samata Party and the Janata Dal (U) in all three regions of the state. It won 39 per cent of the seats contested and polled an average of 29 per cent votes in these seats. The Samata Party won 28 per cent seats and polled an average of 23 per cent votes in the seats it contested. The Janata Dal (U) performed badly, winning only 24 per cent of the seats contested and polling an average of only 13 per cent votes. Both the alliance partners, the BJP and the Samata Party, had a setback in their traditional strongholds, south and central Bihar. Though BJP polled the maximum number of votes in south Bihar, it failed to win a sizeable number of seats from the region. Similarly, the Samata Party contested the largest number of seats in its traditional stronghold of central Bihar, but won only one-fourth of these. The Janata Dal (U) had its presence only in north Bihar (Table 13.7).

Did the multiplicity of NDA candidates in a large number of seats account for the setback to the BJP and its allies in the 2000 assembly elections? The NDA leaders would like us to believe that. But a careful look at the constituency-level results indicates that this factor did not contribute too

Table 13.6: Bihar Vidhan Sabha Elections, 2000: Region-wise Analysis

Region	Seats	Turn-out 2000 (%)	Change over 1995 (%)	RJD				BJP+Samata Party				INC				Left				Others			
				Won	Gain/loss	Vote share	Swing	Won	Gain/loss	Vote share	Swing	Won	Gain/loss	Vote share	Swing	Won	Gain/loss	Vote share	Swing	Won	Gain/loss	Vote share	Swing
North Bihar	156	66.8	+5.3	74	-31	32.8	-2.4	53	+39	29.9	+11.6	10	0	9.6	-7.0	3	-15	4.4	-1.2	16	+7	23.3	-1.0
South Bihar	84	52.5	-10.1	10	-5	12.2	-3.2	41	+18	32.1	+10.3	11	-2	19.1	+1.4	3	-1	4.7	-1.2	19	-10	31.9	-7.3
Central Bihar	84	65.1	+3.7	40	-7	32.5	+5.5	27	+16	27.6	+6.2	3	-3	7.6	-6.8	1	-9	4.1	-3.3	13	+3	28.1	-1.6
Total	324	61.1	+0.8	124	-43	28.2	0.2	121	+73	29.8	+9.8	24	-5	11.1	-5.1	7	-2.5	4.4	-1.8	48	0	26.5	-3.0

Source: CSDS Data Unit, Delhi.

Table 13.7: Comparative Performance of BJP and Its Allies in Bihar

Region	BJP Seats contested	Seats won	Vote (%)	Samata Party Sears con-tested	Seats won	Vote (%)	Janata Dal (U) Seats con-tested	Seats won	Vote (%)
North	55	23	11.9	48	14	8.2	52	16	9.9
South	73	31	24.5	20	7	5.5	14	3	2.1
Central	39	12	11.4	52	13	12.5	21	2	3.8
Total	167	66	14.5	120	34	8.8	87	21	6.5

Source: CSDS Data Unit, Delhi.

greatly. The affiance partners contested against each other in 37 assembly constituencies. In 11 of these constituencies on of the alliance partners won the election; in 15 one was runner; but a united NDA would have made a difference to the electoral outcome, only in two assembly constituencies (Mohiuddin Nagar and Kurtha) which were won by RJD by a narrow margin. In other constituencies. the victory margin of the winning party was too big to be overcome even if the votes of all the alliance partners were combined.

Change of Seats

Looking at the pattern of how seats changed hands between different parties from the 1995 assembly elections to the 2000 assembly elections, one finds a lot of churning of seats from one party to another. Of the total of 324 seats, 182 seats changed hands between the 1995 and 2000 elections. Although in the 2000 assembly elections the NDA won more than twice the number of seats won by its various partners in the 1995 elections, it did not retain even half of its own seats. In 2000, the Congress managed to retain only seven of the 29 seats won in the 1995 assembly elections and lost 10 seats to the NDA and six to the RJD. The left parties not only lost a large number of seats, but their retention rate was also very poor. The RJD retained 94 of the seats won in the 1995 assembly elections and lost 57 seats to the NDA (Table 13.8).

Evaluation of MLAs

There seems to be growing dissatisfaction among the people towards their political representatives. A post-poll survey conducted after the 2000 assembly elections tried to measure people's satisfaction with the performance of their MLA who had completed their term after being elected in the 1995 assembly elections. Nearly one-third were dissatisfied with their MLA while only 15 per cent were very satisfied with them. This trend was more or less even across all sections of the people. The literate were more dissatisfied than the illiterate. Dissatisfaction with the MLA was higher among the upper caste and the Dalits as well. The majority of the women did not hold any opinion on the issue (Table 13.9).

Support Base of The RJD

In the 2000 assembly elections, the RJD performed badly in terms of winning seats, but it polled the highest number of votes. The party saw ups and down

Table 13.8: Change of Seats: Vidhan Sabha Elections, 1995–2000

Winner 1995	Winner 2000						Total
	Congress	RJD	CPI+ CPM	BJP+	JMM	Others	
Congress	7	6	–	10	1	5	20
RJD	7	94	–	57	–	9	167
CPI + CPM	1	7	4	16	–	4	32
BJP+	5	9	3	23	1	7	48
JMM	3	–	–	4	3	–	10
Others	1	8	–	11	7	11	38
Total	24	124	7	121	12	36	324

Source: CSDS Data Unit, Delhi.

Table 13.9: Level of Satisfaction with the MLA

Category	Not satisfied (%)	Somewhat satisfied (%)	Very satisfied (%)	No opinion (%)
All	33	29	15	23
Illiterate	30	22	13	35
Graduate	36	35	21	8
Male	37	34	19	10
Female	28	23	11	38
Upper caste	40	29	10	21
Dalit	40	26	8	26

Source: Bihar Assembly Election Survey, 2000.

in the elections held during the period 1990–2000 in terms of seats, but it polled more or less the same share of votes. This gives an indication of a solid support base for the party, which remained static during the elections held between 1990 and 2000. But does this mean that the same group of people had voted for the party over the years? The survey conducted following the 2000 assembly elections tried to find out the social profile of the RJD vote.

There is a sharp contrast between the profile of those who had always voted for RJD and those who had never voted for the party. While more than 50 per cent of RJD votes came from the Yadavs and the Muslims, of those who had never voted for the RJD, only 6 per cent belonged to these two social groups. There was divided loyalty for the RJD among the other backward castes. There was practically no change in the composition of the RJD vote and the opposition parties failed to make any inroads among the Laloo supporters. The firm opposition for the RJD came from the upper castes as they constituted half of those voters who had never voted for the RJD during the past 10 years. There were sections among Dalits and Adivasis too that had never voted for the party (Table 13.10).

CHANGING SOCIAL BASE OF POLITICAL PARTIES

The results of the elections held in the state during the period 1990–2000 clearly indicate that the Janata Dal, which had remained the most dominant party till the 1996 Lok Sabha elections, started witnessing a decline after the 1998 Lok Sabha elections. The party suffered a humiliating defeat in the 1999 Lok Sabha elections. The BJP, which had polled 15.9 per cent votes in the 1991 Lok Sabha elections, made heavy inroads into Bihar politics during and after the 1996 Lok Sabha elections following its alliance with the Samata Party. The party polled 20.5 and 23.1 per cent votes in the 1996 and 1998 elections respectively. In the 1999 Lok Sabha elections, the formation of the Janata Dal (U) with the merger of the Samata Party and the Janata Dal added to the success of the BJP. With the alliance, the BJP managed to make inroads among Yadav and Dalit voters, who constitute a big section of the electorate in Bihar. The increase in support in terms of votes polled might not look very impressive, but it should be noted that the votes for the party increased even if it contested fewer seats in subsequent elections on account of the seat-sharing arrangement with its partners. The survey revealed that the Janata Dal drew greater support from backward castes, Dalits and Muslims as compared to other sections of society, while the BJP drew greater support from upper-caste voters. The BJP and Samata Party alliance also made the party a popular choice of two backward castes, the Kurmi and the Koeri. The coming together of the Janata Dal and the Samata Party also led to a movement of sections of Dalits towards the BJP–Janata Dal (U) alliance in the 1999 Lok Sabha elections.

Table 13.10: Profile of RJD Voters (%)

Caste	Never voted for RJD	Always voted for RJD	Voted for RJD in the 1999 Lok Sabha elections	Voted for RJD in the 2000 assembly elections
All	28	20	26	27
Upper caste	45	7	9	11
Yadav	2	32	28	27
Muslim	4	26	21	23
*Other OBC	26	21	22	20
Dalit	11	13	19	18
Adivasi	12	1	1	1

*Includes all backward castes except the Yadav.
Source: Bihar Assembly Election Survey 2000.

During the past few years, the popularity of the Congress has declined among all sections of society. CSDS surveys clearly show that the social groups which formed the solid support base of the Janata Dal started deserting the party after the 1998 Lok Sabha elections, though there are still sections among whom the party seems to be very popular. The majority of RJD votes come from Yadav and Muslim voters. The survey also helps us understand the changing social base of different political parties in the state.

The increasing presence of the BJP in Bihar is largely attributed to its growing popularity among upper-caste voters. Traditionally Congress supporters, they have moved in a big way towards the BJP and its alliance partner, the Samata Party, since the 1996 Lok Sabha elections. The survey reveals that the BJP which got only 28.7 per cent of the upper-caste votes in 1995, got more than 75 per cent votes in the Lok Sabha elections of 1998 and 1999, though the alliance suffered some setback among the upper-caste voters during the assembly elections in 2000. The Janata Dal did manage to get some support from the upper castes till the 1996 Lok Sabha elections, but after that the party's popularity among upper castes has declined enormously (Table 13.11).

Table 13.11: Shift Among Upper-caste Voters, 1995–2000

Party	1995	1996	1998	1999	2000
Congress	39.1	10.1	8.7	8.3	15.0
BJP+	28.7	59.5	77.6	76.7	60.7
JD+	20.9	29.1	11.6	–	–
RJD	–	–	Negligible	Negligible	10.5

Source: Bihar Assembly Election Survey 1995; National Election Study 1996, 1998 and 1999; Assembly Election Survey 2000.

OBCs have come to play an important role in the politics of the state over the past decade. The Congress has not been very popular among OBC voters who have traditionally largely supported socialist; formations. With the formation of the Janata Dal before the 1989 Lok Sabha elections a large section of OBC voters moved towards the party. Surveys indicate that OBCs voted for the Janata Dal in large numbers in the 1995 Vidhan Sabha and 1996 Lok Sabha elections. The BJP-Samata Party alliance drew OBC voters. In the 1998 elections, 42.5 per cent of OBC voters voted for the BJP alliance, while support for the Janata Dal alliance went down from 50.3 per cent in 1996 to 17.3 per cent in 1998. The RJD managed to poll 28 per cent of the OBC votes, but in the 1999 Lok Sabha elections, with the merger of the Samata Party and the Janata Dal, OBC support for the RJD went further down to 22 per cent. With the parting of the two parties just before the assembly elections, a section of the OBCs again moved towards the RJD. Support for the Congress among OBC voters, which was just 13.7 per cent in 1995, went down to 7.9 per cent in 1998; however, in alliance with the RJD, the Congress managed' to get 15 per cent of the OBC vote, which went down to just 5 per, cent in the assembly elections of 2000. This is an indication that the alliance of the Congress with the RJD did help the party get so e OBC votes (Table 13.12).

The decade 1990–2000 witnessed a decline in Muslim support for the Congress. The alienation of Muslims from the Congress began soon after the Bhagalpur riots and continued after the demolition of the Babri Masjid. Disenchanted with the Congress, the Janata Dal and its allies became the natural choice of Muslim voters in the state. Survey figures indicate enormous support for the alliance in the 1995 Vidhan Sabha and 1996 Lok Sabha elections among Muslim voters. But the split in the Janata Dal has led to the erosion of this support. From 68.9 per cent Muslim votes in the 1996 Lok Sabha elections, the alliance got only 19 per cent in 1998 with 59.6 per cent Muslims voting for the RJD. The Samata–BJP alliance barely attracted Muslim voters till the 1998 Lok Sabha elections, but with the formation of the Janata Dal (U), the BJP allies did manage to get some Muslim votes in the 1999 elections. However,

Table 13.12: Shift among OBC Voters, 1995–2000 (%)

Party	1995	1996	1998	1999	2000
Congress	13.7	9.9	7.9	14.9	5.0
BJP+	26.2	36.2	42.5	50.3	38.7
JD+	49.8	50.3	17.3	–	–
RJD	–	--	28.0	22.0	40.8

Source: Bihar Assembly Election Survey 1995; Assembly Election, National Election Study 1996, 1998 and 1999; Assembly Election Survey 2000.

the Samata Party and Janata Dal parted ways just before the assembly elections in 2000 and a large number of Muslim voters went back to the RJD (Table 13.13).

Over the elections held during the period 1990–2000, there was a shift among upper-caste voters towards the BJP while the majority of OBC and Muslim voters favoured the Janata Dal till 1996 and RJD since the 1998 Lok Sabha elections. But does this mean that the various castes within these groups have similar party preferences?

It is important to note that neither the upper caste nor the OBCs constitute one monolithic group; rather, they are composed of various castes. While the Rajputs, Bhumiars, Brahmins and Kayastha constitute the upper caste, there are a larger number of castes that are categorised as OBC. The Yadavs, Kurmis and Koeris constitute the upper OBC, while the Kahar, Kumhar, Lohar, Tatwu, Teli, Dhanuk, etc. constitute the lower OBC. Even within Muslims, there are upper and lower castes. Again, the question is: is the voting pattern of the castes within these three groups—that is, the upper caste, the OBCs and the Muslims—similar despite the immense social and economic disparities among them?

A detailed analysis of the data reveals that unlike the four upper castes, there was great internal variation in the voting pattern across the castes of the OBC. The Janata Dal was very popular among the Yadav till the 1996 Lok Sabha elections, but after the party split, it was the RJD that cornered the majority of the Yadav votes. It may be noted that the Yadavs were extremely polarised in favour of the Janata Dal till the 1996 elections, but the 1998 elections also marked the split of the Yadav vote between the Janata Dal, the RJD and the BJP–Samata alliance. Still, the majority of the Yadavs voted for the RJD in 1998. Interestingly, the BJP–Samata alliance got more Yadav votes than did the Janata Dal. Their vote was badly split between the BJP allies, the Congress and the RJD. The Congress did manage to get a sizeable proportion of the Yadav vote because of its alliance with the RJD, but with the breaking up of the alliance, the Yadavs consolidated behind the RJD in the 2000 assembly elections (see Table 13.14).

Table 13.13: Shift among Muslim Voters, 1995–2000 (%)

Party	1995	1996	1998	1999	2000
Congress	21.9	23.3	14.9	33.9	6.6
BJP+	7.5	5.6	4.2	13.4	7.9
JD+	57.3	68.9	19.0	–	–
RJD	–	–	59.6	48.2	61.4

Source: Bihar Survey 1995, National Election Study 1996, 1998 and 1999, Assembly Election Survey 2000.

The voting pattern of the Kurmi and Koeri was quite in contrast to that of the Yadavs. They voted in large numbers for the BJP–Samata alliance, the traditional rival Janata Dal which drew support from the Yadavs. But survey data reveal that though the majority of the Kurmi and Koeri voted for the BJP allies, there were elections in which they had voted for other parties. The 1996 and 1999 Lok Sabha elections witnessed extreme polarisation of the Kurmi and Koeri in favour of the BJP allies, but during the 2000 Vidhan Sabha elections, they voted in sizeable numbers for the RJD (See Table 13.14).

In the elections held between 1990 and 2000, the lower OBCs displayed a divided loyalty towards different parties. There was a clear pattern of movement of the lower OBCs towards the BJP-Samata alliance; however, only a little over 50 per cent of them voted for the alliance in the 1998 Lok Sabha elections and about 63 per cent in the 1999 elections. There was a distinct movement of the lower OBCS away from the Janata Dal, but during the Vidhan Sabha elections in 2000, a sizeable number of them voted for the RJD and the support for the BJP allies among these sections declined. There was a rapid decline in the support for the Congress among the lower OBCs (see Table 13.14).

During the period 1991–2000 the structure of support for political parties was different among upper-caste and lower-caste Muslims. Over the years the Congress lost support among upper-caste Muslim voters, but it is important to note that the party continued to be popular among lower-caste Muslims. The support for the Congress among lower-caste Muslims declined only marginally over the 1995, 1996, 1998 and 1999 elections, but in the 2000 Vidhan Sabha elections it eroded greatly. The survey indicates that Muslims still preferred to vote for the Congress rather than for the BJP–Samata alliance.

The majority of both upper-caste and lower-caste Muslims supported the RJD in the 1998 Lok Sabha elections while the Janata Dal and its allies lost their support to a great extent. The lower-caste Muslims consolidated behind the RJD in the 1999 Lok Sabha and the 2000 Vidhan Sabha elections. However, while the majority of the upper-caste Muslims voted for the RJD, a section of them voted for other parties as well (see Table 13.14).

There was also a considerable shift among Dalit voters in the elections held between 1990 and 2000. Traditionally Congress voters, nearly half of the Dalits voted for the Janata Dal and its allies while 23 per cent voted for the Congress in the 1995 Vidhan Sabha elections. The BJP was not the popular choice of Dalit voters in the 1995 assembly elections. But in that election the state witnessed a slow but constant movement of Dalit voters from the Congress to other parties. While a large number of them voted for the Janata Dal and its allies, a sizeable number even shifted their loyalty towards the BJP and its allies. The split in the Janata Dal before the 1998 elections resulted in a three-way division of the Dalit vote between the Janata Dal and its allies, the BJP and its allies and the RJD.

Table 13.14: Voting Pattern of Muslims and Different Jatis among OBCs, 1991–2000 (%)

Jati	Congress					BJP+					JD+			RJD		
	1991	1996	1998	1999	2000	1991	1996	1998	1999	2000	1991	1996	1998	1998	1999	2000
Yadav	8.2	1.6	7.9	36.3	1.9	4.1	16.1	18.4	21.6	9.2	87.8	80.6	7.9	65.8	39.2	79.6
Kurmi + Koeri	28.0	5.3	24.0	8.3	5.9	40.0	73.7	56.0	70.8	58.3	28.0	17.5	–	18.0	10.4	24.5
*Other OBC	31.6	2.4	–	7.1	9.8	26.3	40.5	23.1	52.4	42.6	31.6	50.0	7.7	23.1	31.0	26.5
Lower OBC	28.6	10.7	8.0	4.2	4.4	20.2	42.0	57.3	62.9	45.0	36.9	35.5	21.3	12.0	11.2	26.5
ST	26.9	24.0	70.2	–	–	–	34.0	8.5	–	–	7.7	28.0	6.4	–	–	–
Lower Muslim	39.1	31.0	31.0	34.0	3.8	–	6.7	6.9	4.3	8.2	47.8	57.8	20.7	37.9	55.3	68.6
Upper Muslim	33.3	16.7	15.7	33.8	13.0	–	3.3	5.9	20.0	7.2	61.1	80.0	17.6	58.8	43.1	44.9

Source: National Election Study 1996, 1998 and 1999; Bihar Assembly Election Survey 2000.
'Other OBC' includes all backward castes except the Yadav, Kurmi, Koeri and the lower backward castes.

But things have changed remarkably since the 1999 Lok Sabha elections. With the merger of the Samata Party and the Janata Dal (U) there has been a movement of the Dalit vote towards the BJP and its allies. The Ram Vilas factor has also made a difference for the BJP and its allies in terms of Dalit support. In Vidhan Sabha elections held in 2000, the RJD managed to regain some support among the Dalits, though the majority of the Dalits still voted for the BJP and its allies in the state (Table 13.15).

The BJP was never popular among illiterate voters. Survey data for the 1995 Vidhan Sabha elections bear testimony to this. But with its alliance with the Samata Party the profile of the party started to change slowly and since the 1996 Lok Sabha elections there has been a constant shift among the illiterate towards the BJP and its allies. The merger worked its magic for the allies during the 1999 Lok Sabha elections, but support for the alliance among the illiterates went down to some extent with the split between the Janata Dal (U) and the Samata Party before the 2000 Vidhan Sabha elections.

The profile of the Janata Dal and its allies is in sharp contrast to that of the BJP allies. The Janata Dal and its allies were very popular among illiterate voters. The split of the Janata Dal before the 1998 Lok Sabha elections led to a split among illiterate voters between the Janata Dal and the RJD. With the 1999 Lok Sabha elections, the RJD started regaining the lost ground among illiterate voters, but support for the party among the illiterate is still low as compared to its popularity among these voters during the early 1990s (Table 13.16).

The BJP and its allies were popular among the educated voters. During the 1990s, the popularity of the alliance among these voters grew. In all the elections held during the period 1990–2000, nearly 50 per cent of the highly educated voters voted for the BJP and its allies. The survey figures are clear testimony that this was on account of the shift of support of these voters from the Congress. Though the Janata Dal and its allies had never been popular among the educated voters they did to get some support from them (Table 13.17).

Table 13.15: Shift Among Dalit Voters, 1995–2000 (%)

Party	1995	1996	1998	1999	2000
Congress	23.0	19.0	13.7	17.3	9.4
BJP+	15.0	24.8	24.5	47.1	38.9
JD+	48.7	31.4	28.4	–	–
RJD	–	–	23.5	26.0	33.1

Source: Bihar Assembly Election Survey 1995; National Election Study 1996, 1998 and 1999; Assembly Election Survey 2000.

Table 13.16: Shift among Illiterate Voters, 1995–2000

Party	1995	1996	1998	1999	2000
Congress	19.8	11.6	15.0	21.7	10.4
BJP+	20.1	38.7	33.2	43.8	33.0
JD+	47.3	40.4	17.0	–	–
RJD	–	–	18.6	22.4	36.0

Source: Bihar Assembly Election Survey 1995; National Election Study 1996, 1998 and 1999; Assembly Election Survey 2000.

Table 13.17: Shift among Educated (graduate and above) Voters, 1995–2000 (%)

Party	1995	1996	1998	1999	2000
Congress	30.1	20.0	Negligible	15.2	9.5
BJP+	34.3	56.0	55.0	45.5	58.3
JD+	20.5	20.0	15.0	–	–
RJD	–	–	20.0	18.2	22.6

Source: Bihar Assembly Election Survey 1995; National Election Study 1996, 1998 and 1999; Assembly Election Survey 2000.

CHANGING SOCIAL PROFILE OF ELECTED REPRESENTATIVES

The 1990s marked a sharp change in the politics of Bihar. Though the numerically strong backward castes had occupied an important place in the state's electoral struggle, never before, except in 1977, had they been able to guide its politics, playing, at best, a secondary role therein.

The implementation of a new reservation policy for the backward castes, based on the recommendations of the Mandal Commission report, witnessed strong opposition nationwide by various upper-caste sections. While in most parts of the country the backward castes generally supported the policy, they nevertheless remained mute onlookers to the violent opposition to it. In Bihar, by contrast, they mobilised and put up a stiff challenge to the anti-Mandal agitationists. There was a prolonged and violent struggle between the anti-reservationists, comprising mainly upper-caste youth, and pro-reservationists, comprising mainly backward caste youth. This led to the externalisation of the undercurrents of age-old and deep-seated antagonism between the upper and backward castes. This was a rare occasion when the divided backward castes joined together to challenge the opposition of the forward castes. One may blame the Mandal Commission for sowing the seeds of casteism, but it also led to a consolidation of castes along only two axes, the upper and backward castes, erasing for a while the numerous internal differences between the two. The immediate fallout of this social change was on the nature of political representation in the state, with more backward castes emerging as people's representatives.

If one looks carefully at the composition of the Bihar legislature over the years, it is clear that the social composition of political representatives changed a great deal. There was a slow and steady decline in upper-caste representation in the state assembly, which went down to as low as 17 per cent in 1995. The Janata Dal registered an impressive victory in the 1995 Vidhan Sabha elections, when OBC representation also went up to 45 per cent. It is noteworthy that not only did the representation of the OBCs increase dramatically, but for the first time OBCs outnumbered the upper castes in terms of representation in the assembly. In 2000, though the proportion of the OBCs declined as compared to the 1995 elections, it was still higher than the proportion of upper-caste representation.

Despite Muslims constituting a sizeable part of the population in the state, their representation in the Vidhan Sabha always remained below 10 per cent. Representation of women also remained below 5 per cent except in the 2000 Vidhan Sabha elections, when it went up to a little over 7 per cent (Table 13.18).

Table 13.18: Changing Social Composition of the Bihar Vidhan Sabha, 1967–2000 (%)

Category	1967	1969	1985	1990	1995	2000
Upper caste	41.8	38.3	26.4	32.5	17.1	29.9
OBC	24.2	26.7	24.6	29.7	45.0	36.4
Muslim	5.6	5.9	10.1	6.1	7.1	9.3
Women	3.4	1.2	4.0	4.0	2.8	7.4

Source: 1967 Statistical Report on General Election to the Legislative Assembly of Bihar, Election Commission of India, New Delhi; 1969 Statistical Report on General Election to the Legislative Assembly of Bihar, Election Commission of India, New Delhi; 1985 Statistical Report on General Election to the Legislative Assembly of Bihar, Election Commission of India, New Delhi; 1990 Statistical Report on General Election to the Legislative Assembly of Bihar, Election Commission of India, New Delhi; 1995 Statistical Report on General Election to the Legislative Assembly of Bihar, Election Commission of India, New Delhi, 2000 Election Commission of India website.

The social composition of the representatives to the Lok Sabha also changed between 1989 and 1999. During the 1989 Lok Sabha elections, 33.3 per cent representatives were upper caste—the figure came down to 18.9 per cent in 1991—whereas the representation of backward castes went up to 43.1 per cent in 1991 as compared to 30.6 per cent in 1989. This was primarily because the backward castes were largely consolidated behind the Janata Dal. The 1996 Lok Sabha elections were unique as they were held against the backdrop of a Congress almost wiped out from the political scene in the state. The Samata Party, which drew its support largely from the Kurmis and Koeris, and which unsuccessfully contested the 1995 Vidhan Sabha elections, entered into an alliance with the BJP. So, in a sense, the upper castes under the banner of BJP put up a challenge to the Janata Dal with the support of two backward castes, the Kurmis and Koeris. The division among the backward castes naturally had an adverse effect on their representation, which went down to 38.7 per cent in the 1996 Lok Sabha elections as compared to 43.1 per cent in 1991. However, it was still higher than the upper-caste representation (Table 13.19).

The 1998 Lok Sabha elections, held after the Janata Dal split and Laloo Yadav formed his own regional outfit, the RJD, further changed the social composition of the elected representatives. The division of votes of the backward castes which had started with the Kurmis and Koeris moving towards the Samata Party in 1996, got a further fillip when even some other backward castes deserted the Janata Dal and voted for the RJD. These elections also marked the beginning of division in the Yadav vote between the Janata Dal and the RJD. The success of the Kurmis and Koeris in the 1996 Lok Sabha

Table 13.19: Changing Social Profile of Lok Sabha Representatives, 1989–1999 (%)

Category	1989	1991	1996	1998	1999
Upper castes	33.3	18.9	27.7	29.6	42.5
OBC	30.6	43.1	38.7	31.4	24.0
Muslim	5.5	4.1	7.4	11.1	5.5
Women	3.7	5.5	5.5	7.4	9.2

Source: 1989 Statistical Report on General Election to the Ninth Lok Sabha Election, Election Commission of India, New Delhi; 1991 Statistical Report on General Election to the Tenth Lok Sabha Election, Election Commission of India, New Delhi; 1996 Statistical Report on General Election to the Eleventh Lok Sabha Election, Election Commission of India, New Delhi; 1998 Statistical Report on General Election to the Twelfth Lok Sabha Election, Election Commission of India, New Delhi; 1999 Statistical Report on General Election to the Thirteenth Lok Sabha Election, Election Commission of India, New Delhi.

elections led to their further consolidation as a political force. The representation of the upper castes also declined marginally, from 27.7 per cent in 1996 to 24 per cent in 1998. The scramble for the sizeable Muslim vote, which can make or mar the prospects of a party, resulted in a considerable increase in the number of Muslim contestants and actually led to an increase in Muslim representation (see Table 13.19).

The consolidation of the anti-Laloo forces continued during the 1999 Lok Sabha elections and the Janata Dal merged with the Samata Party, which as in earlier elections contested in alliance with the BJP. The BPP also entered this alliance. The BJP and its allies' massive victory resulted in an increase in upper-caste representation; more than 42 per cent of the representatives to the Lok Sabha were from the upper castes, while OBC representation went down to 24 per cent. Muslim representation went down to just 5 per cent, but representation of women went up to over 9 per cent, the highest in the past five Lok Sabha elections.

The changing social composition of political representation is an indication of the fact that the backward castes have come to play a major role in Bihar politics. Some may argue that this is largely due to the change of the party in power. The elections held between 1990 and 2000 demonstrated that parties can change but it is hard to visualise a future scenario where the backward castes would be denied political power. Unless the backward castes get their fair share in political representation, no aspiring ruling party is going to be able to get their support. The BJP, which is viewed as a party of the upper castes, achieved great success in the 1996 Lok Sabha elections, winning 18 seats. But this was possible primarily due to the overwhelming support of two backward castes, the Kurmis and Koeris. The phenomenon of the rise of the backward castes in Bihar politics is here to stay. The backward castes enjoy political power today but they may not remain satisfied with being at the fringes of the political system. In fact, 'backwardism' may not have a place in politics in the future. Hence 'backwardism' must take a back seat and its assimilation and integration into larger social groups ensured.

14

Dalit Assertion through Electoral Politics *

Pushpendra

With the 1996 elections to the eleventh Lok Sabha, Indian polity seems to
have embarked upon a phase of fierce competitive politics. The era of one-party
dominance made way for coalition politics. The gradual decline of the Congress,
leaving behind its murky shadow; the growing strength of the Bharatiya Janata
Party (BJP) edging past the Congress in terms of seats in Parliament and its
expansion all over the country; the emergence of regional parties as important
political players in a number of states; the strengthening of smaller parties
(such as the Samajwadi Party, Samata Party, Janata Dal, Rashtriya Janata Dal
[RJDI, Bahujan Samaj Party [BSPI) with their specific group followings and
limited areas of influence, are changes in party politics that are in themselves
expressions of the larger changes in Indian society today. Different sections of
society are desperately trying to assert themselves In politics. The social
composition of parties and articulation of group interests by them too have
undergone major transformation. Their failure to get accommodated in
established national political parties has given rise to a number of smaller
parties. The upper castes, particularly in northern India, have by and large
deserted the Congress and instead chosen to rally behind the BJP. The ongoing
processes of the political rise of the backward castes, despite their inter- and

* This essay is based on the 1996 and 1998 national election surveys conducted by the
Centre for the Study of Developing Societies (CSDS). The author is thankful to the CSDS
for allowing him to use the National Election Survey data. This study was sponsored by
the Centre for Social Studies, Surat. The author is thankful to Ghanshyam Shah, jean
Dreze, Prathama Banerjee and Robert S. Jenkins for their comments on earlier drafts of
the essay. The author also acknowledges the support and assistance of V.B. Singh, Sanjay
Kumar, Himanshu Bhattacharya, Arun Kumar, Anup Kumar Karan and Pankaj Naithani
at various stages of the study.
* *Economic and Political Weekly*, 34 (36), 4 September 1999, pp. 2609–18.

intra-caste divisions and conflicts, have found strong political representation in the form of parties like the RJD, Janata Dal, Samajwadi Party, Samata Party, the regional parties and the left. Muslims have also deserted the Congress and appear to have allied with other parties in order to ensure the defeat of the Congress and the BJP.

In this context, understanding the electoral behaviour of the Scheduled Castes (SCs) has become very important. The general elections of 1996 and 1998 saw a powerful assertion of Dalit politics. What we observed in these two elections was, to our surprise, a different SC voter who was no longer a 'captive' follower of the Congress. These elections highlighted a new phase in the political consciousness, and in the mobilisation and organisation of the SCs. There began a concerted effort by the SCs to create a new political identity for themselves by using the levers of competitive politics. Increased voting by the SCs, shifts in their party preference and a complex pattern of voting, their general support for the left or left-of-centre parties, rise of the BSP, efforts to emerge as a political bloc despite internal class differentiation, and increase in the level of legitimacy given to democratic institutions are some of the important expressions of their political assertion.

This essay attempts to examine the data on the voting behaviour of SCs and traces the changes in their party preference. To explain why this assertion took place through elections I have analysed the opinion of the SCs about the legitimacy of the political system. A further attempt is made to find internal differentiation among SCs regarding their voting behaviour. I have also tried to explain the phenomenon of the rise of the BSP. The concluding part reflects upon the implications of SCs' assertion through electoral politics.

This study is based on the post-poll survey data of the 1996 and 1998 Lok Sabha elections, collected by the Centre for the Study of Developing Societies (CSDS), Delhi. In the 1996 post-poll survey, the total number of respondents was 9614, of which 1791 belonged to the SCs and 3357 to the upper castes. The respective figures for the 1998 elections were 8133, 1312 and 2039. This caste division applies to all religious groups. Interestingly, of the total respondents in the 1998 post-poll survey, 5138 were those who had been interviewed in 1996. This, of course, provides an opportunity to look at the swing in terms of party preference by the same voter. This essay is confined to analysing the aggregate samples of these two election surveys.

An important feature of the 1996 election survey data was the detailed information on the personal backgrounds of the respondents, such as age, education, occupation, housing, landholding, asset holding, and self-assessment of required income to meet household expenses. This helped determine the class position of the respondents and enabled a class-in-caste analysis. Unfortunately, in the 1998 post-poll survey, the background information required to determine the class of the respondent was restricted to only three variables—landholding, occupation and type of house. Further, the landholding data were completely unusable. Occupation details were classified at the time of data entry in a way that greatly undermined their sensitivity as an indicator. Using the background information of the 5138 (panel) respondents could have been one option. But this has its own problems as we cannot rule out the possibility of at least some households having undergone changes in class status between the two elections. I have therefore used the class analysis based on 1996 background details as a proxy for 1998 elections too.

The figures reveal the presence of a sizeable section of a middle class and even a small elite class among the SCs. Since the sample size of the upper class, in the case of the SCs, is very small and in a number of instances, though important, statistically not valid for offering any analysis, for the sake of convenience I have merged both the upper and the middle-class categories. Moreover, a careful look at the financial/occupational background of the respondents suggests that the upper class, as categorised here, for all practical purposes resembles the upper middle class.

The samples of the two post-poll surveys were drawn at the national level. Naturally, while taking up the analysis to the state level, certain differences/ gaps were observed between the CSDS and the Election Commission (EC) figures with respect to the voting percentage and party preference of the voters. In the case of states like Madhya Pradesh, Karnataka and Assam the gap was really significant. The sample size was relatively small for taking up any rigorous interpretation at the state level, which led to underrepresentation of regional variations within the states. One way could have been to adjust the variation for the actual figures released by the EC. However, I have preferred the post-poll figures because most of the analysis here is done at the all-India level for which the authenticity of data cannot be doubted. Adjusting the variation in the case of certain states may result in some other distortions particularly in issues like perception of the legitimacy of the system, and influence of age, sex, locality, education, occupation and caste on party preference. Moreover, the EC data do not contain this information to make adjustments in disaggregated data.

Table 14.1: Caste-Class Division of Respondents, 1996

Class division	SC	Upper caste
Upper class	32 (1.8)	408 (12.2)
Middle class	412 (23.0)	1559 (46.4)
Lower class	1341 (74.9)	1380 (41.1)
Class could not be ascertained	6 (0–3)	10 (0–3)

Note: Figures in parentheses denote percentage.

Also, there is no solid reason to believe that the difference between the two dataset in terms of percentage of votes secured by political parties can be evenly attributed to all the variables.

It is also necessary to point out some of the other limitations of the database with respect to the present study. The national election surveys of 1996 and 1998 conducted by the CSDS were not focused primarily on studying the specific features of SC voting behaviour. For this, a different type of sampling procedure is required keeping in mind the variation in the SC population across states and within states, adequate sample size, nature of political parties, nature and extent of political participation of the SCs in different states, etc. In fact, indicators also need to be sharply focused to study the various dimensions of Dalit politics. However, this does not undermine the importance of the available data that I have culled out according to the needs of the study wherever sample size permitted me.

CONTEXTUALISING SCHEDULED CASTE VOTING

Changes in the voting behaviour of SCs acquire great significance in view of the fact that the SCs find themselves in a web of socio-economic deprivation. The political system, at least theoretically, grants political equality to all, irrespective of caste, wealth, privileges, etc., to be exercised through voting, contesting elections and other forms of participation. Political equality, as opposed to social and economic equality, opens up, in principle, opportunities to utilise political democracy for sharing the power and material benefits accruing from it. However, social and economic inequality is an impediment in the way of taking advantage of equal political opportunities. Hence, a brief account of the socio-economic deprivation of the SCs is in order.

According to the 1991 census, the literacy rate of the SCs was 37.41 per cent as compared to 52.21 per cent of the total population. A smaller proportion of the SCs reside in urban areas as compared to the upper castes—18.7 per cent of SCs to 29.2 per cent of the total population reside in urban areas. Of the total SC population, 45.4 per cent are agricultural labourers and only 23.6 per cent are cultivators. The reverse is true of the general category for whom the respective figures are 20.1 per cent and 40.5 per cent.

According to the Agricultural Census, 1991, the average size of landholding was one acre in the case of SCs, and 1.61 acres for the general category. The ratio of share in land to share in population stood at 0.48 for SCs, and 1.07 for the general category. The size-wise distribution of operational holdings for the SCs and the general category suggests an acute inequality in land distribution. Among the SCs, 71.8 per cent of holdings were less than one acre, covering only 25.7 per cent of the cultivated area. In the case of the general category, there was better distribution of landholdings in different size groups, with the highest concentration in the size class of 4–10 acres. In the general category, 5 8.6 per cent of holdings were less than one acre and the area covered by them was 14.5 per cent. This inequality is illustrative of the structural barriers to the economic development of the SCs.

The political deprivation of the SCs is no less important. Political participation of Dalits is largely confined to casting of votes and has not been effective in bargaining. Their overwhelming support to the Congress offered little and failed to reduce their political deprivation. One expression of their frustration and anger at their deprivation has been their organised protest movements in the states of Bihar, Andhra Pradesh, and parts of Madhya Pradesh, Maharashtra, Orissa, etc.

However, there have been slow and steady changes in the socio-economic and political status of the SCs. Because of a host of proces-ses of upward mobility like sanskritisation, diversification of occupations, migration, urbanisation, and so on, and also due to the decline in the upper castes' dominance, the SCs have been able to make some advancement towards minimising their various deprivations, particularly their political deprivation. In addition to a gradual improvement in their educational level, the policy of protective discrimination has contributed in creating a small elite and middle class, mostly in the service sector, and thus, led to internal differentiation on class lines. Getting organised under trade unions, political parties and various protest movements has increased their level of participation. Such organisations and movements are more politicised—different from the Congress variant of welfare-oriented politics—militant and uncompromising, and assert a distinct Dalit identity.

Normally, political deprivation is considered relatively less difficult to fight against. This assumption is validated by the ascendance to power of the other backward castes (OBCs). Yet, political mobilisation need not take the route of organising communities on traditional identities only. It can base itself on class lines cutting across the traditional structures of caste, tribe, religion, etc. However, in both cases, the underlying logic is that it is collective strength that will compensate for other disabilities, and further lead to the complex strategic issues of political formation, coalition, and so on. This is the art of real politicking. Collective internalisation of this art by a community and the maturity of its political leadership in mastering this art, plays a key role in the political rise of that community.

Scheduled Castes' Voter Turnout

Voting provides the most important opportunity to the common electorate to choose the government it wants to install in Parliament and in the assemblies.

Theoretically, political parties try to woo voters with their policies and programmes and voters, in turn, try to influence the policies and programmes of the parties. In practice, as Weber puts it, if voting is left out of consideration, the number of individuals and social groups with additional channels of influence over the decision-making process falls substantially.[1] The SCs would have virtually none. Many empirical studies in the past, particularly in the initial decades following independence, show that the Dalits lagged behind the upper castes in terms of exercising their franchise for various reasons, the most important being the denial of voting opportunity by the upper castes and the fear of backlash, whenever their candidatural preference seemed to come into conflict with that of the SCs.

Conditions began to change in the early 1990s. In 1971 the SC voter turnout was 78.7 per cent (CSDS Data Unit, CSDS, Delhi). These figures disprove the popular notion that the overall SC vote is small—be it on account of either their ignorance about their voting status, or their fear of violence or denial of voting right. The percentage of SC votes steadily went up. In the 1996 general elections, the SC turnout was 89.2 per cent as against the national average of 87.3 per cent in the case of upper castes.[2] This trend continued in the 1998 elections in which the figures for the SCs and the upper castes were 93 per cent and 91.9 per cent respectively. They are also indicative of the strong political aspirations of the Dalits, and their effort to assert in a democratic polity via the electoral process. Of the 1791 SCs interviewed, only 16 cited the above-mentioned reasons for not casting their vote. Further, they clearly establish that the upper castes show less inclination to vote in reserved constituencies on account of 'indifference' which can best be explained as a result of their not having the option to vote in favour of their caste candidates.

One plausible explanation for the steady rise in the SC voter turnout may be that voting is no longer a passive activity for the SCs. The rise in educational levels, greater awareness of their rights, the realisation of the strength of the adult franchise to create a space for assertion, growing stake in the electoral outcome, lowering of the voter age from 21 to 18, all account for the increasing number of SCs exercising their franchise. Most important, casting vote has become an issue of social status for the Dalits.

The high SC voter turnout was significant in the light of the various restrictions the EC had imposed on poll campaigns. First, the duration of the poll campaign had been reduced by one week. Second, there was a ban on putting posters on private walls, and restriction on the number of vehicles to be used for campaigning. There was also a ban on using loudspeakers in public places, because of which candidates had to rely mostly on door-to-door campaigning. As a result, political parties complained of difficulties in reaching the people. There was general apprehension that weaker sections like the SCs who did not have much access to modern means of communication like TV and radio would find it difficult to get information about local candidates and the programmes and promises of the parties/candidates, and this might affect their turnout on the day of voting. But the fact that they surpassed the upper castes in terms of voter turnout testifies to the SCs' increased political awareness and their determination to assert.

Changes in Party Preference

The most important feature of the recent upsurge in Dalit politics has been the change in their party preference. Since independence, the SCs were considered a 'committed' vote-bank of the Congress, which, in the pre-independence period, did provide political space for the SCs to participate in the freedom struggle. This is not to deny the role of the power, hegemony and dominance of the upper castes, who comprised the upper layers of the Congress leadership. At times the SCs waged anti-feudal struggles against the local landlords. At many places, it was the communists who attracted them. Ambedkar too had a following among them. Nonetheless, it was the Congress that assured the Dalits that the political system of independent India would offer them a bright future. The Republican Party of India (RPI) did try to challenge this dominance through the most part of the 1960s, but its influence was restricted only to Maharashtra and Uttar Pradesh, that too only in a few districts of these states. By the end of the 1960s, even the RPI had lost its sheen. SC voters remained loyal to the Congress even through the troubled times of 1967 and 1977 (the percentage of SC votes polled by the Congress was 45.2 in 1967, 47.8 in 1971, 52.8 in 1980). Only in 1977, could the Congress manage 35.7 per cent of the SC votes.[3] Some fluctuations notwithstanding, the Congress never faced any serious threat to this 'captive' vote-bank except in a few states under left rule. However, decline in its SC vote share set in during the elections held in the late 1980s and early 1990s. The 1996 Lok Sabha elections finally presented a changed electoral landscape, wherein the SCs had deserted the Congress in many states, particularly in important north Indian states like Uttar Pradesh and Bihar. This is also one of the reasons why for the first time the Congress failed to become the single largest party in the Lok Sabha. The 1998 elections closely reflected the SC voting pattern of the 1996 elections. Except in a few states, the Congress is no longer the choice of the majority of the SCs.

The pattern that emerges is that wherever the SCs could find a viable alternative, they have preferred it to the Congress. The BSP has become their first choice; in its absence, the Left Front and the regional parties are preferred in states where they are dominant. However, on account of its all-India presence, the Congress still polls the largest share of SC votes—31.4 per cent in 1996 and 29.9 per cent in 1998. In contrast, the percentage of SC votes in the total votes polled by the Congress was 21.6 and 22.8 per cent in the 1996 and 1998 elections respectively. Compared to this, the Congress was able to get 47.8 per cent of SC votes in 1971. The left parties together polled 11.6 per cent and 10.4 per cent while the BSP polled 12.1 per cent and 10.9 per cent of SC votes in 1996 and 1998 respectively. Clearly, the BSP depends mostly on its SC votes: in 1996, 67 per cent of votes polled in its favour came from the SCs, while this figure was 60.6 per cent in 1998. None of the other parties relies solely on SC votes. The BJP cornered approximately 13 per cent of SC votes in both 1996 and 1998 as against 45.6 per cent and 38.4 per cent of the upper caste votes in 1996 and 1998 respectively. The Congress, the Left Front, the Janata Dal/RJD, and the BSP together accounted for 60.7 per cent and 58.1 per cent of the SC votes polled all over the country in 1996 and 1998 respectively. These are the parties that polled a larger percentage of SC votes as compared to their overall vote share. Thus, the secular, left and left-of-centre together emerged as the choice of SC voters in the general elections of 1996 and 1998.

In Uttar Pradesh, the rapidly emerging BSP captured most of the SC votes. In the 1996 elections, the party polled 59.5 per cent of SC votes while the Congress, the BJP, and the Samajwadi Party–Janata Dal alliance could manage only 9.4, 10.4 and 10.3 per cent respectively. In 1998, the BSP's share in SC votes registered a decline of 9 per cent, while the BJP improved its SC vote share by 8 per cent. In 1996, the Left Front walked away with 61.6 per cent of SC votes in West Bengal, leaving the Congress to rest content with 24.7 per cent of SC votes. While the SCs' preference for the Left Front remained steady, an important change was observed when the Congress vote base among the SCs declined sharply to 10.7 per cent. The gains, instead, were made by the breakaway Trinamul Congress. In Kerala, the Left Democratic Front (LDF) proved too good for the Congress in 1996—their respective voting percentages among the SCs were 69.2 per cent and 20.5 per cent. In 1998, the LDF further improved its SC vote share at the cost of the Congress. In the 1996 elections in Tamil Nadu, the DMK–TMC alliance convincingly won the. confidence of SC voters, polling 68.1 per cent of SC votes as against the Congress–AIADMK alliance poll of 21.3 per cent. However, in 1998, the DMK–TMC alliance had to be content with 41.5 per cent of SC votes, while the Congress suffered further erosion of its base among the SCs.

In 1996, the SC votes were divided in the multi-polar contests in Bihar, Madhya Pradesh and Maharashtra. In Bihar, the Janata Dal and its allies got 24.1 per cent, the BJP–Samata alliance 18.4 per cent, the Congress 14.9 per cent and the CPI(ML) 14.2 per cent of SC votes. The erosion in the Congress votes amongst SCs was once again more than evident. In its strongholds, for example, the Arrah and Aurangabad parliamentary constituencies, the CPI(ML) got 37.7 per cent of SC votes, which was more than the party's percentage of the total votes polled. In Madhya Pradesh, the Congress got 28.1 per cent, BSP 22.9 per cent and the BJP 11.5 per cent of SC votes. A similar trend was observed in Maharashtra's sample. In 1998, the Congress made massive gains in Madhya Pradesh and Maharashtra, where its SC vote share soared to 40.4 and 46.9 per cent respectively. In Madhya Pradesh, the BSP also consolidated its position. In Bihar, the RJD emerged as a strong force among the SC voters.

In 1996, the Janata Dal was able to get 25 per cent of SC votes in Karnataka. The percentage of SC vote share for major parties/alliances in some other states was as follows: the Telugu Desam–left alliance 37.3 per cent in Andhra Pradesh; the BJP–HVP–Samata alliance 36.6 per cent in Haryana; the BJP 36.5 per cent in the state of Delhi; and the Shiromani Akali Dal (SAD) 21.1 per cent in Punjab. In 1998, the Congress won the lion's share of the SC votes in Karnataka (58.9 per cent), while the BJP too improved its position with 14.4 per cent. While no major changes were observed in Andhra Pradesh, in Haryana the Congress succeeded in getting 58.1 per cent of SC votes. In Delhi it got 67.9 per cent SC votes, mostly at the expense of the BJP and other parties. In Punjab, interestingly, both the Congress and the BJP–SAD alliance registered a decline in their SC votes, as the BSP cornered 18.2 per cent of the SC votes.

In the case of Gujarat, the survey data of 1996 are not helpful since a large number of the respondents refused to disclose their party preference. However, the available figures suggest that the BJP got 37.8 per cent of SC votes as compared to 21.6 per cent got by the Congress. In 1998, the Congress improved its performance with 39.1 per cent of SC votes though the BJP remained ahead with 41.3 per cent. As far as Himachal Pradesh is concerned, the sample size in 1998 was too small to suggest any trend. In 1996, 75 per cent of SC votes had gone in favour of the Congress.

The inference to be drawn here is that the Congress lost its support base among SC voters mostly to the left, or to the BSP and the regional parties. The BJP failed to make big inroads among the SCs. As for the SCs' preference for the victorious/emerging regional parties, it reflects the general trend of taking the non-Congress option. The question that arose was of how to classify the regional parties in shifting alliance politics. Many regional parties that were averse to the BJP in the 1996 elections or before the 1998 elections, joined the National Democratic Alliance (NDA) led by the BJP. I still prefer to classify the majority of them as 'left-of-centre' parties in so far as their basic character has remained secular.

Table 14.2: Party Preference of SCs, 1996 (%)

State	Congress		BJP		Left		Regional		JD		BSP		Others*		Sample size (n)	
	SC	UC	SC	UC	SC	UC	SC	UC	SC	UC	SC	UC	SC	UC	SC	UC
Andhra Pradesh[2]	51.8	43.8	–	–	–	–	37.3	35.1	–	–	–	–	10.9	21.1	83	208
Bihar[3]	14.9	7.8	18.4	35.0	14.2	–	–	–	24.1	22.5	–	–	27.3	24.7	141	218
Delhi	47.2	25.2	36.5	53.9	–	–	–	–	–	–	–	–	16.3	20.7	178	317
Gujarat	21.6	11.3	47.7	–	–	–	–	–	–	–	–	–	40.3	41.1	111	151
Haryana[4]	39.0	18.4	36.6	53.1	–	–	–	–	–	–	12.2	2.0	12.2	26.5	41	49
Himachal Pradesh	75.0	64.5	25.0	32.3	–	–	–	–	–	–	–	–	0.0	3.2	28	32
Karnataka	46.7	13.8	1.7	27.6	–	–	–	–	25.0	39.7	–	–	26.6	18.9	60	58
Kerala[5]	20.5	46.4	5.1	5.1	69.2	33.3	–	–	–	–	–	–	5.2	15.2	39	99
Madhya Pradesh	28.1	33.7	11.5	32.5	–	–	–	–	–	–	22.9	–	37.5	33.7	96	83
Maharashtra[6]	33.3	34.8	22.2	34.9	5.6	1.4	16.7	0.7	–	–	–	–	16.6	27.5	18	558

Orissa	74.7	42.0	7.7	14.8	—	—	—	9.9	27.3	—	—	7.7	15.9	91	88
Punjab[7]	47.9	32.3	—	8.6	21.1	22.6	—	—	2.8	3.2	28.1	33.4	71	93
Rajasthan	72.4	39.4	14.5	46.5	—	—	—	—	—	—	13.2	14.1	76	310
Tamil Nadu[8]	21.3	8.1	—	—	68.1	48.6	—	—	—	—	10.6	43.3	160	37
Uttar Pradesh[9]	9.4	7.1	10.4	52.7	—	—	10.3	18.1	59.5	1.7	10.4	20.4	309	537
West Bengal	24.7	44.0	10.0	6.6	61.6	45.1	—	—	—	—	3.7	4.3	271	364
All India	31.4	28.3	13.2	27.1	11.6	7.2	8.5	5.6	7.0	12.1	0.4	6.1	10.6	1791	3357

Notes: *'Others' include independent candidates, other parties and respondents who refused to answer or those who said, 'don't know'. The states where the sample size of the SC respondents was 10 or less than 10, do not Figure in this table.

1 UC stands for upper castes.

2 Regional parry here denotes the alliance of the Telugu Desam Party (Naidu) and the left parties.

3 The vote percentage of the BJP includes that of the BJP–Samata Parry alliance; 14.2 per cent SC votes polled by the left are the votes polled by the CPI(ML) only.

4 The vote percentage of the BJP includes that of the Haryana Vikas Party and the Samata Party.

5 The vote percentages of the Congress and the left include those of the UDF and the LDF respectively.

6 The vote percentage of the BJP includes that of the Shiv Sena. Here the left is represented by the CPI(M). The vote percentage of the Peasants and Workers Party is given under the regional party. 'Others' include the RPI which polled 5.6 per cent SC votes.

7 In the case of Punjab, the regional party indicates the Shiromani Akali Dal.

8 The vote percentage of the Congress indicates that of the Congress–AIADMK combine. The vote percentage for the regional party represents the votes of the DMK–TMC alliance.

9 The vote percentage of the Janata Dal includes that of the Janata Dal–Samajwadi Party alliance.

Table 14.3: Party Preference of SCs, 1998 (%)

State	Congress		BJP		Left		Regional		JD		BSP		Others		Sample size (n)	
	SC	UC	SC	UC	SC	UC	SC	UC	SC	UC	SC	UC	SC	UC	SC	UC
Andhra Pradesh[1]	47.9	34.3	8.3	21.6	6.3	4.4	25.0	31.3	–	–	–	–	2.1	0.7	48	134
Bihar[2]	12.0	7.8	21.3	68.9	8.5	2.6	–	–	41.9	7.8	–	–	16.2	13.0	117	116
Delhi	67.9	36.7	24.5	49.0	–	–	–	–	1.9	–	–	–	5.7	14.3	53	98
Gujarat3	39.1	10.4	41.3	62.4	–	–	4.3	8.0	2.2	–	–	–	13.0	19.2	46	125
Haryana[4]	58.1	17.4	–	17.4	–	–	22.6	54.4	3.2	–	–	–	16.1	10.9	31	46
Karnataka	58.9	18.6	14.4	34.9	2.2	–	4.4	20.9	11.1	16.3	1.1	–	7.7	9.3	90	43
Kerala[5]	10.8	28.6	2.7	26.0	67.5	37.7	16.2	3.9	–	–	–	–	2.7	3.9	37	77
Madhya Pradesh	40.4	26.4	24.6	62.5	–	–	–	–	–	–	24.6	5.6	10.6	5.6	57	72
Maharashtra[6]	46.9	46.4	30.6	40.0	–	0.3	–	–	–	0.3	2.0	–	20.4	13.0	49	330

Orissa	67.1	28.6	2.6	14.3	–	1.4	17.1	37.1	6.6	5.7	–	6.6	10.0	76	70
Punjab[7]	33.0	54.1	–	–	–	–	17.0	16.4	25.0	11.5	18.2	9.8	6.8	8.2	88	61
Rajasthan	62.2	35.8	36.5	59.5	–	–	–	–	–	–	–	1.4	4.7	74	215
Tamil Nadu[8]	9.1	12.2	12.2	34.2	–	–	41.5	29.3	–	–	2.4	–	34.7	24.4	164	41
Uttar Pradesh[9]	8.0	6.1	18.4	70.0	2.4	0.4	9.0	3.6	0.5	–	50.5	3.2	16.9	11.7	212	280
West Bengal[10]	10.7	10.3	28.0	39.0	58.0	45.0	–	–	–	–	–	–	3.4	5.7	150	282
All India[11]	29.9	24.8	13.5	34.5	10.4	8.6	16.4	19.2	6.9	1.4	10.9	0.9	12.0	10.6	1312	2039

Notes: [1] Regional party here denotes the Telugu Desam Party (Naidu).

[2] The vote percentage of the BJP includes that of the BJP–Samata Party alliance. The votes polled by the left parties denote the votes polled by the CPI and the CPI(ML).

[3] Regional party in Gujarat denotes RJP (Vaghela).

[4] The regional parties in Haryana include the Haryana Vikas Parry and HLD (R).

[5] The vote percentages of the Congress and the left include those of the UDF and the LDF respectively. The regional party here mentioned denotes the Muslim League.

[6] The vote percentage of the BJP includes that of the Shiv Sena. Here the left is represented by the CPI(M). 'Others' include the RPI which polled 4.1 per cent of SC votes.

[7] In Punjab the regional party indicates the Shiromani Akali Dal (Badal).

[8] The vote percentage of the regional party represents the votes of the DMK–TMC alliance.

[9] The vote percentage of the regional party denotes that of the Samajwadi Party (Mulayam Singh).

[10] The percentage of BJP votes includes that of the Trinamul Congress. The BJP polled 14.7 per cent and the Trinamul Congress 13.3 per cent of the SC votes.

[11] Regional parties are included independent of their alliance.

In conclusion, the party preference among SCs varied across states. In this respect, SC politics was passing through a phase of transition. Dalits seemed to have understood the importance of their collective strength in electoral bargaining. At least in the states where their are larger numbers, their votes have acquired increasing significance in deciding the electoral outcome. Shift in SC voting towards the left and non-conservative parties is remarkable. Rejection of the Congress by the SCs in many states, particularly Uttar Pradesh and Bihar, symbolises their rejection of the vertical integration process perpetrated by the upper castes. This is the most important change that manifested in the 1996 parliamentary elections and the process continued in 1998. It appears that the SCs no longer follow the voting preference of the upper castes or the local notables that have characterised the elite politics since independence. In fact, no party in these two states could replicate the upper-caste–SC coalition formed earlier under the Congress leadership. This shift signifies a rupture in the patron–client relationship, at least in the realm of party politics.

Party Preference by Economic and Demographic Variables

A further break-up of the SC voters according to age, sex, locality and class throws light on the undercurrents of the transition process. The SCs cannot be considered a homogeneous group, and their internal divisions do influence their party preference. Let us take the indices of influence developed for 1996 (Table 14.4). As the data reveal, voters who preferred the Congress showed least bias for age, sex, locality and class divide. In this sense, the Congress still had an all-encompassing appeal, while all other parties had a narrow, partisan vote base in terms of the divisions mentioned above. Here, however, it is more important to understand the changing partisan characteristic of the SC voting pattern.

Age, on the whole, seemed to have little impact on the party preference of SCs, the most consistent being the age group 26–35 years whose vote was by and large evenly distributed among all the major parties. In other age groups, the standard deviation was slightly higher but more or less equal. In the age group of 18–25 years, the BSP was the most favoured party, followed by the BJP, the left being the least favoured. The standard deviation was low in the case of the Congress, which implies that it was the only party whose voters were evenly distributed across all the age groups. The standard deviation was highest in the case of the BSP. The BSP and the BJP were more favoured by voters in the younger age groups. On the contrary, the left parties and the Janata Dal were preferred mostly by the older age groups.

There was little variation in the pattern of party preference among male and female voters. The standard deviation was only 5.56 and 6.07 for male

Table 14.4: Indices* of Influence on Party Preference, 1996

	Party preference						
	Congress	BJP	JD	LF	BSP	Others	
Age-wise							
Up to 25 years	99.13	108.93	100.92	88.04	120.72	86.90	12.82
26–35 years	94.16	100.37	98.94	111.63	101.79	101.70	5.74
36–45 years	106.30	105.97	87.93	95.51	78.80	105.36	11.42
46–55 years	94.91	80.76	111.04	115.58	99.23	112.32	13.28
56 years or above	110.84	91.02	107.27	89.32	85.20	103.08	10.62
Standard deviation	7.28	11.54	8.87	12.80	16.29	9.32	
Sex-wise							
Male	97.02	103.52	104.32	102.78	108.64	93.13	5.56
Female	103.25	96.16	95.28	96.97	90–57	107.49	6.07
Standard deviation	4.40	5.20	6.39	4.11	12.78	10–15	
Locality-wise							
Rural	95.97	81.12	103–39	118.98	107–70	103–09	12.62
Urban	115–7	1173.61	86.80	26–03	69.97	87.96	49.18
Standard deviation	13–95	65.40	11–73	65.72	26.68	10.70	
Class-wise							
Very poor	96.28	60.48	137.72	123.44	81.07	127.70	30.16
Poor	101.89	114.04	59.42	89.64	137.12	73.51	28.06
Middle	111.56	161.14	74.73	54.28	93.41	70.27	38.28
Rich	75.30	268.66	43.66	63.42	58.21	79.27	84.64
Standard deviation	15–33	88.65	41.23	31–03	33–16	26.93	

Note: *The calculation is based on age group (party-wise)/party total × rand total/age group total × 100.

and female voters respectively. However, there was greater variation in the case of the BSP, which was preferred more by men than women. The same was the case with other parties too. The converse was true for the Congress which was still favoured more by women than men.

On the other hand, the rural–urban divide has a strong influence on SCs' party preference in elections. The variation in the case of urban votes is very large. There is a strong preference for a particular party and rejection of others in the urban areas. The standard deviation was exceptionally high for the BJP and the left. Although the BJP had expanded into rural areas, its vote base was concentrated in urban areas. The gap in the urban indices was close to 100. The left was almost entirely confined to rural areas with negligible supporters from urban areas. The BSP's constituency was also more rural than urban. The Congress and the Janata Dal showed consistency in terms of votes in both rural and urban areas.

However, the strongest influence on voting preference was observed in terms of class division. There was uneven distribution of voters in all class groups, the most uneven being in the middle and, of course, the rich class. The BJP was highly preferred among the middle class and the rich SCs. The BSP, the left and the Janata Dal were clearly the favourite parties of the poor SCs. The Congress was the exception in the sense that it had a wide vote base across all the class groups. Since the middle and the rich classes constitute a small section of the SCs (see Table 14.1), there can be no doubt that the changed preference for the BSP, left or the RJD/Janata Dal indicates the assertion of the poor and deprived among them.

As against the 10 per cent lower-class SC votes going to the BJP, 22.75 per cent of the middle- and upper-class SCs preferred to vote for the BJP. Conversely, only 7.21 per cent of the SC voters of the middle and upper classes voted for the BSP. From among those claiming to vote for the BSP, 85.3 per cent belonged to the lower classes. Similarly, 83.6 per cent, 84.2 per cent, 73 per cent and 90.1 per cent votes of the total SC votes polled by the Left Front, the Janata Dal, the Congress and the regional parties respectively came from the lower classes among the Dalits. In the case of the BJP, this figure was 56.5 per cent. The BJP and the Congress accounted for 56.5 per cent of the middle- and upper-class SC votes. Another 15.1 per cent SC votes in this class group were accounted for by those who did not reveal their party preference. Interestingly, the upper-class SCs resemble the upper class of the upper castes in terms of their voting preference. The election data also show that the lower class belonging to the upper castes voted relatively more in favour of the Congress, the Janata Dal and the left parties. In this sense, the BJP may be termed as not only a party of the caste Hindus, but also as a party of the upper class cutting across all caste groups. The poor SCs preferred parties that took up the cause of the weaker sections. Thus, there was a two-directional shift in the SC votes—the poor SCs preferring the broad left and the well-off SCs opting for the BJP and the Congress.

This trend has serious implications for our understanding of the caste–class discourse. What underlies the newly found attraction among the upper-middle and middle-class SC votes for the BJP? With further economic differentiation, what will be the future of the Bahujan coalition of the SCs, STs, lower-class Muslims and most backward castes and OBCs? Is the question of identity and self-respect adequately addressed by economic prosperity? Can this trend be explained by concepts like elite emulation and imitative reference group or should it be taken as simply a case of class transcending caste? These questions cannot be addressed by the election data alone. However, they require the attention of all researchers concerned.

In the 1996 elections the BSP showed greater probability of support among the youngest age group, which support base became enlarged by 1998. (see Table 14.5). Similarly, among the supporters of the Left Front, the probability of support among the older age group increased further. However, the most important change was that the lowest standard deviation was in the case of the BJP, meaning that its support base was more evenly distributed among all the age groups than that of other parties. Till 1996 this was a characteristic feature of the Congress. Another new feature was the high standard deviation value in the age group 18–25 years implying that this group was the most unstable in deciding its party preference. The age group 46–55 years came next in exhibiting much volatility.

As far as the influence of sex division on voting behaviour is concerned, the support of males and females was largely evenly distributed among parties as it had been in 1996 (see Table 14.5). However, there was a change in the support for the Left Front among females. This shows that more women were likely to be influenced to support the party than men. The standard deviation for the BJP had risen because its influence among male voters had gone up. Otherwise, the standard deviation for all other parties decreased, indicating a trend of sex-wise homogenisation in the support base of the parties.

As far as the rural–urban divide in vote base is concerned, urban voters continued to remain in a situation of flux, though their instability had reduced considerably since 1996. As far as parties are concerned, except for the RJD/Janata Dal, the standard deviation declined in the case of all other parties. The RJD/JD seemed to have further influenced voters in rural areas while its influence among urban voters went down. The Left Front improved dramatically in its vote catching probability in urban areas. Most remarkably, however, the BJP improved its influence in rural areas though there was a decline in its influence over its traditional urban voters. To conclude, the indices

Table 14.5: Indices of Influence on Party Preference, 1998

				Party preference			
	INC	BJP	JD/RJD	LF	BSP	Others	
Age-wise							
Up to 25 years	90.18	107.89	106.24	79.11	147.60	102.24	23.33
26–35 years	100.07	101.64	98.26	93.08	89.74	101.99	4.98
36–45 years	98.95	97.41	98.07	110.18	88.91	102.40	6.94
46–55 years	102.41	97.90	110.08	123.97	74.46	93.019	16.65
56 years or above	112.72	91.47	87.78	105.50	92.94	96.33	9.47
Standard deviation	8.08	6.044	8.61	17.07	28.23	4.29	
Sex-wise							
Male	95.23	109.33	99.59	89.98	100.23	99.68	6.39
Female	104.49	90.23	100.43	110.49	99.76	100.33	6.70
Standard deviation	6.91	13.50	0.60	14.50	0.33	0.46	
Locality-wise							
Rural	98.21	94.51	110.66	111.81	104.43	100.30	6.93
Urban	105.63	117.26	66.47	62.87	86.06	99.05	21.79
Standard deviation	5.25	16.08	31.25	34.61	12.99	0.89	

based on the 1998 data show that the BJP entered a phase of transformation, increasingly acquiring the characteristics of the Congress, and enjoying a wider support base cutting across age, sex and locality.

THE RISE OF THE BSP

The BSP's improved performance was one of the remarkable features of the 1998 elections. This is a typical case of SC assertion in electoral politics, through a party which mainly has a base among them. In 1996, 67.4 per cent and in 1998, 60. per cent of the BSP's votes came from the SCs. In the states of Uttar Pradesh, Haryana, Madhya Pradesh and Punjab, the party performed exceedingly well. In Uttar Pradesh it performed exceptionally well, in terms of both vote share and the number of seats won. The 1996 all-India election figures show that the BSP contested 201 seats, won 11, and was able to get 3.8 per cent of the total valid votes. Of the 11 seats, the BSP won six seats in Uttar Pradesh, three in Punjab and two in Madhya Pradesh. Of these 11 seats, only three belonged to reserved constituencies. Of the all-India SC votes, the party's share was 12.1 per cent. The EC data show that the party secured 20.16 per cent of the total votes in Uttar Pradesh. There were 52 seats in the state where the party polled more than 100,000 votes. It stood second in 17 seats and secured more than 20 per cent of the total votes polled in 46 seats (Table 14.6).

The BSP's vote share showed a steady increase. The party got 4 per cent of the total votes in the 1985 assembly elections, 9.4 per cent of the total votes in the 1989 assembly elections, 9.9 per cent in the 1991 Lok Sabha elections and 10.8 per cent in the 1993 assembly elections.[4] In the 1998 elections, the party performed even better in terms of percentage of votes secured, though in terms of seats, it lost considerably. It contested 249 seats, won five and secured 4.68 per cent of the total valid votes.

The BSP's vote share increased in all four states, namely, Uttar Pradesh, Punjab, Madhya Pradesh and Haryana where the party was known to have a strong base (see Table 14.6). It secured over 100,000 votes in three constituencies in Haryana, nine constituencies in Madhya Pradesh, four constituencies in Punjab and 66 constituencies in Uttar Pradesh. The party polled more than 20 per cent votes in two constituencies in Haryana, six in Madhya Pradesh, 43 in Uttar Pradesh, and more than 40 per cent votes in all the four constituencies of Punjab it contested.

The BSP emerged strong in states where there was a sizeable concentration of SC population. According to the 1991 census, SCs constitute 21.05 per cent of the population in Uttar Pradesh, 28.31 per cent in Punjab, 14.5 per cent in Madhya Pradesh, and 19.75 per cent in Haryana. The all-India average

Table 14.6: Performance of BSP, 1996 and 1998

State	1996		1998	
	Seats won	Total votes	Seats won	Total votes
Punjab	3	8.96	12.65	
Madhya Pradesh	2	6.73	8.70	
Haryana	–	6.59	1	7.68
Jammu & Kashmir	–	5.95	–	5.05
Uttar Pradesh	6	20.16	4	20.90
All India	11	3.80	5	4.68

of SC population to the total population is 16.48 per cent. Other states with SC population above the all-India average are Himachal Pradesh (25.3 per cent), Rajasthan (17.3 per cent), Tamil Nadu (19.2 per cent), West Bengal (23.6 per cent) and Delhi (19. 1 per cent). In Himachal Pradesh and Rajasthan, the Congress has a comfortable hold over SC votes, while Tamil Nadu and West Bengal are the stronghold of the DMK-TMC alliance, and the CPI(M) respectively. In Delhi, both the Congress and the BJP are contenders for SC votes. The BSP is nowhere in the picture in, these states. In Bihar, Andhra Pradesh, Orissa, Tripura and Karnataka the SC population is near the all-India average. Here too the BSP has no foothold. But, importantly, in contrast to 1996, for the first time, in 1998, the BSP succeeded in attracting backward caste votes. For example, in Uttar Pradesh, despite the decline in its SC vote share, the BSP's total vote share increased because of additional backward caste votes cast in its favour. One possible explanation for this is that the number of SC candidates fielded by the BSP in 1998 came down while the share of its backward caste candidates grew.

Dalits' assertion in party politics and governance through their own party is not a new phenomenon. The Jatavs in the Agra region keenly followed the debate of Dalit emancipation between Gandhi and Ambedkar. In 1944–5, they formed the Scheduled Castes Federation (SCF) of Agra which was linked to the All India Scheduled Caste Federation. Till the formation of the RPI in 1958, Dalit politics in Uttar Pradesh kept swinging between the accommodative policies of the Congress and radical politics of the SCF. These two tendencies of integration and separatism continued in the SC movement in postcolonial India.[5] The RPI phase lasted just a decade, its influence being confined to Uttar Pradesh and Maharashtra. The party won three parliamentary seats and eight assembly seats in Uttar Pradesh in the 1962 general elections. Its performance was marginally better in 1967 when it won 10 assembly seats. After winning only two assembly seats in the 1969 elections, the RPI finally declined to a non-entity in the subsequent elections. In this context, Sudha Pai describes the 1970s as 'a phase of integration and a hiatus between two periods of separatist political activity by the SCs in Uttar Pradesh'.[6] The Congress was able to co-opt both of them.

However, the BSP's emergence in the 1980s and 1990s as a force to reckon with in the four north Indian states has its causality in the altered political context and the changes in the SC community itself. The steady decline of the Congress, which earlier used to more or less represent the majority of the SCs all over the country, created a political vacuum. This space has not been occupied by the BJP as it is dominated by the twice-born castes. Precisely because of this the SCs' party preference is quite dispersed. This may be true of some other marginalised social groups also, which probably explains the presence of not less than 30 parties in the eleventh Lok Sabha.

It is necessary to dispel the commonly held belief that the BSP had a powerful electoral appeal among urban educated middle-class SCs. The 1996 figures on voters' background in Uttar Pradesh reveal that 62.7 per cent of the BSP's votes came from illiterate voters though they constituted only 44.8 per cent of the total sample of respondents. The next large share came from voters with secondary education who constituted 27.4 per cent of the total BSP voters. Voters, having completed graduation or above, constituted only 2 per cent of BSP voters though their representation in the sample was 5.6 per cent. In fact, only 6.3 per cent of the graduates preferred to vote for the BSP, whereas this figure was as high as 51.3 per cent for the BJP. This finding proves that education has no direct connection with political consciousness. The assertion of Dalit identity in politics is essentially the assertion of illiterate but politically conscious Dalits.

Occupationally, BSP voters are mainly unskilled workers, agricultural and allied workers, artisans, and small and marginal farmers. Persons engaged in business and white-collar jobs constitute only 2.6 and 1.6 per cent of the BSP voters respectively. The all-India figures also reflect the trends observed in Uttar Pradesh. For example, the all-India figures reveal that 85.3 per cent of the BSP's votes came from the lower classes, suggesting that the BSP is primarily a party of the rural poor.

The other party known for representing mostly SCs was the RPI. In the 1996 parliamentary elections, the party emerged as the obvious choice of SC voters wherever it contested elections in Maharashtra. Though the party failed to win a single seat in the state, of the 11 it contested, its vote share was more than 20 per cent in five seats (the highest being 33.19 per cent in the Akola constituency) and between 10 and 20 per cent of the votes polled in four other constituencies. The party polled more than 200,000 votes in two constituencies (Election Commission of India, 1996). But after entering into an alliance with the Congress in the 1998 elections, the RPI won all four seats it contested in Maharashtra. Its vote share in these constituencies ranged between 47 and 50 per cent. The Peasants and Workers Party of India (PWP) won the Kolaba seat in the coastal Konkan region of the state, securing about 33 per cent of the total votes. However, in the case of Maharashtra, it should be remembered that Dalits constitute only 11.09 per cent of the total population, making it imperative for any party to, form a broader social and political coalition for success.

This section examines the perception of SC voters regarding the legitimacy of the political system. This helps us understand why the political movements of the SCs tend to take the route of electoral politics and in the process reflect a justification for the political system.

The figures of the two election surveys clearly show that there was no substantial divergence of opinion between SCs and the upper castes regarding the efficacy[7] of their votes. In 1996, about 610 per cent of the SCs and 62 per cent of the upper-caste respondents expressed faith in the power of their vote. In terms of class, the figures were, by and large, the same. The second important indicator of legitimacy of the system was the credibility of the elections themselves. In 1996, a sizeable proportion—45.4 per cent of the SCs and 51.3 per cent of the upper castes—affirmed the usefulness of elections. The figures remained more or less the same in 1998. Class-wise, 53.1 per cent of the SCs and 56.9 per cent of the upper castes belonging to the upper and middle classes, described elections as useful. The corresponding figures for the lower class according to their respective caste groups were 43 per cent and 43.6 per cent. However, it is noteworthy that despite a relatively high percentage of voting and moderate faith in its efficacy, elections were not the only choice of an overwhelming majority as far as articulation of political issues was concerned. This might have been because of the persisting problems with the election system, like the lack of choice of good candidates, absence of any accountability of the elected candidates, misuse of money, etc.

On the indicator of voters' perception of the usefulness of parties, significantly, only 41.4 per cent of the SC respondents in 1996 felt that political parties could make government pay attention to them as against 46.9 per cent of the upper-caste people. The response in 1998 was no different. Data reveal that upper- and middle-class respondents who expressed confidence in the usefulness of political parties were 48.9 per cent from the SCs and 51.8 per cent from the upper castes. This confidence level was far more than that of their respective lower-class respondents which was 39.1 per cent and 39.9 per cent respectively. In both years, only 17 per cent of SC voters confirmed meeting any political leader, and only 20 per cent knowing any leader personally. The figures in this respect were more or less similar for the upper castes, except that in 1998, 26.7 per cent of them reported knowing any leader personally. In the 1996 survey, when asked whether any political party cared for the interests of their caste group, only 21.8 per cent of SC respondents and 18.1 per cent of upper-caste respondents replied in the affirmative. These figures were marginally better among SCs in 1998, as 24.4 per cent of them responded positively compared to 15.8 per cent of the upper-caste respondents. Similarly, an overwhelming majority (about 65 per cent) of both castes responded in the negative in both election surveys when queried about the party they felt close to. The upper and middle classes were found better placed than the lower class in these respects.

Thus, the CSDS data reveal that the *legitimacy of the political parties is much lower than the legitimacy of the system in general.* The National Election Survey Report of the CSDS (1996) puts it as a typical example of *high* legitimisation of the system and *low* legitimisatioin of the actors.[8] In contrast, both scholars and political leaders in the 1950s and early 1960s presumed the legitimacy of the new institutions as largely depending on the legitimacy of the parties themselves.[9] One reason for distrust of political parties may be that, as Max Weber says, 'the party is alive only during election periods. The parliamentary delegates and the parliamentary party leaders know to which local notables one turns if a political action seems desirable.' In India, too, upper-class voters tend to participate- less in direct political activities but have developed powerful stakes in the system. This points to the continuing elitisation of Indian politics. The message to political parties is loud and clear: they cannot take the support of the SCs for granted because the low level of trust in the parties may lead the SCs to further changes in party preference.

However, asked the question, 'Suppose there were no parties or assemblies and elections were not held, do you think that the government in this country can be run better?' an impressive 68.8 per cent of the respondents across caste lines in 1996 answered in the negative, whereas this figure stood at 43.4 per cent in 1971 (CSDS Data Unit, Delhi). Although no baseline is available, it can be safely presumed that the increase in percentage came mainly from the weaker sections of society, namely, the SCs, STs and OBCs. Still, 74 per cent of the upper-caste respondents approved of this system as against 67.3 per cent of the SCs. The response remained almost the same in the 1998 elections as well. The foregoing analysis important, considering the conflicting responses with respect to the legitimacy of the different political agencies and institutions. This shows that despite being dissatisfied with the agencies of the system, the SCs see no clear alternative to the multiparty parliamentary democracy. This gives them an added impetus to assert themselves as a political bloc in the electoral arena. On the whole, the Indian political system enjoys moderate legitimacy among the SC electorate, largely from the upper and middle classes.

Nevertheless, its legitimacy among the lower castes has been increasing. This perhaps partly explains why the SCs now throng electoral booths as never before.

CONCLUSIONS

There is an effort on the part of the SCs to carve out a distinct political niche, indeed an identity, in so far as their voting behaviour is concerned. Their assertion in electoral politics in order to occupy political and economic space and, thereby, also enhance their social status, is bound to face stiff opposition—physical as well as political. As a result, the SCs have adopted multidimensional strategies ranging from social measures, such as acquiring education, to getting organised for both electoral as well as non-electoral exigencies.

There is a definite pattern in the party preference of SCs, who have gradually shifted from the Congress and opted for alternatives wherever they could find them. This change in allegiance is guided more by secular concerns in order to derive benefits than by mere parochial interests. These are no longer prepared to be passive voter-supporters in an environment of subjugation and subordination. Though they have realised that the Congress has politically nothing to offer, they do not at the same time opt for any party irrationally or indiscriminately and are not intransigent either.

The exercise of their voting right and its effective application to strengthen exclusively SC-based parties like the BSP, and the left and the left-of-centre parties have been major highlights of their political ascendance. Though there are internal cleavages within the SCs in the form of growing class differentiation, both the lower and upper classes among them are in the process of change so far as party preferences go, with the former mostly inclining to the left and the latter to the BSP.

While political institutions of Indian democracy seem to enjoy the support of the SCs, the political actors stand more or less discredited. This is an alarming signal for political parties, which cannot afford to take the current overwhelming support of the SCs for granted. They will have to show genuine concern for the issues of the SCs lest the SCs find that non-parliamentary methods are more rewarding than electoral means.

PART IV

Caste and Social Transformation

Introduction

The caste system legitimises and perpetuates hierarchy and inequality based on birth. Those who strive for the democratic transformation of Indian society, irrespective of political ideology, have to fight against the prevalent caste ideology. Some wish to annihilate it, others want to reform the caste system—do away with ascribed status and unequal relationships. How to attain this objective is the challenge.

Those who wish to reform caste structure and ideology focus on ethics, arguing that people must change their attitudes and belief system. Others emphasise changes in the economic and political structure so as to create equal opportunities for majority populations. In this context, besides state intervention, struggles of the oppressed have been advocated: there is a long history of the struggles of deprived castes for equality.

As a result of the pressures built up by deprived groups, certain native rulers and the British government provided reservations in jobs and political offices for vocal sections of deprived groups during the colonial period. Their struggles and pressure on the state continued on the eve of independence. The constituent assembly made several provisions in the Constitution, providing protective discrimination to these groups. Ghanshyam. Shah examines the politics of reservation and anti-reservation. He argues that reservation is one of the methods of state intervention to provide a helping hand to those who have been traditionally deprived in the caste structure. This is not enough; it has to be accompanied with the support of other socio-political forces.

Gail Omvedt examines the anti-caste movement of the Dalit and Bahujan Samaj (OBCs) groups led by Jyotirao Phule, Dr Ambedkar, Dalit Panthers, and the Bahujan Samaj Party.

15

Social Backwardness and the Politics of Reservations *

Ghanshyam Shah

SOCIAL BACKWARDNESS

The social backwardness of an individual and/or a group is society and time specific. The social structure places certain individuals/groups in a particular position of disadvantage. Among the factors that determine social backwardness are, one, the objective position of a group in terms of its economic condition in the structure, and two, the prevailing value system related to traditional position, occupation, and lifestyle.

Social backwardness is not insurmountable. Though the factors responsible for it change with change in the economic structure, they do not get eradicated automatically. This requires intervention in the socio-cultural milieu and the economic and political structure. Those who suffer from deprivation make efforts to obviate the factors responsible for their plight. And, the state in the interest of overall social development, takes actions to change the social structure and create conditions whereby socially backward groups and individuals can overcome their backwardness. The range of actions and ideologies adopted for reducing social backwardness fall in the political arena. This essay seeks to examine the nature of social backwardness and the politics pursued by backward castes/communities and the ruling elite for its eradication in India.

The caste system is *sui generis* of the social structure in the Indian subcontinent in general and of Hindus in particular. In this system group identity supersedes individual identity. The position of an individual in society cannot be separated from the position of the 'jati' or social group to which he or she belongs. Homo *hierarchicus is* a central and substantive element of the

*Economic and Political Weekly, 26 (11–12), Annual Number, March 1991, pp. 601–10.

caste system which differentiates it from other social systems. Broadly speaking, the system has been governed by the concept of purity and pollution. It is obligatory for members of a caste to confine their relationships and interaction within the restricted circle of jati, so as to maintain purity in contracting marriages, exchanging food and pursuing occupations. 'The principle of the opposition of the pure and impure,' Louis Dumont argues, 'underlies hierarchy, which is the superiority of the pure to the impure, underlies separation because the pure and impure must be kept separate and underlies the division of labour because pure and impure occupations must likewise be kept separate. The whole is founded on the necessary and hierarchical coexistence of the two opposites.'[1]

Historically, the division of labour in society has divided castes into the haves and the have-nots. The former owned and continue to own greater means of production and also political power. They form the privileged classes in society. The latter constitute the deprived or underprivileged classes. This division of labour enables the privileged castes to exploit the toiling masses.

However, all haves are not equal and do not constitute a homogeneous category. The same is true of the have-nots. The have-nots are traditionally called 'Sudras'. They are broadly divided into 'clean' and 'unclean' or 'aniravasita' and 'nirvasita', or 'Sudras' and 'Ati-Sudras'. The latter are outside the varna system and treated as untouchable or 'achhut'. There are layers within each of these categories. Among the Sudras, there are peasant castes, artisan castes and nomadic castes. The subjective perception of one's position in the varna system varies and changes from time to time, place to place and context to context. For instance, the Patidars of Gujarat were considered Sudras until a few decades ago, but now they call themselves Vaishyas, and are acknowledged as such by others. It is significant that they are not have-nots. Similar is the case of the Vokkaligas and Lingayats of Karnataka, Reddys and Kammas of Andhra Pradesh, Marathas of Maharashtra and to some extent the Yadavas of Bihar.

The system of division of labour based on hierarchy is legitimised by the religious-legal system laid down by the dominant castes. The Dharmashastras and the Puranas give elaborate rules for observation of their respective distinctions between purity and impurity according to one's station in life and prescribe punishment for those who violate the rules. And these rules favour the upper castes. There was no rule of law applicable equally to all. Sudras and women irrespective of caste, were punished much more severely than were male Brahmins for committing the same crime.

Perpetuated by religious sanction, this system has become a cultural system in which members of upper and lower castes have internalised caste ideology. This ideology has two components: 'karma', and hierarchy and social status.

According to the karma theory, one accepts one's station in life and performs the duty prescribed by religion in this life so as to reap rewards in the next. Social status and hierarchy are closely linked, so that castes are not only arranged in hierarchical order, but also strictly stratified according to functions. Members of upper castes cannot do certain types of work without endangering their caste standing. The 'pure' tasks entail less physical labour and more material gain as well as prestige than do the 'impure' tasks. Many scholars observe that there is some kind of cultural 'consensus' from top to bottom among all castes both globally and locally. Michael Moffatt argues,

> Untouchables do not necessarily possess distinctively different social and cultural forms as a result of their position in the system. They do not possess a separate subculture. They are not detached or alienated from the 'rationalisation' of the system. Untouchables possess and act upon a thickly textured culture whose fundamental definitions and values are identical to those of more global Indian village culture. The 'view from the bottom' is based on the same principles and evaluations as the 'view from the middle' or the 'view from the top'. The cultural system of Indian untouchables does not distinctively question or revalue the dominant social order. Rather, it continuously recreates among untouchables a microcosm of the larger system.[2]

The exploitative caste system is backed by legal, religious and cultural sanctions which enable the ruling classes and castes to continue their dominance and maintain the status quo in their favour. As the system has continued for centuries, the Sudras and Ati-Sudras who are theoretically expected to labour and produce surplus, and serve the privileged *dwija* castes, remain deprived of educational benefits, economic opportunities and political power, crucial components that perpetuate their low position in the hierarchy and consequently their social backwardness.

However, it is naive to view the caste system as rigid and stubborn and to believe that it has remained intact in its structure and spirit, or that the laws prescribed in the Dharmashastras have always been enforced uniformly and against all forces. There are, for instance, vast variations in the caste structure in north India and south India, in Bihar and West Bengal. There is mobility within the structure. Castes that have improved their condition or gained political offices have sanskritised their rituals and lifestyle to move up the ladder of the caste structure. Even ex-untouchables such as the Nadars have successfully crossed the boundaries of untouchability. Obviously, such cases of mobility are few. The process of upward mobility in India, however, has been a group process within the caste framework in which the group, and not the individual, is important for recognition of status.

The attempts of Sudras and Ati-Sudras to achieve a higher social status indicate that the cultural consensus is hollow. Those at the bottom endorse it so long as they are unable to challenge it, but whenever possible it is opposed and challenged from below and enforced from above. In doing so they accept the principle of hierarchy but reject the karma theory—a recognition of the principle that status is not ascribed according to the karma of previous birth but can be changed and achieved in this life. There are instances where a Sudra became a 'raja' and called himself a Kshatriya, and the ruling classes of the time recognised his new status as either a *fait accompli* or a strategy to co-opt the conqueror. The 'raja' used to take his close relatives into the new fold of Kshatriya to counter the existing ruling class. Similarly, there are cases of Sudras sanskritised into Vaishyas. However, all those who attained higher status did not necessarily sanskritise their lifestyles and rituals, as in the case of the Kshatriyas who wielded power. Thus, political power and ownership of economic resources are the major sources of mobility. M.N. Srinivas observes about the pre-British period that,

> One of the sources of mobility lay in the system's political fluidity. Any caste that achieved political power at the local level could advance a claim to be Kshatriyas. Second, the king in traditional India had the power to promote as well as to demote castes, and he occasionally exercised this power to bestow a favour on a caste or to punish it. It is presumed that the king consulted the Brahmins learned in the law before he promoted or demoted a caste, but this meant only that the power exercised had to be subject to certain conditions. Third, the availability in pre-British India, of land which, with some effort, could be brought under the plough enabled families that were dissatisfied with local conditions to move out into new areas.[3]

During the last 150 years, political and economic structures have undergone changes. The British introduced a western legal–administrative system which has theoretically undermined caste authority and the principle of ascribed status. It has increased the scope for individual and collective mobility and paved the way to developing individual identity, and weakening the collective identity of the jati. Though traditional customs continue, cases of deviations have increased. More important, formal authority of the caste over its own members and of the upper castes by virtue of their being upper castes over members of other castes has diminished considerably since independence. What was the rule in the past has now become the exception, though the hold of the upper castes, who also constitute the upper classes, over society as a whole has not weakened. Caste councils have been replaced by caste associations and the traditional village *panch* constituted of elderly members of the dominant caste has been replaced by the elected village panchayat.

Parliamentary democracy with adult franchise has changed the locus standi of the backward castes in politics. Theoretically, they have not only attained equality with others in the decision-making process but also have an edge over them in this arena as far as their numerical strength is concerned. Their numbers have increased in the assemblies, local bodies and Parliament. Members of backward castes have become conscious of this attainment. However, there is one contradiction here. Though the political system, like the legal system and the market economy, emphasises individual rather than a caste/community identity, in practice in electoral politics group/collective action controls the action of individuals. This provides scope for reinforcing group identity. Caste identity in politics is, however, not the same as traditional primordial identity. For political purposes a confederation of castes replaces the importance of caste as a localised endogamous group. It is interesting that according to a survey by the Anthropological Survey of India the number of castes has declined in the country: small castes have merged to form larger units. Caste confederations have begun to assert their economic rather than social and cultural rights—a new role of caste, which some scholars call politicisation or secularisation of caste.

Capitalist production relationships introduced by the British to serve their imperialist interests have become a dominant mode in post-independence India. The market has penetrated into the countryside affecting agrarian relationships. The *jajmani* system which kept the deprived castes in bondage to the dominant castes has cracked in many parts of the country. Though many members of the artisan castes continue to be engaged in their traditional profession, their relationship with clients has, by and large, changed from bonded to contractual. All caste members do not necessarily remain confined to their traditional occupations. As early as 1950, F.G. Bailey observed in a village in Orissa, which is a relatively backward state, that all caste members were not engaged in hereditary occupations. Distillers gave up distilling liquor; the Kond potters did not know how to make pots; the fishermen did not fish; the warriors became cultivators.[4] In the 1950s, Kathleen Gough observed a similar pattern in Madras. She noted:

> The caste community is no longer homogeneous in occupation and wealth, for caste is today a limiting rather than a determining factor in the choice of occupation. Exactly half of Kumbarpettai's adult Brahmins are now employed in towns as government servants, school teachers or restaurant workers. Of the remainder, some own up to thirty acres of land, others as little as three. One runs a grocery store and one a vegetarian restaurant. Among the non-Brahmins, the fishermen, toddy-tappers, Marathas, Kallans, Koravas and Kuttadis have abandoned their traditional work.[5]

Village studies of other parts of the country also bear out the trend that caste is no longer a determining factor in occupations, though availability of one's choice occupation is limited and capitalist development goes on at a snail's pace. But that is a different aspect.

Notwithstanding that the caste system in contemporary India has no relation with the means of production, and there have been changes in the main components of the system, the caste of an individual still matters, even if it does not always determine his life chances. Those who owned the means of production and dominated society in the past are in an advantageous position not only to retain their economic hold but also to get more access to new sectors. Industrial entrepreneurship, modern professional occupations and management have a western cultural bias. With their gradual entry into these sectors the upper castes have, to some extent, brought in their own cultural ethos. Those who belong to a different cultural milieu initially require special effort and training to enter these sectors which are limited in size. The upper castes have an edge over the back-ward castes in these sectors because of their early entry. Despite well-laiddown criteria for recruitment in these spheres, social linkages play an important role in the caste-ridden society (perhaps it is true for the so-called *homo equatus* class society of the West also). Who knows who is important not only at the entry point but also influences dissemination of information and culture. This is evident from the fact that since independence white-collar jobs in the public and private sectors have been monopolised by the upper castes. In the 1980s, 68 per cent of the Indian Administrative Service officers belonged to the upper castes. The Sudras by contrast are represented at a minimal level of 2 per cent. The same situation is found in the private sector.[6]

Village studies in various parts of the country carried out in the 1950s and thereafter, and macro-level aggregate data (NSS data of 1952 for the country and Gujarat data collected by me in 1984) reveal the following: first, there is a positive relationship between caste and occupational status; the rich and middle farmers belong largely to the upper and middle castes. Second, diversification of occupations is primarily in business, professions and white-collar jobs among the upper and middle castes, and only marginal among the backward and lowest castes.

However, there is a deviation in the caste–class relationship which should not, for the purpose here, be ignored as statistically insignificant. There is no perfect relationship between caste and occupational ranking. A small proportion of backward castes, Scheduled Caste and Scheduled Tribe households are 'rich' farmers (owning more than 15 acres of land), and cultivate land with hired labour. Similarly, there are a few households among the upper castes which earn their livelihood through agricultural and other manual labour.

On the other hand, the rich of the upper and the rich of the backward castes, or the poor of the upper and the poor of the backward castes cannot be put at par with each other. Cultural factors like exposure to modern forces inhibit or facilitate, at least at the initial stage, entrepreneurship or access to education. For instance, a large landowner from a backward caste lacks the technical know-how for developing agricultural and trading skills due to lack of experience. He is in a minority among large landowners of the upper castes and suffers from an inferiority complex in interpersonal relationships. In fact, he is often looked down upon and ridiculed by upper-caste members of his own class. Moreover, diversification of occupation is more prevalent among members in large landowning upper-caste households than among similar landowners of the lower castes. In Gujarat, for example, as far as large landholding households are concerned, higher education has reached 9 per cent of the Brahmin and 7 per cent of the Patidar (middle caste) as against 2 per cent of the Koli (backward caste) and 3 per cent of other backward castes. Co-operative credit societies, marketing societies, co-operative banks, agricultural producers' societies, etc. are fully controlled by the rich Patidar peasants who use these institutions for strengthening their economic base. At the same time, however, they cannot debar the rich of the backward castes for long from access to the benefits of these institutions. This is partly because of the common class interests between the two and partly because the latter also hold political positions at the state and district levels.

The contrast is more striking between the poor of the upper and lower castes. A poor Brahmin has more contacts among elites in administration who distribute divisible and indivisible benefits and have a greater say in recruitment of personnel than does the poor Koli or Harijan, because public and private sector administration is dominated by bureaucrats from the upper and middle castes. As a result, the poor Brahmin has more opportunities to improve his life chances than a poor person from the low castes. He has better linkages in modern sectors like education, mass media and government administration than the poor from the lower castes. Moreover, an upper-caste boy or girl has a more favourable social milieu for pursuing schooling than the milieu in which his or her counterpart from a lower caste socialises. It should be noted that the latter has traditionally been denied the right to education. Consequently, an illiterate male Brahmin is more an exception than the rule, whereas a large number of males—not to speak of females—of the low castes are still illiterate. It may also be noted that in Gujarat higher education has reached (in the sense of at least one member per household) 12 per cent of the landless Patidars as against only 1 per cent of the Koli landless households.[7] In addition to a favourable social milieu, a Patidar boy not only receives encouragement and guidance from his family, but also gets financial support in the form of loans or scholarships from the funds of the caste organisation to pursue his studies. On the other hand, a poor Koli or Harijan boy has neither the cultural nor material means for pursuing higher education. Needless to say, formal education is an important avenue for diversification of occupation.

All members of the backward castes do not suffer from the same degree of backwardness. Those among them who own land or whose skills have marketable value have acquired education and white-collar jobs. They have become a part of the middle class whose values they have begun to share. Political positions are also cornered by them. Their caste status, however, occasionally makes them vulnerable to caste discrimination. Their social backwardness diminishes as their participation in secular institutions and interaction with class-fellows of upper castes increases. But the poor of the backward castes suffer from multitudinous disadvantages, both social and economic. Since social backwardness stems from economic backwardness, once the latter is removed the former becomes easier to overcome.

Another relevant question is: Can an individual overcome social backwardness without eradicating backwardness of caste as a whole or a large part of the caste? In the present economic and political structure I think one can. By improving one's economic condition and/or getting access to political position one can improve one's own life chances. Improving status in a secular sphere is not the same as sanskritising status. What is often needed is initial support to overcome social backwardness. This is precisely what is happening, though on a very limited scale. Those from the backward castes who have become a part of the middle class, share the values and lifestyle of the middle class. They are alienated, in more ways than one, from their traditional caste-mates who are poor. Such a process paradoxically fractures caste structure and ideology. Without reservation, this would not have happened in the existing structure.

POLITICS OF RESERVATIONS

Reservation in political positions, educational institutions and white-collar jobs is one of the devices to tackle the problem of social backwardness. In India the demand for such a provision came first from the backward castes and has been accepted by the state. Such provisions have been opposed by upper castes who have monopolised these sectors for centuries. What follows is a brief analysis of the politics of backward castes and the ruling elite. Due to constraints of space, however, the discussion will be confined to reservation in jobs and educational institutions.

Politics of Backward Castes

Backward caste movements have a long and uneven history of struggle against the dominant upper castes. They began in south India in the nineteenth century and became a major political force by the first quarter of the twentieth century. In Uttar Pradesh and Bihar the movements began in the early part of the twentieth century but took longer than their counterpart in south India to acquire political influence. There is so far no backward castes movement of any significance in Orissa, West Bengal, Madhya Pradesh and Assam. The movements in both south and north India were initiated and led by the upper strata, mainly landed peasantry, of the backward castes. Having improved their economic conditions thanks to the change in the agrarian structure, and/or penetration of the market economy and/or access to education, they first of all aspired for a higher status in the caste hierarchy. In the political sphere both in the south and the north, the backward caste elite demanded positions in parties, state assemblies, the cabinet and public institutions. Simultaneously, they pressed for reservation in government jobs and educational institutions. Various back-ward castes, particularly the upper castes among them, launched separate struggles for sanskritisation and political positions on caste lines. They finally came together under the banner of backward castes, and mobilised the lower backward castes for enlarged support in the political sphere.

In south India the backward castes under the leadership of Vellala demanded reservation of government jobs and also challenged Brahminical religion and the caste system. The movement succeeded in attaining its demand in 1927 and to a great extent weakened the dominance of Brahmins. But it did not proceed to its logical end of sustaining and expanding its base for eradicating the caste system, which would also have destroyed the traditional status superiority of upper backward castes over lower backward castes in general and the untouchable castes in particular. The leaders of the movement raised the issue of imperialism of north Indians or Dravidians vis-à-vis Aryans, which side-tracked the cause of backward castes who are at the bottom. And, in course of time, the Dravid Munnetra Kazhagam leadership, which led the movement in the 1950s, 'shifted its emphasis in Tamil nationalism from that of race, which would have emphasised downward alliances with the "Adi-Dravidas" or former untouchables, to that of language which permitted an accommodation upward to include Tamil Brahmins'.[8]

In Mysore state, initially the Praja Mitra Mandali and then the Praja Paksha spearheaded the anti-Brahmin movement in the 1920s. Led by landed Lingayats and Vokkaligas, the demands among others included reservations for non-Brahmins in government jobs. Split between the upper and lower backward castes, the backward castes and the Lingayats and Vokkaligas of the upper backward castes fought against each other to be included in or excluded from the list of other backward castes (OBCs) in the 1970s. In Tamil Nadu when the M.G. Ramachandran government superimposed an income criterion of Rs 9000 on the OBC list in 1979, the backward caste elite protested and the order was withdrawn. In Karnataka as long as the Lingayats had been classified as backward, there was not much public agitation. But their exclusion first in the Havanur Commission Report and then in the government's orders based on the report provoked the ire of the community.

As the competition among backward castes intensified and new castes began to assert their claim with the dominant backward castes, the backward castes got split, for the purpose of reservation, into backward communities and backward castes in Karnataka, non-Brahmin Hindu and backward Hindus in Tamil Nadu, and OBCs and most backward classes in Bihar. When the dominant stratum realised that it was not possible for them to get reservation on the basis of caste, they demanded that economic criteria be considered. For example, the Gujarat Kshatriya Sabha which mobilised Kshatriyas—forward and backward—demanded backward caste status for all Kshatriyas before the First Backward Classes Commission in the 1950s. But having failed to get this status for forward Kshatriyas who dominated the caste organisation, it demanded that the status be given on the basis of economic criteria. Prominent leaders of the sabha argued that because of the reservation, except 82 castes/communities identified as backward castes, poor Brahmins, Rajputs, Luhanas, Patidars, Muslims, etc. would remain as they were. The same organisation later repeated its argument that all Kshatriyas should be considered backward, because they were economically backward and the various castes among the Kshatriyas share a common culture and social customs. In other words, the Rajputs, particularly those unable to compete openly, should get the benefit of reservation, be it based on economic criteria or caste criteria. Similarly, the Lingayat and Vokkaliga communities, realising that they would not get 'backward status' as a caste, insisted that the Chinnappa Reddy Commission adopt economic criteria to identify social and educationally backward classes.[9]

The backward caste elite mobilise caste members and pressurise the government to serve their own political interests. To them, caste sentiments and solidarity are a means to political power. They follow the Brahminical ideologies, symbols and idioms. Francine Frankel observes of Bihar:

> Outside the legislative assembly, Yadav, Kurmi and Koeri leaders conformed to the pattern set by the forward castes, and carried out mobilisation within their constituencies among their own caste groups. Many of these politicians, moreover, aimed to strengthen their hold on Yadavs, Kurmis and Koeris in the localities for the limited purpose of enhancing their own bargaining power with party leaders. As one Kurmi politician put it, 'Kurmi leaders just wanted things for

themselves. They were not in conflict with the upper castes. They were just for self.'[10]

The Mandal Commission's approach to the problem of social backwardness and the commission's recommendations suggest that it subscribed to caste ideology. The commission recommended reservation of jobs for backward castes not as an egalitarian measure or a step towards secularism or social justice but primarily to boost the morale of backward castes. It argued:

> It is not at all our contention that by offering a few thousand jobs to OBC candidates we shall be able to make 52 per cent of the Indian population as forward. But we must recognise that an essential part of the battle against social backwardness is to be fought in the minds of the backward people. In India government service has always been looked upon as a symbol of prestige and power. By increasing the representation of OBCs in government services, we give them an immediate feeling of participation in the governance of this country. When a backward class candidate becomes a collector or superintendent of police, the material benefits accruing from his position are limited to the members of his family only. But the psychological spin-off of this phenomenon is tremendous, the entire community of that backward class candidate feels socially elevated. Even when no tangible benefits flow to the community at large, the feeling that now it has its 'own man' in the 'corridors of power' acts as a morale booster.[11]

The Mandal Commission was aware that the benefits of reservation would be 'cornered by the more advanced sections of the backward communities' (read communities as castes). The commission legitimised this as a 'universal phenomenon' in all reformist remedies, and that is fair enough. One would also agree that morale boosting is necessary for developing self-identity, but despite knowing that, the commission ignored the fact that all backward castes are neither socially nor economically equal—some castes do not have even a handful of college-educated persons, not to speak of an advanced section, to get any benefit of reservations. They have been and will continue to be obstructed by the advanced sections of the upper backward castes wherever the latter have a hold. Hence, the base for cornering positions would be narrow, being confined to a few families or castes in the name of 'social justice' for backward classes. More important, all backward castes would not feel elevated by having a collector from a caste other than their own backward caste. Perhaps that is one reason why an overwhelming majority (more than 85 per cent) from backward castes expressed the opinion that along with caste, economic criteria should be introduced.[12]

The elite of the backward castes, thanks to the personalised nature of politics, are not greatly interested in expanding their base to fight against the dominant classes and castes, perhaps fearing that this might endanger their own class interests. Their strategies, like those of upper-caste politicians, are ad hoc and for immediate gain. They use sentiments of their caste-mates for seeking support but corner the material base for themselves and their relatives and friends. Their ideology for social change is within the caste framework and capitalist production relationship in which status hierarchy, either ascribed or achieved, is in-built.

Politics of the Ruling Elite

The British, who introduced reservation, like all rulers, had double standards in values and objectives. They were liberal and followed the principle of social justice in their society but were not concerned with equality and social justice in their colonies. There, as far as possible, they did not wish to disturb the existing social order. They primarily focused on managing forces, broadening their base and legitimising their rule. As non-Brahmins began to express their grievances against Brahmins, in 1881 the Madras Revenue Board instructed the district collector to restrict the number of Brahmin entrants into the services and give preference to non-Brahmins. Though extended by the justice Party in 1920 to all departments, the instructions remained only on paper. The fiat government order on reservations based on caste and community came into existence in 1927 in Madras. Till 1947 the major proportion of the reservation was allotted to non-Brahmin Hindus who led the justice Party. Similarly, the Mysore government also gave into the pressure of the non-Brahmin lobby and appointed a committee under the chairmanship of Sir Lesley Miller, chief justice of the chief court of Mysore, 'to consider steps necessary for the adequate representation of communities in public service'. The committee recommended that as far as possible preference should be given to duly qualified candidates from non-Brahmin communities. The government, though it did not introduce any reservation system by order, abolished competitive examinations for jobs and asked recruitment agencies to give preference to non-Brahmins. Some other native rulers also introduced reservation, partly as a tension-management technique and partly as a benevolent gesture towards the backward castes.

However, the framers of the Indian Constitution were neither colonial masters nor 'rajas' interested merely in maintaining the balance of power in society to facilitate their rule. Their mission, at least on the ideological plank, was to build an egalitarian and secular society. This presupposed abolition of the caste system. Articles 15(4) and 16(4) of the Constitution empower the state to make provision for reservation in jobs for backward classes so as to remove the in equality between advanced classes and the weaker sections of society. There were three viewpoints on this. One section opposed the provisions on the grounds of merit and efficiency, secularism and national integration. They expressed the fear that reservation on the basis of birth would strengthen casteism and communalism. The second section did not oppose the provisions but felt that reservation was not the answer to the problem of inequality. What was needed was socialistic development. The third section supported the provisions on the grounds that backward castes had suffered from discrimination for centuries and they continued to do so on the eve of independence. Dharam Prakash argued that

> The atmosphere in the country today is such as compels us to demand reservation not in the services but also in the legislatures. Otherwise I am of the opinion that in a country, which has become free and the Constitution of which is being framed with full freedom, there is no necessity for reservation. But the great difficulty which forces us to make a demand for reservations is that there is no such generosity and impartiality in our society as society needs for its welfare nor is there any possibility of it being there in the near future.[13]

Like him, others supported reservation not as a principle, or an ideal solution, but as a device that could narrow the gap between the advanced and deprived sections of society. H.V. Kamath said, 'Members and even friends outside may dispute the wisdom of this course, but practical politics and statesmanship is guided not always by absolute ideal considerations; our policy and our course are often guided by expediency and the exigencies of the prevailing situation. The situation today dictates to us this course.'[14]

Kamath and other members of the constituent assembly were referring not merely to caste discrimination and the dominance of the upper castes, but also to the rising aspirations of the backward castes. When the subcontinent was divided into India and Pakistan, Muslim leaders created a feeling among their community members that Muslims would lose their identity in independent India under the dominance of the Hindus who constituted the majority. Some of the tribes in the northeast frontier regions expressed similar apprehensions. The tribal political leaders of the Chhota Nagpur region in Bihar demanded a separate electorate for the tribals. A small section of the tribals in Gujarat also asked for a separate state outside the Indian Union. At the same time, the SCs were demanding a separate electorate. The tribals and depressed classes asserted their political identity as indigenous people of the country. S. Nagappa, a member from Madras, asserted in the constituent assembly: 'We, the Harijans and Adivasis are the real sons of the soil and we have every right to frame the Constitution of this country. Even the so-called caste Hirndus who are not real Indians, can go, if they want . . . We know how to assert ourselves.' Political leaders felt that separate political identities would strengthen the segregated status and/or separatist aspirations of the depressed classes which would endanger the unity of the country. Thus, in order to give the deprived sections a 'fair deal' and to satisfy the political aspirations of their elite, the ruling elite evolved the strategy of reservation for them. D.N. Sandanshiv, an SC jurist, observed that, 'In 1947, on independence of India, Hindus got India, Muslims got Pakistan and the Scheduled Castes and the Scheduled Tribes got reservations.'[15] There is not much exaggeration in this statement. The provisions necessary to reconstruct an egalitarian social order are either absent in the Constitution or are at most relegated to the Directive Principles.

Ordinances promulgated in 1950 identified the SCs and STs, but not the other backward classes, though the Constitution uses the term 'backward classes' or 'weaker sections'. The ruling elite was also not in a hurry to define and identify the backward classes so as to make special provisions for them. Except in south India, there was no pressure from the OBCs for reservations. But in Madras, Periyar E.V. Ramaswamy and his party, the Dravida Kazhagam, launched an agitation against the quashing of the 'communal' government order by the Supreme Court in 1950 as this decision affected the prospects of the backward classes adversely. The agitation spread throughout Madras. It was so 'severe and persistent, that the Government of India under the prime ministership of Jawaharlal Nehru, within two months of the Supreme Court's decision moved the First Amendment to the Constitution'.[16] A new clause, clause (4), was incorporated in Article 15, empowering the state government to make special provision for the advancement of the socially and educationally backward classes of citizens and SCs and STs. The Madras government then passed an order in 1951 providing reservations to the backward classes and the SCs.

The Government of India appointed the First Backward Classes Commission in 1953. The commission submitted its report in 1955, identifying 2399 castes as socially and educationally backward. The majority of the members of the commission recommended reservation for the OBCs among other things in government jobs and educational institutions. The government did not accept the recommendations on the grounds that the commission had not applied any objective tests for identifying backward classes. However, by the early 1960s, it was difficult for the Congress, the ruling party, to ignore the clout of some of the backward castes in north and south India. The Socialist Party in the Hindi-speaking belt mobilised OBCs. In 1967, the monopoly of the Congress was challenged and the party lost power in several north Indian states. This was also the time when the Naxalite movement was at its height and the land grab movement had mobilised the backward castes against exploitation.

The Congress party split in 1969 into the Congress (I) and the Congress (O), the former, led by Indira Gandhi being more radical than the latter. It evolved a strategy to win over the OBCs. Jagjivan Ram, the Congress (S) president, said in 1970, 'Hindu society is a confederation of different castes. . . . . And the dominant castes which have so far been enjoying the fruits of all governmental measures even today try to expropriate to themselves the advantage provided by the government. . . . . We have the challenge from the dominant castes in certain areas and we have the challenge from what is known as left adventurism. We have to meet all these challenges. . . .'[17] Later in 1971, he appealed to the Congress, saying: 'It is the duty of Congressmen to strengthen the organisation, broaden its base and bring those persons within the fold who have been so long standing outside it.'[18] In order to woo the deprived communities and the minorities, the Congress manifesto of 1971 declared: 'The Congress is pledged to promote with special care the educational, employment and economic interests of the weaker sections of the people particularly the Scheduled Castes, the Scheduled Tribes and the backward classes.'

In the early 1970s several state governments appointed socially and educationally backward class (SEBC) commissions to assess the conditions of the various groups and report which sections of society should be treated as OBCs. These commissions were also asked to recommend what special treatment and/or concessions similar to those enjoyed by SCs and STs should be granted to the OBCs. On the basis of the reports, certain castes were identified as OBCs and granted reservations in educational institutions and government jobs.

At the national level, the Second Backward Classes Commission, under the chairmanship of B. P. Mandal, was appointed by the Janata government in 1978. However, the Janata government lost power before the commission could complete its report. The Congress government not only gave two extensions but gave full support and cooperation to the commission. Though the commission submitted its report in December 1980, the report was placed before Parliament only in April 1982 when backward class members of Parliament protested against the delay and held a *dharna* outside Parliament House. The Congress government neither took any decision on the Mandal Commission report nor did it reject the report. But for the anti-reservationists; in Gujarat in 1985, the then prime minister Rajiv Gandhi promised to develop a national consensus on the issue. No effort was, however, made in that direction either. Rajiv Gandhi was waiting for a political opportunity to use the report as Madhavsinh Solanki had done in Gujarat with the Rane Commission report.[19]

The National Front government began to face a number of challenges from within and outside. It had failed to check the price rise and inflation, the increasing violence in Punjab and Kashmir, and the growing communal emotions on the. Ram Janmabhoomi issue. With the departure of the deputy prime minister Devi Lal, the Janata Dal faced an internal crisis and prime minister V.P. Singh feared for his rural vote base. On the other hand, powerful backward caste politicians in the Janata government pressurised the government to implement the report so as to strengthen their base. V.P. Singh, once a critic of the Mandal Commission report and no champion of backward castes, announced on 7 August 1990 that: his government had decided to implement the 'first phase' of the commission's recommendations. In this phase, 27 per cent jobs were to be reserved for the socially and educationally backward classes in all central government departments and offices and public sector undertakings, including government-run banks and financial institutions. As the anti-reservation agitation began in educational institutions, the government declared that the recommendations of the report would not be implemented in the educational sphere. This raises the question whether there were a sufficient number of qualified backward class candidates available for government jobs. If they were available in large numbers, it could be assumed that social backwardness had not prevented them from availing of education, in which case social and economic backwardness of the backward castes was not that severe. And if qualified candidates were not available, reservation for jobs was just an eyewash.

When Raja Ramanna, a minister in the National Front government, argued that reservations would adversely affect scientific institutions, V.P. Singh announced that the Mandal recommendations would not apply to services related to science, technology, space and atomic energy. Later, military services were also exempted. Further, the government declared that state governments were free to accept or reject the recommendations of the Mandal Commission. In the states which had their own OBC list, the state list would prevail if it was different from that of the Mandal Commission. The Congress party, which was responsible for sponsoring caste-based reservations In various states, was now talking about economic criteria. One Congress leader alleged that 'caste-based reservations rent the fabric of our nationhood. What the states can get away with, the Centre can't'.[20] He feared that the administrative efficiency and probity of the central government would be jeopardised—as if the union government had preserved these virtues much more than the states. The Chandra Shekhar government was not against the recommendations of the Mandal Commission but had no courage to complete the task left unfinished by V.P. Singh. The ruling elite thus bent this way or that depending upon pressure and political exigency. Political ideology was the last priority in determining their political decisions, functioning as they did on an *ad hoc* basis without a long-term perspective of the country's development.

The politics of forward castes

The forward castes, the majority of whose members belong to propertied classes, have continued to be dominant in white-collar jobs in the public and private sectors since independence. Their interests are obviously adversely affected by reservations as they have to share the limited positions of income and power with the backward castes against whom they bear deep-rooted prejudices.

Though spokespersons of the forward castes wax eloquent on secularism and against the caste system, their secularism extends only to sharing power and position among themselves and the caste system with its ideology of status and hierarchy is perpetuated by them to serve their own economic and cultural interests. In fact, when traditional deprived groups start demanding their berth, they accuse them of being casteist or communal. But they know that the traditional caste structure, its boundaries and functions are redundant to meet the new forces of market economy and competitive polity. They abolished caste panchayats and formed caste associations which are often confederations of endogamous jatis.

The bureaucracy and the intelligentsia articulate the views of the upper castes and whenever possible protect their economic interests. The bureaucracy opposes the provisions of reservation on one or another ground. In 1989, the All India Confederation of Central Government Officers' Association, representing 40,000 class I central government officers, asked the central government to not only reject the recommendations of the Mandal Commission but to withdraw even the existing reservations of all kinds including those for SCs/STs', saying that 'reservation is a retrograde step as it discourages initiative and development and encourages inaction and parasitism'.

The intelligentsia—both of Marxist and liberal hues, not to speak of conservative—opposes reservation and argues for applying the principles of merit and efficiency, and equality and secularism. They apprehend caste and class war and propagate maintaining culture by nurturing hereditary and traditional skills. Some take a blatant racist position. They argue that merit and efficiency, necessary for progress, are prerogatives of the elite class/castes. Some others who subscribe to the notion of 'elasticity' and 'resilience of caste' now advise that caste be ignored entirely in policy prescription. They advocate economic criteria for identifying social backwardness and favour reservation for all poor irrespective of caste. Such a prescription would in reality, as I have argued elsewhere,[21] enable the upper and the poor sections of the forward castes to close their ranks and, in the process, become much more cohesive than they are today. This in turn will not only strengthen upper-caste dominance but also perpetuate the caste system.

OVERVIEW: A STEP TOWARDS SECULARISM

Caste is an important though not the determining factor of an individual's life chances in Indian society. It can thus not be ignored when identifying social backwardness of a group or an individual. Of course, the caste system has undergone changes with capitalist development and parliamentary democracy. It has no relationship with the means of production. Again, it is a limiting but not the determining factor in deciding one's occupation. Economic and contract relationships have increasingly replaced the *jajmani* system. Interdependence of castes in social and economic relationships has weakened in many parts of the country. Traditional legal sanctions of the Dharmashastras and Puranas regarding the conduct of an individual and the duties and responsibilities of castes towards one another are increasingly being challenged. The secular legal system has been accepted though it is not being fully adhered to in practice. While the principle of karma, which prescribes the ascriptive status of an individual, has lost its credibility, the principles of hierarchy and status continue to be applied where they serve the interests of those who dominate the economic and political spheres.

The central concern of those who subscribe to an egalitarian social order is to weaken if not completely eradicate the caste system—its structure as well as ideology, particularly the ideology of hierarchy and status—and also to dismantle the dominance of proprietary classes. Both are interdependent in the Indian situation, therefore they have to be attacked simultaneously. Economic development via greater access to economic opportunities is a necessary though not sufficient condition for eradication of social backwardness. But economic development in the present structure does not move at the desired speed. And the political elite are not inclined to change the structure in favour of the have-nots. Struggle by the depressed sections is therefore the best course of action. Legal measures and institutional rearrangements with welfarism are not substitutes for struggle: they may provide only temporary respite. Reservation too is one such measure. It has very limited potential for transformation of society. That is possible only if it is used judiciously.

The British used reservation as a device to manage social tension and to perpetuate their own power. Reservation in the post-independence period has to be used to serve altogether different objectives. For that, the strategy has to be modified. The time has come to think afresh on the issue, taking stock of the changing nature of caste and class and also the experiences of reservations post-independence.

The reservation system in the current economic and political structure is meant only for backward class families who are relatively better off—having viable land with infrastructure and/or marketable skills. Despite its laudable objectives, it cannot help small and marginal farmers, or landless labourers in the farm and unorganised sectors. To get a job one requires to study at least up to the 12th standard. For that, some financial support from the family is a prerequisite. Consequently, the majority from the backward castes cannot even enter primary school. There are a number of backward castes without a single member who has studied up to the secondary level. For them, reservation is only notional.

Nevertheless, the system of reservation has the potential to challenge the hegemony and cultural dominance of the upper castes. Reservation has paved the way for some members of the backward castes to enter the middle class and share power and positions with the upper castes. Possibilities of interaction as colleagues among persons of upper and lower castes have increased. On the other hand, economic differentiation within the backward castes has grown. Also, the backward caste elite who entered the middle class imbibed middle-class values and lifestyles and became alienated from their castes-fellows. This has the potential to weaken the traditional caste structure.

This process howsoever meagre has to be accelerated and not thwarted. With the facility of reservation, upward mobility for a backward caste person is relatively easy. And if he moves up and becomes a member of the middle class his social backwardness, though not eradicated, is reduced. Nevertheless, with the class into which he has moved up his original caste identity will keep him in the minority. This is so because, besides casteism of upper castes, the base of backward castes within the middle class is largely confined to a limited number of castes and further to small segments within them. Hence the individual should try to expand his class–caste base and not delimit it. To facilitate this, measures should be taken so that a backward caste entrant to the middle class does not cling to his traditional jati and does not develop a vested interest in maintaining caste sentiments. Of course, as mentioned above, the majority of members of backward castes in a given structure—reservation or no reservation—cannot move up. And even if they move as a caste and not as individuals it will not alter the existing caste system. Therefore, what is needed is to facilitate individual mobility from backward castes and at the same time obstruct the forces that compel one to cling to caste. That is, the existence of the caste system and its strength have to be recognised and delegitimised.

Such dual tasks are possible along among other thing through reservation on caste basis and dereservation by family; that is, once a member of a family holds a white-collar job that family should cease to get the benefit of reservation. This will create the possibility for larger number of families from various backward castes to enter the middle class, and discourage those who have so entered from using caste as a crutch and generate in them the confidence to forge a new identity. However, if an adequate number of candidates from different families of various backward castes are not available, the positions should not be dereserved, but offered only to the backward caste families who were once beneficiaries. It might be argued that since the reservation quota has so far remained unfilled, such dereservation is meaningless. Admittedly, such policy decisions should not be taken till the quota is filled, but what is needed is to accept dereservation as a principle. Though it will likely remain as notional as reservation is for many backward castes, it will certainly check the growth of vested interests among the backward castes to perpetuate reservation. This is the least the reservation system can do to accelerate the process of secularisation and challenge the cultural hegemony of the dominant upper castes. To expect much more would be to entertain an illusion.

16

The Anti-caste Movement and the Discourse of Power*

GAIL OMVEDT

We do not want a little place in Brahman Alley. We want the rule of the whole country. Change of heart, liberal education will not end our state of exploitation. When we gather a revolutionary mass, rouse the people, out of the struggle of this giant mass will come the tidal wave of revolution. . . . To eradicate the injustice against Dalits, they themselves must become rulers. This is the people's democracy.

—From *Dalit Panther*, 1973

Events of 1990–1 placed the issue of caste squarely at the centre of Indian politics, with a newly solidified 'left and democratic front' (the National Front–Left Front alliance) taking as its principal identifying programme, under the name of 'social justice', a major demand of the Dalit and non-Brahmin movements from the time of their origin: reservations in education and public service. It began when a minority Janata Dal–National Front government was elected to power in 1989; its manifesto had included implementation of the Mandal Commission report, which polarised reservations for 'backward classes' (mainly the Shudra castes, estimated [by the Mandal Commission] at 52 per cent of the population) in addition to those already existing for Scheduled Castes (SCs) and Scheduled Tribes (STs). Even then, 'anticipatory' riots broke out in northern cities. Then in August, in the context of a growing confrontation with Devi Lal, then deputy prime minister and self-proclaimed spokesperson of the peasants, who was also at the centre of a series of corruption charges, V.P. Singh announced the implementation of the commission's recommendations.

*Region, Religion, Caste, Gender and Culture in Contemporary India, ed. T.V. Satyamurthy (Delhi, 1996), pp. 334–54.

This unleashed a storm of protest, with upper-caste youth throughout northern Indian cities demonstrating and rioting; then, a wave of 'self-immolations' followed, spurred by tremendous newspaper publicity and intellectual support, and by the desperation of many lower-middle-class upper-caste youth who had seen their future in terms of government jobs. There was a chorus in the press against V.P. Singh, talk of the 'Mandalisation of India', and respectable social scientists who had made their careers analysing the reality of caste in India now rediscovered the economic factor and threatened a 'brain drain' of high-caste talent abroad. The Bharatiya Janata Party (BJP), whose 'Hindu unity' was most threatened by the unleashing of contradictions between Dalits/other backward castes (OBCs), on the one hand, and the upper castes on the other, then unleashed its forces in a massive onslaught to build a temple to Rama at Ayodhya, and when this was halted by the police forces of the state, withdrew its support from the government.

The minority National Front government fell; but V.P. Singh, far from withdrawing his backing, began a tour of the country, drawing huge crowds not only in the north, to which his own mass appeal had been limited in 1989, but also in the south and west. The events established his personal hegemony over the Janata Dal, and whereas earlier he had identified himself with various toiling sections, speaking of participation in management for workers and remunerative prices for farmers, he now began leaving aside all other concrete issues and centring on the single issue of the Mandal Commission and reservations for the Shudra caste groups. He was, in the words of an article in *Sunday*, turning the Janata Dal into an 'up-market Bahujan Samaj party', and though there have been numerous Janata Dal leaders and activists unenthusiastic about reservations, there has been little they could do about it. And he has been using the language of power to justify his stands. As he stressed in a *Frontline* interview, 'the greater debate is not about government jobs . . . The point is of share in the decision-making and power structure'.[1]

In doing so, 'in rendering 'Dalit' parties like the Bahujan Samaj Party (BSP) irrelevant, and forcing the left into the position of simply rallying around him without an ability to devise any alternative programme (that the left has no relevant programme today is another matter), V.P. Singh, the politician, has learned what most Marxists have not, namely, that: (i) the abolition of caste is a core question of any democratic or revolutionary movement in India; (ii) it is not a question simply of a Dalit movement but of an anti-caste movement in which Dalits must play a leading role, while forging a Dalit–Shudra (OBC–non–Brahmin) alliance; (iii) that the central term of its discourse is not jobs, ending atrocities, and certainly not 'uplifting the oppressed', but that of power.

The outcome of the elections (in which Congress [I] emerged as the largest, but not majority, party and BJP became the largest single opposition party) has been heralded in many quarters as a setback for the National Front and 'Mandal'; certainly large sections of the bourgeoisie and bureaucracy as a whole, and a major section of the intelligentsia is breathing a sigh of relief. Yet, it is worth stressing that the National Front—Left alliance won 127 Lok Sabha seats, making it the largest opposition force—in spite of extreme lack of funding in comparison to the other fronts, lack of party organisation, and the sympathy factor after Rajiv Gandhi's death which played a significant role especially in the southern states. What the events of 1990–1 and the stress on 'social justice' has accomplished is to create, for the first time in Indian political history, a stable national political platform of democratic and left parties, with no section of socialist/communist forces able to ally with the Congress or the BJP under the rubric of 'opposition unity'. This alliance should not be overrated; it is centred on a 'one-point' programme of caste justice without any effective economic programme to give this a base, any new vision of socialism capable of overcoming the crises of the period, or any ability to really draw in other new social movements and the constituencies they represent.

But it is an important step forward, and it has been accomplished by taking up one of the basic issues of the anti-caste movement, in the context of forging an alliance of non-Brahmins (OBCs) and Dalits (Shudras and Ati-Shudras) which has been a concern of this movement from the beginning. And it has adopted a central theme of this movement's discourse, that of power. Throughout its history, the anti-caste movement has engaged in dialogue with the Marxist Left, but it has its own history, analysis and discourse. This chapter will briefly examine some of the moments of that history.

THE NINETEENTH CENTURY: JOTIRAO PHULE

Jotirao Phule, the Maharashtrian middle-caste social revolutionary whose death centenary was celebrated in 1989–90, is regarded by both Dalits and radical non-Brahmins alike as their forerunner. In Maharashtra, the peasant movement and the women's movement also look upon him as a founder. Indeed, he inaugurated a new discourse, a new understanding of Indian history from the viewpoint of the Shudra and Ati-Shudra (Dalit) peasantry which continues to be relevant today.[2]

Phule took up the 'Aryan theory' which the Brahminic and nationalist elite at the time was using to justify its ascendancy and equivalence with Europeans, and turned it around to celebrate the middle and low castes as descendants of an original non-Aryan peasant community, which had had it traditions of equality and prosperity until it was conquered by the cruel invading Aryans. For Phule, the history of caste in India is a history of violence, *force majeure*, and subjugation. The holding of state power, and the use of religious deception in order to consolidate their position, is the hallmark of Brahmin–Aryan rule, or the *bhatshahi*. The British were but another set of conquerors in this line, after the Aryans and the Muslims; only Phule sees their conquest (that of both the British and the Muslims) as having certain liberatory aspects because their religion, unlike the caste system imposed by the Aryans, is egalitarian. Under the British too, though, exploitation of the Shudra peasantry is primarily a function of Brahmin control of the state bureaucracy (which extracts taxes and bribes, while at the same time cheating the peasants in the courts), backed by Brahminic cunning and religious justification: Brahmins are the moneylenders who ensnare the peasant in debt, and the priests who cheat him on his very deathbed.

The central figure of this new ideology–mythology for Phule is that of Bali Raja. To the Brahminic myths, Bali is a *rakshasa* or demon-king, and the boy Waman who sends him down beneath the earth is an incarnation of Vishnu. To peasants in Maharashtra, though equally so in south India, Bali is the symbol of an ideal king and an era of happiness, and Phule celebrates him as such, weaving into his reinterpretation the names of the various Maharashtrian peasant and nomadic gods (Vithoba, Khandoba, Jotiba) as his lieutenants. From Waman through Parashuram and all the avatars, history is thus one of conquest and deception. Phule also adds that about the non-Aryans who fought against this conquest, who were all Kshatriyas as well as peasants. The bravest of these were the Mahars and Mangs (the untouchable castes of Maharashtra) who, in return for their heroism, were thrown down into the lowest position in the system.

For Phule, the crucial preconditions for the defeat of the exploitative *bhatshahi* are the rejection of the inegalitarian Brahminic religion and the unity of the Shudras and Ati-Shudras. He very often lists these, including Kunbis, Malis, Kalis, Dhangars, down to Bhils, Mahars and Mangs; in the process denying the Kunbis the more status-claiming title of 'Maratha', and normally laying special emphasis on the (Dalit) Mahars and Mangs. He also explicitly opposes the Indian National Congress (INC), then in the days of its first formation, as Brahmin dominated, and raises the point that India can become a 'nation' only when caste is overcome and the masses of Shudras and Ati-Shudras are able to come forward.

These themes—the need for Dalit–Shudra unity; the need for a new religion to transcend Brahminism;[3] and characterisation of the Congress as a party of Brahminism (and later, also of capitalism)—were subsequently adopted by anti-caste movements.

In addition, in analysing Phule's ideas, a useful comparison can be made between his stress on violence, conquest and state power in the history of exploitation, and Marx's emphasis on the role of primitive accumulation prior to and outside the sphere of factory production, the arena in which most of the third world peasantry finds itself, where 'violence is the midwife of history'.

AMBEDKAR: DALITS AND NON-BRAHMINS DURING THE INDEPENDENCE MOVEMENT

After 1917, non-Brahmin and Dalit movements arose as separate movements, though interlink-ed, and drawing on common ideological themes. Non-Brahmin movements were strongest in Maharashtra, in the Madras Presidency (Tamil Nadu and coastal Andhra) and in Mysore with differing impact.[4] Dalit movements were actually wider in spread if weaker in resources, including not only south and west India, but also movements such as the Ad-Dharm in Punjab, Adi-Hindus in western Uttar Pradesh, and Namashudras in Bengal.[5]

Let us look at the common fate of anti-caste movements from the viewpoint of the Dalit movements. These arose separately and always expressed their autonomy because of the obvious contradictions with the middle castes. Yet they shared common traditions with the non-Brahmin movements, stressed common themes, used a common language, and nearly always looked to alliances. Ambedkar, the towering figure of the Dalit movement, at times even spoke of himself as a part of the 'non-Brahmin movement' and consistently argued for alliance with the non-Brahmin leaders of Maharashtra. A common theme of the Dalit movements was the *adi* theme, drawn from Phule, that of being original non-Aryan inhabitants, oppressed through conquest and subjugation.

Nearly all the regionally diverse Dalit movements had both an economic and a social thrust: they tried to get land for Dalits (normally forest and 'waste' land), and freedom from *vethbegar* or the caste-enforced caste-specific imposed labour; and became involved in organising the working class where Dalits were employed as wage labour in the mills in cities such as Nagpur and Bombay. They also fought for education and tried to generate internal social reform, including marriage between subcastes and the ending of customs such as the *devadasi*-type prostitution.

But power was the key. Ambedkar's statement that 'we must become a ruling community' has become one of the most famous sayings of the movement. At the 1930 Round Table Conference, Ambedkar made his position clear with regard to independence in precisely these terms, arguing that Untouchables, more than any other section, needed freedom from British rule, because only under Swaraj would they have an opportunity of garnering power, and that was the key to their liberation.[6]

But how was power to be achieved? Ambedkar took political strategy very seriously, and he was clear about two aspects of the prevailing political situation: first, that the Congress was irrevocably a party of the Brahmins and the bourgeoisie, and that Dalits should remain independent of and from it. And second, that the struggle of the Dalits could not be waged by the Dalit party alone, but as part (and hopefully the leading part) of a political party uniting peasants and workers, Dalits and the *bahujan samaj* (middle castes).

His first and most vigorous political effort consisted of the formation of the Independent Labour Party (ILP) during the 1930s, and its campaigns against the *Mahar watan*, against the *khoti* landlord system in the Konkan spearheaded by activists in that region from 1930 onwards, and against the anti-working class 'black bill' of 193 8. The anti-*khoti* struggle united both Mahars and Kunbi tenants, and produced one of the biggest peasant marches of its time to the Legislative Council in Bombay in 1938.[7] The massive textile workers' strike in 1938 was initiated by Ambedkar's party and carried out in alliance with communists and moderate trade union leaders.

Throughout this period, Ambedkar continually urged Maharashtrian non-Brahmin leaders (for example, Jedhe) not to join the Congress; and continually sought allies from among similar forces throughout India—for example, with Periyar, making an effort to revive the Justice Party, and with Swami Sahajanand, leader of Bihar's militant peasant movement. Ambedkar's effort to forge fraternal links with Swami Sahajanand produced an almost paradigmatic meeting between the two. It was at a time (1938) when Jagjivan Ram, a Congress protege, was both trying to wean Dalits away from Ambedkar by forming a 'Depressed Classes League' and to split agricultural labourers from the Bihar peasantry with his Khetmajoor Sabha.

But Ambedkar ignored Jagjivan Ram. His paper had been praising the militancy of the Kisan Sabha, which was becoming autonomous and moving away from 'Gandhism'; but he urged that it should also move away from Congress and that 'peasants and workers must have their own political party'. When the two leaders met in Bombay, Ambedkar reiterated these points. The Swami argued that Congress was an 'anti-imperialist united front', and that the leadership could be changed; Ambedkar argued that it was simply a party of Brahmins and the bourgeoisie, and was not even truly 'anti-imperialist'. The alliance failed on this point of political strategy—and not on 'class' or 'caste' differences between Dalits and non-Brahmins, agricultural labourers and peasants.[8]

Throughout this period also, Dalits in various parts of the country, and Ambedkar, were carrying out a fight against 'atrocities' in which it was normal for them to directly confront the non-Brahmin middle peasant castes such as the Kunbis. Nevertheless, both Ambedkar and other Dalit leaders of the time followed a policy of alliance with nonBrahmins and peasants and workers as a matter of political strategy. Thus Punjabi Ad-Dharm leaders joined forces with the Unionist Party in the 1930s, and the Bengali Namashudras with the Muslim Krishak Praja Party. All these parties and groups realised that unity among them was a precondition for winning power. Ambedkar's ILP, with its strong rhetoric of 'worker-peasant' struggle, can also be seen as constituting a practical application of what the communists had proposed in the 1920s but never carried through, namely, 'worker-peasant parties'.

The demand for reservation also saw Dalits and non-Brahmins by and large acting together, in spite of considerable tensions. Ambedkar himself has, in his writings, referred to himself as a 'Shudra' and part of the non-Brahmin movement; and his eloquent defence of reservations referred to both the Dalits and the non-Brahmins—and, strikingly, used the language of power and self-determination:

> Now, [what] one would like to ask those who deny the justice of the case of the Backward Classes for entry into the Public Services is whether it is not open to the Backward Classes to allege against the Brahmins and allied classes all that was alleged by the late Mr Gokhale on behalf of Indian people against the foreign agency? Is it not open . . . to say that by their exclusion from the Public Services a kind of dwarfing or stunting is going on? Can they not complain that as a result of their exclusion they are obliged to live all the days of their lives in an atmosphere of inferiority? . . . Can they not lament that the moral elevation which every self-governing people feel cannot be felt by them, and that their administrative talents must gradually disappear owing to sheer disuse till at last their lot as hewers of wood and drawers of water in their own country is stereotyped.[9]

However, Ambedkar's radical strategy of a united struggle against Brahminism and capitalism in the 1930s did not succeed. His political activities and much of his theoretical writing during the 1940s must be seen in the light of this failure. Instead of a revolutionary democratic political movement of workers and peasants, Dalits and Shudras, the Congress strategy won hegemony, for a time succeeding in co-opting elements from all sections, from 'Harijans' to many of the non-Brahmin peasantry. It should also be noted that the post-independence Congress political strategy (which has basically consisted of uniting 'Harijans, Adivasis and minorities' with the upper castes against the middle castes, or agricultural labourers with the bourgeoisie against the peasantry) had its first glimmerings in the organising tasks that it had carried out during the 1930s and the promotion of leaders such as Jagjivan Ram.

Against the background of this failure, Ambedkar also took a step backward and formed the Scheduled Castes Federation (SCF) as a party exclusively consisting of Dalits, in order to gain whatever concessions and benefits that could be won out of India's inevitable independence under Congress raj. Instead of workers' and peasants' struggles and attempts to unite Dalits and middle castes, its activities focused on demands for reservations and separate village settlements. In other words, the overall radical liberatory strategy was given up for one of constituting Dalits as simply an 'interest group' in an otherwise pluralistic system. The whole period of the drafting of the Constitution has to be seen in this light, as well as Ambedkar's very pessimistic conclusions about unity. Thus, in his unpublished writings he could state that

> [i]t is obvious that these three classes [Dalits, Shudras, and Tribals] are naturally allies. There is every ground for them to combine for the destruction of the Hindu social order. But they have not . . . the result is that there is nobody to join the untouchable in his struggle. He is completely isolated. Not only is he isolated he is opposed by the very classes who ought to be his natural allies.[10]

Ambedkar did not fully give up the effort; his 1951 election manifesto for the SCF stated that it might 'dissolve itself' into a 'Backward Caste federation' if this seemed viable; before his death, he recommended the transformation of the SCF into a republican party whose declared intention (which was, however, unrealised in practice) was to become a broader party of all oppressed sections; and one of his last actions was to join the Samyukta Maharashtra movement (the first rd left–democratic front in Maharashtra) in spite of the fear of the 'dominance of Marathas' in a united Maharashtra state.

Nevertheless, independence occurred against a backdrop of failure of unity attempts, in a process controlled by the Brahmin/bourgeois-dominated Congress party which had begun a process of co-opting and integrating lower-caste representatives and of speaking in the name of 'agricultural labourers' and the 'rural poor', but without giving these sections any real power. It was an independence dominated by capital and a large-scale bureaucracy— controlled, predictably, by Bania Castes and an aristocratic Brahmin elite—in which the Nehru model of heavy Industrialisation based on a public sector and planning was to structure an unbalanced, inegalitarian, and environmentally destructive and unsound course of development.

THE 1970S: DALIT PANTHERS PROCLAIM REVOLUTION

The formation of the Dalit Panthers in 1972 took place against a background of such oppressive developments—namely, the repeated failure of the

Republican, Party to fulfil any of the hopes of the Dalits, of rising tensions in the countryside, and of the revolutionary inspiration provided by the Naxalbari insurrection which was crushed by the state. It was a year of the beginning of all kinds of new movements—the year of the formation of the All Assam Students' Union (AASU), of the Jharkhand Mukti Morcha (JMM), of the new farmers' organisations in Punjab and Tamil Nadu; it was also the year of the rise of the Chipko movement and of the beginnings of the women's movement with the establishment of the Self-Employed Women's Association (SEWA), and the year in which the Anandpur Sahib Resolution was drafted. In this ferment, Dalit youth in Bombay set out to organise a revolution.

In spite of their proclamation of the goal of power in the manifesto, however, the Dalit Panthers did not really have a political strategy. Instead, they fought battles on two fronts and against two enemies: at the symbolic level, against Brahminism; and at the concrete level, against the caste Hindu peasants and artisans who were directly responsible for numerous atrocities committed against Ati-Shudras. Indeed, the 1970s were a decade in which the 'principal contradiction' seemed to be shifting, due to the development of agricultural capitalism and the coming forward of kulaks belonging to 'backward castes', to one between Dalit agricultural labourers/poor peasants and a middle-caste non-Brahmin rich peasant/landlord section. Most left intellectuals at the time (which includes me) believed this to be the case, and stressed that the 'rich peasants' were becoming the main enemy, and that a 'non-Brahmin movement' or movements of middle castes—as opposed to the Dalit movement—had exhausted its historically progressive role. The massive rioting that spread throughout Marathwada. in 1978, when Maratha-Kunbis attacked and assaulted Dalits over the issue of renaming Marathwada University after Ambedkar clearly appeared to be a confirmation of the validity of such a view.

Statistics (and even village-level experience) fail to show a real increase in differentiation; the growing numbers of agricultural labourers represented not a true proletariat but an 'immiserated' section, a large proportion of which was 'landless', thrown back on agriculture due to lack of employment opportunities elsewhere. The real growing differentiation appeared to be between agriculture and industry/services, and the unorganised and organised sectors (see Tables 1–8 in appendix). Yet, left activists and intellectuals spoke about the tremendously increasing number of 'landless agricultural labourers', of 'rich peasants' (or even 'rich and middle peasants') as the rising rural ruling class, and of 'caste Hindus' as the enemies of Dalits. Thus, not only was the movement of peasants for higher crop prices attacked as being in the interest of kulaks, but reservations for 'backward classes' were said to be nothing but a 'class' strategem of the same sections, of the 'rich and affluent OBCs' responsible for the principal atrocities on Dalits.

The effect of this analysis and the strategy that it implied was to throw the largest section of toiling people into the ranks of the class enemy and to propagate the notion that Dalit–bahujan unity would be impossible to achieve. One of the results of such a reading of the political horizon was to make it easier for Dalit leaders to justify their alliance with the Congress, which continually claimed to speak in the name of the 'rural poor'. Most Dalit Panther leaders have, in fact, taken this route sooner or later. But several aspects of the developing situation went unnoticed. Thus, many failed to realise that the success of Congress strategy in dividing Dalits and 'other backwards' was making unity difficult. The constant reiteration of propaganda to the effect that 'reservations' were for Dalits and that they were responsible for the unemployment and misery of other low-caste poor was effective. But precisely this situation was becoming transformed by the Mandal Commission proposals to extend reservations to various Shudra sections—proposals that provoked violent and widespread opposition from higher castes, including higher-caste intellectuals A who continued to emphasise that the 'backwards' were the principal enemies of the Dalits.

The Mandal Commission, appointed in 1978 by the first opposition (Janata) government at the centre, was in part a culmination of attempts of certain state (including a few Congress) governments, since 1971, to extend reservations to 'backward classes'. It was also, in part, an outgrowth of the tradition harking back to Ram Manohar Lohia's interventions in India's politics, as well as an upsurge of Dalits and OBCs in north India. It is worth noting that the commission also located the reservation issue in the context of power: 'In a democratic set-up every individual and community has a legitimate right and aspiration to participate in ruling this country. Any situation which results in a near-denial of this right to nearly 52 per cent of the country s population needs to be urgently rectified.'[11]

The Marathwada riots were the last of their kind to range the middle castes and the Dalits against each other on a mass scale. The Gujarat reservation riots of 1981 and 1985 have sometimes been placed in the same category, but in fact they represent a different phenomenon. In Gujarat, Dalits were attacked not by the middle castes but by the upper castes, which blamed the former for the state government's proposals to extend reservations to the OBCs. While this seems ironical, it illustrates the degree to which reservations are seen as a Dalit issue (and in which ending reservations for Dalits remains the principal goal of any anti-reservation movement, despite disclaimers), whilst the Shudra castes for whom reservation is intended have been normally less aware of their implications than the Dalits.

Thus, in the first riots, the backward castes themselves apparently remained passive, but gradually OBC and Dalit organisations began to work together. In the second round of rioting, however, a significant change was observable. The OBCs attacked upper castes (although this was to some extent distorted by the fact that the police force which attacked the press and the upper-caste neighbourhoods was primarily composed of recruits drawn from the OBCs). Finally, the Dalit/OBC–upper-caste conflict was given a communal twist with the engineering of Hindu–Muslim riots. The text and the subtext became inversions of each other. This was a clear indication of the shape of things to come at the start of the 1990s. After the events in Gujarat, the upper castes will never again dare to attack the Dalits and OBCs directly, but rather will attempt to push the ideology of 'Hindu unity' in order to maintain their power.

KANSHI RAM AND THE DALIT MOVEMENT IN THE 1980s

'We have a one-point programme—take power.' This statement, by the office secretary of the BSP, illustrates the principal thrust of the strongest Dalit organisation to emerge in the 1980s. And, indeed, the BSP, under Kanshi Ram's leadership, was envisaged precisely as a party of Dalits and backwards and minorities, with Dalits playing a vanguard role; and, from the outset, it has been projected as an organisation based on practical politics and not on sentiment. Power was within its grasp precisely because the Dalits and Shudras together constituted a majority.

'We are 85 per cent—we don't need to make any alliances; we can rule on our own.' This statement echoes the view which Arun Kamble (one of the few of those who eventually joined the Janata Dal!) had propagated as a leader of the Dalit Panthers—namely, that 'Dalits and backwards and minorities together, we are 85 per cent. We are the majority. We don't want a separate Dalitsthan— India should become Dalitsthan.' But the BSP went further than other Dalit organisations of the time by projecting itself not as a 'Dalit' party but as a 'Bahujan' party, using the terminology of the non-Brahmin movement of the 1920s in order to project itself as a party of Dalits and non-Brahmins—and minorities. And, with a solid base among north Indian Chamars, it also succeeded in attracting significant backing from OBCs and minority communities.

The 1980s were, in fact, the decade in which Dalit–Shudra unity gradually came to be constructed. The need for it was forcefully proclaimed not only by Kanshi Ram and Kamble, but also by Rajshekar of *Dalit Voice,* by Sharad Patil of the Satyashodhak Communist Party, by the Dalit Sangharsh Samiti (DSS) of Karnataka as it examined the issue of reservations and its relations to the Ryotu Sangh, asserting the need for the two movements to come together even though the latter was dominated by the 'main enemies of Dalits at the village level'. Rajshekar put this strongly in one of his early booklets:

Dalits are born Marxists. Because we have not understood the law of contradictions, we get confused and therefore come to the wrong conclusion. . . . As Dalits, we become the natural leaders of the Indian Revolution, and therefore it is out responsibility not to commit any mistakes. . . . We have to convince the OBCs that fighting Brahminism is as much their duty as freeing themselves from Shudra slavery. The enemies of OBCs are not Dalits. . . . Similarly, every Dalit organisation is pointing out that Dalits are victims of Brahminism. . . . Hence, the contradiction between Dalits and OBCs is non-antagonistic.[12]

Dalits, throughout this period, were in the process of articulating strategies of alliance; rather than simply fall in line behind the middle-caste Shudras, they wanted to pursue specific goals germane to their struggle. 'We support reservations for Jats,' stated a Backward and Minority Classes Employees Federation (BAMCEF) activist of the anti-Kanshi Ram group, 'provided they stop acting like Thakurs.' Or, in Arun Kamble's terms, 'There should be a Kunbi-isation of Marathas.'[13] Or, as the DSS argued in relation to the Ryotu Sangh, they must stop being 'economistic'. Generally, such demands amount to urging the middle castes to de-sanskritise themselves, as Guru has pointed out in a paper on Phule and reservations:

Mandal Commission might forge the unity of all the exploited non-Brahmin castes as against those exploiting castes . . . this process, instead of consolidating the caste structure, would devour it from within. Moreover, the introduction of Mandal Commission would radically undermine the process of sanskritisation which had helped in maintaining the heirarchised structure like pure Marathas (shannavkuli) versus impure Marathas. . . . The whole development is making Phule's category of absorbing the 'local great tradition' representing so-called Maratha into 'little tradition' representing the vast Bahujan Samaj masses . . . .[14]

For some time, it was the BSP which was most successful in capturing the new anti-caste upsurge. A look at the 'discourse' of Kanshi Ram's principal slogans illustrates BSP's appeal: *brahmin bania thakur chor/baki sab DS-4*[15] in fact contains a formulation of the alliance strategy, identifying the 'main enemy' and the 'allies'; *mat hamara raj tumara nahi chalega nahi chalega*[16] is a clear statement of the thrust to political power, while the more recent *vote se lenge PM/CM, arakshan se SP/DM*[17] illustrates the limited nature of the drive to power.

'Politics' in the end was the undoing of the BSP's success, as Kanshi Ram's support of Devi Lai and Chandra Shekhar lost him much of the prestige he had won earlier in the Dalit community. Though the BSP still remains a party to be reckoned with in Uttar Pradesh and Haryana, in the rest of the country V.P. Singh has emerged as the effective spokesperson of the Dalit and low-caste aspiration to power through reservations. The responses at a massive rally in Pune (28 November 1990) were significant:

> Dondiba, a backward-caste farmer from Sangli who had waited in the blazing sun for four hours to hear V.P. speak . . . angrily told this correspondent, 'For centuries we have been dehumanised and oppressed . . . When V.P. Singh announced one little step in our favour it could not be tolerated by the Brahminical parties which have never stood for the Dalits. V.P. Singh has sacrificed his gaddi for our sake, now we must stand by him.' 75-year-old Savitribai of Pune was attending the meeting. . . . Why had she, despite failing vision, ill-health and arthritis made it a point to come? Savitribai answered, 'I have come to see and hear V.P. Singh. He belongs to the same caste as me. . . . I am a Dalit and I consider V.P. Singh as a man of my caste because he has stood up for us, spoken of social justice for us'.[18]

THE 1991 THRESHOLD

A major transformation has taken place in Indian politics. Congress hegemony has apparently vanished for good—not in the sense of a major decline in share of the popular vote, but in the sense that it can no longer parley as 30–45 per cent share of the popular vote into 60–70 per cent Lok Sabha seats, and also, in the sense that its ideology, derived from Nehru's time in power, stands thoroughly discredited. No longer can the Congress(I) convincingly appear as the party of the toiling masses; at best, it can promote 'stability', the only alternative to Hindu fundamentalism; it is, more clearly than before, the party of the more secular bourgeoisie and Brahmin-dominated bureaucracy.

And this has happened in a context in which a left–democratic political alliance has focused on anti-caste issues and has brought together the uncomfortable allies: Dalits and OBCs.[19] Yet the lack of a full programme remains a serious problem. The question of an alternative socialist vision stands, and just as revolutionary communists for decades have been describing the parliamentary communists as 'reformists', so the peasants and other sections of labourers involved in the 'new social movements'—the women's movement, the farmers' movement, and the environmental struggles—have reason to see the National Front-Left coalition as essentially representing yet another betrayal of their interests. This is a crisis for the movements: the crisis of how they will obtain political representation; and it is a crisis for the democratic and left parties of winning a solid mass base.

In part it is specifically a crisis of the anti-caste movement which has been partly embodied in the National Front—Left alliance—for this movement never took reservations: as its sole goal; it always saw economic issues (land, wages, relief from exploitation by the bureaucracy, etc.) as central. Yet, from Phule to Ambedkar, there has been a history of uncertainty and ambiguity as to the root causes of exploitation and the path to overcome it. Ambedkar's argument for 'state socialism' (which assumed only private property as the root of exploitation, and overlooked the question made so poignant in the crisis of state-socialist societies today), as much as the Mandal Commission report's statement that 'exploitative relations of production' had to be dealt with—even as it stressed only exploitation within agriculture and not within industry or between agriculture and industry—reflects these problems of analysis. These movements leave out environmental issues, questions of the exploitation of peasants' and women's subsistence labour, and indeed the entire question of 'alternative development' now being raised so strongly.

These issues will have to be dealt with. Until then, there can be no transformation of Indian politics; there will only be a prolonged impasse.

POSTSCRIPT (JUNE 1995)

Editors Note

Since this chapter was written, the BSP has appeared to have grown into a political force wielding a considerable degree of power in Uttar Pradesh, India's most important state. It has also made significant attempts (as in the state legislative assembly elections held towards the end of 1994 and in early 1995) to extend its influence beyond Uttar Pradesh. These attempts are yet to yield positive results.

However, in Uttar Pradesh the BSP entered into a coalition with the Samajwadi Party to form a government after the Uttar Pradesh state assembly elections held in 1993. The ostensible purpose of the Samajwadi Party–BSP coalition was to keep the BJP (the largest single party elected to the Uttar Pradesh legislative assembly with 177 MLAs out of a total of 425) out of power.

However, within eighteen months of assuming power, the coalition foundered on a clash of personalities between the chief minister (Mulayam Singh Yadav of the Samajwadi Party) and the BSP leader (Kanshi Ram) who was not in the government. Mulayam Singh Yadav had other enemies too, and these included the Congress (I) leaders of Uttar Pradesh (especially Narain Dutt Tewari), the BJP leaders, and the Janata Party leaders including (in particular) V.P. Singh and Laloo Prasad Yadav, the powerful chief minister of neighbouring Bihar.

The animus, rooted in such a combined opposition to Mulayam Singh Yadav, was too strong to let the government last out the normal lifetime of the legislature. Not surprisingly, a crisis suddenly developed in the relations between the coalition partners in May 1995. Soon thereafter the government fell.

With the removal of Mulayam Singh Yadav from power, a new government was formed with the BSP going it alone under the chief ministership of Mayawati (who had been a member of the ousted government). Even though the absolute strength of the BSP in the legislature is small (44, after the sudden defection of 25 MLAs during the crisis), the new ministry enjoys the support of the BJP. This is indeed a curious phenomenon which may have a significance that stretches beyond momentary opportunism. Kanshi Ram's recent declaration that the BJP is not, in his view, a communal party, may mean that the BJP's efforts to project an un-Brahminical image have something in common with the BJP's general communal orientation.

The recent *bouleversement* in Uttar Pradesh politics is indicative of the fragility of coalitional politics in India. The appropriate metaphor for this phenomenon is osteoporosis. The proliferating bourgeois class with its inner contradictions, and the political parties (at the national and state levels) are so brittle that they have a tendency to flake off at the slightest opportunity. The proclivity towards frequent fragmentations followed by ersatz reconstitutions of coalitions based on no discernible principle cannot but carry a gloomy portent for the future of 'democratic' politics in India.

Appendix to Chapter 16

Table 16.1. Income of Organised and Unorganised Sector Workers, 1981

	Workforce (0000)	Income (Rs crore)	Average annual income per worker (Rs)
1. Wage and salary earners	965	43,121	4468
A. Organised sector	229	24,850	10,851
(Public)	155	16,495	10,643
(Private)	74	8354	11,289
B. Unorganised sector	736	18,271	2482
(Agricultural workers)	555	9454	1703
(Non-agricultural workers)	181	8817	4871
2. Self-employed	1260	24,719	3549
A. Cultivators	925	27,754	3000
B. Non-cultivators	335	16,971	5066

Source: Centre for Monitoring the Indian Economy (CMIE), Basic Statistics on the Indian Economy 1985, vol. 1: All India, 1985 (Bombay, 1985), Table 10.1.

Table 16.2. National Income by Sectors of Industrial Origin
(% distribution)

	1950–1	1970–1	1984–5
Agriculture and allied activities	54.04	49.19	37.91
Manufacturing, construction, and mining	17.14	20.62	22.17
Tertiary activities (of which) defence and public administration	24.81	31.19	39.91

Source: A. Mitra, 'Disproportionality and the Services Sector', *Social Scientist*, 16 April 1988, pp. 3–8.

Table 16.3. Occupational Classification of Workers by Sector
(% distribution)

	1901	1951	1961	1971	1981*
Agriculture and allied activities	71.7	72.1 7	1.8	72.2	68.8
Manufacturing, mining, etc.	12.6	10.7	12.2	11.2	13.5
Tertiary: Trade, commerce, transport, other services	15.7	17.2	16.0	16.7	17.7

Source: Basic Statistics on the Indian Economy 1987, Volume 1: All India, 1987 (Bombay: CMIE, 1987), table 9. 1 B.

Dalit Panther, 1973, Manifesto (Bombay: Model Art Printing). Translated (from Marathi) by G. Omvedt (n.d.).

*excludes Assam.

Table 16.4. Caste and Rural Class: Distribution of Caste Groups among
Hindu Rural Households (late 1950s)

	Scheduled Caste	Lower Caste	Middle Caste	Upper Caste	Total
Agriculture:					
Farmers	0.18	1.69	0.93	1.09	3.89
	(6.95)	(6.95)	(7–57)	(24–38)	(7–35)
Cultivators	3.19	10.20	6.52	1.96	21.87
	(27.05)	(41–79)	(53–30)	(43–91)	(41–35)
Sharecroppers	1.00	1.51	3.76	0.17	3.44
	(8.50)	(6.17)	(6.18)	(3–91)	(6.50)
Agricultural labourers	4.27	4.11	1.46	0.05	9.89
	(36.19)	(16.85)	(11.91)	(1.09)	(18.70)
Forestry, fishing,	0.28	0.81	0.17	0.02	1.28
livestock	(2.38)	(3.31)	(1–39)	(0.62)	(2.42)
Others	2.87	6.09	2.39	1.17	12.52
	(24.34)	(24.93)	(19.65)	(26.09)	(23.47)
Total	11.79	24.41	12.23	4.46	52.89
	(100.0)	(100.0)	(100.0)	000.0)	(100.0)

Source: P.C. Joshi, 'Perspectives on Poverty and Social Change: The Emergence of the Poor as a Class', Economic and Political Weekly, 14 February 1979, nos. 7–8, p. 363.

Definitions: farmers = those cultivating mainly with hired labourers

cultivators = mainly cultivating owned or rented land, etc,

upper castes = those who use sacred thread by custom

middle castes = those from whom Brahmins take water by tradition

lower castes = other castes who were not scheduled

Table 16.5. Estimated Operational Farm Holdings and Area Operated

	1970–1	1980–1	1985–6
Percentage of operational holdings			
Marginal (0–1 hectare)	50.9	56.4	58.1
Small (1–2 hectares)	18.9	18.1	18.3
Semi-medium (2–4 hectares)	15.0	14.0	13.5
Medium (4–10 hectares)	11.2	9.1	8.1
Large (over 10 hectares)	3.9	2.4	2.0
Percentage of area operated			
Marginal (0–1 hectare)	9.0	42.1	13.2
Small (1–2 hectares)	11.9	14.1	15.6
Semi-medium (2–4 hectares)	18.5	21.1	22.3
Medium (4–10 hectares)	29.75	29.6	28.7
Large (over 10 hectares)	30.17	23.0	20.2

Source: Basic Statistics Relating to the Indian Economy, 1989 (New Delhi: Central Statistical Organisation, GOI, 1989).

Table.16.6. Distribution of Rural Households in Relation to Landholding

	Percentage of households		Percentage operated	
	1953–4	1970–1	1953–4	1970–1
Not operating land	28.2	27.5	–	–
Small holding (0–2.49 acres)	28.2	32.9	5.4	9.2
Medium (2.5–9.9 acres)	28.0	29.4	28.6	37.5
Large (10 acres and above)	14.6	10.4	65.9	53.2

Source: G. Omvedt, 'The New Peasant Movement in India', *Bulletin of Concerned Asian Scholars*, 20 April 1988, no. 2, p. 18.

Table 16.7. Agricultural Labourer Households by Caste as a Percentage
of Rural Households

	1956–7	1964–5	1974–5	1977–8
Total	24.5	21.8	25.9	29.9
With land	12.2	9.6	12.8	14.5
Without land	12.3	12.2	13.2	15.3
Scheduled Castes				
With land		40.5*	40.3*	34.3*
Without land		40.7*	41.9*	39.1
Scheduled Tribes				
With land		9.8*	10.4*	12.9*
Without land		9.3*	9.5*	12.2*

* Percentage of all agricultural labourer households in the category.

Sources: My rearrangement of tables contained in Government of India, 1954, *Agricultural Labour Enquiry* (1953–1954) (New Delhi: Ministry of Labour, GOI); GOI, *Rural Labour Enquiry* (1964– 1965) (New Delhi: Ministry of Labour. GOI, 1965); GOI, *Rural Labour Enquiry* 0974–1975) (New Delhi: Ministry of Labour, GOI, 1975); GOI, *Rural Labour Enquiry* (1977–1978) (Chandigarh: Labour Bureau, Ministry of Labour, GOI, 1978); GOI, *Final Report on Indebtedness among Rural Labour Households* (Delhi: GOI, 1978a).

Table 16.8: Agricultural Labourer Households as a Percentage of Rural Households

	Scheduled (lakh)*	(%)	Scheduled (lakh)	(%)	Others (lakh)	(%)	Total (lakh)	(%)
1. Agricultural sector (a+b)	289 (19.5)	(76.4)	192 (13.0)	(87.1)	999 (67.5)	(61.4)	1,480 (100.0)	(66.5)
a. Cultivators	107 (11.6)	(28.2) (13.0)	120	(54.4) 75.4	698	(42.9) (100.0)	925	(41.5)
b. Agricultural labourers	182 (33.8)	(48.2)	72 (13.0)	(32.7)	301 (53.2)	(18.5)	555 (100.0)	(24.9)
2. Non-agricultural sector	89 (12.0)	(23.6)	8 (3.8)	(12.9)	628 (84.2)	(38.6)	745 (100.0)	(33.5)
Total (1+2)	378 (17.0)	(100)	220 (10.0)	(100)	1627 (73.0)	(100)	2225 (100.0)	(100)

Source: Centre for Monitoring the Indian Economy, 1985, Table 1.8c.

*1 lakh = 100,000

Notes

Chapter 1: Introduction: Caste and Democratic Politics

1 R.N. Saksena, *Scheduled Castes and Tribes: Founding Fathers' Views*, New Delhi: Uppal, 1981, pp. 408–409.

2 Address to the Congress Parliamentary Party, 2 November 1954, *The Collected Writings of Jawaharlal Nehru*, Delhi: Nehru Memorial Fund.

3 J.H. Hutton, *Caste in India: Its Nature, Function and Origins*, Cambridge: Cambridge University Press, 1946.

4 G.S. Ghurye, *Caste, Class and Occupation*, Bombay: Popular Book Depot, 1969, p. 1.

5 Louis Dumont, *Homo Hierarchicus*, Chicago: University of Chicago Press, 1970, p. 43.

6 Ibid., chapter 3.

7 Michael Moffatt, *An Untouchable Community in South India: Structure and Consensus*, Princeton: Princeton University Press, 1979, pp. 3–5.

8 Kathleen Gough; 'The Social Structure of a Tanjore Village', in McKim Marriot, ed., *Village India*, Chicago: University of Chicago Press, 1955, p. 846.

9 Joan Mencher, 'The Caste System Upside Down', *Current Anthropology*, 15 (1975), p. 436. See also Gerald Berreman, 'The Brahmanical View of Caste', *Contributions to Indian Sociology*, N.S. 5, 1971.

10 Robert Deliege, *The World of 'Untouchables' Paraiyars of Tamil Nadu*, Delhi: Oxford University Press, 1997.

11 N. Sudhakar Rao, 'Structure of South Indian Untouchable Castes', in Ghanshyam Shah, ed., *Subaltern Studies VI*, Delhi: Oxford University Press, 1989.

12 M.N. Srinivas, *Religion and Society among the Coorgs of South India*, Bombay: Oxford University Press, 1952.

13 D.D. Kosambi, *An Introduction to the Study of Indian History*, Bombay: Popular Book Depot, 1956, p. 95.

14 Morton Klass, *Caste. The Emergence of the South Asian Social System*, Philadelphia: Institute for the Study of Human Issues, 1980, p. 132.

15 Tapan Raychaudhury, 'The Mid-Eighteenth-Century Background', in Dharma Kumar, ed., *The Cambridge Economic History of India, Vol. 2, 1757–1970*, Cambridge: Cambridge University Press, 1982.

16 See McKim Marriot, *Village India: Studies in the Little Community*, Chicago: University of Chicago Press, 1955; M.N. Srinivas, *India's Villages*, Calcutta: Government of West Bengal, 1955; Kathleen Gough, op. cit.; and Andre Béteille, *Caste, Class and Power*, Bombay: Oxford University Press, 1966.

17 M.N. Srinivas, *Social Change in Modern India*, Bombay: Allied Publishers, 1966, p. 19.

18   K.L. Sharma, *The Changing Rural Stratification*, Delhi: Orient Longman, 1984, p. 114.

19   K.S. Singh, *People of India: An Introduction*, Calcutta: Seagull, 1993, p. 79.

20   F.G. Bailey, *Caste and the Economic Frontier*, Manchester: Manchester University Press, 1957.

21   Gough, op. cit., p. 42.

22   Government of Gujarat, 1976.

23   Ghanshyam Shah, 'Middle Class Politics: The Case of the Anti-Reservation Agitation in Gujarat', *Economic and Political Weekly*, 22, 19–26 May 1987.

24   O. Lewis, *Village Life in Northern India: Studies in a Delhi Village*, Urbana: University of Illinois, 1958, p. 81.

25   R.S. Khare, *The Changing Brahmans: Associations and Elites among the Kanya-kubjas of North India*, Chicago: University of Chicago Press, 1980.

26   G.S. Ghurye, op. cit., p. 342.

27   R.L. Hardgrave, *The Nadars of Tamil Nadu: The Political Culture of a Community in Change*, Bombay: Oxford University Press, 1969.

28   Ghanshyam Shah, *Caste Association and Political Process in Gujarat*, Bombay: Popular Prakashan, 1976.

29   Francine R. Frankel, 'Caste, Land and Dominance in Bihar: Breakdown of the Brahminical Social Order', in R. Frankel and M.S.A. Rao, *Dominance and State Power in Modern India: Decline of Social Order*, vol. 1, Delhi: Oxford University Press, 1989.

30   Shah (1976), op. cit.

31   James Manor; see his essay in the present volume.

32   Rajni Kothari and Tarun Sheth, 'Extent and Limits of Community Voting: The Case of Baroda East', *The Economic Weekly*, 15 September 1962; Rajni Kothari and Ghanshyam Shah, 'Caste Orientation of Political Factions, Modasa Constituency: A Case Study', *The Economic Weekly*, Special Number, July 1963.

33   Selig S. Harrison, *India: The Most Dangerous Decades*, Madras: Oxford University Press, 1960, p. 72.

34   M.N. Srinivas, 'The Future of Indian Caste', *Economic and Political Weekly*, 14 (7–8), Annual Number, February 1979, p. 241.

Chapter 2: Features of the Caste System

Note: In this chapter I have quoted many authorities that are chronologically later, by half a century or more, than the period I have here in view. But other and older authorities are almost everywhere indicated. The reason is that the later authorities give more details and are easily accessible to most people.

1   Athelstane Baines, *Ethnography Castes and Tribes*, 1912, p. 11.

2   Quotation from Megasthenes' account in John Wilson, *Indian Castes* vol. I, p. 347.

3   P.R.M. MacIver, *Community*, 1920.

4   *The New Statesman, Special Supplement*, 28 April, 1917, p. 38.

5   Gujarat Brahmins do have such councils. See Borradaile's *Gujarat Caste* rules, translated into Gujarati by Mangaldas Nathoobhoy.

6   E. Hultzsch, ed. and trans., *South Indian Inscriptions*, 1890, vol. I, no. 56.

7   *United Provinces Census*, 1911, p. 337; *Panjab Census*, 1911, pp. 420–1; also cf. Hamilton, *A Geographical Description of Hindustan*, 2 vols, 1820, I, p. 110; James Kerr, *The Domestic Life, Character and Customs of the Natives of India*, 1865, pp. 316–19; R.M. Martin, *The History of Antiquities and Statistics of Eastern India*, vol. III, 1938, pp. 179–80; and Arthur Steele, *The Law and Custom of Hindu Castes*, 1868, pp. 150–1.

8   The result of this fact is to be seen in the departure of the customs of many castes from the rules laid down in the Hindu sacred laws. See Steele, *The Laws and Customs of Hindu Castes*, p. 124 and Appendix A.

9   *United Provinces Census*, 1911, p. 337.

10 *Bengal Census*, 1911, pp. 467–9.

11 Ibid., p. 487.

12 *Godavari District Gazetteer*, vol. I, p. 48.

13 Russell, *Tribes and Castes of the Central Provinces of India*, 1916, vol. II, p. 31.

14 Crooke, ed., *The Tribes and Castes of the North- Western Provinces and Oudh*, 1896, vol. I, pp. 45, 109; vol. II, pp. 93, 326; vol. III, 247, 332; vol. IV, 33, 43.

15 M.R. Majumdar and K.M. Kapadia (eds), *Ghurye Felicitation Volume*, 1954, p. 282.

16 *Madras Census*, 1871, p. 137.

17 M.G. Rànade in *Journal of the Bombay Branch of the Royal Asiatic Society*, vol. XX, P. 476.

18 *Madras Census*, 1871, p. 151 and footnote.

19 *Mysore Census*, 1901, p. 400.

20 Martin, op. cit., vol. II, p. 466.

21 UP *Census*, 1901, p. 227.

22 UP *Census*, 1911, p. 328.

23 UP *Census*, 1901, p. 212.

24 H.H. Risley, *The People of India* (2nd edn 1915), p. 159.

25 UP *Census*, 1911, p. 329; E.A.H. Blunt, *The Caste System of Northern India*, 1931, pp. 90–4.

26 UP *Census*, 1911, p. 331.

27 H.H. Risley, *Tribes and Castes of Benga4 Ethnographic Glossary*, 1891 (1), vol. II, p. 270.

28 *Bengal Census*, 1901, p. 367.

29 Ibid.

30 Ibid.

31 A.K. Forbes, *Rasa Malt*, vol. II, 1856, edited by Rawlinson (1925), p. 240

32 J. Bhattacharya, *Hindu Castes and Sects*, 1896, p. 255.

33 Wilson, op. cit., vol. II, pp. 74–5.

34 *Encyclopaedia of Religion and Ethics,'* vol. X, p. 491 (b).

35 Slater Gilbert, *Some South Indian Villages*, 1918, p. 38.

36 *Trichinopoly District Gazetteer*, vol. I, p. 8 1.

37 E. Thurston, *Castes and Tribes of Southern India*, 1907–9, VI, p. 16.

38 *Bellary District Gazetteer*, p. 58.

39 H.H. Mann and N.V. Kanitkar, *Land and Labour in a Deccan Village*, no. 2, 1921, p. 108.

40 Russell, op. cit., vol. IV, p. 189.

41 Thurston, op. cit., vol. IV, p. 88.

42 Russell, op. cit., vol. I, pp. 72–3.

43 *Panjab Census*, 1911, p. 413.

44 G.W. Briggs, *The Chamars*, 1920, p. 231.

45 *Encyclopaedia of Religion and Ethics*, vol. IX, p. 636 (b); also compare Forbes, vol. II, p. 238.

46 M.G. Ranade, *Journal of the Bombay Branch of the Royal Asiatic Society*, p. 478.

47 Bhattacharya, op. cit., p. 259.

48 W. Logan, *Malabar*, vol. I, 1887, p. 85.

49 Bhattacharya, op. cit., p. 259.

50 Wilson, op. cit., vol. II, p. 77.

51 Ibid., p. 79.

52 *Madras Census*, 1891, p. 224.

53 G.W. Forrest, *Official Writings of Mountstuart Elphinstone*, 1884, pp. 310–11.

54 *Madras Census*, 1871, p. 129.

55 D.V. Potdar, *Marathi Gadyacha Ingraji Avatar*, Appendix, pp. 42–3.

56 Vad, *Sawai Madhavrao*, vol. III, p. 280.

57 Ranade, op. cit., p. 478; Vad, ibid., p. 287.

58 Ibid., p. 478.

59 *Madras Census*, 1891, p. 299.

60 Bhattacharya, op. cit., pp. 19–20.

61 Ranade, op. cit., p. 456; Vad, *Bataji Bajirao*, vol. I, pp. 306, 309, 3377.

62 Ibid., p. 455.

63 James Forbes, *Oriental Memoirs*, vol. I, 1834, p. 256.

64 Holt Mackenzie in *Minutes of Evidence Taken Before the Select Committee on the Affairs of the East India Company*, vol. III, 1832, p. 215.

65 R. Rickards, *India*, vol. I, 1892, p. 29.

66 Campbell, *Ethnology of India*, p. 216.

67 Wilson, op. cit., vol. II, 151; also compare Martin, op. cit., vol. I, p. 111.

68 Bhattacharya, op. cit., note 32, p. 39.

69 Wilson, op. cit., vol. II, p. 115.

70 Ibid., p. 59.

71 Ibid., p. 188; also compare Sir John Malcolm, *Memoirs of Central India and Malwa*, 1823, vol. II, pp. 122–3.

72 Wilson, op. cit., vol. II, p. 67.

73 Bhattacharya, op. cit., pp. 50–1.

74 Baines, op. cit., p. 28.

75 *Madras Census*, 1871, p. 133.

76 P.N. Bose, *History of Hindu Civilisation during British Rule*, vol. II, 1894, p. 27, quotation from *Ain-i-Akbari*.

77 *Salem District Gazetteer*, 139–64; *Tanjore Dist. Gaz.*, 81–8.

78 Baines, op. cit., p. 59.

79 Russell, op. cit., vol. I, p. 9.

80 Quoted in the *Encyclopaedia Britannica* (11th edn), vol. V, p. 465 (a).

81 B.A. Irving, *The Theory and Practice of Caste*, 1853, p. 19.

82 Bains, op. cit., note 1, p. 11.

83 E.A. Westermarck, *History of Human Marriage* (5th edition, 1921), vol. II, p. 59.

84 Baines, op. cit., p. 59.

85 Compare Sir John Malcolm, *Memoirs of Central India and Malwa*, 1823, op. cit., vol. II, p. 162.

86 *Encyclopaedia. of Religion and Ethics*, 1913, vol. III, p. 234.

87 V.N. Martin, ed., *Vyavahara Mayukha* 1880, vol. I, p. 110.

88 *Panjab Census*, 1911, p. 417.

89 *Bengal Census*, 1901, p. 351.

90 UP *Census*, 1911, p. 333.

91 Ibid., p. 353.

92 Russell, op. cit., vol. I, p. 10.

93 *Madras Census*, 1901, p. 128; also compare Kerr, op. cit., p. 279: 'You may sometimes hear a native say that he is a Brahmin. But not unfrequently when you ask him to name his caste, he mentions the minor subdivision, or perhaps the trade or profession, to which he belongs.'

94 *Salem District Gazetteer, pp. 123–4.*

95 Rev. M.A. Sherring, *Hindu Tribes and Castes*, vol. I, 1872, p. XXII.

96 *Madras Census*, 1891, p. 234.

97 E.A. Gait, 'Caste', *Eniyclopaedia of Religion and Ethics*, 1913, p. 232.

98 UP *Census*, 1811, p. 354; Gait's observation may apply only to Gujarat.

Chapter 3: Hierarchy: The Theory of the 'Varna'

1 We take hierarchy as our starting point both because we are starting from the whole and not the parts, and because we are starting from that which is more conscious (hierarchy) rather than that which is less conscious (division of labour). Compared with other aspects of the same level, hierarchy is in this sense the most fundamental. This primacy implies a relationship to ourselves, and is thus, at bottom, more a matter of methodology than ontology. We aim to go beyond existing views which appear inadequate, rather than attain a definitive statement of the truth of the matter, which would require, in particular, comparison with societies other than our own.

2 The *Shorter Oxford English Dictionary* is more logical on this point than the positivist *Littré* (*s.v.*): '(1) the orders of the various degrees of ecclesiastical estate; (2) the order and subordination of the different choirs of angles; (3) by extension, subordination of powers, authorities, ranks.' The *Grand Larousse* quotes Bossuet: 'The holy subordination of ecclesiastical powers, in the image of celestial hierarchies.' *Cf.* also *Grande Encyclopédie, s.v.* (applied by extension, as early as the time of the Byzantine Empire, to government and social organization as a whole).

3 Here is an example of lack of understanding on the part of modern Indian authors. In a studious work, K.M. Kapadia (*Marriage and Family in India*, London: Oxford University Press, 1955, p. 159, beginning of Chapter VIII) finds that the ancient texts rank the purposes of marriage hierarchically as) follows: religious duty (dharma), progeny *(praja)*, pleasure *(rati)*. He takes it that 'sex . . . is the least

desirable aim of marriage', and he adds: 'Marriage was desired not so much for sex or for progeny as for obtaining a partner for the fulfilment of one's religious duties'. It is very questionable to interpret duty as excluding progeny, and there is a complete misunderstanding. As so often, this list indicates a hierarchised totality, in which the lowest item (pleasure) is both limited and consecrated by its association with the superior purposes. Obviously duty includes progeny, as progeny presupposes pleasure. Pleasure is not 'less desirable', it is desirable- in its subordinate place. As interpreted by modern individualists, the datum is atomised, because they lose sight of the need felt by the authors of the ancient texts: to order everything rationally in relation to the supreme and permanent ends.

Add a good measure of sociocentricity, and you have these lines by Kardiner (The Individual and His Society, New York [1939], 1947, p. 447): 'The absence of such [social] mobility, as exists in caste systems, ought theoretically to augment anxiety about achievement of prestige; but practically this anxiety eventually disappears and is replaced by attitudes of resignation and submission.'

4 For the distinction between hierarchy and distribution of power, see Parsons, 'A Revised Theoretical Approach to the Theory of Social Stratification', in Reinhard Bendix and Seymoler Martin Lipset (eds), Class, Status and Power: A Reader in Social Stratification, London, 1954, p. 95 and also pp. 108, 128 and note 1, p. 665.

5 Emile Senart, Les castes dans l'Inde, Les of castes, et les systeme, Paris, 1894 (trans. Ross), pp. 114–19. Senart, whose starting point is the modem caste, may be regarded as the initiator of the modern tendency to undervalue the varnas. For him, these (classical) varnas represent an arbitrary expression in an older (Vedic) language of a reality which had become basically different. At the same period Oldenberg, more open to ethnology in general, is less clear-cut (see his critique of Senart's work in the light of Fick). Max Weber, in The Religion of India. The Sociology of Hinduism and Buddhism, Glencoe, 1958, still often translates varna by 'caste'.

6 'This, we are constantly told, bears no resemblance to reality . . . the four-caste system [sic] is a pure figment' (A.M. Hocart, Caste. A Comparative Study, London, 1950, pp. 23–4).

7 For details and references, see Coll, Pap. no. 4. The arrangement is equivalent to that noted in the case of the castes; thus the Brahmans and Kshatriyas taken together are opposed to the rest in that they preside over the society.

8 In order to give a racial explanation of the system of varnas, play has sometimes been made with the primary sense of varna, colour, and with the fact that the aborigines are described in the Veda, as being dark-skinned. This explains only the distinction between the twice-born and the Shudras, and not the threefold division of the former. See Hocart, Caste, pp. 27ff; Srinivas ('Varna and Caste'), Caste in Modem India, and others consider the varnas as given hereditary groups to which certain functions would have been reserved. However, it can be seen from the outset to be a matter of function, a necessity, so to speak, for social organisation which governs the identity of persons. Ketkar convincingly shows the importance, in this case especially, of attributive status (op. cit., pp. 45ff). According to Manu (I, 28–9), these functions were 'allotted at the first creation'.

9 P.V. Kane, History of Dharmasastra (Ancient and Mediaeval, Religious and Civil Law), Poona: Bhandarkar Oriental Research Institute, 1930, II, no. 1, pp. 19–179, etc.

10 It is certain that, as in the case of the Shudras, modifications came about in the status of people attached to the class of Vaishyas; they should be identified and

their history traced with reference to the general movement which has been briefly indicated. In a recent work, R.S. Sharma attempts to trace the evolution so far as the Shudras alone are concerned *(Shudras in Ancient India,* Delhi: Motilal Banarsidass, 1958). This is a substantial work, conscientious and well documented. But apart from the fact that the author endeavours to find change at all costs, where probably there is none (it seems gratuitous to regard the Shudras as the product of Indo-European society by the degradation of their status, when on the contrary aggregation by some of the indigenous population is more likely), he is wrong in the main because he studies the category as if it existed by itself independently of the whole—another instance of the mistake we have so often encountered. On the contrary it should be obvious that the following is necessarily essential to the evolution of the status of the Shudras: the actual emergence of a fifth category, long unrecognised in theory, which eventually replaced the Shudras as the excluded category, the Shudras having been excluded in the system of the varnas just as the Untouchables are excluded in the caste system. One will retain mainly an attractive view of the period of the Laws of Manu. According to Sharma, the Shudras were on the ascendant in this period and acquired new rights, yet at the same time their incapacities were reasserted in the doctrine to the point of caricature. If this phenomenon were corroborated, it would have to be more strictly linked to the competition between Hinduism and the more or less heretical sects, for the Shudras were assimilated to the heretics sufficiently clearly to suggest that they were deeply indebted to them for their promotion.

11   I have discussed this point elsewhere *(Coll. Pap.,* no. 3) from the point o view of its implications for the 'political' domain, but it was essential to mention it briefly here. The extent to which the comparative perspective is lacking in these studies can be seen by reading in a work by a master of Vedic studies that there had been a 'usurpation of sacerdotal offices by the layman' (Renou Louis and Jean Filliozat, 1953, *Inde Classique,* 1, 375). To suppose that the king is generally or essentially a layperson is to have a strange idea of royalty. It is true that anthropologists do much the same thing in a more subtle way; thus it is one of the tendencies of the classic *African Political Systems* (Evans-Pritchard and Fortes, eds, Introduction) to reduce the religious functions of the king to his political functions.

12   The differentiation between status and power enables us to place the development in India in relation to simpler societies and to draw together some of its characteristic aspects. Hocart, as has been said, compared the system to chieftainship in Fiji, where some degree of religious division of labour is encountered, centred on the chief. For India, the distinction under consideration needs to be added, and Hocart (power) must be introduced into Bouglé (status). Compared with a tribe with moities, whether totemic or not, it can be said roughly that in Fiji chieftainship replaces complementarity by division of labour, and correlatively emphasises the distinction between the sacred and the profane. As compared with chieftainship (in Fiji), the caste system both differentiates status and power (king and priest), and also in practice replaces the opposition between sacred and profane by the opposition between pure and impure. Roughly speaking, the sacred is differentiated into pure and impure, which up to then were identified with one another, but it must be immediately remembered that whilst in the case of chieftainship, and in other cases, states which correspond to that of impurity in the caste system are dangerous in themselves, they are not dangerous, but only *socially degrading,* in the caste system. Moreover, as is natural in a world in which differentiation has been

carried further, the division of labour is more developed, and more important, in India than in Fiji. But above all one must bear in mind the correlation between two phenomena: (1) the replacement of the king by the priest on the topmost rung of the status ladder; (2) the introduction of the opposition between pure and impure, with the innovations it entails. This opposition represents a ritualistic point of view: it originated historically in Vedic ritual and spread to the whole of social life, and it represents access to the sacred rather than the sacred itself. It is natural that such a point of view should be the work of the priest, and a logical connection between the two phenomena can be perceived.

It is quite natural that the distinction between priesthood and royalty, between status and power, while allowing the expression of hierarchy in a pure form, should permit the progress of differentiation in religious matters.

In an unexpected way we thus arrive at a plausible hypothesis about the origin of the system; pre-Aryan India would have had a system similar to that in Fiji, as Hocart suggested; Brahmanism, starting with Vedic development, and subordinating king to priest, would have encompassed it in a strict hierarchy, at the same time developing it and making it more precise.

13 Srinivas, 'Varna and Caste' (reprinted in Caste in Modern India). He insists on the fact that the varnas provide a common reference, and thus a means of comparison, for actual localised caste systems. But how would this be possible if, as he also claims, two quite heterogeneous things are involved? According to Gait, the varnas represent the 'external view' of the social organisation (Census of India, 1911, India Report, p. 366, quoted by Blunt, Caste System, p. 8). One sometimes still finds the idea that the castes were the product of the subdivision of the varnas (A.R. Desai, Social Background of Indian Nationalism, Bombay: Oxford University Press, 1948, p. 223).

14 For example, the interesting pamphlet mentioned by Weber: A.C. Das, The Gandhavaniks of Bengal, Calcutta, 1903.

15 'Ranks and degrees, order and regularity, are essential to the well-being of every community. The regulations of caste are nothing else than these, carried to an excess of refinement' (B.A. Irving, The Theory and Practice of Caste, London, 1857, p. 4).

Kathleen Gough Aberle, in her article 'Criteria of Caste Ranking in South India' (Man in India, XXXIX, no. 2, 1959, pp. 115–26), tries to reduce caste ranking in Kerala (Malabar) to what she calls 'relationships of servitude', in the extremely broad sense of personal dependence extending from a quasi-feudal relationship to servitude proper. This hypothesis does not account for the superiority of the Nambudiri Brahman over the king, whether or not Kshatriya. In this sense, the dualism which is discussed later in the present work is also present here. However, Miller had shown, for the same region, that whilst the princes were confined to limited territories, only the Brahman transcended these divisions and unified them ('Caste and Territory in Malabar', American Anthropologist, LVI, no. 3, 1954, pp. 410–20), which may be regarded as symbolic: the ranking which Gough calls 'ritual', far from being simply the expression of relationships of force, modifies and limits the impact of these relationships.

Ramkrishna Mukherjee, in The Dynamics of a Rural Society, Berlin: Akademic Verlag, 1957, tried to demonstrate a kind of statistical congruence between the caste system and three major economic classes which he distinguished in Bengal. Two of the classes in question are considered to have resulted from the British domination.

However, were there not castes before this? By contrast, see the clear recognition of the subordination of the phenomenon of class to that of caste in Marian Smith, 'Structured and Unstructured Class Societies' (*American Anthropologist*, LV, no. 2, 1953, p. 304): 'Indian society is structured in terms of caste but not in terms of class.'

16 This duality can be seen in terminological usage. These authors constantly speak of 'ritual status' and 'secular status', whereas from the indigenous point of view, and in the strong sense of the word, there is only one status, that is, 'ritual' status. M.N. Srinivas has given us at least the concept of the 'dominant caste', which is useful provided it is well defined: the dominant caste to a greater or lesser extent reproduces the royal function on a smaller territorial scale and 'dominance' is opposed to 'status', as fact is to right, or the dominant caste is to the caste of the local Brahmans.

17 This relates to a remote village of Orissa, where land is very cheap: F.G. Bailey, *Caste and the Economic Frontiers*, Manchester: Manchester University Press, 1957, pp. 266–7. Notice especially the inversion of the usual sense of 'validate'. In the text we have spoken only of 'power' (legitimate force, strictly linked to control of the land). Wealth in movables and chattels is indeed quite another matter: its emancipation was achieved by the British domination (Coll. Pap., no. 5).

Chapter 7: Caste, Class and Property Relations

1 Karl Marx, 'The British Rule in India, *New York Daily Tribune*, June 1883.

2 R. Palme Dutt, 'India Today', Calcutta, 1970, p. 327.

3 M.K. Gandhi, *Young India*, October 1921.

4 'Colonial Theses', Sixth Congress of the Communist International, 1928.

5 Communist Party of India (Marxist), 'Memorandum on National Integration', 1968.

6 M.K. Gandhi, *The Story of My Experiments with Truth*.

7 B.R. Ambedkar, 'Address to All India Depressed Classes Congress', 1930.

8 See Gail Omvedt, 'Cultural Revolt in a Colonial Society: The Non Brahmin Movement in Western India', Bombay, 1976.

9 N. Ram, 'Pre-History and History of the DMK', *Social Scientist*, December 1977.

10 Draft Five Year Plan, 1978–83, p. 11.

11 Ibid., pp. 2–3.

Chapter 8: The Transformation of Authority in Rural India

1 M.N. Srinivas, 'The Social System of a Mysore Village', in McKim Marriot, ed., *Village India*, Chicago: University of Chicago Press, 1955, p. 8.

2 Srinivas, op. cit., p. 6.

3 Louis Dumont, *Homo Hierarchicus*, Delhi: Vikas, 1970, pp. 161–2.

4 S.C. Dube, 'Caste Dominance and Factionalism', *Contributions to Indian Sociology* (New Series), no. 2, December 1968, p. 59.

5 Bernard S. Cohn, 'Anthropological Notes on Disputes and Law in India', *American Anthropologist*, vol. 67, no. 6, pt II, December 1965. Reprinted in Cohn, *An Anthropologist among the Historians and Other Essays*, Delhi: Oxford University Press 1987, pp. 594–9.

6 C. Metcalfe, 'Minute', in *Report from Select Committee, Evidence, III, Revenue*, App. 84, pp. 328ff.

7   It scarcely seems necessary to document this observation. The theme comes through in innumerable conversations and interviews I have had over the years with untouchables and other persons in many different regions. See, for example, Oliver Mendelsohn, 'Life and Struggles in the Stone Quarries of India', *The Journal of Commonwealth and Comparative Politics*, vol. XXIX (1991), no. 1.

8   James C. Scott, *Weapons of the Weak Everyday Forms of Peasant Resistance*, New Haven: Yale University Press, 1985.

9   Srinivas, op. cit., p. 15.

10 Malinowski was the first anthropologist to argue a rigorous case for the existence of law in stateless societies, and his *Crime and Custom in Savage Society* (Bronislaw Malinowski, London: Routledge and Kegan Paul, 1981), was a crucial work in the development of a conception of legal pluralism. But it has long been objected that Malinowski was really trying to find the source of *order* in Trobriand society and that he assumed that whatever produced order must be called *law*. The argument is that despite his seeming lack of ethnocentrism and his rejection of Maine's evolutionary legal history, Malinowski had not freed himself from a nineteenth-century positivist jurisprudence which assumed that order always arises from law.

11 Srinivas, op. cit., p. 8.

12 Cohn, op. cit., pp. 269–73, n. 5.

13 Dumont, op. cit., p. 181, n. 3.

14 Ibid., p. 169.

15 Ibid., p. 167.

16 Ibid., p. 182.

17 Ibid., p. 287.

18 Ibid., p. 180.

19 Anand Chakravarti, *Contradiction and Change—Emerging Patterns of Authority in a Rajasthan Village*, Delhi: Oxford University Press, 1975.

20 Ibid., p. 95.

21 Ibid., p. 191.

22 Ibid., p. 58.

23 Ibid., p. 61.

24 Ibid., pp. 58–9.

25 Ibid., p. 59.

26 Ibid.

27 Cohn, op. cit., p. 87.

28 Chakravarti, op. cit., p. 67.

29 Bernard S. Cohn, 'The Changing Status of a Depressed Caste', in Mckim Marriot (ed.), *Village India*, Chicago: University of Chicago Press, 1955.

30 Ibid., p. 66.

31 Ibid.

32 From late in the nineteenth century the land administration of Alwar state was reorganised by British officials along the lines pursued in Punjab. So the object was to make peasants the primary landholders of the state, rather than to pursue the zamindari model of eastern India.

33   The only serious effort to write the history of a village is Kessinger (Tom G. Kessinger, *Vilayatpur 1848–1968*, New Delhi: Young Asia, 1979). Valuable though this study is, it is highly sketchy on the matter of juridical authority or dispute settlement. The basic problem in developing historical accounts of this is the absence of documentary materials.

34   W. Wiser, and C.V. Wiser, 1930, *Behind Mud Walls*, Berkeley: University of California Press, 1963.

35   The first systematic account of the system is in W.H. Wiser (*The Hindu Jajmani System*, Lucknow: Lucknow Publishing House, 1936). Wiser is concerned only with the reciprocity of the arrangements, not with questions of domination and subordination. M.N. Srinivas ('The Dominant Caste in Rampura', *American Anthropologist*, vol. 61, 1959), on the other hand, talks of *patrons* as members of the dominant caste.

36   Kessinger, op. cit.

37   F.G. Bailey, *Caste and the Economic Frontier*, Manchester: Manchester University Press, 1957; Andre Bétêille, *Caste, Class and Power*, Bombay: Oxford University Press, 1965.

38   Oliver Mendelsohn, 'The Pathology of the Indian Legal System', *Modern Asian Studies*, pt 4, October 1981; 'Life and Struggles in the Stone Quarries of India', *The Journal of Commonwealth and Comparative Politics*, vol. XXIX, no. 1.

39   Ibid.

40   A recent two-volume set of studies is devoted to consideration of the theme of dominance and its decline in the post-independence period. The evidence of decline is seen, of course, to be far from uniform across India. One of the weaknesses of the volumes is that they generally fail to take much notice of what has been happening in villages. The argument of the present essay suggests that evidence of the decline of dominance is far stronger at this level and that this perspective is crucial to an overall assessment of the problem. We are rightly past the era when village studies are seen to be *the* way of penetrating to the *real* India. But there is a danger that we are failing into the opposite trap of thinking that village studies tell us very little about the developing character of India.

41   Kessinger, op. cit.

42   Zoya Hasan, 'Patterns of Resilience and Change in Uttar Pradesh Politics, in Francine R. Frankel and M.S.A. Rao (eds), *Dominance and State Power in Modern India*, Delhi: Oxford University Press, 1989, vol. I, pp. 170–85.

43   W.H. Moreland, *India at the Death of Akbar*, London: Macmillan, 1920; M.F. O'Dwyer, 1901, *Final Report on the Alwar Settlement*.

44   P. Saran, *The Provincial Government of the Mughals 1526–1658*, 2nd edn, London: Asia Publishing House, 1973.

45   Irfan Habib, *The Agrarian System of Mughul India*, New York. Asia Publishing House, 1963; S. Nurul Hasan, 'Zamindars Under the Mughals', in R.E. Frykenberg (ed.), *Land Control and Social Structure in Indian History*, Madison: University of Wisconsin Press, 1969.

46   Cohn, op. cit.

47   Richard G. Fox, *Kin, Clan, Raja and Rule: State–Hinterland Relations in Preindustrial India*, Bombay: Oxford University Press, 1971; Francine R. Frankel and M.S.A. Rao, *Dominance and State Power in Modern India* vols I and II, Delhi: Oxford University Press, 1989 and 1990.

48 Burton Stein, *Peasant State and Society in Medieval South India*, Delhi: Oxford University Press, 1980; Nicholas B. Dirks, The Hollow Crown: *Ethnohistory of an Indian Kingdom*, Cambridge: Cambridge University Press, 1987. David Ludden, *Peasant History in South India*, Princeton: Princeton University Press, 1985; Bronislaw Malinowski, *Crime and Custom in Savage Society*, London: Routledge and Kegan Paul, 1926.

49 Dirks, op. cit., pp. 4–5.

50 Dirks, op. cit.; Ludden, op. cit., p. 66.

Chapter 9: Caste and Class: Social Reality and Political Representations

1 For a detailed discussion on changes in caste under British rule in India and the impact the colonial policies had on the caste system, see G.S. Ghurye, 'Caste During the British Rule', in his *Caste and Race in India*, Bombay: Popular Prakashan, 1962, pp. 270–305. Also see Marc Galanter, 'Reform, Mobility, and Politics Under British Rule', in his *Competing Equalities: Law and Backward Classes in India*, Delhi: Oxford University Press, 1984, pp. 18–40.

2 Collective self-awareness among the lower castes as a people, oppressed socially and economically by the ritually high-ranking castes, developed and found organisational articulation through their participation in anti-Brahmin movements which grew in the early decades of the twentieth century. See Gail Omvedt,*Cultural Revolt in a Colonial Society: The Non-Brahman Movements in Western India—1873 to 1930*, Bombay: Scientific Socialist Education Trust, 1976; see also F. Bugene Irshick, *Politics and Social Conflict in South India: The Non-Brahman Movements and Tamil Separatism* 1916–29, Berkeley: University of California Press, 1969.

3 For an elaboration of this point, see D.L. Sheth, 'Politics of Recognition and Representation', *Book Review*, vol. 19, no. 11, pp. 34–5.

4 Galanter sees this development during the colonial rule as having brought about some important changes in the caste system: 'caste organisation brought with it two important and related changes in the nature of castes. The salient groups grew in size from endogamous jatis into region-wise alliances. Concomitantly, the traditional patterns of organisation and leadership in the village setting were displaced by voluntary associations with officials whose delimited authority derived from elections.' Galanter, 'Reform, Mobility, and Politics Under British Rule', p. 23.

5 For a recent argument articulating a contrary position emphasising that the caste system has, even in the face of such changes, maintained systemic continuity, see A.M. Shah, 'A Response to the Critique on Division and Hierarchy', in A-M. Shah and I.P. Desai, *Division and Hierarch: An Overview of Caste in Gujarat*, Delhi: Hindustan Publishing Corporation, 1988, pp. 92–133. Shah sees horizontal divisions as intrinsic to the caste system itself, representing another principle of caste organisation which has always operated in juxtaposition with hierarchy. The horizontal divisions in caste, in his view, are thus produced and reproduced as part of the continuous process within the system, a kind of change that a system undergoes for its own survival and maintenance. Whereas for his interlocutor in the debate, I.P. Desai, the horizontal divisions which are prior to caste but were integrated in the system of castes by the principle of ritual hierarchy, are now breaking away from that hierarchy and are interacting in horizontal social and political spaces. In this sense, for Desai, horizontal divisions re present a new

principle for the emerging stratificatory system which has undermined the caste principle of ritual hierarchy, I.P. Desai, 'A Critique of Division and Hierarchy', in the above-cited *Division and Hierarchy*, pp. 40–9.

6   In this essay, I have used the term 'affirmative action' to refer to the larger package of social policies, but particularly that of reservations in jobs and educational institutions, devised for the 'weaker sections' of society. For a detailed discussion of the policy, see D.L. Sheth, 'Reservations Policy Revisited', *Economic and Political Weekly*, 14 November 1987, pp. 1957–87.

7   For an illuminating discussion on the changed relationship between ritual status and occupation and its implications for the emergence of a new type of stratificatory system in India, see I. P. Desai, 'Should "Caste" be the Basis for Recognizing Backwardness?' *Economic and Political Weekly*, vol. 19, no. 28, July 1984, pp. 1106–16.

8   Of late, recognition of systemic changes in caste is reflected in the mainstream sociological writings. For example, M.N. Srinivas in one of his latest writings has characterised the changes that have occurred in the caste *system* as systemic in nature:

As long as the mode of production at the village was caste based, denunciation of inequality from saints and reformers, or from those professing other faiths proved ineffective. It was only when, along with ideological attacks on caste, education and employment were made accessible to all, and urbanisation and industrialisation spread that *systemic changes* occurred in caste (emphasis mine).

See M.N. Srinivas (ed.), 'Introduction', in *Caste. Its Twentieth Century Avatar*, New Delhi: Viking, Penguin India, 1996, p. XIV.

9   For an overview of comprehensive, systemic changes that have occurred in local hierarchies of castes in rural areas, G.K. Karanth, 'Caste in Contemporary Rural India', in M.N. Srinivas (ed.), *Caste: Its Twentieth Century Avatar*, pp. 87–109. Karanth, in his concluding remarks to the essay (p. 106), observes: 'In the first place, it may not be appropriate any more to refer to caste in rural India as a "system". Castes exist as individual groups, but no longer integrated into a system, with the dovetailing of their interests.'

10 The writings and politics of Ram Manohar Lohia, a renowned socialist leader, however, constituted an exception to this approach of the left parties to political mobilisation. In his view, horizontal mobilisation of lower castes on issues of social justice had greater political potential for organising the poor and deprived populations of India than the ideology of class polarisation which, in his view, lacked an empirical, social basis for mobilisational politics. See Ram Manohar Lohia, *The Caste System*, Hyderabad: Ram Manohar Lohia Samata Vidyalaya Nyas, 1964. Also see D.L. Sheth, 'Ram Manohar Lohia on Caste in Indian Politics', *Lokayan Bulletin*, vol. 12, no. 4, January–February 1996, pp. 31–40; also see D.L. Sheth, 'Ram Manohar Lohia on Caste, Class and Gender in Indian Politics', *Lokayan Bulletin*, vol. 13, no. 2, September–October 1996, pp. 1–15.

11 D.L. Sheth, 'Social Bases of Party Support', in D.L. Sheth (ed.), *Citizens and Parties: Aspects of Competitive Politics in India*, Delhi: Allied Publishers, 1975, pp. 135–64.

12 Rajni Kothari in his pioneering work on the Congress party saw this aspect of Congress politics, that is, expanding its social base through management of caste-based political factions regionally and seeking consensus on issues of development and modernisation nationally, as crucial to the Congress party's

prolonged political and electoral dominance. See Rajni Kothari 'The "Congress System" in India', *Asian Survey,* vol. 4, no. 12, December 1964, pp. 1161–73; see also 'The Congress System Revisited', in Rajni Kothari, *Politics and People: In Search of Humane India,* vol. 1, Delhi: Ajanta Publishers, 1989, pp. 36–58.

13   See D.L. Sheth, 'Social Bases of the Political Crisis', *Seminar, Annual Number: India 1981,* January 1982, no. 269, pp. 28–36.

14   For detailed empirical studies of interaction between caste and politics, see Rajni Kothari (ed.), *Caste in Indian Politics,* Delhi: Orient Longman, 1970.

15   The concept 'politicisation of castes' was first used by Rajni Kothari in the early 1970s to describe changes that had occurred in the caste system with its involvement in democratic politics. See Rajni Kothari, 'Introduction', in *Caste in Indian Politics,* pp. 3–25.

16   See D.L. Sheth, 'Reservations Policy Revisited', pp. 1957–87.

17   M.N. Srinivas, 'Varna and Caste' in M.N. Srinivas, *Caste in Modern India and Other Essays,* Bombay: Asia Publishing House, 1962, pp. 63-9. Also see, Andre Béteille, 'Varna and Jati', Sociological *Bulletin,* vol. 45, no. 1, March 1996, pp. 15–27.

18   It must be noted that percentage figures reported below showing representation of social formations in different middle-class positions are based on a preliminary analysis of the survey data. They are likely to change, albeit in a small measure, when a composite index of middle-class membership is constructed and representation of different formations is then shown in a single middle-class category. For example, the upper-caste formation might show a higher degree of representation in the middle class, and the Dalits lesser, than they do now on separate indicators.

Chapter 10: Federating for Political Interests: The Kshatriyas of Gujarat

1   For an authoritative statement on the concept of dominant caste, see M.N. Srinivas, 'The Social System of Mysore Village', in McKim Marriot (ed.), *Village India,* Chicago: Chicago University Press, 1955, and 'The Dominant Caste in Rampura', *American Anthropologist,* February 1959. The concept and the analysis underlying it have also attracted adverse criticism. See, for instance, Louis Dumont and D. Pocock, 'Village Studies', in *Contributions to India Sociology,* April 1957. Although the empirical viability of the concept of dominant caste has been a matter of continuous debate, it seems to us that the political significance of a dominant-caste situation has not been adequately stressed so far. Where splits and factions occur within the general framework of a dominant caste sharing a common heritage and a common idiom of communication, politics serves as a medium of integration through adaptation and change. Factions within the same dominant caste also make it easy to bring in other castes to strengthen the support base of rival factional leaders. The task is much more difficult where rival groups are made up of whole castes that between them have little in common. A dominant-caste model of politics makes cross-cutting loyalties more easy to develop than in the case of a confrontation of exclusive caste groups (for example, the Nairs and Ezhavas in Kerala, or Kammas and Harijans in Andhra, or Rajputs and Bhumihars in Bihar until very recently). In cases like the latter, although the development of political attitudes ultimately leads to some flexibility in caste relations, the process is far more strenuous and often destroys the forces of cohesion in the antecedent social structure.

2   It has been emphasised, and quite rightly, that the operating caste system in India functions not along the varna typology found in the texts but along the jati lines of primary marriage groups. (Thus see Iravati Karve, *Hindu Society: A New Interpretation*, Poona: Deccan College, 1061; David G. Mandelbaum, 'Concepts and Methods in the Study of Caste', *The Economic Weekly*, Special Number, January 1959.) This ignores and thus puts in proper perspective, the varna symbolism employed by some castes for social and political mobility. The symbol of Kshatriya is both sufficiently indigenous and hallowed by tradition and sufficiently loose and nebulous to be invoked for claims to status and power. Because of the traditional claims of the Kshatriya to be the class of warriors and rulers, the label is particularly handy for political purposes. It has been invoked by ritually differently placed groups for functionally the same purpose, namely, a claim to high status and power. (Examples: Coorgs in Mysore, Jars in Rajasthan and Punjab, Marathas in Maharashtra, Kammas and Reddys in Andhra, Ahirs, Kurmis and Koeris in Bihar and Uttar Pradesh, Kathis in Saurashtra and Bariyas in Gujarat, alongside Rajputs everywhere.)

3   This included acceptance back into the Hindu fold. Thus the Moresalam Rajputs who had been converted into Muslims in the Mughal period were 'purified' through a religious ceremony in March 1953 by which they reentered the Hindu Kshatriya community. The Kshatriya Sabha took the initiative in this move.

4   'Sanskritisation' is an influence that leads lower castes to emulate the Brahminic castes in their search for status and prestige while the latter are exposed to another influence, namely, 'westernisation'. M.N. Srinivas, *Religion and Society among the Coorgs of South India*, Oxford: Clarendon Press, 1952, see also his *Caste in Modern India and Other Essays*, Bombay: Asia Publishing House, 1962, Chapter II; and 'A Note on Sanskritisation and Westernisation', in *Far Eastern Quarterly*, vol. xv, no. 4. A feature of the simultaneous operation of the two influences is that while 'Sanskritisation' leads to a narrowing of the gap between castes, 'westernisation' may narrow the gap, widen it, or leave it as before, depending upon the differential impacts on upper and lower castes.

5   A subject too large for discussion here.

6   The term 'talukdar' refers to a class of small estate holders most of whom were Rajputs with a background of political rule. The British under the Gujarat Talukdar Act of 1889 gave protection to this class and appointed a special officer called the Talukdar Settlement Officer for this purpose. There were also attempts to redeem their debts and help them by establishing schools and hostels for raising their educational levels. Natvarsinh Solanki was the first talukdar to pass the matriculation examination. See, however, in this connection, F.G. Bailey, *Tribe, Caste and Nation*, Manchester: Manchester University Press, 1960, pp. 186–93.

7   Charotar is the name of a prosperous part in the Kaira district of Gujarat, well known for its agricultural yield and for the powerful caste of peasant-proprieters known as Patidars who emerged from this area to be one of the most influential communities in Gujarat. The Kshatriya movement, having its roots in this area, was directed against Patidar dominance from its inception. Solanki inherited the Charotar Rajput Samaj from his father and, true to his reformist ideas, changed the Charotar name to Kshatriya Samaj.

8   It is interesting to·note that the other leaders agreed to most of what Solanki proposed when setting up the organisation—except its name. They insisted that the term 'Rajput' should be retained. Apparently, they were still afraid of being

polluted by the lower castes who were presumably to be included in the 'Kshatriya' ideology. They agreed to give scholarships to members of the lower castes but were not prepared to give up their own identity as Rajputs.

9   Because of his Brahmin origin, the Maharaj enjoys the status of a revered priest in the Kshatriya community. At the same time, his association with reformist activities and with Gandhi and the Congress during the independence movement has been an influencing factor in the sabha's approach to politics. His non-political posture in politics has been a convenient device for linking the Kshatriyas to politics while at the same time asserting that they were a non-political organisation. He has also influenced the techniques adopted by them in the programme of mass awakening. He has been to them both a prophet and a man of their own. He has provided the spiritual symbol for attracting the Kshatriya masses who may not have been amenable to the usual reformist jargons. The weapons of *satyagraha* and non-violence, usually anathema to the Rajputs and the Kshatriyas, became acceptable when taught by the Maharaj.

10   The figure 22 provided an emotional symbol. It represented the 22,000 courageous soldiers of Rana Pratap, who fought against the Mughal Empire at Haldighat. It was a symbol of Kshatriya prowess. The uniform consisted of a sword, a saffron-coloured turban and the traditional Kshatriya apparel, the '*surval*' and the '*bhet*'. Thus the appeal for unity and discipline was made by invoking tradition. It was the caste spirit that would make for unity and discipline.

11   For the last of these, 1,00,000 signatures were collected.

12   The first tour lasted thirty-seven days, the next, twenty-six days in four batches, after which there were two tours every year.

13   Their conflict with the administration made the Kshatriyas realise the importance of political power. And as they knew too well, they could get their demands accepted by the administration through their association with the Congress. There are several instances in which redress against grievances was sought through influential men in the Congress. Quite often this led to further disappointment, with Congressmen refusing to favour, which only made men like Natvarsinh Solanki more determined to build up the Kshatriya organisation as a power in itself. Indeed, as will be seen from what follows, the sabha's policy kept fluctuating between the 'political line' of wooing the Congress and the 'organisation line' of building its own power. In the outcome, the latter approach succeeded but only by expressing itself politically against the Congress party.

14   Saurashtra and Kutch are unions entirely consisting of former princely states. Each had a separate existence for some time until they were merged with the bilingual state of Bombay. They are now part of Gujarat state.

15   It should be noted here that the social status of the Patidar community differs between different regions of Gujarat. Thus in central Gujarat, in Ahmedabad, Kaira and Baroda districts, the Patidars are very prosperous and have achieved high status. In north Gujarat and Saurashtra, on the other hand, especially in princely regions, the Patidars, still under the domination of the mercantile community, have until recently enjoyed a low status. It is only lately, largely owing to land legislation, the operation of adult franchise, and the fraternal support of the Patidars of central Gujarat, that their condition is beginning to improve. See Rajni Kothari and Ghanshyam Shah, 'Caste Orientation of Political Factions—Modasa Constituency: A Case Study', The *Economic Weekly*, Special Number, July 1963.

16   It has been observed since independence that special privileges granted to backward class communities, especially Bhils, weakened the appeal of such a process of assimilation. Bhils found it convenient to remain classified as 'backward' and to be placed lower than the Kshatriyas in order to take advantage of economic privileges. Here, economic interests cut across social aspirations.

17   The two quotations are from Mahida's appeals to Kshatriya leaders of Saurashtra, one before and one after the election, as reported in the issues of *Rajput Bandhu* of 11 November 1948 and 16 December 1948, respectively. The last few words represent an anxiety to obtain recognition from the Congress through an identification with democratic institutions and values.

18   From the leading article in *Rajput Bandhu* dated 29 September 1949. During the same period the Kutch Rajput Sabha also resolved to join the Congress. The resolution justified the decision by saying that 'the economic problems of Kshatriyas are decided in accordance with policy decisions at the national level. This requires us to make our demand felt at the national level. This can only be done through a national organisation like the Congress.' *Rajput Bandhu*, 13 October 1949.

19   Again note, that affiliation with the Congress is justified in terms of the Sarvodaya ideology, which is essentially the non-political and 'Gandhian' aspect of the Congress programme.

20   Partly, this was the result of the direct impact of Mahida. Partly, however, it arose from their experience of conflict with the district administration, and the failures of the sabha to press their demands with the state government. Its failures as a pressure group led it, under Mahida, to adopt the 'political line'.

21   Ultimately a compromise was arrived at through the efforts of Ravishankar Maharaj.

22   The demand shows the levelling effect of this caste federation's attempt to expand its numerical base by bringing in more and more caste groups. Only, two years ago the sabha was fighting for the restoration of land rights to the Rajputs of Banaskantha, a northern district of Gujarat. It now demanded the benefits due to backward communities. Clearly, both its strategy and its social composition had undergone a substantial change.

23   It is noteworthy that Mahida introduced Chhasatia as 'a representative of the lower sections of the Kshatriya community'. Although a pure Rajput, Chhasatia came from very poor conditions, and worked his way up. He thus represented a large section of 'lowly' Rajputs, indistinguishable from other Kshatriyas.

24   'We have seen during the last General Elections that the organisational strength for social work that we had built through the Gujarat Kshatriya Sabha was shattered owing to internal political differences … In times like this, organisations which lack unity of thought cannot survive. This is clear. Hence for the sake of the organisation it is imperative that all Kshatriyas should adopt a single political ideology.' *Kshatriya Bandhu*, 16 December 1957.

25   The amended article under the head Purposes, now reads as follows: 'This institution will work for strengthening the Indian National Congress to achieve a classless social order and to strengthen the basis of democracy.'

26   This difference in temperament and approach of the two leaders is reflected even today in the respective roles they play in the Swatantra Party. While Solanki (bored by his term in the Bombay legislature) has refrained from contesting elections and has preferred to work as the organisational secretary of the state Swatantra Party,

Mahida has chosen to be a colourful addition to the Lok Sabha (his lustrous turban being second only to the glamour and beauty of Maharani Gayatri Devi of Jaipur). On the other hand, Solanki's son, a polished young man who received his education abroad, perfectly at home with the tenor of upper-level politics in India, has gone to the Lok Sabha as an MP on a Swatantra Party ticket.

27   The Patidar leaders of the Congress regarded the Kshatriya approach as an attempt on their part to capture the Congress. They were apprehensive of such a prospect. Tribhuvandas Patel, president of the Kaira District Congress Committee, in 1962, and later, president of the Gujarat Pradesh Congress Committee, in interviews with us, explained that he could not allow the sabha to nominate Kshatriya candidates, as that would have compromised the integrity of the Congress.

28   It may be noted that the Congress was put in the same dilemma when faced by the Kshatriya demands in allocating seats. It could have given more seats to them only by denying the same to its Patidar activists. The Congress, of course, chose not to do so as it had miscalculated the power of the sabha's leaders on the Kshatriya masses.

29   To complete our account, we must also add that political divisions within the Patidars also helped the Swatantra Party, as for instance in Kaira.

30   Similarly, the prince of Kutch went against the Congress and helped the Swatantra Party bag all the five seats from Kutch.

31   For a study of this by election and the role of the Kshatriya movement in its outcome, see Rushikesh Maru, 'Fall of a Traditional Congress Stronghold', *The Economic Weekly*, vol. XVII, no. 25, 19 June 1965.

32   As a result of this mobilisation in the last four years, the Swatantra Party made handsome gains in the 1967 general elections. In Saurashtra, it won 19 out of 46 assembly seats and four out of six parliamentary seats. As against this, in the 1962 general elections, the Swatantra Party had failed to gain a single seat from Saurashtra in both the assembly and Parliament.

33   Lloyd I. Rudolph and Susanne Hoeber Rudolph, 'The Political Role of India's Caste Associations', Pacific Affairs, vol. 33, 1960.

34   Even in the West it has been noticed that voluntary organisations have been losing their autonomy and are increasingly turning to the government for concessions. See Reinhard Bendix, 'Social Stratification and the Political Community', *European Journal of Sociology*, vol. I, no. 1. At any rate, there is need to distinguish between voluntary associations that are self-sufficient and those that are politicised. The classic presentation of the role of voluntary associations in a democracy as principally being one of minimising governmental interference is to be found in Alexis de Tocqueville's account of American democracy. The caste groups in India have traditionally performed a somewhat similar role and have managed to keep the government at arm's length. Both in America and in India, however, the current trends are against de Tocqueville's ideal type and towards greater politicisation.

35   Robert Dahl, in *Who Governs* (New Haven: Yale University Press, 1962), uses the concept of 'dispersed inequalities' to describe the phenomenon discussed here.

36   F.G. Bailey, *Caste and the Economic Frontier*, Manchester. Manchester University Press, 1957.

37   Other forms include caste association, regional conference of one or more castes, specialised agencies of a caste to promote employment, educational and other interests of caste members, and the systematic use of caste and ascriptive symbols

to mobilise pressure, resources, or votes. Sometimes caste symbols are substituted by occupational and class symbols for the same purpose.

Chapter 11: Pragmatic Progressives in Regional Politics: The Case of Devraj Urs

The author wishes to thank the UK Social Science Research Council for supporting the research for this essay. Many comments here are based upon necessarily off-the-record interviews with politicians and civil servants, mainly in Bangalore, during January 1980. Special thanks are due to G. K. Karanth, M.N. Srinivas and Francine Frankel for criticisms and information. They are, however, not to blame for what appears here.

1   Interviews with politicians, social scientists and journalists of diverse views, Calcutta, late January 1980. See also, B. Sen Gupta, 'CPI-M: Promises, Prospects, Problems', New Delhi and Stockholm, 1979.

2   See J. Manor, 'Where Congress Survived: Five States in the Indian General Election of 1977', *Asian Survey*, August 1978. Interviews with four senior officials, Bangalore and Delhi, January 1980.

3   Interview with D. Devraj Urs, Bangalore, 16 January 1980.

4   J. Manor, 'Structural Changes in Karnataka Politics', *Economic and Political Weekly*, 29 October 1977, pp. 1865–9. For background on the development of the system Urs displaced, see J. Manor, 'Political Change in an Indian State: Mysore, 1917–1955', New Delhi, Canberra, London, 1977.

5   In some backward areas, vote-banks still operate. (Interview with G.K. Karanth, Bangalore, 17 January 1980.) But they are now quite exceptional.

6   These lectures were later published as *The Agrarian Prospect in India*, second edition, New Delhi, 1976. See particularly pp. 31–46.

7   Interviews with Kadidal Manjappa, Bangalore, 6 July 1972 and 16 January 1980; M.A.S. Rajan, 'The Land Reforms Law in Karnataka', Bangalore, 1979, pp. 3–11.

8   Ibid., pp. 11–18. See also M.A.S. Rajan, 'Land Reforms in Karnataka: Contexts and Relationships', Bangalore, 1979.

9   Rajan, 'The Land Reforms Law . . .', pp. 17–19, 26–8, 35. Also, interview with B. Basavalingappa, Bangalore, 15 January 1980.

10   Ibid., pp. 36–50; interviews with opposition leaders and civil servants, Bangalore, 17 and 19 January 1980.

11   These figures are extrapolated from interviews with officials in the land reforms section, Karnataka Revenue Department; a typescript on statistics on land reforms to the end of November 1979 by H.N. Ranganathan, Assistant Special Officer for Land Reforms, Revenue Department (hereafter 'Ranganathan Typescript') and from Rajan,' . . . Contexts and Relationships', p. 41.

12   Ranganathan Typescript and Rajan, . . . Contexts and Relationships', p. 41.

13   Ibid.

14   Rajan, '. . . Contexts and Relationships', p. 7.

15   This is based on interviews with a wide range of social scientists, journalists, civil servants, lawyers dealing in land cases and politicians of all parties in Karnataka. See also S.X.J. Melchior's reports, *Economic and Political Weekly*, 5 May and 18 August 1979.

16   Rajan, '. . . Contexts and Relationships', p. 43. We exclude Kodagu and Chikmagalur districts from this comment because the large plantations there which are excluded from the Land Reforms Act (because of their economic importance) markedly distort the figure.

17 Ranganathan Typescript. Of the recipients, 3966 were members of the Scheduled Castes and 3161 were from other groups.

18 'A Bird's Eye View of Land Reforms in Karnataka', Briefing Paper, p. 3.

19 I am grateful to M.N. Panini for this information.

20 For a discussion of various occupational groups within the Lingayat category or sect, see J. Manor, 'The Evolution of Political Arenas and Units of Social Organisation: The Lingayats and Vokkaligas of Mysore', in M.N. Srinivas (ed.), *Dimensions of Social Change in India*, New Delhi, 1976.

21 H.W. Blair, 'Rising Kulaks and Backward Classes in Bihar: Social Change in the Late 1970s', *Economic and Political Weekly*, 12 January 1980, p. 66.

22 Ibid., p. 67. Blair's essay offers an interesting contrast to the case of Karnataka.

23 Interview with Devraj Urs.

24 I am grateful to Francine Frankel for this information.

25 For useful information on 'backward class' policies in Karnataka and India, see L. Dushkin, 'Backward Class Benefits and Social Class in India, 1920–1970', *Economic and Political Weekly*, 7 April 1979 and references therein to her other work.

26 See, for example, *The Statesman* (Delhi), 4 January 1980 and *Indian Express,* 18 January 1980. These reports were confirmed by officials of the Election Commission, New Delhi, 29 January 1980.

27 I am grateful to Bashiruddin Ahmed for this information.

28 Interview with Devraj Urs.

29 I am grateful to Mumtaz Ali Khan for this information. As further evidence of this effort, see 'Reservations in Promotional Vacancies—Defects: Remedies with Reasons', 1978, Typescript, Government of Karnataka.

30 Interview with Devraj Urs.

31 Interviews with Mumtaz Ali Khan, Bangalore, 17 January 1980 and with Karnataka civil servants, 15 and 19 January 1980. Also, Mumtaz Ali Khan, 'Seven Years of Change: A Study of Some Scheduled Castes in Bangalore District', Bangalore, 1979, pp. 184, 191, 194–215.

32 Mumtaz Ali Khan, 'Seven Years of Change . . .', pp. 185–7.

33 Interviews with G.K. Karanth and two Karnataka civil servants, Bangalore, 17 and 18 January 1980.

34 Interviews with seven Karnataka civil servants, Bangalore, January 1980. Also, D.M. Nanjundappa, 'A New Deal for the Poor: A Position Paper', Bangalore, 1979.

35 I am grateful to G.K. Karanth for this point.

36 Interview with Devraj Urs. This of course raises questions about the adequacy of Urs's party organisation to build and integrate grassroots organisations. But a discussion of this must wait for another occasion.

37 See, for example, *The Times of India*, 23 January 1980.

Chapter 12: The BJP and Backward Castes in Gujarat

1 *Sadhna*, 6 March 1993 (Gujarati).

2 Ghanshyam Shah, 'Caste Sentiments, Class Formation and Dominance in Gujarat', in Francine Frankel and M.S.A. Rao (eds), *Dominance and State Power in Modern India*, vol. II, Delhi: Oxford University Press, 1990.

3 Raymond Williams, *A New Face of Hinduism: The Swaminarayan Religion,*

Cambridge: Cambridge University Press, 1984. See also Makrand Mehra, 'Sampradayaki Sahitya and Samajik Chetana: Swaminarayan Sampradayano Abhyas 1800–1840', *Arhat* 5(4), October–December 1986 (Gujarati). David Hardiman, 'Class Base of Swaminarayan Sect', *Economic and Political Weekly*, 23(37), 10 September 1988.

4 Swami Sachchidanand, *Dharma*, Ahmedabad: Nav Gujarat Publications, 1987 (Gujarati), p. 92.

5 Ibid.

6 Ibid., p. 30.

7 Swami Sachchidanand, *Adhogatinu Mul Varna Vyavastha*, Ahmedabad: Samanvay Prakashan, 1988 (Gujarati), pp. 274–6.

8 Ibid., p. 291.

9 Sat Vichar Darshan, *The Systems*, Bombay: Sat Vichar Darshan, 1992, p. 12.

10 *Tatvagyan* 31(7), Gujarati monthly journal of the sect.

11 Sat Vichar Darshan, op. cit., pp. 20–211.

12 Ibid., p. 25. Swami Shraddhanand, Arya Samajist and militant Hindu nationalist also advocated in the 1920s a need for a temple with a larger hall which can provide a meeting place to a larger number of people as such facilities are available in mosques and churches. See Gyanendra Pandey, 'Hindus and Others: The Militant Hindu Construction', *Economic and Political Weekly*, 26(52), 28 December 1991.

13 Pandurang Shastri Athavale, *Vijigishu Jivanvad*, Bombay: Sat Vichar Darshan Trust, 1992, p. 38.

14 Ibid.

15 Ibid., p. 101.

16 *Sadhna*, 7 November 1992.

17 Quoted by Asghar Ali Engineer and Tanushri, 'Gujarat Bums Again', *Economic and Political Weekly*, 21(31), 2 August 1986.

18 Swami Atmanand, *Hindu Samaj Samanvaya*, Ahmedabad: Bharat Sevashram Sangh, 1982, p. 63.

19 Ibid.

20 Ibid., p. 46.

21 Ibid., pp. 43–62.

22 Dattopant Dhengadi, *Samajik Samrasata*, New Delhi: Kamavati Samajik Samrasata Manch, 1992, p. 18.

23 Ibid., p. 14.

24 Ibid. No such statement has been found in Ambedkar's speeches and writings or from his major biographers. According to the author, Ambedkar said so at the Bombay airport to Hindu Mahasabha workers of Bombay. No other evidence of this nature is available from Ambedkar's works.

25 B.R. Ambedkar, 'Pakistan or the Politics of India', in *Dr Babasaheb Ambedkar: Writings and Speeches*, vol. 12, Bombay: Education Department, Government of Maharashtra, 1990.

26 Ghanshyam Shah, 'Strategies of Social Engineering: Reservation and Mobility of Backward Communities of Gujarat', in Ramashray Roy and Richard Sisson (eds), *Diversity and Dominance in Indian Politics*, Delhi: Sage Publications, 1990.

27 Ghanshyam Shah, 'Middle Class Politics: A Case of Anti-Reservation Agitation

in Gujarat', *Economic and Political Weekly*, 22 (19–21), Annual Number, May 1987.

28 Gajendraprasad Shukla, 'Rajkiya Pakshni Vicharsarani Ane tena Adhar' (unpublished Ph.D. thesis), Surat: Centre for Social Studies, 1991.

29 Personal interview.

30 Ghanshyam Shah, 'Protests by the Rural Poor', in Alok Bhalla and Peter Bumke (eds), *Images of Rural India in the Twentieth Century*, Delhi: Sterling Publishers, 1992.

31 Shukla, op. cit.

32 Lancy Lobo, 'Communal Riots in Tribal Dediapada and Sagbara during October–November 1990: A Report' (typescript), Surat: Centre for Social Studies, 1991.

33 See Ghanshyam Shah, 'Tenth Lok Sabha Elections: BJP's Victory in Gujarat', *Economic and Political Weekly*, 26 (51), 21 December 1991.

Chapter 13: New Phase in Backward Caste Politics in Bihar, 1990–2000

All the three surveys were conducted by the Centre for the Study of Developing Societies, Delhi, during the 1995 and 2000 Vidhan Sabha elections and during the 1996, 1998 and 1999 Lok Sabha elections. The 1995 Vidhan Sabha election survey was conducted in 16 assembly constituencies spread across all three regions of the state. The total number of completed interviews was 817. The 2000 Vidhan Sabha election survey was conducted in 36 assembly constituencies spread across all three regions of the state. The total number of completed interviews was 2220.

The 1996, 1998 and 1999 surveys were conducted during the Lok Sabha elections retaining the same sample. The survey was spread across 44 polling booths of 22 Vidhan Sabha segments of 11 Lok Sabha constituencies selected through the Stratified Random Sampling adopting the Probability Proportionate to Size (PPS) method. The total number of completed interviews are 880 in 1996 and 833 in 1998 and 881 in 1999.

During the 1995 Vidhan Sabha elections the Janata Dal had an alliance with the CPI and CPM. The BJP and Samata party contested the elections separately. For a meaningful comparison with the 1996 and 1998 elections both the parties have been looked at as an alliance even for the 1995 Vidhan Sabha elections.

During the 1991 Lok Sabha elections the JMM had an alliance with the Janata Dal, but the alliance broke down during subsequent elections. During the 1998 Lok Sabha elections the BJP and the Janata Dal maintained their alliance while the RJD entered into a half alliance with the Congress and the JMM.

Chapter 14: Dalit Assertion through Electoral Politics

1 Sidney Verba, and Norman Nie, *Participation in America: Political Democracy and Social Equality*, New York: Harper and Row, 1972.

2 A very high percentage, 87.3 per cent, overall voter turnout was reported in the CSDS sample as against the actual figure of 57.9 per cent. The CSDS Report (Report of the National Election Survey, 1996 submitted by the CSDS to the Indian Council of Social Science Research [ICSSR]) explains this gap as follows: Since voting is generally considered an act of responsive citizenry, there is a tendency of slight overreporting in all such surveys. However, a wide gap of about 30 per cent in the present survey can be explained largely by two factors. One, span of survey period in a given locality was restricted, to about 30 hours only including the night

failing in between the days. Therefore, only those present during this period barring refusals were interviewed. The people thus interviewed distinguish themselves as generally present in the locality and thus more likely to vote than others. Fully aware of this problem the interviewers were asked to ascertain, at least, voting/ non-voting information about not-interviewed respondents as well. Interestingly, only 36.9 per cent of the not-interviewed respondents were found to have voted. This brings down the turnout figure from 87.3 per cent to 70.6 per cent. Finally, as a by-product of this survey we came to know that as much as 12.7 per cent names in the voter list were non-eligible voters. That is, either they were dead, permanently migrated, working and residing far away from their native place or were untraceable to the extent that they could be characterised as ghost voters. If these non-eligible voters too are excluded from the potential list of voters the actual turnout figure goes up from 57.9 per cent to 66.2 per cent which is very close to the revised figure of 70.6 per cent.

3   V.B. Singh, 'Harijans and Their Influence on the Elections in Uttar Pradesh', in Subrata Kumar Mitra and James Chiriyankandath, eds, *Electoral Politics: Changing Landscape*, New Delhi: Segment Books, 1947, p. 247.

4   Data released by the Election Commission of India on the respective elections.

5   Sudha Pai, 'From Harijan to Dalits: Identity Formation, Political Consciousness and Electoral Mobilisation of the Scheduled Castes in Uttar Pradesh', in Ghanshyarn Shah (ed.), *Dalit Identity and Politics*, Delhi: Sage Publications, 2001.

6   Ibid.

7   This concept was first well developed by election analysts at the Survey Research Centre, University of Michigan in the form of a scale of political efficacy, and subsequently applied in electoral research in many countries.

8   V.B. Singh, Report of the National Election Survey, 1996, submitted by the CSDS to ICSSR.

9   Paul R. Brass, *Caste, Faction and Party in Indian Politics* (Volume Two: Election Studies), Delhi: Chanakya Publications, 1985.

Chapter 15: Social Backwardness and the Politics of Reservations

[An earlier draft of this paper was presented at a faculty seminar at the Centre for Social Studies, Surat. I thank all the participants of the seminar for their comments. I specially thank Anjana Desai for her careful reading of the paper and her comments on it.]

1   Louis Dumont, *Homo Hierarchicus*, Chicago: University of Chicago Press, 1966, p. 43.

2   Michael Moffatt, *An Untouchable Community in India: Structure and Con sensus*, Princeton: Princeton University Press, 1979, p. 3.

3   M.N. Srinivas, *Social Change in Modem India*, Bombay: Allied Publishers, 1966, p. 93.

4   F.G. Bailey, *Caste and the Economic Frontier*, Manchester: Manchester University Press, 1957.

5   Kathleen Gough, 'Caste in a Tanjore Village', in E.R. Leach (ed.), *Aspects of Caste in South India, Ceylon and North-West Pakistan*, Cambridge: Cambridge University Press, 1960, p. 32.

6   Santosh Goyal, 'Social Background of Officers in the Indian Administrative Service', in Francine Frankel and M.S.A. Rao (eds), *Dominance and State Power in Modem*

India, vol. I, Delhi: Oxford University Press, 1989; Santosh Goyal, 'Social Background of Indian Corporate Executives', in Francine Frankel and M.S.A. Rao (eds), *Dominance and State Power in Modern India*, vol. II, Delhi: Oxford University Press, 1990.

7   Ghanshyarn Shah, 'Caste, Class and Reservation', *Economic and Political Weekly*, vol. II, 1985, no. 3.

8   Francine Frankel, 'Middle Classes and Castes in India's Politics: Prospects for Political Accommodation', in Atul Kohli (ed.), *India's Democracy*, Princeton: Princeton University Press, 1988, p. 245.

9   Chinnappa Reddy, *The Justice-Journey of the Karnataka Backward Classes: The Report of the Third Karnataka Backward Classes Commission*, Bangalore: Government of Karnataka, 1990.

10 Francine Frankel, 'Caste, Land and Dominance in Bihar', in Francine Frankel and M.S.A. Rao (eds), *Dominance and State Power in Modern India*, Delhi: Oxford University Press, 1989, p. 87.

11 Government of India, *Report of the Backward Classes Commission*, Delhi: Government of India Press, 1980, p. 57.

12 *India Today*, 30 September 1990.

13 R.N. Saksena, *Scheduled Castes and Tribes: Founding Fathers' View*, New Delhi: Uppal Publishing House, 1981.

14 Ibid.

15 D.N. Sandanshiv, *Reservations for Social Justice*, Bombay: Current Law Publishers, 1986, p. 3.

16 T. Venkatswamy, Report *of the Second Backward Classes Commission*, Bangalore: Government of Karnataka, 1986, p. 21.

17 A.M. Zaidi, *The Encyclopedia of the Indian National Congress*, vol. XXI, 1970–1, New Delhi: S. Chand and Company, 1984, p. 27.

18 Ibid., p. 240.

19 Ghanshyam Shah, 'Middle Class Politics: A Case of Anti-Reservation Agitation in Gujarat', *Economic and Political Weekly*, Annual Number, 1987, p. 199.

20 Mani Shankar Aiyar, 'Mandalam! Mandalam!', *Sunday*, 16–22 September 1990.

21 Shah, 'Caste, Class and Reservation', note 7.

Chapter 16: The Anti-Caste Movement and the Discourse of Power

1   'We are the Force of Change', *Frontline*, 16 February–1 March 1991. Interview with V.P. Singh by N. Ram.

2   R. O'Hanlon, *Caste, Conflict and Ideology: Mahatma jotirao Phule and Low-Caste Social Protest in Nineteenth Century Western India*, Cambridge: Cambridge University Press, 1985; G. Omvedt, *Cultural Revolt a Colonial Society. The Non-Brahman Movement in Western India: 1910–1930*, Pune: Scientific Socialist Education Trust, 1976; 'Report on the History of Dalit Movement in Maharashtra, Andhra and Karnataka, New Delhi: Indian Council of Social Science Research, 1990 (mimeo); J. Phule, *Samagrah Wangmay* (in Marathi), Bombay: Government of Maharashtra, 1986.

3   Phule was to formulate what he called a *sarvajanik satya dharm*; Periyar was to choose atheism, Ambedkar Buddhism, and so forth.

4   The south Indian movement had a large base amongst landlords; the Mysore

movement was more popular among the educated urban section; the Maharashtra movement had a base among the peasantry.

5   Omvedr, op. cit.; M. Juergensmeyer, *Religion and Social Wisdom: The Movement Against Untouchability*, Berkeley: University of California Press, 1982; E.F. Irschick, *Politics and Social Conflict in South India: The Non-Brahmin Movement and Tamil Separatism*, Berkeley: Centre for South and Southeast Asia Studies, 1970.

6   B.R. Ambedkar, *B.R. Ambedkar: Writings and Speeches*, 7 vols, Bombay: Government of Maharashtra, 1979–91, edited by Vasant Moon (vol. 2 published in 1981; vol. 5 in 1989).

7   This struggle has been neglected by left historians, perhaps because it was outside the framework of the Kisan Sabha of the time.

8   *Janata*, 1937–8. A Marathi weekly published by Dr B.R. Ambedkar (partial set available in the Vasant Moon collection, Nagpur).

9   Quoted in Omvedt, op. cit., p. 211.

10 Ambedkar (1979–91), 1989, pp. 115–16.

11 Government of India, *Report of the Backward Classes Commission (Mandal Commission Report) (7 vols in 2 parts)*, New Delhi: Backward Classes Commission, Government of India, 1980.

12 V.T. Rajshekar, *Dilemma of the Class and Caste in India*, Bangalore: Dalit Sahitya Academy, 1989.

13 This is almost what, in fact, happened with the Mandal Commission's classification. In Maharashtra, this includes 'Kunbis' but not 'Marathas'. Maratha opposition to reservations has, as a consequence, been effectively silenced. One of the significant reasons for the lack of anti-reservation riots in Maharashtra stems from this irony.

14 G. Guru, 'Mahatma Jotirao Phule and Reservations', Surat: Centre for Social Studies 1991 (mimeo).

15 Meaning, colloquially, 'Brahmins, Banias and Thakurs are thieves, the rest are with us'. DS-4 refers to the Dalit Shoshit Samaj Sangharsh Samiti, (DSSSS), a front organisation under Kanshi Ram's leadership, prior to the formation of the BSP.

16 Meaning, 'No longer "We vote—you rule" '.

17 'We shall take the posts of PM and CM through the vote; we shall take the posts of DM and SP through reservation.'
    PM = Prime Minister; CM = Chief Minister; SP = Superintendent of Police; DM = District Magistrate.

18 *Sunday Observer*, 2 December 1990.

19 It has to be added that this alliance is also taking a regional-national form, with even the Janata Dal and the CPI (M) becoming almost de facto regional parties.

Select Bibliography

Bailey, F.G., *Caste and the Economic Frontier: A Village in Highland Orissa.*
Manchester.

———, 1960. Tribe, *Caste and Nation: A Study of Political Activity and Political Change in Highland Orissa.* Manchester.

Bayly, Susan, 1999. *The New, Cambridge History of India. Caste, society and Politics in India from the Eighteenth Century to the Modern Age.* Cambridge: Cambridge University Press.

Berreman, Gerald, 1979. *Caste and Other Inequalities.- Essays on Inequality.* Delhi: Manohar.

Bétèille, Andre, 1981. *The Backward Classes and the New Social Order.* Delhi: Oxford University Press.

———, 1965. *Caste, Class and Power: Changing Patterns of Stratification in a Tanjore Village.* Delhi: Oxford University Press.

———, 1991. *Society and Politics in India. Essays in a Contemporary Perspective.* Delhi: Oxford University Press.

Bhatt, Anil, 1975. *Caste, Class and Politics: An Empirical Profile of Social Stratification.* Delhi: Manohar.

Brass, Paul R., 198 5. *Caste, Faction and Party in Indian Politics,* Vol. 2, Election Studies. Delhi: Chanakya Publications.

Breman, Jan, 1979. *Patronage and Exploitation.* Delhi: Manohar.

Centre for Social Studies (ed.), 1985. *Caste, Caste, Conflict and Reservation.* Delhi: Ajanta Publications.

Chatterjee, Partha, 1999.'Caste and Subaltern Consciousness', in Ranajit Guha (ed.), *Subaltern Studies VI. Writings on South Asian History and Society.* Delhi: Oxford University Press.

Cox, Oliver C., 1948. *Caste, Class and Race.- A Study in Social Dynamics.* New York: Monthly Review Press.

Fox, Richard G., 1979. *From Zamindar to Ballot Box. Community Change in a North Indian Market Town.* Ithaca, New York: Cornell University Press.

Frankel, Francine and M.S.A. Rao (eds), 1989. *Dominance and State Power in Modern India: Decline of a Social Order,* vols I and II. Delhi: Oxford University Press.

Frankel, Francine, 1988. 'Middle Classes and Castes in India's Politics: Prospects for Political Accommodation', in Atul Kohli (ed.), *India's Democracy.* Princeton: Princeton University Press.

Galanter, Marc, 19 84. *Competing Equalities: The Indian Experience with Compensatory Discrimination.* Berkeley: University of California Press.

Gokhale, Jayashree B., 1979, 'The Dalit Panthers and Radicalisation of the Untouchables', *Journal of Commonwealth and Comparative Studies,* vol. 17. no. 1.

Gould, Harold A., 1990. *The Hindu Caste System.* Delhi: Chanakya Publications.

Gupta, Dipankar (ed.), 199 1. *Social Stratification.* Delhi: Oxford University Press.

Gupta, S.K., 1985. *The Scheduled Castes in Modern Indian Politics: Their Emergence as a Political Power.* New Delhi: Munshiram Manoharlal.

Hardgrave, Robert L., 1969. *The Nadars of Tamilnad- The Political Culture of a Community in Change.* Berkeley: University of California Press.

Harrison, Selig S., 1960. *India: The Most Dangerous Decades.* Madras: Oxford University Press.

Jaffrelot, Christophe, 1996. *The Hindu Nationalist Movement and Indian Politics, 1925 to the 1990s,* London: Viking.

Joshi, Barbara R., 1982. *Democracy in Search of Equality: Untouchable Politics and Indian Social Change.* Delhi: Hindustan Publishing.

_____, (ed.), *The Untouchable! Voices of the Dalit Liberation Movement.* London: Zed Books.

Karve, Iravati, 1968. *Hindu Society: An Interpretation.* Poona: Deccan College.

Klass, Morton, 1980. *Caste. The Emergence of the South Asian Social System.* Philadelphia: Institute for the Study of Human Issues.

Kolenda, Pauline, 1984. *Caste in Contemporary India. Beyond Organic Solidarity.* Jaipur: Rawat Publications.

Kothari, Rajni (ed.), 1970. *Caste in Indian Politics.* New Delhi: Orient Longman.

Kothari, Rajni and Ghanshyam Shah, 1963. 'Caste Orientation of Political Factions: Modasa Constituency: A Case Study', *The Economic Weekly,* Special Number, July.

Leach, Edmund (ed.), 1971. *Aspects of Caste in South India, Ceylon and North West Pakistan.* Cambridge: Cambridge University Press.

Lynch, Owen M., 1969. *The Politics of Untouchability: Social Mobility and Social Change in a City of India.* New York: Columbia Press.

Mahar, J. Michael (ed.), 1972. *The Untouchables in Contemporary India.* Tucson: University of Arizona Press.

Marriot, McKim (ed.), 1969. *Village India.* Chicago: Chicago University Press.

McGilvray, D.B. (ed.), 1982. *Caste Ideology and Interaction.* Cambridge: Cambridge University Press.

Meillassoux, Claude, 1973. 'Are There Castes in India?, *Economy and Society, 2, 1.*

Mendelsohn, Oliver, and Marika Vicziany, 1998. *The Untouchables: Subordination, Poverty and the State in Modern India.* Cambridge: Cambridge University Press.

O'Hanlon, Rosalind, 1985. *Caste, Conflict and Idrologr Mahatma jotirao Phule and Low Caste Protest in Nineteenth-century Western India.* Cambridge: Cambridge University Press.

Omvedt, Gail, 1976. *Cultural Revolt in a Colonial Society: The Non-Brahmin Movement in Western India, 1873–1930.* Bombay: Scientific Socialist Educational Trust.

———, (ed.), 1982. *Land, Caste and Politics in Indian States.* Delhi: Authors Guild Publications.

Rudolph, Lloyd 1. and Susanne H. Rudolph, 1960.'The Political Role of India's Caste Associations', *Pacific Affairs,* 33.

———, 1967. *The Modernity of Tradition: Political Development in India.* Chicago: University of Chicago Press.

Searle-Chatterjee, Mary and Ursula Sharma, 1994. *Contextualising Caste.* Oxford: Blackwell Publishers.

Sharma, K.L. (ed.), 1994. *Caste and Class in India.* Jaipur: Rawat Publishers.

Shah, Ghanshyam, 1975. *Caste Association and Political Process in Gujarat.* Bombay: Popular Prakashan.

Srinivas, M.N., 1979. 'The Future of Indian Caste', *Economic and Political Weekly,* Annual Number.

———, 1989. *The Cohesive Role of Sanskritisation and Other Essays.* Delhi: Oxford University Press.

———, 1987. *The Dominant Caste and Other Essays.* Delhi: Oxford University Press.

———, (ed.), 1996. *Caste: Its Twentieth-century Avatar.* Delhi: Viking. Templeman, Denis, 1996. *The Northern Nadars of Tamil Nadu: An Indian Caste in the Process of Change.* Delhi: Oxford University Press.

Zelliot Eleanor, 1992. *From Untouchable to Dalit: Essays on the Ambedkar movement,* New Delhi: Manohar.